# The psychology of social class

*The Psychology of Social Class* gives a comprehensive account of psychological and other research into social class using data from Britain, the USA and elsewhere. By addressing differences in social class, it broadens the perspective of social psychological research. It uses sociological research, but fills important gaps, such as the effect of achievement motivation and other personality variables on social mobility. It also provides explanations for sociological findings such as the effect of social class on health.

The book describes the class system in Britain and compares it with others in the modern world. Michael Argyle also looks at the historical development of class and some attempts to abolish it. Psychological models of class are discussed, and hierarchies in small groups and social organisations are examined.

A detailed account is also given of class differences in behaviour and beliefs and covers such aspects as marriage, friendship, speech style, personality, sexual behaviour, crime, religion and leisure. Finally, Michael Argyle examines the images people have of the class system.

*The Psychology of Social Class* also looks at the effects of class on well-being and discusses possible explanations of class differences in terms of genetics, socialisation, work experience, differences in lifestyle and the sheer effects of social status.

**Michael Argyle** is Emeritus Reader in Social Psychology at the University of Oxford, a Fellow of Wolfson College and Emeritus Professor of Psychology at Oxford Brookes University. He is the author of sixteen books, including *The Social Psychology of Everyday Life, Cooperation, Bodily Communication* and *The Psychology of Happiness*.

Other titles by Michael Argyle available from Routledge:

**Bodily Communication**

**The Social Psychology of Religion** *(with B. Beit-Hallahmi)*

**Social Skills and Mental Health** *(with P. Trower and B. Bryant)*

**The Psychology of Happiness**

**Cooperation**

**The Social Psychology of Everyday Life**

# The psychology of social class

## Michael Argyle

London and New York

First published 1994
by Routledge
11 New Fetter Lane, London EC4P 4EE

Simultaneously published in the USA and Canada
by Routledge
29 West 35th Street, New York, NY 10001

Typeset in Garamond by J&L Composition Ltd, Filey, North Yorkshire
Printed and bound in Great Britain by
Mackays of Chatham PLC, Chatham, Kent

*British Library Cataloguing in Publication Data*
A catalogue record for this book is available from the British Library

*Library of Congress Cataloging in Publication Data*
Argyle, Michael.
    The psychology of social class / Michael Argyle.
    p.   cm.
    Includes bibliographical references and index.
    1. Social classes–Psychological aspects.   2. Social classes–Great Britain–
    Psychological aspects.   I. Title.
    HT609.A685 1993
    305.5′0941–dc20                                                    93–3445
                                                                        CIP

ISBN 0–415–07954–3
       0–415–07955–1 (pbk)

# Contents

# Illustrations

## FIGURES

# Preface

Social class is one of the most interesting and important issues in the social sciences. Many social problems are connected to it – crime, poverty, ill-health, mental disorder and political unrest, for example. In order to tackle such problems we need to find their explanation, which often lies in psychology. However, psychologists have neglected it. Sociologists have done excellent work on it, but have left out the psychology, for example on the causes of social mobility, or of inter-class attitudes. Class is important to psychology, because many of the phenomena which we study are very different in different classes – relationships, language and sex, for example.

The topic of class has great intrinsic interest and even entertainment value, as is shown by the numerous TV programmes, novels and jokes on this theme. I hope that this book will have some entertainment value as well as being a serious contribution to the subject. Above all, I hope it will help people to understand the various ramifications of social class.

I have drawn extensively on recent social survey and other data, mainly from this country, but also from others, to illuminate the main psychological issues about class.

I am indebted to a number of colleagues for reading chapters – Nicholas Argyle, Geoff Evans, Yair Hamburger and Peter Robinson. And I have been greatly helped by the books by a number of sociologists – John Goldthorpe, Anthony Heath, Gerhard Lenski and Harold Kerbo, and the compilation of survey data by Ivan Reid. Again Ann McKendry did a superb job with her word processor.

Michael Argyle
*Oxford*
*October 1992*

# Chapter 1

# The study of class: class in Britain

## THE CONTRIBUTION OF PSYCHOLOGY TO THE STUDY OF SOCIAL CLASS

Social class has hitherto been studied mainly by sociologists; indeed, it is one of the central concerns of sociology. They have been very successful here, and have developed increasingly sophisticated methods of analysing the differences between classes, in behaviour and outcomes, the causes of social mobility, class consciousness and conflict, and other aspects of social class. Psychologists have a great deal to learn from them; indeed, we have been remiss in neglecting the great variation between classes in the phenomena that we study. We are aware of some class differences, for example in speech style, but less aware of class differences in social relationships, sexual behaviour, child-rearing, personality and self-esteem.

However, sociologists have failed to recognise the importance of psychological variables in this field. In the study of social mobility for example, they take account of education, and sometimes of intelligence, but not of other abilities and skills, nor of individual differences in motivation, personality or physique. There has been little study by sociologists of interaction between classes, at the level of language, non-verbal communication, of the detailed indicators of social distance and deference. The analysis of class consciousness has not looked at the attitudes and stereotypes which classes have of one another. In these and other ways psychology can enlarge the field of study, the data to be collected, the phenomena to be described.

Sociologists have been successful in discovering many differences between classes, in lifestyle and outcomes (e.g. Reid, 1989). However, they have made much less progress in explaining these differences. It is very important to do so. Consider for example class differences in mental health: it is clear that working-class people have worse mental health than middle-class people, but if anything is to be done about it we need to know why. If it is due to 'downward drift', as may be the case with schizophrenics, nothing can be done. If it is caused by stress due to poverty, unemployment, etc., only wider social measures could help. But if it is due to personality differences caused by socialisation, e.g. poor methods of coping, then improvement of parental socialisation might help. And if it is due to lack of social support, improved social support networks could be organised. If it is caused by unhappiness and low self-esteem, which are also class-related, we need to know the causes of these in turn. Similar questions arise in connection with the explanation of class differences in health and happiness, and there are great differences in health in particular.

These examples concern 'outcome' variables, where the existence of large class differences constitutes a social problem. Other areas of class differences are primarily of academic interest to those of us who want to understand human behaviour. Why are there substantial differences in sexual behaviour for example? Working-class people engage in much more premarital inter-course. Is this because, as in the animal world, where there is an uncertain future, males invest less in a single relationship, in order to make sure that their genes are reproduced? Or is it because working-class child-rearing is more permissive, produces less internal restraint? And, if so, why does child-rearing vary by class in this way? It might be because middle-class families value family stability, responsibility and domesticity more, because they have had more positive experience of it, or in order to control future family fortunes and the inheritance of property. Unless we can decide between such theories we can have no understanding of class differences in sexual behaviour.

Similar considerations apply to the explanation of other areas of class differences. Why do classes differ so much in leisure activities, attitudes to work, social relationships, religious beliefs and other aspects of ideology? Is it because of class differences in personality, child-rearing, subcultural patterns of behaviour or experiences produced by position in the class system, for example at work? And what in turn is the cause of such class differences in personality, child-rearing and the rest? I believe that much of the explanation of the differences established by sociologists lies outside sociology, and is often to be found in psychology.

Sociologists have taken a lot of interest in class conflict and class consciousness, but social psychology has found that these inter-group phenomena have a number of surprising features. As in other cases of relations between groups of different status, like racial groups, members of the lower-status group often accept the superiority of the other group, and believe that the status quo is fair; some are not aware that the other group is doing any better. A theory in social psychology – social identity theory – can help here, though it needs some extension.

Sociologists have explained the apparently universal existence of class systems in human society in terms of the functional requirements of all societies (Davis and Moore, 1945). However, such theories are incomplete unless we know the motivations which drive some people to seek positions of higher status, and the rewards which they provide. And why do they often behave in a way which distances them from the lower orders when they get there?

Several fields of psychology are needed to answer these questions, including:

*Social psychology*, especially the study of social relationships, inter-group attitudes and behaviour, the analysis of attitudes and beliefs.

*Personality*, especially self-image and self-esteem, assertiveness and power motivation, coping mechanisms, certain personality traits, the effects of socialisation.

*Individual differences*, especially intelligence and other abilities, biological differences in height, attractiveness and other measures.

We shall make use of several other fields of psychology – industrial psychology, health psychology, social psychiatry, the psychology of religion and of politics and criminal psychology. Reference will also be made to other fields such as biological anthropology and ethology.

## THE MEANING AND MEASUREMENT OF CLASS

Everyone knows what class is – as we shall see, 95 per cent of people can say what their own class is for example. However, the exact meaning of the term is more elusive. Sociologists are not agreed. Some define class as status or prestige, others as power, or income, or wealth and property, or say that class is what people think their class is. In some smaller community studies, a more social psychological approach has been used, where class is based on which individuals accept each other as equals and which defer to others. The best predictors of such reputational status are occupation, education, income and area of housing. More recently, 'lifestyle', or leisure activities, consumption and other aspects of behaviour, has been identified as an indicator of class. For social survey purposes class is usually measured in Britain by occupational status, but in the USA by income or education. We shall start with the class people think they are.

*Subjective social class.* Part of the evidence that there *is* a class system is that about 95 per cent of the population think there is, and can say which class they belong to themselves. Table 1.1 shows how a national sample placed themselves: 'If you were asked what social class you belong to, what would you say?' Note that putting the question in this way does not impose any concepts or theories on the respondents. Notice also that about 95 per cent of the sample were able to answer this question.

This study allowed respondents to use their own words. If fixed alternatives are offered the results can vary a lot. In the USA, if the choices were between upper, middle and lower, nearly 80 per cent thought they were middle-class in the 1940s; if working was added to the list only 43 per cent

*Table 1.1* Unprompted self-ratings of social class (percentages)

| | Upper/ Upper middle | Middle | Lower middle | Upper working | Working | Other[1] | Rejected class[2] | No/hazy concept |
|---|---|---|---|---|---|---|---|---|
| Men | 1.7 | 32 | 5 | 1.6 | 50 | 5 | 4 | 1.3 |
| Women | 1.5 | 39 | 4 | 1.4 | 43 | 5 | 4 | 1.6 |
| All | 1.6 | 36 | 4 | 1.5 | 46 | 5 | 4 | 1.5 |

*Source:* Reid, 1989
*Notes:* 1. Included poor, ordinary, lower, lowest; 2. Some of these subsequently acknowledged class and applied it to themselves.

opted for middle (Vanneman and Cannon, 1987). There is quite a strong, though far from perfect, correspondence between subjective social class and class as measured by social scientists. For example, self-description as middle-class or working-class corresponds quite well to having non-manual or manual jobs respectively. While occupation is commonly used in Britain to put people into classes, other criteria are commonly used by the public, especially income and education. So a person with a manual job who also earns a large salary may regard himself as middle-class and have a middle-class lifestyle and attitudes. Jackman and Jackman (1973) found that subjective social status in the USA could be predicted from occupation, but also from education and income. Social contacts, i.e. the class of friends, was an important factor, and itself dependent on occupation, education and income. Owning capital had no direct link with subjective class, but it did have an indirect one, through affecting social contacts.

Another source of mismatch between subjective and objective social class is that some individuals simply place themselves incorrectly. For example, an upwardly mobile person, who has retained left-wing attitudes but has a middle-class job and lifestyle, may regard himself as working-class. He is describing his class of origin, not his current class.

Several surveys have been carried out in Britain in which people were asked which criteria they could use to tell which class people are in. Townsend (1979) found the following order of criteria, in answer to the question 'What decides what class you are in? Is it mainly job, education, the family you are born into, your way of life, money, or anything else?' (these were the first choices).

Way of life   (31 per cent)
Family   (18 per cent)
Job   (17 per cent)
Money   (17 per cent)
Education   (10 per cent)

Another survey offered a large choice, in answer to the question 'Which two of these would you say are the most important in being able to tell which class a person is?'

*Table 1.2* Rank order of social class criteria

| (a) Men and women | (b) Women only |
| --- | --- |
| 1 The way they speak (33) | 1 Appearance and behaviour (53) |
| 2 Where they live (28) | 2 Family background (50) |
| 3 The friends they have (27) | 3 Attitudes, beliefs and political views (45) |
| 4 Their job (22) | 4 Style of life (42) |
| 5 The sort of school they went to (21) | 5 Education (38) |
| 6 The way they spend their money (18) | 6 Occupation (31) |
| 7 The way they dress (12) | 7 House/area in which they live (13) |
| 8 The car they own (5) | 8 Income (13) |
| | 9 Prestige/standing in the community (11) |

| (c) Men | Women | Men and women |
| --- | --- | --- |
| 1 Way of life (29) | 1 Way of life (33) | 1 Way of life (31) |
| 2 Job (22) | 2 Family (21) | 2 Family (18) |
| 3 Money (17) | 3 Money (16) | 3= Job (17) |
| 4 Family (15) | 4 Job (12) | 3= Money (17) |
| 5 Education (10) | 5 Education (11) | 5 Education (10) |

*Source:* Reid, 1989
*Note:* Figures in brackets are the percentages giving each item.

An important series of studies was carried out by Lloyd Warner and associates, first in a New England town of 17,000 which was called 'Yankee City' (Warner and Lunt, 1941), later in 'Jonesville', pop. 6,000 (Warner *et al.*, 1949). The social status of families was established by interviewing others who knew them or knew of them. A high degree of agreement was reported, and it was concluded that there were six classes in these small towns. In Jonesville, 339 of the 2,095 families were interviewed. This method gives a kind of reputational status, 'Evaluated participation', or esteem, which reflects the level at which people are accepted in the community, the clubs they belong to, the people with whom they mix as equals. This method has been criticised by some sociologists on the grounds that it can be used only in small communities, that it does not measure class in the Marxist sense of economic and political groups in conflict, and that people are assessed as individuals not class members (Pfautz and Duncan, 1950; Kornhauser, 1953).

Hollingshead (1949) used a more systematic but similar method. Out of a sample of 535 families in 'Elmtown', twenty were located who were well known and who were at different points in the prestige scale. Other families were rated by over twenty raters each for their position on a prestige scale defined by these families, and a very high level of agreement was found.

Warner devised an 'Index of Status Characteristics', which predicted his laboriously obtained class measures very economically. Occupation was weighted 4, sources of income was weighted 3, house type weighted 3 and dwelling area weighted 2. From his research data he could well have included income and education, both of which had high correlations with Evaluated Participation.

These measures were applied to larger communities by Coleman and Rainwater (1979) in surveys of Kansas City and Boston in 1971–2. People were asked to estimate the social status of eighty-four hypothetical families, who had various combinations of occupation, income and education. Statistical analysis showed that income was the strongest predictor of prestige (r = .57), followed by job (r = .29) and education (.10). From these data a scale for measuring social status was produced, with weighted scores for each type of job and levels of income and education. It would be interesting to know how occupation, income and education would be weighted in Britain.

These methods are very attractive to social psychologists, who are interested in the social behaviour of individuals, though we are also interested in identification with groups and feelings of conflict between them. If people think that they are of the same or similar social status they will feel at ease in each other's company, are happy to belong to the same club, become friends or marry. If they do not think they are of the same status, these things are less likely to happen, they will keep a certain 'social distance', and one will behave differentially to the other, in extreme cases calling them 'Sir', standing aside or taking their hat off, for example. And social status is not just a property of individuals; it is shared by their families. Usually wives and children are treated with the same respect that is given to the husband if he is the main earner. Families try to pass on their social status to their children, particularly by seeking the appropriate level of education and training and by financial help.

## Assessing class by occupation

We have seen that both subjective class and reputational class can be predicted quite well from occupation – though also, and perhaps equally well, by income, education, area of residence, etc. However, sociologists in Britain in particular usually measure class by occupation, and this is used in government official statistics. As a result much of the research which will be cited in this book has used class as defined by occupation. Sociologists like occupation for theoretical reasons, partly of Marxist origins – occupation represents capital v. labour and, in addition, degrees of authority over other people.

This is not the practice in the USA, where class is usually assessed by education or income now. There is a lot to be said for using occupation: different jobs have a different social standing which is widely agreed; the social standing of jobs correlates with level of skill needed, and hence length of training, with amount of power or influence within working organisations and with level of earnings. We have seen that it is correlated with

*Table 1.3* Typical occupations[1] of each social class

*I Professional, etc.*
Accountant, architect, chemist, company secretary, doctor, engineer, judge, lawyer, optician, scientist, solicitor, surveyor, university teacher, veterinarian.

*II Intermediate*
Aircraft pilot or engineer, chiropodist, farmer, laboratory assistant/technician, manager, proprietor, publican, member of parliament, nurse, police or fire-brigade officer, schoolteacher.

*IIIn Skilled non-manual*
Auctioneer, cashier, clerical worker, commercial traveller, draughtsman, estate agent, sales representative, secretary, shop assistant, typist, telephone supervisor.

*IIIm Skilled manual*
Baker, bus driver, butcher, bricklayer, carpenter, cook, electrician, hairdresser, miner (underground), policeman or fireman, railway engine driver/guard, upholsterer.

*IV Partly skilled/semi-skilled*
Agricultural worker, barman, bus conductor, fisherman, hospital orderly, machine sewer, packer, postman, roundsman, street vendor, telephone operator.

*V Unskilled*
Chimney/road sweeper, kitchen hand, labourer, lift/car park attendant, driver's mate, messenger, railway stationman, refuse collector, window/office cleaner.

*Source:* Devised from pp. 1–89 and appendixes B1 and B2, Registrar General's *Classification of Occupations* (1980).
*Note:* 1. In alphabetical order. These are mainly basic occupation titles; foremen and managers in occupations listed are allotted to different classes.

subjective social class. We shall see in Chapter 8 that it is associated with education, which is both a cause of occupational class and an effect of class of origin, i.e. of parents.

The most widely used occupation scale in Britain is the Registrar General's. The current revised version used in the census is shown in Table 1.3. This scale was used in a number of the studies referred to later in this book.

*Table 1.4* Percentage distribution of occupational classes (Great Britain, 1990)

| | Professional | Employers and managers | Intermediate and junior non-manual | Skilled manual and own-account non-professional | Semi-skilled manual and personal service | Unskilled manual |
|---|---|---|---|---|---|---|
| Males | 7 | 19 | 18 | 36 | 15 | 4 |
| Females | 6 | 18 | 25 | 29 | 18 | 5 |

*Source:* Reported current occupation or last job, *General Household Survey*, 1992

The population is distributed between occupational classes as shown in Table 1.4.

A number of other ways of classifying occupations have been devised. Goldthorpe and Hope (1974) devised a 36-category scheme, which was then reduced to several shorter versions. The 5-category list is as follows:

Salariat
Routine non-manual
Petty bourgeoisie
Foremen and technicians
Working class

The interest of this scale is that it is theoretically derived reflecting both ownership and authority, and it is successful in predicting voting. So, for example, the 'petite bourgeoisie', i.e. employers and self-employed, are the most Conservative, the 'working class' the most Labour. This division of occupations predicts voting better than the Registrar General's scheme. There are many other occupational category schemes, which have been used in different studies, and these have been reviewed by Reid (1989).

Marx and some other sociologists have argued that class is really based on power. Power is mainly derived from positions in organisations, where people are able to direct the behaviour of others, so that occupation is an important source of power. Wright (1985) devised a scheme for classifying occupations entirely in terms of power and control, and this has been used in some studies of class behaviour. The law is another source of power. We shall see how in England during the nineteenth century the law was extensively changed to give working-class people more power, starting with being able to vote (p. 32).

It is common to regard some people who are in the same kind of job as nevertheless being of different class. One may be richer for some reason, live in a grander house and have a different way of life. This could be through family background, school or college attended, inherited wealth or the spouse's job, for example. Occupation is not the only basis of class.

Sociologists are well aware that occupation is not the only source of social status. In earlier times being related to a noble family was the main source of status for some. Today non-work roles, in local government, including becoming lord mayor, or in voluntary associations, can raise a person's status. Imitating the lifestyle of a higher class, as done by the *nouveau riche* and their many followers, is another. Belonging to the right or wrong racial or religious groups is another important source of social status, independently of occupation, in many countries (Parkin, 1971).

## Wealth

'The rich are different from us, they have more money.' So they do, but how much more? Table 1.5 shows the earnings of the main family earner, total family income and final income after benefits have been added and taxes subtracted, for the top to bottom fifths of households by income. This table is based on 7,625 families, studied in 1988. The final incomes, after benefits and taxes have been taken into account, show a ratio of 4.31:1 from top to bottom. The similar ratio for total family income is 24.1:1, and that for earnings of main earner 26.4:1. The effect of redistribution, by benefits and taxes, is considerable.

Table 1.5 Income from each fifth of households (1988)

|  | Bottom fifth | Next fifth | Middle fifth | Next fifth | Top fifth |
|---|---|---|---|---|---|
| Earnings of main earner | 740 | 3,090 | 7,400 | 10,830 | 19,500 |
| Total family income | 1,210 | 4,440 | 10,750 | 16,260 | 29,170 |
| Final income | 4,800 | 6,570 | 9,700 | 12,360 | 20,700 |

Source: Social Trends, 1992

The best-paid men (in April 1992) were doctors (av. £39,291), the worst-paid were kitchen porters (£8,767). The best-paid women were doctors (£31,985), the worst-paid were hairdressers (£6,640). The average salary for non-manual workers was £17,313, and for manual workers £11,398 (New Earnings Survey, 1992). There are some higher salaries than this, those of some financiers and a small number of managing directors. But within the main occupations the top ones are paid less than five times as much as the bottom ones.

However, income and status are often out of step. Plumbers, bookmakers and many other small businessmen earn more than clergymen, school teachers or nurses, but are judged by the public to be of lower social status. However, as Parkin (1971) points out, school teachers, clergy and nurses have other economic benefits – such as security of employment and promotion prospects. In successive American studies the correlation between income and class has become progressively smaller, and is now about .45. In addition to the reason given above, some families are well-off because there are several earners, others are badly-off as a result of divorce or illness. When there are several earners they tend to have similar occupations, and their income, but not their class, is enhanced (Coleman, 1983).

So much for earnings. Wealth is a very different story. The distribution of wealth in Britain is shown in Table 1.6. The top 1 per cent of wealth holders in Britain owned 18 per cent of property and other wealth in 1989, or 11 per cent if pension rights are included. A smaller group, the top 0.1 per cent, owned 7 per cent of wealth in 1986, about £740,000 each, and the top 1 per cent owned about £190,000 each. For the top 5 per cent the corresponding figure is £73,600 each, and for the bottom 50 per cent of the population it was only £845 each (New Society, 1987).

However, wealth is much more equally distributed than earlier in the

*Table 1.6* The distribution of wealth (Great Britain, 1989)

|  | Top 1% | Top 5% | Top 10% | Top 25% | Top 50% |
|---|---|---|---|---|---|
| Marketable wealth (including houses) | 18% | 38% | 53% | 75% | 94% |
| Marketable wealth plus occupational and state pension rights | 11% | 26% | 38% | 62% | 83% |

Source: *Social Trends*, 1992

century, when the top 1 per cent owned 69 per cent (as opposed to 18 per cent in 1989). Changes towards greater equality of incomes have been much smaller, and during the Thatcher years salary differentials became greater again (Heath *et al.*, 1991).

Inherited wealth was important in previous times, when most members of the upper class and some of the middle class did no work, and consequently had no income, but lived on rents from land and interest from investments (pp. 30–1). Wealth is now much less important than income, though middle-class families create continuity of their social position partly through inheritance, and people with well-paid jobs usually accumulate some wealth.

## Consumption and lifestyle

We have seen that middle-class people earn a lot more than working-class people. We now consider how much they *spend*. *The Family Expenditure Survey* (1990) reports the following class differences in average expenditure a week, per household and per person.

|  | I | II | III | IV | V |
|---|---|---|---|---|---|
| Per person | 97 | 90 | 64 | 61 | 60 |
| Per household | 278 | 268 | 202 | 176 | 159 |

These class differences are much smaller than the differences in earnings (see p. 9). There are several reasons for this – heavier taxation of larger incomes, more money put into saving schemes, welfare benefits of various kinds for poorer people and more multiple earners in working-class families. As a result class I expenditure per head is only 60 per cent greater than class V, though the income ratio is more like 4:1.

If class I people spend 60 per cent more, what do they spend it on? The different areas of expenditure are shown in Table 1.7.

It can be seen that richer people spend more on everything except tobacco, where the lowest classes spend most. There is little difference in food, fuel or alcohol. There are much greater class differences in housing, transport,

Table 1.7 Class differences in household expenditure (£ per week)

| | Professional | Employers and managers | Intermediate non-manual | Junior non-manual | Skilled manual | Semi-skilled manual | Unskilled manual | All households with employed head |
|---|---|---|---|---|---|---|---|---|
| Housing | 71.3 | 72.6 | 61.4 | 51.0 | 48.4 | 42.9 | 36.4 | 55.5 |
| Fuel, light and power | 13.0 | 15.0 | 12.2 | 11.6 | 12.2 | 11.3 | 12.4 | 12.6 |
| Food | 61.7 | 65.0 | 52.3 | 47.0 | 54.4 | 45.2 | 42.8 | 54.0 |
| Alcohol | 13.7 | 17.7 | 13.2 | 11.8 | 14.9 | 10.8 | 9.6 | 13.9 |
| Tobacco | 2.6 | 4.3 | 4.9 | 4.8 | 8.3 | 8.2 | 7.7 | 6.2 |
| Clothing and footwear | 23.2 | 27.6 | 19.6 | 22.0 | 18.4 | 14.8 | 11.1 | 20.3 |
| Household goods | 32.2 | 29.6 | 24.0 | 24.6 | 21.2 | 19.3 | 14.5 | 23.9 |
| Household services | 20.9 | 21.6 | 20.4 | 13.7 | 11.4 | 10.3 | 10.9 | 15.5 |
| Personal goods and services | 13.6 | 15.8 | 12.2 | 11.6 | 10.4 | 9.4 | 7.5 | 11.8 |
| Motoring | 62.2 | 54.0 | 53.2 | 39.1 | 45.3 | 31.1 | 24.4 | 45.5 |
| Fares and other travel | 11.8 | 9.4 | 10.1 | 7.0 | 5.3 | 4.8 | 5.6 | 7.4 |
| Leisure goods | 26.9 | 19.8 | 15.1 | 14.6 | 11.5 | 11.4 | 9.2 | 15.1 |
| Leisure services | 43.7 | 51.2 | 28.1 | 22.0 | 11.8 | 13.2 | 10.2 | 27.9 |
| Miscellaneous | 3.1 | 2.9 | 2.2 | 2.0 | 1.8 | 1.5 | 1.1 | 2.1 |
| Total | 399.9 | 406.8 | 328.8 | 282.8 | 282.3 | 234.1 | 203.3 | 311.7 |

Source: Family Expenditure Survey 1990

services and household goods. (And, as we shall see later, leisure.) However, we should distinguish between class and income, which we have seen correlate only at about .45. Individuals of the same income but different class spend their money differently, because they have different lifestyles. In the USA, middle-class families with incomes above the average for their class, in 1983, were buying motorboats, campers, swimming pools, sports cars for their children and large American cars for themselves. Upper-class families with similar incomes (below the average for *their* class) instead spent their money on private club memberships, special educational experiences for their children, high culture objects and events, participation in civic affairs and smaller foreign cars (Coleman, 1983).

Middle-class spending on vehicles and transport reflects the greater number of cars – in Britain 96 per cent of professional families have one car or more, 52 per cent have two or more, compared with 57 per cent and 8 per cent of unskilled. This in turn reflects the geographical dispersion of middle-class people and their longer journeys to work. Expenditure on housing reflects middle-class ownership of larger houses, with corresponding mortgages and upkeep, compared with council rents. Expenditure on services reflects greater middle-class private education and private health, and more frequent visits to restaurants, more holidays and other outings. Middle-class people nearly all have basic amenities such as unshared bathroom, lavatory, a garden and a hot-water system. Over time, the lower classes catch up with the equipment of higher classes. By 1990 home computers were possessed by 45 per cent of professional families, 12 per cent of unskilled, dishwashers by 36 per cent of professional and 4 per cent of unskilled. Most families had a refrigerator, colour TV, central heating and a telephone (*General Household Survey*, 1989).

Most middle-class families own their homes (90 per cent), many of them with a mortgage. So do quite a lot of working-class families, including 42 per cent from class VI. This is mainly because local authority tenants have been encouraged to buy the houses which they were renting. Renting from the local authority is almost entirely confined to class IV and below.

Market research people make a lot of use of class in their surveys and marketing strategy. What they are interested in is which sections of the population will buy various products. The ACORN scheme is a classification of households by different kinds of housing area, which of course correlates with social class. It is found that there are large differences in product use between different areas. For example, consumption of red wine and brown sauce varies as seen in Table 1.8.

For marketing purposes it is important to take account of the age, sex and composition of family, as well as social class.

We saw earlier that members of the public take account of 'way of life', and we shall see later that they use clothes and accent as cues for class. Could

Table 1.8 Consumption of red wine and brown sauce by housing area

| | | Numbers of families with frequent use/population average | |
|---|---|---|---|
| | | Red wine | Brown sauce |
| I. | High-status non-family areas | 207 | 58 |
| J. | Affluent suburban housing | 156 | 48 |
| K. | Better-off retirement areas | 138 | 87 |
| B. | Modern family housing, higher incomes | 112 | 62 |
| A. | Agricultural areas | 97 | 129 |
| H. | Mixed inner metropolitan areas | 95 | 87 |
| C. | Older housing of intermediate status | 82 | 92 |
| E. | Better-off council estates | 59 | 155 |
| F. | Poorer council estates | 53 | 143 |
| D. | Older terraced housing | 52 | 124 |
| G. | Poorest council estates | 38 | 217 |

Source: Ford, 1988

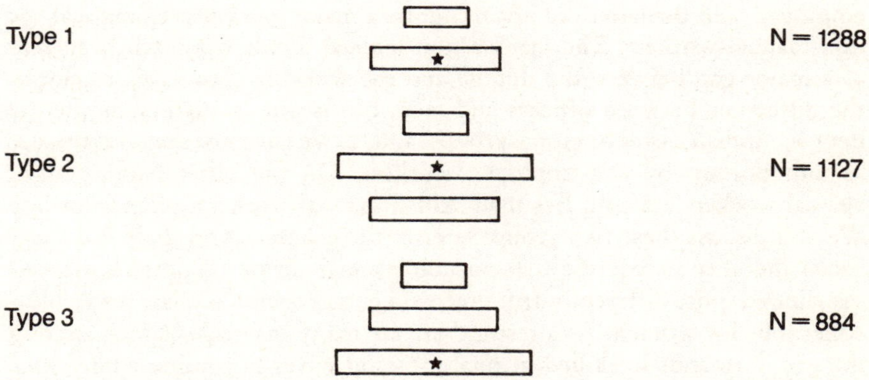

Type 1                                                                N = 1288

Type 2                                                                N = 1127

Type 3                                                                N = 884

Figure 1.1 The three most popular models of the class structure, with the survey members' self-placement (marked with an asterisk)
Source: Britten, 1984

an index be constructed for use in research? We shall discuss later various attempts to do so from analysing the contents of living rooms (p. 116).

## HOW MANY CLASSES ARE THERE?

If people are asked, a variety of answers are forthcoming. A few think there is only one or don't know what class is, but most think that there are two or three. A large British survey of perceptions of the class system was carried out by Britten (1984). Out of 2,575 26-year-olds the three models of the class system shown in Figure 1.1 were the most popular.

The first model was widely held by male manual workers, the second by non-manual workers and the third by women in classes I and II. Seven other models were found, but all these were less widely held. Social scientists think that there are three with sub-divisions (as in the Goldthorpe occupational scheme, Table 1.4), or five, as in the Registrar General's scheme (Table 1.3). These divisions are made on the grounds that there are major differences in occupation, income and lifestyle between these occupational groups.

Are there any sharp breaks, or discontinuities, in the class hierarchy, or is it better described as a kind of continuous gradient? These two models have been held by different social theorists, and also by different sections of the public. Marxists thought of two classes in opposition, owners and workers, while Warner and Hollingshead thought of a continuous gradient of prestige. Vanneman and Pampel (1977) tried to test these alternative models by seeing which was the best predictor of various kinds of behaviour. The dichotomy model was the best predictor of voting, but the continuous gradient model predicted life satisfaction better. Their respondents were more likely to use the dichotomy model if they worked in large bureaucratic industries, but used the gradient model if they were self-employed, and the latter did not recognise a major gap between manual and non-manual workers. The manual/non-manual divide has often been seen as a major gap between the middle and the working class. This resembles the difference between officers and men, but is not so marked as the gap between Indian castes or ethnic groups and, as we have just seen, is regarded as unimportant by self-employed workers. On the other hand, routine clerical workers are paid less than skilled manual workers, often a lot less. We will discuss these two groups later in the chapter. And there is a lot of social mobility across the manual/non-manual divide. Women's jobs are distributed quite differently from men's, i.e. more white-collar, fewer blue-collar jobs for women. As a result there are many marriages which straddle the gap, husbands in skilled manual jobs and wives in routine white-collar ones (pp. 20–1).

Nevertheless the manual/non-manual gap is an important one. It shows up clearly in studies of occupational prestige in all countries, though the division is less clear in Communist countries. And although skilled manual jobs are often paid more than white-collar clerical ones, the latter are more likely to have benefits like pensions, better promotion prospects and security, annual salary increases and cleaner, safer, working conditions (Wedderburn and Craig, 1969, cited by Parkin, 1971). Do well-paid manual workers become middle-class? According the the theory of 'embourgeoise-ment' they do; this will be discussed later.

According to Marxist thinking the main gap should be between owners or employers and workers. Something like this is found in agricultural communities, between the farmers and the farm workers (p. 210). Elsewhere however there are several grades of employees, and any conflict is between the lower grades and the managers, who are themselves employees. The 'owners' are likely to be relatively invisible directors or shareholders, or the government, in the case of nationalised industry. Workers may be shareholders themselves, at least via their pension funds.

There may be another gap, between the upper and middle classes, especially between the top 0.1 per cent of the population who own all that wealth, for example, and the rest. They certainly have an expensive lifestyle that puts them apart from other people.

## THE MAIN CLASSES IN BRITAIN

*The upper class.* In previous centuries the upper class in Britain consisted of the landed aristocracy. Despite an earlier aversion to business, in the second half of the nineteenth century this group became integrated with those who ran commerce and industry (Giddens, 1973). For a time 1 per cent of the population in Britain owned a third of the country's wealth; it is now less, but still 28 per cent of wealth apart from dwellings. There is an even smaller group, 0.1–0.2 per cent, who own a very large slice of wealth. This wealth is owned by families rather than individuals, since it is shared out, and above all inherited by some of the next generation. We shall meet this group again in the analysis of social mobility. Many people move in and out of other social classes, but very few enter this one. It is difficult to become a company chairman, a director of a bank or a top civil servant unless father had a similar position. The upper class includes those at the top of the main social organisations, including senior politicians, judges and bishops (Heath, 1981). It is much smaller than the class I of the occupational schemes described above, and too small to fall into social surveys, which they might not answer anyway.

In several ways the upper class is a real social group, since the members are linked by kinship and marriage. They own shares in each other's firms, and there are many interlocking directorships. It is difficult to get into since the members recruit their own children and groom them for membership by sending them to the same schools and universities, where they get to know each other and establish an old boy network with a shared outlook.

The upper class has a very distinctive and expensive culture and lifestyle – large houses, elaborate entertainments, expensive sports (shooting, polo, etc.) and annual rituals – Ascot, Henley. Though different from the aristocratic upper class of an earlier period, some of them do live in country houses and own land, and some acquire titles, through their status in politics, industry or other organisations (Scott, 1991; Abercrombie and Warde, 1988).

*The middle class.* We have seen that most people think that there is one, that 1.6 per cent of the population think they are upper middle (or upper) class and 36 per cent that they are middle class. The 'old' or traditional middle class consisted of families who owned property and usually their own businesses. During this century there has been a great increase in salaried managers and professionals.

The Registrar General's scheme defines class I as higher professionals, managers and administrators, some employed by government, others by private firms. It includes 5 per cent of men, 1 per cent of women, so is mainly male, though families usually share the same class. The work situations of doctors, lawyers, etc., on one hand, and managers and administrators, on the other, are different. They are grouped together since they have similar earnings, live in similar neighbourhoods and have the same kind of outlook, for example of a 'code of service', and they are trusted and given authority (Goldthorpe, 1982).

Surveys of consumption and lifestyle suggest another way that the middle class can be divided. Those employed in 'education, health and welfare' earn less than industrial employees and managers, but have a lifestyle which is stronger on health and culture. Rather than spending their money on skiing, drinking and expensive restaurants, they eat and drink less, but go to opera, plays and classical concerts, and engage in skating, climbing, jogging and hiking. This style is being copied by other sections of the middle class and they have been described as the vanguard of a new healthy lifestyle (Savage et al., 1992).

The Registrar General's class II consists of lower professionals, like nurses and teachers, and makes up 22 per cent of the population. These two classes between them have been described by Goldthorpe as the 'service class' and by others as the 'salariat'. Members of the middle class have little capital wealth; with the exception of the small group of employers, they earn salaries, which are a good deal larger in class I than in class II, and certainly greater than in class III. They have careers, and they have favourable conditions of work, their jobs require a high level of skill and at higher levels a lot of autonomy.

'Yuppies' (young, upwardly mobile professionals) belong somewhere in classes I and II, though by skill level they might fit a lower class. They are typically employed in various financial and commercial organisations, and are highly paid for the use of certain specialist skills. They are interesting since by origins and education they often belong to some lower class, i.e. they have been upwardly mobile, though not by the usual educational route, and are not always socially acceptable to other class I individuals, as in the case of the despised 'Essex man'.

The lower middle class consists mainly of fairly routine, 'white-collar', i.e. clerical, workers and has been the object of a great deal of interest from sociologists. It forms an increasing proportion of the work-force (17 per cent), and is mainly female (74 per cent). While members appear to occupy a status between the middle and working classes, they are on average paid less than skilled manual workers, but on the other hand they have more secure jobs, fringe benefits like pension schemes and much better conditions of work. Most manual workers can earn more only by doing overtime. Very few of the women get promoted and many leave to have a family, but over half the men are promoted out of clerical into usually low-grade managerial jobs by the age of 30. It has been argued that white-collar jobs have been 'proletarianised' or 'deskilled' by the introduction of computers and other office equipment. On balance however the degree of autonomy is similar to that of skilled manual workers, and new equipment has on the whole led to upgrading of jobs (Lockwood, 1989).

On the other hand, personal service workers like shop assistants, check-out people and receptionists have very little autonomy, feel that their work has been deskilled, and it has been concluded that their work is indistinguishable from working-class work (Marshall *et al.*, 1988).

The *'petite bourgeoisie'* are people who are self-employed, or who own their own small business, and have a small number of employees, typically shop-keepers and small builders, decorators and other craftsmen. They are in some ways outside the class system, in that they combine manual work with ownership. They are often manual workers who have found a form of social mobility, which takes a few a long way upwards (Scase, 1982).

*The working class* are seen by themselves and others as 'the workers', especially as manual workers. We have seen that 46 per cent of the British population regard themselves as working-class, plus 1.5 per cent 'upper-working-class' (Table 1.3), and that there are 52 per cent of people in the Registrar General's classes III(m)–V. The gap between skilled manual workers, class III(m), and the others is an important one. There is an 'aristocracy of labour', and those at the top are regarded by their employers as an important form of capital investment, with the result that skilled workers are not only better paid, but have better job security (Giddens, 1973). In an interesting study in Rochdale, Penn (1985) found that differences of skill played an important role at work; for example, different unions defended the interests of their group by restricting entry to it. On the other hand, differences of skill did not create social divisions within the working class, and did not affect marital choice.

*The traditional working class* consists of people working in traditional industries, like textiles, coal, steel, ship-building, and their families, who live in Victorian row houses near the works, typically in large industrial towns. They are mostly semi- or unskilled and poorly paid. They have a strong feeling of solidarity with kin, neighbours and work-mates, and of class solidarity, belong to trade unions and vote Labour. They have a strong we–they attitude to employers and bosses.

*The 'new' working class.* According to the theory of *embourgeoisement* prosperous workers may adopt the lifestyle of the middle class. We discuss the evidence for this later in relation to work behaviour (p. 98). The *Affluent Worker* study by Goldthorpe *et al.* (1968–9) was partly intended to test this hypothesis. It was concluded that well-paid manual workers and their families were different from traditional workers in having little identification with other workers or the unions. They worked and belonged to unions for instrumental, i.e. money-earning, reasons. However, they were not middle-class, they mostly voted Labour, did not associate with middle-class people and did not regard themselves as middle-class, or aspire to be. They were an example of the 'new' working class. Marshall and colleagues (1989) argue that this instrumental attitude to work is by no means new. On the other hand, they found that over half of British manual workers saw work as more than just a way of earning a living. This topic will be taken up again in Chapter 5.

In an American survey of 3,275 white workers and their spouses it was found that the great majority of manual workers saw themselves as working-class. Income and education had only a small effect for them; the only exception was that going to college produced a substantial increase in middle-class identification, but it is possible these respondents were only doing temporary jobs. For the professional, business and white-collar subjects, income and education had a much larger effect. Comparison with an earlier period showed that the manual–non-manual gap in class identification had increased (Dalia and Guest, 1975).

The concept of a new working class has also been put forward to explain the high level of working-class Conservative voting. It is found that there are certain factors which bring about a shift away from Labour, such as buying a house, not belonging to a union and working in private industry (pp. 219–20). Very often these people are living in new housing estates and have bought their council houses, so are no longer living near their kin or taking part in the old working-class solidarity (Lockwood, 1966).

*The 'underclass'* was first noticed in the USA, during the 1970s. The term was used to describe what appeared to be a 'culture of poverty', outside normal society, consisting mainly of blacks and Hispanics, who had migrated to northern cities and did the worst-paid and least desirable jobs, or no jobs at all. Some American sociologists interpreted this as a subculture, produced by the breakdown of the family and teenage pregnancy, resulting in inadequate socialisation, not knowing the difference between right and wrong, dependence on welfare and young people turning to crime, drugs and violence instead of work. Others saw the main cause as unemployment, poverty and the decline of the environment, houses, schools and recreation centres. Later research has found that the American underclass is not only a black and Hispanic problem, whites are involved too, and that it embraces a great variety of social failures, misfits, the homeless, mentally ill and physically handicapped (Marks, 1991).

Critics of the underclass doctrine argued that many children reared in the underclass were able to escape from it. An extensive study was made of 456 men in Boston, who had been in the control group for the famous study of delinquency by the Gluecks; they were themselves *non*-delinquent, but of low IQ, and from very poor areas of the city. Long and Vaillant (1984) found that by the age of 47 many of these men had left the underclass, 9 per cent to class II. Those from the worst homes had spent more time in prison and were more anti-social, but otherwise were not any worse off than those from better homes in this group. The transmission of the underclass was not due to economic factors but more to the passing on of low IQ, depression, alcoholism and other aspects of physical and mental illness. Much of the disadvantage arises anew (Rutter and Madge, 1976).

Charles Murray (1990) argued that an underclass developed in Britain during the 1980s, similar to the American ones, though less dominated by ethnic minority groups. He showed that there was a rapid increase during this period of three key features of underclass culture – dropping out of work, violent crime and illegitimate births. Members were not only out of work, many were able-bodied young men who made no attempt to find work. There has been an increase in poverty in Britain during the last thirteen years. The British underclass is mainly white and lives on council estates, where there is a lot of unemployment and many single parents (*The Economist*, 1992). Research in Britain has also found that at least half of the children born to disadvantaged homes do not repeat this pattern in the next generation – much of the disadvantage arises anew (Rutter and Madge, 1976).

## CHANGES IN THE BRITISH CLASS SYSTEM SINCE 1900

There have been considerable changes in the distribution of jobs. There has been a big decline in manufacturing industry, with a consequent fall in the proportion of skilled manual workers by 30 per cent and of semi-skilled by 35 per cent between 1911 and 1971. This is partly because of the introduction of automation, partly because labour-intensive work can be done more competitively in Third World countries, in the Far East. At the same time there has been an increase in the number of higher and lower professionals, managers and administrators, and clerical workers, especially female clerical workers (Routh, 1980). There have been large increases in all kinds of middle-class work, but especially of clerical workers and jobs in service industries – medicine, education, entertainment, travel, sport and finance.

The distribution of incomes has changed, so that the top 10 per cent earn less, the middle 60 per cent more and the bottom 30 per cent much the same. Tax changes have done little to equalise things. The distribution of wealth on the other hand has changed more. The richest 1 per cent owned 69 per cent of the nation's wealth in 1911–13, but only 18 per cent in 1989 (*Social Trends*, 1992).

The composition of social classes has changed a little. The upper is no longer dominated by the aristocracy, but by wealthy business families. Different occupations make up class I, which now includes accountants and city finance workers, scientists and architects, as well as doctors and lawyers. We have seen that there is a new working class, which is distinct from the traditional one, but which is not middle-class. The manual working class is smaller, but there are more unemployed, and working-class people are much more at risk here.

Has social mobility increased? Heath (1981) concludes that upward mobility has increased a little: for those born before 1890 it was 16.5 per cent, for those born in 1938–47 it was 30.5 per cent. Downward mobility fell from 33 per cent to 21 per cent. This reflects the increasing size of the middle class at the expense of the working class, so that more upward mobility is needed to fill the jobs. Access to the upper class is still very limited, though it has become a little easier to become a higher civil servant, a bishop or a senior Army officer, only a little easier to become a company director and no easier to become the chairman of a bank or other large corporation (Abercrombie and Warde, 1988).

Have the relations between classes changed at all? There are several indications that they have. The kind of 'Upstairs–Downstairs' situation shown on TV, of an immense social gap between the gentry and their servants, is so remote from present-day experience as to make it a suitable topic for entertainment. The world of work has changed profoundly, through the activities of trade unions and of social scientists. The earlier authoritarian and hierarchical forms of organisation have been modified by industrial democracy, the power of employers and managers has been reduced and supervisors have been taught more skilled and less authoritarian styles of working.

## THE SOCIAL CLASS OF WOMEN

The traditional approach has been to take the family as the unit of class and to assess its class from the husband's job. It is argued that women usually have part-time jobs and are away from work for the period of child-bearing. On the other hand, in only 19 per cent of families is the husband the only earner; often the wife is in a different occupational class, and sometimes in a higher one, than her husband. Not all women put their family and domestic duties first, many are career women and postpone or abandon having children. If sociologists measure the class of families by husband's occupation they will be wrong some of the time. It may be a mistake to assume that husband and wife have the same class – they may be treated very differently at work, and some aspects of their behaviour can be predicted better from their individual class (Haralambos and Holborn, 1990).

In an Australian study Graetz (1991) found that in the great majority of households the husband was the main earner, and his job the best indicator of class. However, in 4–5 per cent of cases the wife had a better job, which was more or less full-time, so her class would not be assessed well from her husband's occupation. A large survey of British Open University students found that for married women, whether employed or not, the husband's job was the best predictor of subjective social class. For single women their own occupation was the best predictor. Other factors which affected the subjective class of women were father's class and own education (Abbott and Sapsford, 1987).

The subjective class of men is unaffected by their wife's job, but the class of women is greatly affected by their husband's job. This explains why women see their jobs less in class terms and women are less divided by class. Women play a much smaller part in trade unions, as would be expected (Vanneman and Cannon, 1987). We shall see later that women in families do not lose contact at all when class differences develop between them, though male relatives see each other less often when this happens (p. 79).

Women are in some ways of a lower class, or rather they belong to a lower caste, like a racial minority group. Their job prospects and pay are worse than those of men, they have less power, and men hold partly negative stereotypes about them, which justifies discrimination, for jobs for example. Marxist feminists have explained the origins of the 'oppression' of women as a coalition between men and capitalists in the nineteenth century to exclude women from work and restrict them to a domestic role (Barrett, 1980). They are certainly not excluded from work now, but they are mainly in low-paid forms of clerical and service work, and have been described as 'the underclass of the white-collar sector' (Giddens, 1973).

The social mobility of women raises a number of important issues, and will be discussed in Chapter 8.

## REFERENCES

Abbott, P. and Sapsford, R. (1987) *Women and Social Class*. London: Tavistock.
Abercrombie, N. and Warde, A. (1988) *Capital, Labour and the Middle Classes*. London: Allen & Unwin.
Barrett, M. (1980) *Women's Oppression Today*. London: Verso.
Britten, N. (1984) Class imagery in a national sample of women and men. *British Journal of Sociology*, 35, 406–34.
Coleman, R.P. (1983) The continuing significance of social class to marketing. *Journal of Consumer Research*, 10, 265–80.
Coleman, R.R. and Rainwater, L. (1979) *Social Standing in America*. London: Routledge & Kegan Paul.
*Classification of Occupations* (1960, 1966, 1970, 1980) Published in the year before a census. OPCS. London: HMSO.
Dalia, J.T. and Guest, A.M. (1975) Embourgeoisement among blue-collar workers? *Sociological Quarterly*, 16, 291–304.

Davis, K. and Moore, W.E. (1945) Some principles of stratification. *American Sociological Review*, 10, 242–9.
*Economic Activity, Census* (1981) Great Britain (1984) OPCS. London: HMSO.
*The Economist* (1992) How the other tenth lives. 12–18 September: 29–30.
*Family Expenditure Survey Report for 1986* (revised) (1990) DOE. London: HMSO.
Ford, R. (1988) The problem with socio-economics. Paper at conference on 'The challenges currently facing research'. London International Business Communications Ltd.
*General Household Survey* (1989) London: OPCS and HMSO.
Giddens, A. (1973) *The Class Structure of the Advanced Societies*. London: Hutchinson.
Giddens, A. (1989) *Sociology*. Cambridge: Polity Press.
Goldthorpe, J. (1982) The service class. In A. Giddens and G. Mackenzie (eds) *Social Class and the Division of Labour*. Cambridge: Cambridge University Press.
Goldthorpe, J.H. and Hope, K. (1974) *The Social Grading of Occupations: A New Approach and Scale*. Oxford: Clarendon Press.
Goldthorpe, J.H., Lockwood, D., Bechhofer, F. and Platt, J. (1969) *The Affluent Worker*. Cambridge: Cambridge University Press.
Graetz, B. (1991) The class location of families: a refined classification and analysis. *Sociology*, 25, 101–18.
Haralambos, M. and Holborn, M. (1990) *Sociology*. 3rd edition. London: Unwin Hyman.
Heath, A. (1981) *Social Mobility*. Glasgow: Fontana.
Heath, A., Jowell, R., Curtice, J., Evans, G., Field, J. and Witherspoon, S. (1991) *Understanding Political Change*. Oxford: Pergamon.
Hollingshead, A.B. (1949) *Elmtown's Youth*. New York: Wiley.
Jackman, M.R. and Jackman, R.W. (1973) An interpretation of the relation between objective and subjective social status. *American Sociological Review*, 38, 569–82.
Kornhauser, R.R. (1953) The Warner approach to social stratification. In R. Bendix and S.M. Lipset (eds) *Class, Status and Power*. Glencoe, Ill.: Free Press.
Lockwood, D. (1966) Sources of variation in working class images of society. *Sociological Review*, 14, 249–67.
Lockwood, D. (1989) *The Blackcoated Worker*. Oxford: Clarendon Press.
Long, J.V.F. and Vaillant, G.E. (1984) Natural history of male psychological health, XI: escape from the underclass. *American Journal of Psychiatry*, 141, 341–5.
Marks, C. (1991) The urban underclass. *Annual Review of Sociology*, 17, 445–66.
Marshall, G., Newby, H., Rose, D. and Vogler, C. (1988) *Social Class in Modern Britain*. London: Hutchinson.
Murray, C. (1990) *The Emerging British Underclass*. London: IEA Health and Welfare Unit.
*New Earnings Survey* (1992) London: HMSO.
*New Society* (1987) Database: personal wealth. 24 April.
Parkin, F. (1971) *Class Inequality and Political Order*. London: MacGibbon & Kee.
Penn, R. (1985) *Skilled Workers in the Class System*. Cambridge: Cambridge University Press.
Pfautz, H.W. and Duncan, O.D. (1950) A critical examination of Warner's work in community stratification. *American Sociological Review*, 15, 205–15.
Reid, I. (1989) *Social Class Differences in Britain*. 3rd edition. London: Fontana.
Routh, G. (1980) *Occupation and Pay in Great Britain 1906–79*. London: Macmillan.
Runciman, W.G. (1966) *Relative Deprivation and Social Justice*. London: Routledge & Kegan Paul.
Rutter, M. and Madge, N. (1976) *Cycles of Disadvantage*. London: Heinemann.

Savage, M., Barlow, J., Dickens, P. and Fielding, T. (1992) *Property, Bureaucracy and Culture*. London and New York: Routledge.

Scase, R. (1982) The petty bourgeoisie and modern capitalism: a consideration of recent theories. In A. Giddens and G. Mackenzie (eds) *Social Class and the Division of Labour*. Cambridge: Cambridge University Press.

Scott, J. (1991) *Who Rules Britain?*. Cambridge: Polity Press.

*Social Trends 17* (1987) CSS. London: HMSO.

Townsend, P. (1979) *Poverty in the United Kingdom*. Harmondsworth: Penguin.

Vanneman, R. and Cannon, W. (1987) *The American Perception of Class*. Philadelphia: Temple University Press.

Vanneman, R. and Pampel, F.C. (1977) The American perception of class and status. *American Sociological Review*, 42, 422–37.

Warner, W.L. and Lunt, P.S. (1941) *The Social Life of a Modern Community*. New Haven: Yale University Press.

Warner, W.L. *et al.* (1949) *Democracy in Jonesville*. New York: Harper & Row.

Wright, E.O. (1985) *Classes*. London: Verso.

# Chapter 2

# Other class systems, past and present

We have just described the class system in Britain, and its recent development. In order to consider the phenomena of class more generally we shall now look at other class systems with a number of questions in mind.

1 Is the British class system similar to others or is Britain more stratified with less chance of social mobility than elsewhere, as has sometimes been claimed?
2 How does class differ in other countries in the modern world, for example in unequal distribution of wealth, social distance between classes, social mobility and who gets to the top?
3 Have there always been class systems in earlier historical periods, and have they taken different forms?
4 Is class inevitable? Two main attempts to abolish it will be described – Communism in the USSR and Eastern Europe and on a smaller scale the Israeli kibbutz.

## CLASS SYSTEMS IN THE PAST

Marx (1984 edit.) thought that there have been four main stages in the history of class: (1) primitive societies – no classes or private property, (2) ancient civilisations – masters and slaves, (3) feudalism – landlords and serfs, (4) bourgeois society – capitalists and labourers. Lenski (1966) also wrote a history of class, and concluded that social differentiation rose and fell, reaching its height in the period of the advanced agrarian empires, like Eygpt, China and India, in the past. In the present century there are a number of mainly agrarian countries where the governing class comprises 1–2 per cent of the population and owns 50–60 per cent of the arable land – Egypt, Jordan, Iraq, Portugal, Chile, South Vietnam, Lebanon and Southern Spain (Lenski and Lenski, 1978).

The detailed history of class is beyond the scope of this book, but a short account will be given of the main kinds of class system. In addition to Marx's four types I shall add caste systems. Another kind, which was found only in dry regions in Asia, was 'oriental despotism'. According to the 'hydraulic model' of oriental despotism, the construction of large-scale irrigation systems led to the emergence of a powerful class of those who controlled the irrigation, which gave them great power over others. It also led to large-scale cooperation and the need for defence (Cohen and Service, 1978).

## Primitive societies

The most primitive societies are the 'hunters and gatherers', nomadic tribes composed of communities of about 50, occasionally up to 500, with very primitive technology. Examples today are the Aborigines, Bushmen, South American Indians and the Andaman Islanders. They are all nomadic – they hunt and gather and move on, so they acquire few possessions. They are very cooperative, which is necessary for hunting, and they share their food and most of their few possessions.

Status is given to the men with the best hunting skills, because they are important to the welfare of the tribe. There are leaders of a sort – part-time headmen and shamans. They have some power over others, and their position depends mainly on their personal qualities, such as hunting and leadership skills. There are no class differences in the sense of different groups with different cultures. There is almost no inheritance of power or status and none of possessions.

These tribes are virtually egalitarian. This is made possible by their small size and lack of material possessions. They are more like the social groups described in the next chapter than class systems (Radcliffe-Brown, 1922; Lenski, 1966).

From about 10–15,000 BC there were very slow changes, starting with cultivating land, first with a digging stick, later with plough and irrigation. This led to the appearance of settled villages, of 100–200 members, sometimes larger, and houses. Examples which still exist today are the Zuni and other American and South American Indians, and Pacific Islanders. These tribes are more prosperous than hunters and gatherers, have more food, build houses and own possessions, have time for leisure including ritual and warfare. There is more specialisation of occupations and skills, such as craftsmen and a commercial class, and there are more full-time leaders and shamans. These individuals have power and privileges, but little more material wealth, though some have larger houses and burial sites. Indeed those who acquire surplus wealth in some tribes give it away or even destroy it, in potlatch ceremonies – this gives them prestige and builds up obligations on the part of others. An important difference from hunters and gatherers is that leadership offices give authority and status, over and above those earned by individual qualities; often the leaders wear special badges or uniforms.

Status can be acquired by religious or magical skills, by being good at hunting or fighting or good at oratory. Status differences are greater than in simpler communities, and the leaders have greater power. However, the range of inequality is still not very great, because there is no shortage of land or food; there is little development of material possessions, and these are often given away (Lenski, 1966).

The next stage of technological and social development takes us to advanced horticultural societies, who use metal hoes and other farming implements, which enable them to dig to a greater depth and produce a lot more food. These societies are larger, up to 3 million, with cities of up to 30,000, supported by the efficient farmers. Examples are societies in West Africa like the Yoruba and Zande and, at an earlier historical epoch in Central and South America, the Incas and Aztecs. Most of these societies have a central authority, above the village or city level, consisting of the king, his family and relations, the staff of the court, tax collectors and other administrators. The king and his family are very wealthy, through collecting taxes, and have great power. They can execute people, for example. In these societies there is far more social inequality than in the simpler ones described so far. Not all of them developed centralised despotism; this is most common under certain conditions: living outside rain forests, having advanced technology and being threatened by aggressive neighbours, with subsequently greater political development (Lenski, 1966).

These societies developed three main classes – (1) those connected to or favoured by the king, (2) officials, technicians and specialists who carried out the tasks of government and (3) the common people. Each class may be divided further, and the lowest class can be divided into slaves and free men. There may also be status groups or castes, based on tribal origins. Social mobility is possible, and people try very hard to become appointed to political offices. However, there is more of a hereditary class system than in simpler societies, since there is more property to inherit – land, slaves, offices, money and cattle in particular.

## Slavery

This was a common kind of class system, in larger agricultural communities in the ancient world. Slaves played an important part in the societies of Athens and Rome, and comprised up to 30 per cent of the population, freeing their owners for a life of leisure and politics. They were mostly prisoners of war, from Africa and Persia. At a later period, between 1600 and 1870, the slave trade imported several million slaves from West Africa to the USA, Brazil and the Caribbean.

Slaves were owned, often bought and sold, had very poor legal rights, and it was believed that their position was justified because they were inferior. Some were captured in wars, others sold in the slave trade, some inherited their status, others had fallen into debt. In most slave societies, the slaves were able to buy their freedom.

In the Roman Empire slaves were employed either by families as servants or for agriculture, mining and other industrial work. In the large workshops and farms working groups were found very difficult to handle, because of the unwillingness of the workers and the large numbers involved. Some of the supervisors were themselves slaves, others monks or soldiers. In any case they found it very difficult to extract efficient work from slaves, the only incentive available being punitive discipline, including lashing, chains and execution, even crucifixion. The slaves were compelled by law to work and were severely punished if they did not; in exchange they were given lifelong board and keep, but were not usually paid. Slaves in domestic work were sometimes treated in a paternalistic way, as part of the family. Some slaves in Athens did well, not only as supervisors, but as teachers and philosophers; some slaves even had slaves.

They were usually treated very badly however, and were despised members of what was seen as an 'inferior' race or culture. They had no political and very few legal rights. Owners were not allowed to kill them or have sexual relations with them for example, but many were killed as part of the 'entertainment' in circuses. Others managed to buy their freedom, and owners gained prestige by freeing slaves. Slavery did not work as a social institution, because the slaves were constantly staging revolts, and because slaves were such unwilling workers, and freedmen who were paid did better work (Hellie, 1989).

In the American Southern states slaves were also a caste, in that all were black, their status was inherited and it was not possible to buy freedom (Kerbo, 1983). In Jamaica in 1795 291,000 slaves were controlled by a white population of 17,000. Freedom could not be bought and the slaves were despised, distrusted, paid almost nothing and often starved to death (Littlejohn, 1972). Slavery was abolished in South Africa, but replaced by *apartheid*, another kind of caste system, the different racial groups forced to live in separate areas, use separate facilities in trains and other public places, legally enforced arrangements to the disadvantage of the black and coloured groups.

The racial situation in Britain and other modern countries is also like a caste system in some ways, in that it is very difficult to move into another group. Being black in particular conveys low social status, but most people would regard a black doctor or member of parliament as of higher status than a white manual worker. There is also quite a lot of intermarriage, with the result that many blacks are partly white; this gives them greater status within the black community and some may 'pass' as white (Brown, 1965).

## Caste systems

Here people are born into a caste, must marry within it, and it is very difficult to leave it. The caste system of India and other countries in South Asia has lasted for 3,000 years, though it has slowly been dismantled since World War II. There are five main castes:

Brahmins, originally priests, but now containing other high status occupations as well
Kshatriyas, soldiers
Vaisayas, tradesmen and craftsmen
Sudras, lower-status manual workers
Harijans, untouchables, who fall outside the caste system.

Each of these main castes is divided into many smaller occupational groups, based on traditional specialisation of jobs, typically of 5–15,000 people over a certain area, each group aware of its social rank.

The relations between castes are defined by their occupational roles, so that interaction and cooperation are demanded. The system is basically hierarchical, the higher castes enjoying greater power and perceived as exploiting the lower ones. In addition, several kinds of distance and deference are required. This is stronger in country villages than in the cities and is particularly strong in Kerala. Here the proper distances to be kept between castes are specified: Brahmins must keep 7 feet from the next caste; the next pairs of castes must keep 25 and 32 feet apart, and the fourth caste must keep 64 feet from the untouchables. Other forms of distance and deference include the use of caste names and terms of address, standing in the presence of Brahmins and other rituals. Some of these rules are enforced by law, others by social convention.

The most rigid boundary in the social hierarchy is between the untouchables and the four 'clean' castes as illustrated by the 64 feet distance in Kerala, although the unclean make up 27 per cent of the population there. If an unclean person touches the water, food, utensils or person of a higher caste individual, this is regarded as insult and pollution, and punishment will follow.

The caste system is closely linked to Hinduism and the belief in reincarnation – to a higher or lower caste depending on performance in the present role, a kind of life-time social mobility. This probably explains the high degree of acceptance of caste, even by the lowest rank and the untouchables; the sanction for breaking the rules is becoming untouchable, or an animal, in the next life. Nevertheless there is quite a lot of deviance.

There is very little individual mobility, but there is some mobility of whole castes, who may succeed in improving their status a little, especially during changing economic conditions. The caste system actually prevents classes being formed, so that privilege is kept intact.

As we shall see later in this chapter, in India today, overall salary differences show more equality than in many other countries, and prestige is on the whole associated with the same occupations as elsewhere (Gupta, 1991).

## Feudalism

This was the kind of class system to be found in England and France in the Middle Ages, from before 1066 to the Peasants' Revolt in 1381. Feudalism was a form of economic and social stratification in which all land was owned by the king. Land was held (and eventually owned) by barons who gave military service in exchange; in turn, smaller areas were held by knights who were usually lords of the manor. Serfs held much smaller strips of land, and also received protection; in exchange they had to provide a certain number of days' work, military service and a proportion of their produce. The system was at its height in Europe round about 1200, when the ranks in the hierarchy became institutionalised, not just a matter of custom.

The power of the higher ranks was based primarily on the ownership of land, helped by their military power, and legitimated by the church (Kerbo, 1983). In principle the king owned all land and in practice kings were extremely wealthy: it has been estimated that King Richard I and King John had incomes equivalent to those of forty of the richest nobles or of 24,000 serfs (who were paid a penny a day). Feudal kings organised large armies, and were much occupied with war and conquest of territory.

The next level in the hierarchy were the lords, who held large territories, and also controlled small armies. Below them came knights, lords of the manor, who each controlled a village with about 400 people, including children. Every person was born into a certain 'estate', and had legal obligations to their superiors, and could be punished if they failed to carry them out. Serfs owned no land and had no political rights; they were usually very poor. Their superiors could make them pay taxes or simply seize their land. What the serfs did get out of the system was a strip of land to farm and protection.

In addition to lords, knights, priests and serfs, there were soldiers and retainers associated with castle and manor, a growing number of merchants, the early capitalists, and an artisan class of skilled craftsmen.

There were great inequalities in the feudal system, of wealth as we have seen, of power and of social status. There was a large social gap between lords and knights, and the peasants. The style of leadership within the feudal system was personal and paternalistic, and was based on a high degree of acceptance of authority, as well as the dependence of subordinates on landowners. There was a hierarchy of management: the bailiff was assisted by a reeve, who was sometimes a representative of the peasants.

The church supported the feudal system, the higher clergy and monks were themselves of high status and the church owned a lot of land, in fact a third of England at the time. They taught the divine right of kings and gave ideological support to the system. They taught that there would be rewards in heaven for those who performed their proper duties in this world. In the sixth century St Benedict founded the first of many monastic orders, with rules condemning idleness in order to avoid sin, and requiring manual work to discipline the soul; in addition, it enabled workers to give to the poor and to the church. However, monks taught later that intellectual and religious work was superior to manual work, a view the upper classes were happy to accept.

There was some social mobility, for example by marriage into a higher rank and by moving into the classes of artisans or merchants. Upward mobility was greater during times of war, famine and economic changes bringing new opportunities.

The peasants were poor and oppressed, they were not free to leave, they were compelled to work a certain number of days for the lord of the manor, who also claimed fines for marriage and numerous other arbitrary and servile dues. These frustrations and the desire for freedom led to the Peasants' Revolt in 1381, one of the main causes of the collapse of feudalism. Another cause was the Black Death of 1347–54, which killed a half to a third of the population; landowners no longer had enough serfs to farm their land, and increased pressure led to their flight to the towns to become craftsmen, artisans or merchants. Others became free yeomen who owned their own land (Trevelyan, 1942).

## Class during the Industrial Revolution (England 1769–1850)

The discovery of steam-power, inventions in the textile industry and the development of iron and coal led to the first factories and other large-scale industry, and massive changes in the shape of society. These changes took place first in England, but European countries soon followed and later the USA. Some historians think this started a move away from the great social inequalities and feudal rigidity of earlier periods (Lenski, 1966), while others draw attention to the poverty and bad working conditions of factory workers (Thompson, 1980).

The Industrial Revolution was created by the inventions mentioned; entrepreneurs built factories using these methods and employed increasing numbers of people, especially in mining, textiles, iron and engineering. There was a very large movement of population from country to town, to live in the new industrial slums, and there was a large increase in the size of the population. What effect did all this have on the class system?

The aristocracy were still in place, about 0.25 per cent of the population, 350–400 families of wealthy aristocrats, and 3,000 lesser squires and gentry. They all owned land and country houses, some were very wealthy, doing little work and deriving most of their income from rents, though some also invested in the new industries. They had an elegant way of life, with large houses and many servants – up to fifty in the richer households. There were balls, the Grand Tour, the London Season and the rest. They were looked up to, in the country in particular, because of their wealth, their titles, their famous ancestors and their impressive way of life. Feudal attitudes of deference to social superiors, no matter how idle, still persisted (Bédarida, 1991). This was the leisured class, the 'idle rich', as portrayed by Jane Austen. There was another urban leisure class, after the Napoleonic wars which ended in 1815, of 'fund-holders', living on the interest from government loans, made to finance the war. However, the Industrial Revolution produced new classes of people with other sources of wealth and power.

The men who created the Industrial Revolution were the entrepreneurs, who owned or borrowed capital, and used the new inventions of steam-power and the rest, and built up the first factories. The early entrepreneurs in England were mostly middle-class merchants with some capital, while a minority were ex-craftworkers or were self-made. They were not well educated, but they knew their own trade. They shared a faith in progress and an enthusiasm for technical inventions. They were a rising prosperous class, despised by the landed aristocracy; many lived austerely, reinvesting rather than spending their profits, and few sought to infiltrate the upper classes (Bendix, 1956). They worked extremely hard, were examples of the Protestant Work Ethic, some were unscrupulous and many were authoritarian, but others like Robert Owen had a Utopian vision of the ideal working community, in which there was cooperation, a happy and healthy environment and character training. However the entrepreneurs, while of great importance, were few in number, and during the nineteenth century declined both in numbers and in power; they were to be replaced by the managers (Lenski, 1966).

The factories were administered by salaried managers, a new class, some of whom were trained as accountants or lawyers. They had the skills of organising supplies, managing the whole production process, controlling an ill-disciplined work-force and marketing the product (Mathias, 1983). They were not professional managers so much as experts in their particular industry. Also important were the engineers, the technical experts, who made the machinery work. The larger the factories became, the more managers and experts were needed, and the more they were paid. The growing middle classes included people in banking and commerce, civil servants and other administrators, and the growing number of professions. In all the middle class was about 4 million strong, one sixth of the English population.

The middle classes felt themselves to be the middle tier of a three-class system. They had great self-confidence and optimism, felt that they ran society, and that they also represented the common interest in opposition to the selfish sectional interests of the aristocracy. They worked hard, in a self-disciplined way, they wanted to better themselves, and some succeeded in becoming propertied members of the upper classes themselves.

Meanwhile there was rapid expansion of the lower middle class of clerical workers, who were still nearly all men during this period. Their social status was well above that of manual workers and their conditions of work much better.

The working class as we know it was partly created by the Industrial Revolution. In 1851 five-sixths of the population belonged to this class, some in the new factories, some in traditional small-scale work and many still in agriculture and service. There were only 2 million in factory work in 1851, out of 5 million in industry and transport, while there were 1.3 million domestic servants and many agricultural workers.

The process of converting craftworkers and peasants into industrial workers was a difficult one. They had previously worked at home and were not accustomed to the conditions of industrial work, in particular having to keep regular hours. In their efforts to control workers, employers used fines for lateness and absenteeism, low wages (so that hunger would keep them at work), long hours (to keep them out of the public houses), corporal punishment (especially for children), dismissal or relegation to worse jobs – and resultant starvation and prison.

Skilled workers were paid quite well, but the less skilled and unskilled were paid no more than before. The wages paid were as low as employers could get away with, enough to keep the workers alive, but with consequent malnutrition and frequent visits to the pawn shop. Wages did not increase until after 1863, following the growth of trade unions and a general increase in the prosperity of industry.

The bad conditions and starvation wages led to great discontent and riots by industrial workers. The Luddites destroyed textile machinery in 1811–12 in the North of England. The Peterloo riot by cotton workers in Manchester in 1819 was savagely put down by the Yeomanry, a kind of militia composed of manufacturers and merchants – on horseback. Out of a large crowd of rioters 421 were injured, 161 with sabre wounds. This was a real class war. The leaders were hanged or transported to Australia (Thompson, 1980). The law had been very unfavourable to the working classes: trade unions were not allowed until 1825, people could be hanged or deported to Australia for small thefts and lower-class people were not allowed to wear smart clothes, of silk for example. In 1832 the Reform Bill gave the vote to rate payers, in 1833 the Factory Act required shorter working hours, safer and cleaner working conditions, in 1834 the Poor Law Act provided the dole and in 1835 the Municipal Bill gave working people a say in local government.

These developments probably averted a revolution. The trade unions and allied movements cooled and re-directed discontent into more peaceful channels, using the power of organised labour to increase wages and improve the conditions of work, but also to increase cooperation with employers, with whom the workers had a common interest. In any case the industrial workers were a minority of the working class, and servants, agricultural workers and workers in traditional workplaces were not interested in revolutionary politics.

Did the Industrial Revolution produce more or less social stratification? In terms of *incomes*, the owners, managers and skilled workers did well, but the semi- and unskilled did very badly until after 1863. *Social mobility* increased, compared to earlier feudal periods. This was partly due to the spread of education, needed to train skilled people of all kinds to man the new industry. There were many possibilities for promotion through competence and hard work, even into the landowning classes. Poor boys could become Lord Mayor of London.

*Social distance* between the three main classes was large. The relationship between the supervisors and the workers was a curious one. On the one hand, the supervisors knew the workers personally and exercised some degree of paternalistic benevolence; on the other hand, workers were clearly treated very badly. The traditional feudal relationship was used as a means of controlling workers by eliciting obedience and deference – but without the duties of the master being taken very seriously (Bendix, 1956). The Navy was famous for the brutal treatment of sailors and their frequent mutinies. The social distance between ranks in industry became larger as factories became larger. However, the power of working people, at first very small, increased with the growth of trade unions, the ability to vote in local and national elections and the repeal of harsh laws favouring the rich at the expense of the poor. There was also a greatly increased geographical separation of classes. Instead of cottages grouped round the manor, the upper classes lived in the country, the middle classes in spacious suburbs and the workers in the industrial slums (Trevelyan, 1942; Bédarida, 1991).

## HOW DOES THE BRITISH CLASS SYSTEM COMPARE WITH OTHERS IN THE MODERN WORLD?

Britain has often been described as 'class-ridden', even by people who live here (Dahrendorf, 1982). Is this true, and if so in what sense? I shall look at several dimensions on which stratification systems can be compared.

### Income inequality

There are large differences between the incomes of different sections of the population in every country. Egalitarianism is simply unknown. The percentage of national income earned by the top and bottom 20 per cent of families is a measure of how much difference there is. Table 2.1 shows ratios

*Table 2.1* Ratios of richest/poorest 20 per cent of households (1989)

| | |
|---|---|
| Brazil | 26.1 |
| Botswana | 23.6 |
| Costa Rica | 16.5 |
| Australia | 9.6 |
| USA | 8.9 |
| UK | 6.8 |
| Israel | 6.6 |
| France | 6.5 |
| Sweden | 4.6 |
| Japan | 4.3 |
| Poland | 3.6 |
| Hungary | 3.0 |

*Source:* World Bank, 1991

of expenditure or income for a number of countries as reported by the World Bank. These figures are mainly based on expenditure. As we saw in the last chapter, the top-to-bottom ratio in Britain, after tax and welfare, is only 4.3:1, probably because middle-class people save more and spend less. The most unequal incomes are consistently found in South American countries, the most equal ones in Communist countries. Britain is in the middle, more equal than the USA, less so than Sweden which has become increasingly egalitarian. Third World countries have shown an 'inverted U' pattern of development: as they get richer, inequality increases at first but declines later. The percentage of very poor people in such countries is usually very high. The percentage of the population with incomes less than $75 per annum was over 20 per cent in some South American countries in 1969 (Fields, 1980).

*Is British class less dependent on money?* In Britain money is rather low on the list of cues for decoding the class of other people, after lifestyle, family background, etc. (p. 5). It is sometimes said that in the USA money is the main cue for class, and it is possible to find anecdotal support for this. I was present when a nervous visitor was being shown a wonderful new computer at Harvard, and on enquiring who was allowed to use it was told 'Anyone who can afford it'. However, the study of Centers (1949), on the criteria people used to decide on another's class, found that money came quite low on the list, and in much the same place as in similar British studies (p. 203). Robinson and Bell (1978) report similar surveys in the two countries. Subjective social class depended slightly *more* on income in the UK ($r = .21$) than in the USA (.16), and on occupation (UK $r = .38$, USA .25), but equally on education in both.

## The status of occupations

According to the 'convergence' hypothesis, the same occupational hierarchy will be found in all industrialised societies. How far is this the case? Treiman

(1977) re-analysed eighty-five surveys of the perceived prestige of different jobs in sixty countries, for 509 occupations in all, later placed in fourteen groups. He was able to produce a universal scale of occupational prestige by averaging across countries. He found a very high level of agreement, in that for nearly all the sixty countries studied, the local order of job prestige correlated at over .87 with the universal scale. However, two groups of countries had a lower level of agreement. Poland and the USSR had lower correlations, though still over .80. We discuss later the high status of skilled workers, and the relatively low status of clerical workers, in Communist countries. The second deviate group consisted of Third World countries, like India, the Congo and Nigeria. The convergence hypothesis was intended to fit only modern industrialised countries, and it is no surprise that Third World countries fit it less well. Nevertheless, the correlation between Indian prestige rankings and the universal scale was as high as .75, and a number of other Third World countries had higher ones, e.g. Indonesia, Thailand, Chile, Ghana, the Ivory Coast and South-West Africa.

Kelley (1990) tackled the problem somewhat differently. He used the fourteen main occupational groupings found by Treiman, but obtained scores for socioeconomic status, based on income and education not prestige, for sixteen representative countries. He too found high correlations between the SES scores for different countries and averaged them across the

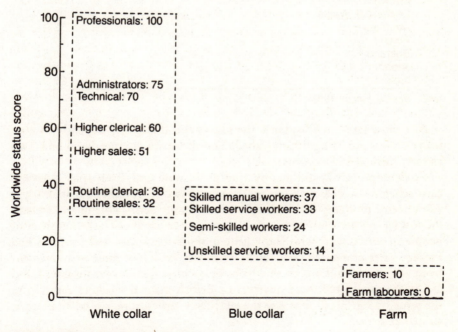

*Figure 2.1* Worldwide status scale
*Source:* Kelley, 1990

world. His Worldwide Status Scale gives scores for many occupations, and is shown in Figure 2.1.

## Social mobility

It is part of the convergence hypothesis that all industrial societies with nuclear families will develop much the same levels of social mobility. The alternative hypothesis is that mobility rates will differ as a result of cultural and political factors: left-wing governments will produce higher mobility, countries with feudal, aristocratic or right-wing traditions will have lower rates.

Heath (1981) used the percentages of people moving across the manual/ non-manual line in nineteen industrialised countries for which recent data were available. The results gave some support to the convergence hypothesis: the highest rate was for Canada (37.5 per cent), the lowest for Italy (25.5 per cent); England and Wales scored 33.7 per cent.

*Table 2.2* Percentage manual/non-manual mobility

| | |
|---|---|
| Canada | 37.5 |
| Sweden | 37.0 |
| USA | 36.5 |
| France | 34.0 |
| England & Wales | 33.7 |
| Australia | 33.2 |
| Poland | 30.7 |
| Bulgaria | 28.5 |
| Japan | 28.0 |
| Italy | 25.5 |

*Source:* Heath, 1981

As I show later, in Chapter 8, the rate of social mobility depends on how many classes are being distinguished. The above study considered only two classes, manual and non-manual.

Goldthorpe (1987) did a similar study of nine countries using a seven–class schema – which of course gives higher rates of 'mobility'; Britain's was 72 per cent. Hungary had the highest rate (76 per cent), Poland and Ireland the lowest (60 per cent, 58 per cent), partly because of the large numbers of people in agriculture, who show little mobility. England and Scotland had average rates compared with other countries, and low rates of movement from agriculture but a high rate from blue-collar families into classes I and II. At the same time three-quarters of British manual workers came from the same backgrounds, because the shift from agriculture had taken place at an earlier period.

Heath found that for his nineteen countries those with the highest mobility also had the highest rates of expansion of the non-manual class, as a result of industrialisation, e.g. Hungary, Bulgaria and Yugoslavia. It is not clear whether industrial change was the main cause of high mobility, or whether the latter was due to political factors. In the USSR however there was high mobility but quite a low rate of increase in the non-manual class, so that politics was probably the cause.

Sweden is another interesting case. It has a high rate of mobility, but a lower rate of change than other industrialised countries: a similar pattern to the USSR and probably due to a social democratic tradition promoting equality of opportunity and outcome. Australia is also a very open society, with a high rate of mobility on several different measures, but a moderately low rate of change. This may be because Australia is a 'new' society, little affected by, indeed rebelling against, European feudal and aristocratic traditions.

Heath (1981) and others have studied the extent of entry into the élite class, variously defined, in different countries. Earlier studies had claimed, for example, that America was a very open society on the basis of the large number of people in this class from manual backgrounds, but this is partly because of the large number of people categorised by investigators as belonging to the élite group. If comparable categories are used, corresponding to our class I, 76 per cent of the England and Wales élite came from a non-élite background, compared with 71 per cent in the USA. Mobility rates into the élite give a slightly different ordering of countries from manual/non-manual mobility. It is hardest to enter the élite group in Italy (of the countries studied), France and Spain, Germany and Japan; easiest are Hungary, Yugoslavia; Britain and the USA have intermediate rates again.

Another way of comparing social mobility in different countries is by path analysis, to show the different predictors of individual mobility (see p. 180). Several such studies have been carried out in a similar way. They show that in Czechoslovakia a son's job, i.e. his occupational status, is not predicted by his father's job, but *is* predicted by his father's educational level, via the son's education. In Spain on the other hand father's occupation is the strongest predictor of son's job, while father's education is a minor factor, as is son's education. This confirms that there is openness and a lot of mobility in Czechoslovakia, and that this is achieved via education; in Spain on the other hand jobs depend more on class of origin than on education. In Britain and the USA, son's education is an important predictor of his job, and his father's education and occupation are also predictors, education being the stronger one.

Kelley (1990) compared the correlation between father's and son's occupational status in fifteen countries with other features of those countries. He found that 'inheritance' of status was greater when there was a lot of educational inequality, and when there was much income inequality between different jobs. Brazil, Bolivia and the Philippines were highest both in the inheritance of status and in these two kinds of inequality; Britain and

*Table 2.3* Power distance

| Philippines | 94 | USA | 40 |
|---|---|---|---|
| Mexico | 81 | Canada | 39 |
| India | 77 | Australia | 36 |
| Brazil | 69 | Germany (FR) | 35 |
| France | 68 | Great Britain | 35 |
| Japan | 54 | Sweden | 31 |
| Italy | 50 | New Zealand | 22 |
| S. Africa | 49 | Israel | 13 |
| Argentina | 49 | | |

*Source:* Hofstede, 1984

Malaysia were lowest in inheritance (i.e. most open) and in the two kinds of inequality. This study shows that mobility depends partly on equality of education. Kelley interprets the effect of income differentials through their effect on inherited privilege.

The conclusion of these various studies of social mobility is that Britain is in the middle of the international scale. The countries with the greatest mobility were the Communist countries, together with Sweden and Canada. The lowest are in South America, Italy and Japan.

### Social distance

By social distance is meant the perceived gap between classes, in terms of inequality of various kinds, the amount of deference or respect, or the unlikeliness of people making friends or marrying between classes.

A notable cross-cultural comparison was carried out by Hofstede (1984), with 116,000 employees in forty countries. His measure of 'power distance' was based on the replies to three questions, about whether employees were afraid to disagree with their boss, whether the boss used an autocratic or paternalistic leadership style and whether employees preferred this to more democratic methods. Some of the national scores are given in Table 2.3.

Hofstede found that power distance was greater for countries which were closer to the equator, which had large populations and were poor. It can be seen that the countries with large power distances tend to be those with large income inequality and low social mobility.

There is less evidence from other measures of social distance. Laumann and Senter (1976) used a Bogardus-style social distance scale to find the social distances between seventeen occupational groups. The results were very similar in the USA and Germany.

There is often said to be less social distance between ranks in the USA, but I could not find any objective evidence for this. Warner and Lunt (1941) in their study of 'Yankee City' found a highly stratified community, with six clear status levels. This study was criticised by other American sociologists on various grounds.

Another approach to social distance is to see how many friends are drawn from the same class. In Fischer's (1977) study of Detroit just over 45 per cent of friends were so chosen in each of four classes. Laumann (1973), also in Detroit but using five classes, found a figure of 41 per cent perhaps equal to 50 per cent for four classes, though it was 74 per cent for class I (top professional and business). In Britain Willmott (1987) found 61 per cent of same class friendships in London, but using only three classes, perhaps equivalent to 45 per cent for four classes. Goldthorpe (1987) used a national sample, and reports a number of statistics for within-class friendships, not all directly comparable, but most of them greater than 45 per cent, especially for class I, and for classes VI–VII, especially for those not socially mobile. This does not demonstrate any clear difference between the two countries in the social distances between classes.

*Titles and feudalism.* Britain still has titles, landed noble families, and other residues of feudalism. The USA does not have titles, no Sirs or Lords, but they do have prominent, rich and powerful families, like the Kennedys. These families were founded by ancestors who either made a lot of money, or were successful in politics, or both, and in the USA money is necessary for political success. At the other end of the social scale, the USA has far deeper racial divisions than Britain, and many blacks and Hispanics form an underclass whose members are out of work and involved in crime and drugs.

*Deference.* Perhaps the lower orders are more deferential to their 'betters' in Britain? The Hofstede study suggests that at work they are not. The only evidence for it comes from agricultural workers, who have been found to be deferential in behaviour if not in attitudes to the farm owners, but this is not true for industrial workers (p. 210). However, the American spirit of 'democracy' and the Australian assertion of equality perhaps lead to a greater rejection of deference in some situations.

*Accent,* and to a lesser extent appearance, mean that a person's class in Britain is easily and rapidly identifiable. The result may be that class has a more pervasive effect on social encounters. In the USA for example accent varies more with region though it also varies with class to some extent (p. 124). It is probably easier to place a person by accent in Britain than in America.

Australia is sometimes claimed to be a classless society. It was founded by people who had fled from or been expelled by Britain, and who were rebellious about traditional class divisions. We have seen in this chapter that Australia is not one of the most egalitarian countries in terms of the distribution of incomes but it has a high level of social mobility. Nevertheless class differences remain. Graetz (1987) carried out a national survey, with nearly 5,000 respondents. Of these 64 per cent thought there was a class system and could answer questions about it, but the remainder either said there were no classes or couldn't answer any questions about them. These were mainly young, lower-class, uneducated, Italian or Greek immigrants. Perhaps they were simply ignorant of Australian life. The majority who knew what class was thought that there was a simple hierarchical system with three to four classes.

Wild (1974) carried out a study, similar to that of Yankee City in scale, of a town of 5,200 which he called Bradstone, in New South Wales. From interviews with 200 people he decided that there were six classes, from the Gentry to the No-hopers. We report the class structure of the leisure groups there later in this book (p. 76). The same criticism could be made as of the Yankee City study, that in such a small town many people know each other and are reacting to each other as individuals, not as members of classes. However I have lived in Sydney and Adelaide, and can report that these cities appear to be just as stratified as any British city, if not more so, in terms of wealth, lifestyle, separate clubs and above all residential segregation.

However, as in the USA, the social distances between classes in Australia seem smaller than in Britain, and deferential behaviour of any kind is unusual.

## TWO ATTEMPTS TO ABOLISH SOCIAL CLASS

### Class in Communist societies

Communist societies were inspired by the ideas of Karl Marx, who taught that taking over private property and control of the means of production would lead to egalitarianism and that class would pass away. Communism has now passed away in most places in which it was established, but it existed in Russia from the revolution in 1917 to 1991 and in Eastern Europe from 1945 to 1991. Did class pass away?

Surveys of the prestige given to different occupations in Russia and Eastern Europe found that they were ranked in a similar way as in other countries though with certain differences (Treiman, 1977). Other evidence suggests that occupations fell into four main status groups.

1 White-collar, intelligentsia (i.e. professionals, senior scientists, technicians, managers and administrators)
2 Skilled manual workers

3 Lower or unqualified white-collar workers
4 Unskilled manual workers

(Parkin, 1971)

The main difference from capitalist societies is that skilled manual workers had higher prestige and income and white-collar workers were below them, though above unskilled manual workers. White-collar clerical workers were not at the lower end of a middle-class group as in capitalist countries, with similar privileges and prospects of mobility into administration. There was no clear division under Communism between non-manual and manual; the more important division was between the white-collar intelligentsia and everyone else. About 10 per cent of the population were in the top group, a third of them party officials or bureaucrats. There were fewer middle-class people and more agricultural workers than in other industrialised countries.

Communist countries form a partial exception to the convergence theory of a universal ordering of occupations. This is because under Communism such things are not determined by market forces, but by central planning, inspired by ideological considerations. In the early days of Communism a high degree of egalitarianism was imposed, with higher earnings for skilled manual workers and lower levels for the former bourgeois class. In the 1930s Stalin changed this policy and turned against 'equality-mongering'; income differentials were introduced to motivate people to acquire the skills and accept the responsibilities of higher administrative and technical jobs (Parkin, 1971)

Inkeles (1950) carried out a detailed analysis of class in the USSR before and during World War II. He describes a number of measures which strengthened the divisions between classes – the introduction of different uniforms for workers of different ranks, the abolishing of inheritance tax, and larger pensions and prizes for higher-status individuals. Social mobility became more difficult because of the structure of tuition fees for college, the drafting of lower-status young people into industrial work and preference for children from middle-class families for management and officer training.

The differences in earnings between occupational levels in Communist countries were less than in capitalist countries. In Eastern European countries in 1964 engineering and technical staff earned only about 50 per cent more than manual workers. In the USSR party officials and military officers earned more than this. In addition to salary differences those of higher status had access to important privileges and perks. Although the actual differences in earnings between occupational groups were smaller than under capitalism, people were much more aware of them, perhaps because of the contrasting ideological message of egalitarianism.

However, in Communist countries membership of the Communist Party was a greater source of prestige, power and privileges than occupation. The party has been described as a new ruling class of political bureaucrats, which replaced the western bourgeoisie in controlling the means of production for its own benefit. The privileges which party members and the intelligentsia received included (1) larger houses, and sometimes a dacha as well, (2) access to restricted consumer goods, (3) special medical facilities, (4) better education for children, (5) better food from special shops, (6) cars and travel. These differences were so substantial that they created a class difference in lifestyle.

Djilas (1957) argued that the intelligentsia had higher earnings and many other privileges because they were party members; others think that there was a single new and favoured class which included those in the professions and management. However, 'the fact that white collar intelligentsia has become increasingly identified with the Communist party tends to enhance the group's privileged position in society' (Parkin, 1971, p. 151).

Social mobility was higher than in capitalist countries, partly as the result of rapid industrialisation, purges of large numbers of the élite class and the abolition of private property. In 1961 over 85 per cent of the Central Committee of the Communist Party in the USSR came from peasant or manual backgrounds (Giddens, 1980). In Hungary in 1963 77 per cent of managerial, administrative and professional jobs were filled by people from such a background. The rate of mobility slowed down, and for doctors, scientists and other professions the figure was lower. Political offices could be attained most easily from the least skilled sections of society; the professions and management increasingly needed university training. The effect of this massive social mobility was that everyone believed that it was possible to rise into the privileged class, though the need for higher education was becoming a barrier. For manual workers however another kind of social mobility was possible, by retraining for more skilled jobs.

The children of the white-collar intelligentsia had privileged access to the best schools and colleges, and most of them stayed on as members of the same class; their parents' advantages were passed on via education though not via inheritance of property.

Inkeles and Bauer (1959) carried out a survey of Russian refugees at the end of World War II. These individuals may have been biased, but most peasants and workers among them did not feel that their interests coincided with those of the intelligentsia. The latter were seen as the most harmful class, while the working class was seen as the most harmful by the intelligentsia. However, other studies suggest that there was a higher degree of acceptance both of the ideology and of the social system (Lenski, 1978).

Was there a class system or not? There was no private property, or class control of the means of production, there was a high rate of mobility, including moving into the top political offices, and the range of incomes was small. On the other hand the white-collar intelligentsia were paid more, and the privileges of housing, travel, cars, education, etc., constituted a considerable difference in lifestyle and social prestige, especially for those who were also party members. Parents could not pass on property to their children, but there was as much 'occupational inheritance' as under capitalism, the result of better access to education and jobs for middle-class children (Kerbo, 1983).

## The kibbutz

The Israeli kibbutz is probably the most enduring and successful attempt at an egalitarian utopian community. Kibbutzim first started in 1909, and employed 3.6 per cent of the Israeli population in 1987, about 120,000 people. They produce about 40 per cent of Israel's food and 7 per cent of her exports. There is a strong ideological basis, of devotion to Israel and to cooperative and socialist ideals, and in some cases religious ones. Here they are unlike many other cooperative experiments, since the kibbutz represents the highest ideals of the society outside, rather than rebelling against them. They are quite small communities, mostly between 250 and 500 adults, with as many children. Originally all were engaged in farming, but now many of them now include small factories, with 50–100 workers; these started as small workshops, but then expanded to provide work for older members and new immigrants. In addition to kibbutz members there are paid workers – taken on partly because of the need for particular skills and partly because of government pressure to employ new immigrants.

The original plan was that the kibbutz should be totally egalitarian and democratic, with collective ownership of all property. There are a number of administrative positions, managers of farms and factories, supervisors and others. These jobs are filled by rotation, for a year at a time, at an annual meeting, and the occupants must consult the others at weekly meetings on important decisions. In practice, those with leadership and administrative skills are repeatedly chosen for these jobs, since it is clearly in the interests of the kibbutz for the most competent individuals to run it. In one case the main offices rotated between twelve of the 140 members (Zweig, 1959). Originally skilled manual work was valued most highly, and there was no great enthusiasm to occupy management positions; however, things have worked out differently.

Managers and other administrators were not supposed to be paid any more or receive any benefits from their positions of leadership, but in practice they do. They have more freedom of movement, go on more trips outside the kibbutz, have some petty cash to spend when they go and have the status of representing the kibbutz outside. In addition they gain status and authority inside and become members of a higher-status group who do no manual work, give orders and make decisions (Rosenfeld, 1957). However, office holders do not form a distinctive group, and they have no power to pass on their social status to their children, so that there is no class system here (Tiger and Shepher, 1975).

Other status divisions have opened up in the kibbutz. Some members have acquired higher status by inheriting wealth, others by having been there longest. There has been increased desire for private possessions, and another room added to the house. Some members are interested in higher education and better jobs than the kibbutz can provide, which has resulted in some leaving.

Another division has appeared, between the kibbutz members and those merely employed, especially in the factories, who may be other Israelis or even Arabs. Finally, it was part of the original plan that women should do all the same jobs as men. Things started that way, but then women slowly gravitated to child-care and cooking, looking after the home. This gave them lower status than production workers, and women are now discontented with this lower status (Ben-Rafael, 1988; Yizher, 1989).

## REFERENCES

Bédarida, F. (1991) *A Social History of England 1851–1990*. London: Routledge.
Bendix, R. (1956) *Work and Authority in Industry*. New York: Wiley.
Ben-Rafael, E. (1988) *Status, Power and Conflict in the Kibbutz*. Aldershot: Avebury.
Brown, R. (1965) *Social Psychology*. New York: Collier-Macmillan.
Centers, R. (1949) *The Psychology of Social Class*. Princeton, NJ: Princeton University Press.
Cohen, R. and Service, E.R. (eds) (1978) *Origins of the State*. Philadelphia: Institute for the Study of Human Issues.
Dahrendorf, R. (1982) *On Britain*. London: BBC.
Djilas, M. (1957) *The New Class*. New York: Praeger.
Fields, G.S. (1980) *Poverty, Inequality and Development*. Cambridge: Cambridge University Press.
Fischer, C.S. *et al.* (1977) *Networks and Places*. New York: Free Press.
Giddens, A. (1980) *The Class Structure of the Advanced Societies*. London: Hyman.
Goldthorpe, J.H. (1987) *Social Mobility and Class Structure in Modern Britain*. Oxford: Clarendon Press.
Graetz, B. (1987) *Images of Class in Australia: Equality, Rank and Status*. Canberra: Australian National University.
Gupta, D. (1991) *Social Stratification*. Delhi: Oxford University Press.
Heath, A. (1981) *Social Mobility*. London: Fontana.
Hellie, R. (1989) Slavery. *Encyclopedia Britannica*, 27, 285–98.
Hofstede, D. (1984) *Culture's Consequences*. Beverly Hills, Calif.: Sage.
Hope, K. (1982) A liberal theory of prestige. *American Journal of Sociology*, 87, 1011–31.
Inkeles, A. (1950) Social stratification and mobility in the Soviet Union. *American Sociological Review*, 15, 465–79.
Inkeles, A. and Bauer, R. (1959) *The Soviet Citizen*. Cambridge, Mass.: Harvard University Press.
Kelley, J. (1990) The failure of a paradigm: log-linear models of social mobility. In J. Clark, C. Modgil and S. Modgil (eds) *John H. Goldthorpe: Consensus and Controversy*. London: Falmer.
Kerbo, H.R. (1983) *Social Stratification and Inequality*. New York: McGraw-Hill.

Laumann, E.O. (1973) *The Bonds of Pluralism*. New York: Wiley.

Laumann, E.O. and Senter, R. (1976) Subjective social distance, occupational stratification, and forms of status and class consciousness: a cross-national replication and extension. *American Journal of Sociology*, *81*, 1304–38.

Lenski, G.E. (1966) *Power and Privilege: A Theory of Social Stratification*. New York: McGraw-Hill.

Lenski, G.E. (1978) Marxist experiments in destratification: an appraisal. *Social Forces*, *57*, 364–83.

Lenski, G. and Lenski, J. (1978) *Human Societies*. New York: McGraw-Hill.

Littlejohn, J. (1972) *Social Stratification*. London: Allen & Unwin.

Marx, K. (1964 edit.) *Precapitalist Economic Formations*, trans. J. Cohen. London: Lawrence & Wishart.

Mathias, P. (1983) *The First Industrial Nation*. 2nd edition. London: Methuen.

Mizoguchi, T. (1991) *Making Economics More Efficient and More Equitable*. Tokyo: Kinokuniya and Oxford University Press.

Parkin, F. (1971) *Class Inequality and Political Order*. London: MacGibbon & Kee.

Radcliffe-Brown, A.R. (1922) *The Andaman Islanders*. Cambridge: Cambridge University Press.

Robinson, R.V. and Bell, W. (1978) Equality, success, and social justice in England and the United States. *American Sociological Review*, *43*, 125–43.

Rosenfeld, E. (1957) Social stratification in a 'classless' society. *American Sociological Review*, *16*, 766–74.

Stark, T. (1977) *The Distribution of Income in Eight Countries*. London: HMSO.

Thompson, E.P. (1980) *The Making of the English Working Class*. London: Gollancz.

Tiger, L. and Shepher, J. (1975) *Women in the Kibbutz*. New York: Harcourt Brace.

Treiman, D.J. (1977) *Occupational Prestige in Comparative Perspective*. New York: Academic Press.

Trevelyan, G.M. (1942) *English Social History*. London: Longmans Green.

Warner, W.L. and Lunt, P.S. (1941) *The Social Life of a Modern Community*. New Haven: Yale University Press.

Wild, R.A. (1974) *Bradstow: A Study of Status, Class and Power in an Australian Town*. Sydney: Angus & Robertson.

Willmott, P. (1987) *Friendship Networks and Social Support*. London: Policy Studies Institute.

World Bank (1991) *World Development Report*. Washington: World Bank.

Yizher, U. (1989) Kibbutz in crisis – a new direction rather than a new model. *Kibbutz Studies*, *29*, 14–19.

Zweig, F. (1959) *The Israeli Worker*. New York: Herzl & Sharon.

# Chapter 3

# Psychological models of social class

We have seen that all human societies have social hierarchies, and that most of them have classes. Bands of hunters and gatherers and Israeli kibbutzim do not have classes, because they are too small for social categories to appear over and above individuals, and because status cannot be passed on to the next generation. We shall try to learn more about how hierarchies work, and how they develop into class systems, starting with small groups, of animals and humans, which develop dominance hierarchies, but do not have social classes. Social organisations provide a much closer model of class systems, and are also the main basis of them in the community.

## SOCIAL HIERARCHIES IN ANIMALS

Most animals who live in groups form dominance hierarchies. This is clearly an innate pattern of behaviour, the result of evolution, and it is possible that human beings have inherited this behaviour to some extent. The phenomenon was first noticed in domestic fowl: as soon as a new flock is formed (by the farmer or experimenter), there is a battle for status, by pecking and threatening gestures, between cocks, hens and chickens; the high-ranking birds get more food, better nest sites, and the dominant cocks mate more often (Schjelderup-Ebbe, 1922).

Dominance hierarchies are common but not universal. Some species are organised by territoriality, and individuals co-exist without conflict. Some of these form hierarchies if placed together, for example in a zoo or laboratory. When there is competition between males, for food or females, dominance hierarchies result. They are found in a wide range of species, including insects, birds, fish, wolves, deer, seals, as well as in baboons and other non-human primates. We will look particularly at the dominance hierarchies in groups of baboons and macaques.

*Measurement of dominance.* A highly consistent index of dominance is the approach–withdraw pattern, where the subordinate animal withdraws. This is correlated with winning fights, leadership, aggression, mounting other animals and being groomed. However, the correlation between these different behaviours can be quite low (Bernstein, 1970).

The hierarchy may consist of one despot, who dominates the whole group, or of a linear chain of animals dominating one another in turn, or of a number of ranks. The most dominant animal is usually the leader of the group, decides where the group will go, protects the group against predators and maintains internal cohesion by breaking up fights (Eibl-Eibesfeldt, 1975). In some species of monkeys, a male 'control' animal keeps order in the group, but without dominating it. In ant communities there is a cooperative dominance hierarchy, where there is division of labour and the lower-rank workers do food gathering and nest-building for the whole colony. However this is a different kind of hierarchy since it is based entirely on genetic differences between ranks, and is not the result of aggressive encounters.

Baboons live in groups up to about forty in size, occasionally more. There is a hierarchy among the males; those higher up in the hierarchy are more aggressive to the others, mate most frequently with females in full oestrus, have first choice of food, receive submissive gestures from the other animals and act as leaders of the group (Hall and DeVore, 1965).

*The advantages of dominance hierarchies.* The evolutionary advantage is usually explained by zoologists in terms of 'inclusive fitness', the survival not so much of individuals but of their genes, held also by progeny and other close kin (Hamilton, 1964). In the examples of dominance behaviour that we have seen so far, the dominant animals get more food and the dominant males copulate with more females. Both of these are obviously advantageous for inclusive fitness. The access to females is very important; a low-ranking male may not be able to copulate at all, and in some species will leave the group, presumably because this is to his genetic advantage. Competition over food can be over 'teat order', where baby pigs or cats scratch their way to occupying their mother's front teats, which produce more milk than the rear ones. Another advantage is access to the best nesting sites and shelters, or other aspects of territory. A dominant jay is first to take over a vacant territory, low-ranking pairs of Canada geese may be evicted from their nest sites by a higher-ranking couple. Another advantage of dominance may be reduced stress, because there is less conflict with the other members of the group, while high-ranking animals can 'enjoy their privileges with a minimum of effort' (Wilson, 1975). Dominant animals receive a lot of grooming from subordinates. This has the biological advantage of cleaning the skin, and may give emotional benefits too.

Dominance hierarchies may also be genetically advantageous to the whole group, they may be a case of 'group selection'. In groups with clear dominance hierarchies the healthiest and strongest males father more offspring, so that the next generation will contain plenty of similar males to defend the group. There is less aggression, and therefore less genetic damage to group members. Food is consumed more rapidly when there is a stable hierarchy. And population density may be restricted (Clutton-Brock and Harvey, 1976).

*Which animals are dominant?* A number of characteristics are regularly found to predict dominance. (1) *Age*. As we have seen older animals are more dominant, and juveniles have to take their turn, especially in access to females. (2) *Sex*. Males are dominant over females. Females may have their own dominance hierarchy, which is all below, or slightly overlaps, the male one. (3) *Size* is a strong predictor of dominance, in all species from insects to primates. In the case of ungulates (deer, sheep, etc.) length of antlers or horns is important. (4) *Rank of mother*. In Japanese macaques and others the sons of high-ranking mothers themselves have high rank. It is not clear whether this is the result of genetics or of socialisation through greater contact with dominant adults (Kawai, 1958). (5) *Aggressiveness*. In addition to age, size, etc., hens vary in aggressiveness and fighting skills. In monkeys the dominant animals have higher testosterone, which may be the cause of their aggressiveness. (6) *Intelligence*, or possibly *social skills*, has been found to be important for chimpanzees and rhesus monkeys who can achieve dominance more by cunning alliances than by brute force (Eibl-Eibesfeldt, 1975).

*The behaviour of dominant animals.* Dominance may depend on actual fighting. A group of laboratory mice may fight for two days before the hierarchy is stabilised. Animals use their teeth, claws or specially developed weapons like horns and antlers. In primates, an animal will sometimes attack a member of its own group, or of another group, or another species. This may take the form of charging, slapping, scratching, stamping on the back, hair-pulling, biting, lifting and slamming down. In wolf packs however during the breeding season, fierce and injuring fights take place. These encounters are usually started by a subordinate animal approaching, for example, food or a female, the higher-ranking animal makes an aggressive response and if the subordinate fails to retreat there is a fight. Aggression is mostly directed towards animals in the next lower rank. There is a 'magnification' process whereby the difference between early winners and losers increases over time. Early successes make later ones more probable. The outcome also depends partly on luck, such as being tired on a particular day (Wilson, 1975).

However, too much fighting would be damaging, and not genetically advantageous, either to individuals and their genes or to the group. To a large extent, in many species, actual fighting is replaced by dominance signals, 'ritualised' versions of actual aggressive acts; biting is replaced and symbolised by wide-open mouth, showing the teeth, in baboons for example. Among deer there are ritual threat displays and fights, using antlers. The repertoire of such dominance signals in non-human primates is:

*facial expression*: bared teeth, lowered eyebrows, staring eyes
*posture*: tense, head lowered, forelegs bent, swaying
*movement*: slow approach
*bodily state*: hair bristling
*bodily contact*: hit, bite
*vocalization*: barking or grunting or other loud noises.

(Argyle, 1988)

Dominant animals may also use homosexual mounting of other males, who submit, female-style. In rabbits and other species chemical signals are used, marking territory with gland secretions. It has been suggested that all these dominance signals communicate to others the animal's past history of dominance encounters and its expectations of future ones (rather like self-confidence and self-presentation in human hierarchies).

It is important to keep up cohesive bonds within the dominance hierarchy. A chimpanzee who has won a fight and dominated another does not kill it. On the contrary he may groom the other, giving 'conditional reassurance', i.e. reconciliation on condition that the other behaves in a subordinate way. The subordinate animal may groom to appease, and attain friendly and harmonious relationships; the dominant animal to reassure that aggression has ceased and non-aggression can resume (de Waal, 1988).

*The behaviour of subordinates.* Some studies suggest that the behaviour of subordinates is more important than that of dominant animals in maintaining the hierarchy (Rowell, 1972). A subordinate signals its submission, thus avoiding attack by a more dangerous animal. It may just turn and flee, screeching, urinating and looking over its shoulder. It may make appeasement signals by cowering, curling up, holding out a hand, facing away and lowering the eyes, presenting for copulation or inviting grooming. Lower-status animals look upwards in the hierarchy, to form an 'attention structure', where infants watch mothers, mothers watch mates and males watch higher-ranking animals, so that the whole group can respond rapidly to leadership initiatives (Chance, 1976).

Young males are kept in a subordinate position, and away from the females. They compete for dominance among themselves and may cooperate to oppose the dominant males. Or they may leave the group entirely. Those that do so may play an important part in the evolutionary process. Presumably they leave when it is to their advantage to do so. They can disperse genes between populations, and they may experiment with life in new habitats and with new kinds of adaptation (Wilson, 1975).

Subordinate baboons have been found to be prone to various diarrhoeal diseases, which have been interpreted as stress-related (Rowell, 1972).

Subordinate females may be for a time 'helpers at the nest' of their siblings, which is found to help the survival of their sisters' progeny, and they can mate later themselves.

Why do lower-rank animals put up with it, and why do they stay in the group at all? They put up with their lower-status position because they have to, because of the aggression and superior fighting power of the dominant animals. For many members of the group the stable social system is advantageous – they have some access to food and females, together with the benefits of a peaceful social group. Subordinate animals are usually younger, smaller and weaker. If they stay, subordinate males may take their turn in the hierarchy and be able to copulate later when the dominant animals grow old, become feeble and die. Age-grades have been found in grouse and some kinds of monkeys and apes: as the top rank weakens or dies, the next rank takes over.

*Other kinds of dominance hierarchies.* Dominance hierarchies do not always take the straightforward form found in hens and baboons, and we will look at some of the other varieties.

*(1) Female hierarchies.* Females may also form hierarchies, for reasons similar to those of males. If successful they get more food and better nesting sites. They are able to approach more dominant males, with success. However, female hierarchies are less clear and less stable. In some species a female's rank depends on that of her mate, for example when there is pair-bonding (most birds, gibbons) or where one male has several females, as with baboons. Chimpanzees are less faithful, so that this does not apply.

*(2) Hierarchies of groups.* So far we have dealt only with dominance hierarchies *within* groups, but there is also inter-group dominance, the formation of miniature class systems. Two groups of the same species may come into conflict over territory; one group may win simply because it is larger. The result is fatal for the smaller group, in the case of insects. For rhesus monkeys, the losers retreat to smaller territory, and the winners fight more among themselves (Marsden, 1971).

*(3) Hierarchies of species.* Dominance hierarchies are formed between related species, e.g. of birds, fish, rodents or deer. The winners are the species which is larger in bodily size or better socially organised. Insects may go a step further and invade the nest of another species, take them prisoners and make them work as 'slaves' (Dawkins, 1976).

What can we learn about human hierarchies from the study of animals? We have seen that there are biological reasons for forming hierarchies, both for the successful individuals and for the whole group. Success depends on size and strength, but also on rank of mother and intelligence, as in human hierarchies. Dominance is established by the use of non-verbal signals, which have some similarity with their human equivalents, e.g. staring and frowning. And, as with humans, the females are less interested in forming hierarchies and often take their mate's status. The close similarities with animals here suggest that there may be an innate basis to human hierarchies.

## HIERARCHIES IN HUMAN GROUPS

Small social groups of all kinds form dominance hierarchies. These are not classes, but dominance relations between a number of individuals. They do not pass their social status on to anyone else, and there are no cultural differences between ranks.

*The meaning and measurement of status in groups.* Groups like committees, juries or working parties, which are engaged in problem-solving or decision-taking, rapidly develop a J-shaped distribution of amount of talk, or number of utterances. This is one index of dominance. One person talks most and the majority speak very little, especially in larger groups. When the top person speaks they address the whole group; when a low-rank person speaks they usually address the person at the top (Bales *et al.*, 1951). In studies of juries, actually 'shadow juries', the top three people out of the twelve have most of the conversation, while the others listen.

The individuals who talk most, in committees or similar groups, are also the most influential. A meta-analysis of seventy-seven studies found that rate of participation correlated overall .69 with leadership status based on ratings by group members (Stein and Heller, 1983). The high-ranking individuals talk more because the others like what they have to say, reinforce their utterances by signs of approval, so they are chosen to be sources of influence by the group. When people have power in a group, they not only talk more, they contribute more to the group task, are highly evaluated by the other members and influence the others a lot; the others develop expectations which legitimate the power of the leaders (Ridgeway and Berger, 1986).

Dominance or leadership status in groups can be assessed by ratings, made by the group member or by observers. Slater (1955) found that in groups of three to seven students, *two* leaders often appeared, a task leader, who was thought to have the best ideas, and a best-liked, or socio-emotional leader. In the meta-analysis of participation rates described above, participation rate had very little relationship (r = .16) with ratings of maintenance measures, i.e. socio-emotional leadership.

Gibb (1950) studied groups of ten student or officer candidate groups, and found quite low correlations between choices as personal friends and ratings as leaders, between .25 and .43, again showing that task and socio-emotional influence are largely independent. Friendships in groups are formed mainly between people of equal status in the group (McPherson and Smith-Lovin, 1987), a small-scale version of what happens in the class system.

Many of these studies are based on groups of men; do women form dominance hierarchies too? In a study of adolescent boys and girls at a summer camp it was found that in the girls' cabins the hierarchies were unstable, in that they changed a lot over time and from one situation to another (Savin-Williams, 1979). We saw that in groups of monkeys dominance hierarchies are mainly based on the male animals. It has been observed that males form dominant structures very readily in clubs, sports teams, politics and armies, possibly reflecting a genetic sex difference here (Tiger, 1969), a point of view which will be discussed later.

In groups of adolescents, or of younger children, dominance hierarchies are found, but based less on amount of talk. Physical size and strength are relevant here, as are direct use of threats and other methods of influence (Lippitt et al., 1952).

*When is a dominance hierarchy formed?* Hierarchies form quite fast. Fisek and Ofshe (1970) observed fifty-nine three–person groups for 40 minutes each. In half of them there was clear differentiation of amount of speech in the first minute, and this increased over time. In the other half there was little or no initial differentiation, but this was quite marked by 5 minutes. In juries, the very first thing they have to do is to elect a foreman. Dominance hierarchies can be established faster than this. Kalma (1991) found that group members could rate their future status in a group before a word had been spoken, but after they had seen the other members. Dominant patterns of gaze behaviour appeared to be one of the cues used.

A more definite hierarchy is formed in groups under certain conditions.

a In larger groups Bales found greater inequality in participation rates the larger the group (Bales et al., 1951). And where there is an appointed leader, his directions are more acceptable in larger groups. The reason is obvious, there will be chaos unless order is imposed.
b When the group is engaged in task rather than social activities, especially complex tasks.
c When decisions must be made quickly. Hamblin (1958) found that in groups of three, when an experimental crisis was induced by a sudden change of the rules, the two subordinate members were influenced more by the informal leader.
d When there are clear and obvious differences of social status, age, competence, etc., within the group.
e Men form hierarchies much more readily than women.

*Do dominance hierarchies make groups more effective?* In a group of three or more, if there is a leader he can coordinate the activities of others. In any group, if the people who are most skilled and knowledgeable about the group's task are allowed to take charge, the group would be expected to be more effective. Fiedler and Meuwese (1963) found that the leaders of tanks were able to influence the effectiveness of the crew, but only when the crew was cohesive. The team must have a hierarchy *and* cohesion. Studies of appointed leaders show that they have more effective groups if they have a style of leadership which includes task-direction and concern for the group members (Argyle, 1989). Savin-Williams (1979), in his study of an adolescent summer camp, found that dominance hierarchies appeared to foster reduction of aggression within groups as well as division of labour, and hence better task cooperation.

*Which individuals become leaders?* Early studies found that there were consistent, though modest, correlations between informal leadership status in groups of students and traits like intelligence, extraversion and adjustment. Studies of juries and similar groups of adults find that occupational status, education, age and race are also important predictors. Strodtbeck *et al.* (1957) found that jury foremen were much more likely to be proprietors than clerical, skilled or manual labourers, in that order. Social skills are important too. Borgatta *et al.* (1954) found, with groups of three airmen, that assertiveness and social acceptability, as well as task ability, were predictors of leadership.

People are more likely to be accepted as leaders if they have been valuable members of the group in the past, by conforming and by useful contributions to the group's task. This gives them what Hollander (1958) called 'idiosyncrasy credit', a kind of permission to deviate. This solves the problem of how a leader can lead without being rejected for deviating: his or her new ideas are taken seriously because he has been successful in the past.

Assertiveness has been thought of by psychologists as a personality trait, and as a social skill, which can be measured and trained (Galassi *et al.*, 1981). It certainly leads to leadership status in groups (Shaw, 1971). There is less agreement over the motivational basis or the origins of assertiveness. McClelland (1987) conceptualised a need for power, measured by a projection test, as a kind of acquired drive. It is produced by certain socialisation experiences, such as permissiveness for sex and aggression and little physical punishment, because this creates greater sympathetic nervous system activity, believed to be behind power motivation. McClelland and his co-workers have found that men who are strong in power motivation are more aggressive, impulsive and competitive. Individuals with high power motivation try to dominate in groups, and surround themselves with low-power friends who can be led; they seek occupations like management and journalism where they can exert influence, but they succeed as leaders in organisations only if they have further, inhibitory, motivations to keep their power in check. However, they are not liked much, they have low self-esteem, drink a lot, have high blood pressure and poor health.

Women express their assertiveness in a way that shows concern for and looks after the interests of the other person – and this is a style recommended by assertiveness trainers (Wilson, 1993). This makes an interesting parallel with dominance behaviour in chimpanzees, who are concerned to sustain social bonds in the hierarchy (p. 49).

Intelligence is a good predictor of emergent leadership, but more important than intelligence or other general abilities is the ability to deal with the group task. Experiments have shown that if a group is confronted by more than one kind of task, the leadership may change (Carter and Nixon, 1949). A real-life example has been found in gangs of delinquents who may shift from crime to football – whereupon the leadership also changes.

A number of experiments have been carried out to see whether external status, task activity or non-verbal dominance signals are most effective as predictors of leadership. For example, Ridgeway (1987) found that a high level of task activity was more effective than non-verbal dominance.

It has often been found that men are more likely to emerge as the leaders of mixed-sex groups, in juries for example. Women are also less likely to seek the leader's role. This is partly because the tasks used have been ones on which men are better and partly because of stereotyped expectations about males and leadership (Hollander, 1983). This situation is changing, and in a recent study of fifty-two task groups studied over fifteen weeks, no such gender differences were found (Schneier and Bartol, 1980).

*The behaviour of dominant members.* We have seen that in many kinds of group dominant people talk more. The way they do this is by getting in first whenever there is a pause, i.e. by having a small reaction time for speech (Skvoretz, 1988). In order to establish their dominance, members operate in the task domain, rather than in the socio-emotional domain. This makes them candidates for leadership; the group selects the one whose ideas and capacities it likes best. We have seen that dominant people are more influential. They do this by trying to influence other group members. Lippitt *et al.* (1952) studied the behaviour of children at summer camps, comparing those rated by each other as having high or low power. It was found that the higher-power children made more attempts to influence other children, did so by more direct forms of influence and were more successful. In some laboratory studies power was manipulated experimentally: high-power members used their influence and felt that they had greater opportunity to help the group towards its goals; they enjoyed their time in the group, and felt more attracted to it than did low-power members (Shaw, 1971). In a study with experimental hierarchies in groups of nineteen to twenty-five students, the high-status people were able to criticise low-status members, but not vice versa (Kelley, 1951).

Individuals who are seeking a leadership position in a group use a special pattern of non-verbal signals:

standing at a height, facing the group
at full height, hands on hips, expand chest
gazing a lot, staring down, looking while talking
non-smiling face
touching others
voice loud, low-pitched
gestures pointing at others or their property.

However, in an established hierarchy leaders are more relaxed, as with monkeys, and may sit in a relaxed posture (Argyle, 1988).

*The behaviour of low-status members.* In the non-verbal domain, low-ranking group members do the opposite of what the dominant people do, for example bending posture, smiling, voice at low volume, looking while the other is speaking, deferential head-nods. Verbally, low-status members speak less, do not interrupt, address high-status individuals rather than the group as a whole and do so politely.

In laboratory groups and in field studies it has been found that low-status members communicate a lot to high-status members, do so in a rewarding deferential, approval-seeking way, perhaps to reduce the threat caused by more powerful people (Shaw, 1971).

Ridgeway and Johnson (1990) argue that the hierarchy inhibits the expression of disagreement on the part of low-status members – only the high-status members are allowed to do this. Both can use agreement. Lippitt *et al.* (1952) in their summer camps studies found that low-power children used indirect methods of influence with high-power children, but did not do this often. Kelley (1951), with his experimental hierarchies, found that low-status members communicated a lot with higher-status members, especially if they had shown a desire to move upwards. This was interpreted as a substitute for real mobility.

*Relationships in the hierarchy.* We have seen that different people are accepted as leaders and as friends; nevertheless there is a tendency for people to say that they like the high-status members of a group. Hurwitz *et al.* (1960) studied the relationships between forty-two mental health workers. The low-status members were ill at ease and defensive, they liked the highs most, over-estimated the extent to which the highs liked them and talked mainly to these members. As we have seen, this upward communication has been interpreted partly in terms of substitute social mobility, partly as an attempt to reduce social unease.

Differences in rank are partly differences of power, that is to give rewards or punishments. Those at the top have more power and those lower down are dependent on them for various rewards (Emerson, 1962). And there can be whole networks of social influence based on the ability to reward and punish.

*Conclusions on human dominance hierarchies.* Human groups, like groups of monkeys, form dominance hierarchies. They use some similar non-verbal signals for dominance and submission to do this. Hierarchies are more stable in groups of males, and males usually dominate in mixed-sex groups. On the other hand, human dominance hierarchies are not decided by fighting (except perhaps in small boys) and are not about competition for females.

In human groups, the high-ranking members participate more and exert more influence, disagree and criticise more, but are not more aggressive. Hierarchies are formed most readily and leadership accepted when there is a group task, and when the group is large. The hierarchy reduces aggression, increases division of labour and other aspects of cooperation, and can be seen as functional. Leaders emerge from the group, with the approval of the others, because they are good at the group task and are socially acceptable; some people want to lead because of their assertiveness or power needs. Dominance hierarchies form very quickly.

These dominance hierarchies show the wider class system operating, in the relationships and interaction between people of different rank, which is partly derived from social class. However, the groups themselves do not have a class system, since there are no ranks or categories: social position depends entirely on the behaviour and attributes of individuals.

## SOCIAL ORGANISATIONS

From early times people have worked not only in small groups, but in larger social units – social organisations. Today these include factories, banks, government departments, hospitals, universities, armies and churches. They often have to be large, because of the scale and complexity of the work – a small group couldn't manufacture airliners or build skyscrapers. Organisations need to have a certain social structure for the work to be coordinated and led effectively. And in every case, they have a hierarchical structure, where there are a number of ranks and where some people at each level supervise those at the level below. (These are the 'line' managers; 'staff' people, professional experts, have a rank but may not supervise anyone.) Those at each level are in turn supervised by others in the rank above. Those at higher levels are paid more, have more comfortable working conditions and are treated more respectfully. This more-or-less universal structure is found in all social organisations, with some variation, and they can be seen as miniature class systems, where the ranks are the classes. They are also part of the basis of the class system itself, in that equivalent ranks in organisations become social classes. The British working class is said by historians to have developed as a group with a name that people were conscious of belonging to in the nineteenth century. The main reason was the shared experience of the social struggles of subordinate groups of manual workers, especially miners and textile workers in the industrial North (Joyce, 1991).

The tendency to form social organisations is probably not innate, but rather the result of slow cultural growth, partly in response to the development of more elaborate technology. All advanced civilisations have produced large-scale organisations for industrial, military, governmental, educational, religious and other purposes. The leaders of armies and the entrepreneurs who created factories built up their rather similar organisations by trial and error, and by copying others. Industrial organisations in America and Britain were greatly influenced by 'classical organisation theory' (Taylor, 1911), which was based on observing the design of armies and said that there should be a rigid hierarchy, a clear chain of command and much division of labour. This model was much criticised, and has been modified by other ideas about the importance of social groups, skilled supervision and adapting organisations to the needs of technology (Argyle, 1989).

As larger tasks are tackled, the working group becomes larger, whether the job is building a railway or fighting a war. When it is larger than, say, twenty, it is difficult for a single supervisor to look after it, so the group splits into smaller groups and there are several supervisors. Now a further level of 'management' is needed to direct the supervisors. It used to be believed that a manager could not supervise more than five to seven subordinates, though this is now known to vary with the technology. However, if we assume that a first-line supervisor can handle twenty subordinates and the managers can handle six, with an army or factory or hospital of 1,000, there would be four ranks, i.e. one managing director or general, and three ranks under him.

The hierarchy depends also on the complexity of the work and the need for division of labour. In a modern factory there may be hundreds of distinct jobs, each with its own special skills, for which selection and training are needed. In addition to a large number of different kinds of manual work there are also many kinds of non-manual work – accounting, computing, clerical, managerial and research work, inspection, time-study and the work of supervisors, shop stewards, management services specialists, financial and legal experts and many others. This means that there have to be corresponding numbers of working sections, whose work has to be supervised and coordinated with that of others.

Organisations inevitably create ranks, a hierarchical social order. Those in the higher ranks have more responsibility and power. Many individuals, though not all, want to be in these ranks. When there are hundreds, thousands or more members, most of them do not know each other, apart from their immediate superior, subordinates and co-workers. They have to deal with other members whom they do not know personally. They do this by categorising them, not only by age and sex, but also by rank, and often by function or speciality. Rank is recognised by badges of office (e.g. in the armed forces), or other aspects of appearance, or title, just as in the class system outside.

*Positions and roles*. To understand how organisations function we have to study the patterns of social interaction between the members. Every member of an organisation occupies a *position*, e.g. supervisor, shop steward, personnel manager. Every position carries a definite rank in the hierarchy. For every position there is a *role*, i.e. a pattern of behaviour typical of the people in that position, and behaviour which is expected of them. Roles include the behaviour expected in relation both to subordinates and superiors.

The pressures to conform to a role can be very strong. Zimbardo (1973) paid a number of normal, middle-class student volunteers to play the roles of prison guards and prisoners, assigned arbitrarily, with appropriate uniforms in an imitation prison. Many of the 'guards' became brutal, sadistic and tyrannical, and many of the 'prisoners' became servile, selfish and hostile, and suffered from hysterical crying and severe depression.

The job requirements are made clear by immediate supervisors, by co-workers and in the course of training. The social behaviour of employees is affected by the interlocking of roles; if a doctor plays the doctor role the patient has to play the patient role, and the same is true of other pairs of roles. The way in which different roles interlock is at the heart of social structures. A supervisor has a relationship of interlocking roles with subordinates and with superiors. It is the interlocking of roles which holds social organisations together. In particular the status hierarchy is held together by the complementary and indeed cooperative styles of behaviour of superiors and subordinates.

Some organisations have many levels in the hierarchy – if they are very large, and if there is a small span of control, giving a 'tall' shape, as in many Japanese firms. When there is a large span of control, as in car factories, there are fewer levels. There may be some major breaks in the hierarchy, marked by different dining rooms for example. In the services there is an officers' mess, a sergeants' mess and an other ranks' mess, creating a kind of three–class system. Traditional Oxford colleges had a senior common room, a middle common room (for research students), hall and junior common room for undergraduates and a different dining room for staff – a four–class system. (My own college, Wolfson, was the first to have a single dining room and common room for everyone.)

Organisations take on one of the key features of classes when they are so large that most people don't know each other and have to identify one another's rank by their uniforms (as in the services and hospitals) or other aspects of appearance, manner or workplace.

*Selection and mobility*. As with class, the members of working organisations enter at different levels; if their family owns the firm they start at the top, if they are graduates they start as management trainees, otherwise they start at or near the bottom. For the better jobs there is a lot of competition and elaborate selection to find the individuals who can do the job best, and thus further the purposes of the organisation.

When a new worker has been accepted, he or she is then trained. This may take years, as in the case of lawyers, pilots and others. Some high-level skills are taught outside in educational establishments, as in the case of doctors and scientists. Those who do well may be promoted, and this is done on the basis of evidence of competence at the job or by formal assessment procedures.

Professionals, managers and other people in good jobs are often very concerned about promotion, success in their careers. In mid-career, around the age of 40, managers have been found to be preoccupied with promotion prospects (Sofer, 1970), or to be in a period of crisis, in which they have to come to terms with their limited prospects. As they get older some people become more committed to their work, which becomes more central to their personality, while others become less committed, and spend more time with family and other interests. For those in the lower ranks there is less prospect of promotion, they have 'jobs' rather than 'careers' (p. 99). In order to do better, to earn more money, they have to join another organisation or start their own business.

*The relations between ranks.* The social distance between ranks may be great or small. By social distance is meant the ease of interaction and the possibility of friendship. It is smaller if there are opportunities for informal interaction, for example from sharing dining and leisure facilities. It is smaller if all wear similar clothes, as in Japanese factories. Social distance may be deliberately increased; for example, in most armies the officers live a kind of unreal upper-class lifestyle, with servants, first-class travel and impressive dress uniforms. A gulf separates the officers from the men, who are put into a lower-class cultural style and usually develop a culture of earthy, masculine sexuality (Van Doorn, 1990).

It is on the whole better to supervise than be supervised. It is a direct source of social status, one of the criteria of social class. People enjoy higher status, having subordinates who will do what they want and the chance of being responsible for task achievements on a larger scale. But it can also involve long hours and the stress of being responsible for others.

The social distance between ranks partly depends on the amount of power a superior has and the kind of power it is. Superiors usually have the power to reward or punish, which in some cases is very large – being able to promote or fire for example. However, organisations differ in the kind of power that is used. In prisons, and some armies, authority rests in the power of punishment. In many places of work it depends mainly on financial rewards (together with the hope of promotion for some). In research establishments, universities, hospitals and voluntary organisations, members work also because they believe in the importance of the goals of the organisation; leaders can appeal to this motivation in subordinates (Etzioni, 1961). In many places of work today, entrepreneurs and senior management have this commitment themselves, but their subordinates do not.

Being supervised can be a frustrating experience – the other has more power and may be unskilled at using it. This is common at lower levels, where many people are supervised by authoritarian or other unskilled types of foremen. Further up the scale the supervision is usually less harsh and more skilled. If supervisors or managers have the right skills they can do a great deal for their subordinates – solve their problems and provide social support (Argyle, 1989).

Organisations differ in the style of supervision and management used. Some are quite authoritarian – subordinates are given orders without explanation, others use the democratic-persuasive style, where subordinates are consulted, able to participate in decisions and orders are explained. They also vary in how much superiors look after those under them. Combined with authoritarian discipline such rewardingness amounts to paternalism, a kind of feudal attitude; combined with democratic-persuasive style rewardingness produces the best kind of management, in terms not only of the job satisfaction of subordinates (together with lower absenteeism and labour turnover) but also of effectiveness and productivity. As with chimpanzees, there has to be bonding as well as hierarchy.

American studies of blacks and whites at work have found that they can work together without difficulty, but they rarely meet socially outside the place of work. The explanation may be that work is structured so that interaction is easy or that cooperation is motivated by wage incentives. Perhaps interaction involving families, in leisure settings, is more intimate or perhaps other members of the family have not had the opportunity to get used to the other groups at work. Similar considerations probably apply to relations between people of different occupational status. They often get on at work without difficulty; not only do they work closely together, but they also take part in the jokes, games, gossip and fooling about that commonly occur during coffee and work breaks, and indeed at other times. This is a more enjoyable and closer kind of interaction between classes than is common outside work, though we shall see later that leisure groups often produce cooperation between members of adjacent classes at least (p. 75).

*Producing organisational change.* Working hierarchies seem to be an inevitable feature of work, but they can take quite different forms. They do not have to be authoritarian, and there do not have to be large social distances between ranks. A lot of thought is being put into the optimal design of working organisations. They are more effective and more acceptable to their members when there are not large social distances between the ranks, when for example those at all levels can participate in decisions, and when supervisors are persuasive and democratic, rather than authoritarian, and when they look after their subordinates (Argyle, 1989).

Social organisations also vary with the technology. In traditional, mass-production industry, e.g. textiles and automobiles, there are large working groups, though they may not be real groups, incentives and machine-pacing and little contact with supervisors. In continuous process working, as in oil refineries and power stations, there are smaller working groups, which operate as teams, and there are better relations in the hierarchy. The introduction of computers and other aspects of automation can have different effects on the social organisation. This can give more or less power and autonomy, to supervisors for example, depending on whether they programme the computers, or someone else does. An individual's job may become more skilled and demanding, or it may disappear.

Organisations may change for economic reasons, or because of changes in government policy, or as the result of social research and theories. An important example is the introduction of industrial democracy in its various forms – inspired by political ideas and also by research showing the benefits of greater participation in decisions (e.g. Miller and Monge, 1986).

Changes in organisations cannot be brought about simply by telling people about the new arrangements. There is great resistance to change as people fear loss of income or status, or changed relationships with other people, while some may choose the even greater upheaval of leaving the organisation entirely. Members need to be taught and persuaded to accept the new arrangements; there are several ways of doing this. A number of procedures have been devised for the introduction of change in organisations, involving presentation of ideas and data, and discussion with personnel at all levels, together often with some social skills training (Argyle, 1989).

*Social organisations as models of the class system.* Working organisations are miniature class systems, where ranks form the classes. We should include other organisations, such as educational, medical, ecclesiastical, sporting and voluntary, where not all are 'working' in a traditional sense. These organisations are also an essential part of the class system, since the ranks and the relationships between them are recognised outside. Supervisors and managers have power to control their subordinates, and the same relationships carry over to non-work relationships – with members of lower classes who are encountered as shop assistants and people in other subordinate roles. A study of a large department store in Oxford found that staff complained about the way that some north Oxford housewives treated them like servants (Woodward, 1960).

The relationships inside organisations are also found outside. Those who have servants can pay them more or give them the sack. Anyone who buys something at a shop can cease to use that shop or make complaints; anyone who uses an office can also complain. And the leaders of leisure groups, and of juries, are usually middle-class. In addition, middle-class people are often deferred to, and their approval and disapproval matters. Their class gives them power to influence other people, perhaps because it is associated with the real power of similar individuals at work.

The ranks in organisations are like social classes, though there are more of them, and the divisions between them are much clearer. However, there are some particularly important divisions, such as between officers and men, which correspond to a major break in the class system, between manual and non-manual.

Organisations are composed of working individuals, and families play little or no part. While children 'inherit' their parents' social status, this happens in organisations only if the family owns the business and can pass on a management position to their children. Senior members of organisations can help their children to get on by giving them a good education, but can't usually give them a job.

## A SOCIAL PSYCHOLOGICAL MODEL OF THE CLASS SYSTEM

A little more needs to be added, to provide an account of the main class phenomena, by using familiar principles of social psychology.

1 Every social organisation develops a hierarchy, including industry, education, medicine, the churches, sporting and voluntary organisations. All of them develop a number of ranks of different status, to provide leadership and administration.
2 Similars attract, and those at similar levels in different organisations will like the company of members of other organisations who enjoy similar status, income, expertise or authority.
3 Groups of similar individuals who spend time together will develop further similar behaviours, including styles of speech, appearance and lifestyle.
4 Similarity of speech and appearance makes membership of classes visible to strangers. There may be some 'self-presentation' in communicating this information, but it is more due to conformity to class norms (p. 112). The attitudes towards senior, equal and junior members of working and other organisations are generalised to strangers whose class is identified in this way.
5 Spouses and children share the same social class as the main earner, or the family members most involved in social organisations, though they may not have earned any rank themselves.
6 Membership of a social class is a major source of self-esteem and self-image, because people react to everyone as a member of a class. However, the self-esteem of low-status individuals is protected by a number of psychological mechanisms (p. 224).

7 Class systems appear to be an inevitable feature of human society. However, as with social organisations, the social distance and other aspects of the relations between classes could quite well be changed.

## REFERENCES

Argyle, M. (1988) *Bodily Communication.* 2nd edition. London: Methuen.

Argyle, M. (1989) *The Social Psychology of Work.* 2nd edition. Harmondsworth: Penguin.

Bales, R.F., Strodtbeck, F., Mills, T. and Roseborough, M.E. (1951) Channels of communication in small groups. *American Sociological Review, 16,* 461–8.

Bernstein, I.S. (1970) Primate status hierarchies. In L.A. Rosenblum (ed.) *Primate Behavior.* New York: Academic Press.

Borgatta, E.F., Couch, A.S. and Bales, R.F. (1954) Some findings relevant to the great man theory of leadership. *American Sociological Review, 19,* 755–9.

Carter, L.F. and Nixon, M. (1949) An investigation of the relationship between four criteria of leadership ability for three different tasks. *Journal of Psychology, 27,* 245–61.

Chance, M.R.A. (1976) The organization of attention in groups. In M. von Cranach (ed.) *Methods of Inference from Animal to Human Behaviour.* Chicago: Aldine.

Clutton-Brock, T.H. and Harvey, P.H. (1976) Evolutionary rules and primate societies. In P.P.G. Bateson and R.A. Hinde (eds) *Growing Points in Ethology.* Cambridge: Cambridge University Press.

Crook, J.H. (1970) The socio-ecology of primates. In J.H. Crook (ed.) *Social Behaviour in Birds and Mammals.* London: Academic Press.

Dawkins, R. (1976) *The Selfish Gene.* Oxford: Oxford University Press.

de Waal, F.B.M. (1988) The reconciled hierarchy. In M.R.A. Chance (ed.) *Social Fabrics of the Mind.* Hove and London: Erlbaum.

Eibl-Eibesfeldt, I. (1975) *Ethology.* 2nd edition. New York: Holt, Rinehart & Winston.

Emerson, R.M. (1962) Power-dependence relations. *American Sociological Review, 27,* 31–41.

Etzioni, A. (1961) *A Comparative Analysis of Complex Organizations.* New York: Free Press.

Fiedler, F.E. and Meuwese, W.A.T. (1963) Leader's contribution to task performance in cohesive and uncohesive groups. *Journal of Abnormal and Social Psychology, 67,* 83–7.

Fisek, M.H. and Ofshe, R. (1970) The process of status evolution. *Sociometry, 33,* 327–46.

Galassi, J.P., Galassi, M.D. and Vedder, M.J. (1981) Perspectives on assertion as a social skills model. In J.D. Wine and M.D. Smye (eds) *Social Competence.* New York: Guilford.

Gibb, C.A. (1950) The sociometry of leadership in temporary groups. *Sociometry, 13,* 226–43.

Hall, K.R.L. and DeVore, I. (1965) Baboon social behavior. In I. DeVore (ed.) *Primate Behavior.* New York: Holt, Rinehart & Winston.

Hamblin, R.L. (1958) Leadership and crises. *Sociometry, 21,* 322–35.

Hamilton, W.D. (1964) The evolution of social behaviour. *Journal of Theoretical Biology, 7,* 1–52.

Hollander, E.P. (1958) Conformity, status, and idiosyncrasy credit. *Psychological Review, 65,* 117–27.

Hollander, E.P. (1983) Women and leadership. In H.H. Blumberg *et al.* (eds) *Small Groups and Social Interaction*. Chichester: Wiley.

Hurwitz, J.I., Zander, A.F. and Hymovitch, B. (1960) Some effects of power on the relations among group members. In D. Cartwright and A. Zander (eds) *Group Dynamics*. 2nd edition. London: Tavistock.

Joyce, P. (1991) *Visions of the People*. Cambridge: Cambridge University Press.

Kalma, A. (1991) Hierarchisation and dominance assessment at first glance. *European Journal of Social Psychology*, 21, 165–81.

Kawai, M. (1958) On the rank system in a natural group of Japanese monkeys (I) The basic and dependent rank. *Primates*, 1, 111–30.

Kelley, H.H. (1951) Communication in experimentally created hierarchies. *Human Relations*, 4, 39–56.

Lippitt, R., Polansky, N., Redl, F. and Rosen, S. (1952) The dynamics of power. *Human Relations*, 5, 37–64.

McClelland, D.C. (1987) *Human Motivation*. Cambridge: Cambridge University Press.

McPherson, J.M. and Smith-Lovin, L. (1987) Homophily in voluntary organizations: status distance and the composition of face-to-face groups. *American Sociological Review*, 52, 370–9.

Marsden, H.M. (1971) Intergroup relations in rhesus monkeys (*Macaca Mulatta*). In A.H. Esser (ed.) *Behavior and Environment: The Use of Space by Animals and Men*. New York: Plenum.

Miller, K.I. and Monge, P.R. (1986) Participation, satisfaction, and productivity: a meta-analytic review. *Academy of Management Journal*, 29, 727–53.

Ridgeway, C.L. (1987) Nonverbal behavior, dominance, and the basis of status in task groups. *American Sociological Review*, 52, 683–94.

Ridgeway, C.L. and Berger, J. (1986) Expectations, legitimation, and dominance behavior in task groups. *American Sociological Review*, 51, 603–17.

Ridgeway, C. and Johnson, C. (1990) What is the relationship between socio-emotional behavior and status in task groups? *American Journal of Sociology*, 95, 1189–212.

Rowell, T. (1972) *Social Behaviour of Monkeys*. Harmondsworth: Penguin.

Savin-Williams, R.C. (1979) Dominance hierarchies in groups of early adolescents. *Child Development*, 50, 923–35.

Schein, E.H. (1978) *Career Dynamics: Matching Individual and Organizational Needs*. Reading, Mass.: Addison-Wesley.

Schjelderup-Ebbe, T. (1922) Beiträge zur sozialpsychologie des haushuhns. *Zeitschrift für Psychologie*, 92, 60–87.

Schneier, C.E. and Bartol, K.M. (1980) Sex effects in emergent leadership. *Journal of Applied Psychology*, 65, 341–5.

Shaw, M.E. (1971) *Group Dynamics*. New York: McGraw-Hill.

Skvoretz, J. (1988) Models of participation in status-differentiated groups. *Social Psychology Quarterly*, 51, 43–57.

Slater, P.E. (1955) Role differentiation in small groups. *American Sociological Review*, 20, 300–10.

Sofer, C. (1970) *Men in Mid-Career*. Cambridge: Cambridge University Press.

Stein, R.T. and Heller, T. (1983) The relationship of participation rates to leadership status: a meta-analysis. In H.H. Blumberg *et al.* (eds) *Small Groups and Social Interaction*. Chichester: Wiley.

Strodtbeck, F.L., James, R.M. and Hawkins, C. (1957) Social status in jury deliberation. *American Sociological Review*, 22, 713–19.

Taylor, F.W. (1911, 1947) *Scientific Management*. New York: Harper.

Tiger, L. (1969) *Men in Groups*. London: Nelson.

Van Doorn, J. (1990) War, the theory and conduct of: modern armed forces. *Encyclopaedia Britannica*, 29, 699–708.

Wilson, E.O. (1975) *Sociobiology: The New Synthesis*. Cambridge, Mass.: Belknap and Harvard University Press.

Wilson, K. (1993) *Assertion and its Social Context*. Oxford: Pergamon.

Woodward, J. (1965) *Industrial Organization: Theory and Practice*. Oxford: Oxford University Press.

Zimbardo, P.G. (1973) A Pirandellian prison. *The New York Times Sunday Magazine*, 8 April, 38–60.

# Chapter 4

# Social relationships

In some ways this is the central chapter of the book, since it takes apart the social life of different classes, and shows some of the causes and effects of the different kinds of relationships formed. Relations between parents and children, for example, result from other aspects of the life of each class and act as causal agents to perpetuate it.

Social psychologists have done the main research on social relationships, but have neglected the effects of social class. For this we have to turn to a number of social surveys, carried out by survey organisations or by sociologists.

I shall concentrate on data which have been collected in Britain during recent years. Some excellent studies have been carried out, and I am indebted to the following principal sources for this chapter.

MORI (1982) 1,801 adults aged 15+ in 178 areas of Great Britain.
Young and Willmott (1973) 1,928 adults aged 15+ in 24 areas of London and S.E. England.
Willmott (1987) 132 married people with children in two areas of London, one middle class, one working class.
Goldthorpe (1987) 333 adult males interviewed in 1972, Great Britain.

I shall also refer to a number of more specialised studies of particular relationships, and to some comparable American investigations, such as:

Veroff, Douvan and Kulka (1981) 2,264, a US national sample in 1976.
Fischer (1977) 3,000 adults in Detroit.

The same range of relationships can be found in each class – friends, neighbours, kin, etc. However, the meaning of these terms and the range of individuals who are included in them vary quite a lot, especially in the cases of friends and neighbours.

We shall see that there are straightforward and quite large quantitative differences, for example middle-class people have more friends. However, several surveys have obtained more detailed data on the frequency of meeting and the shared activities; although working-class people have a smaller number of friends, they live near them and see them more often. We shall examine the origins of these relationships and the amount of help and support given. For example, working-class people depend for help more on kin than on friends. And we shall examine how far these relationships can cross class boundaries, in the case of kin for instance.

The earliest studies of class differences in relationships were more intensive, qualitative local studies, like that of Stacey (1960) in Banbury, and Young and Willmott (1957) in East London. The social class scene has changed since then and I shall draw as far as possible on more recent and representative studies. The earlier work produced a number of interesting ideas, and I shall try to test these against the more recent data. For example Allan (1979) concluded from his local surveys that working-class friendship was based on groups, like those met in pubs and clubs. However, more extensive surveys like those by MORI and Goldthorpe, including those in the USA like Fischer's, found exactly the opposite – middle-class people belong to more clubs and leisure groups, though working-class individuals know more people from pubs and purely social clubs.

## FRIENDSHIP

Does 'friendship' mean something different in different classes? Allan (1979), among others, concluded that working-class people in Britain had few friends; they had close relationships with kin, and less close ones with 'mates', drawn from neighbours, work-mates and club members. We shall see that working-class people do have friends (though not so many), but that they are different in a number of ways. For example, Willmott (1987) found support for a weaker version of Allan's thesis: his middle-class respondents most often described a friend as 'someone whose company you enjoy' (30 per cent v. 6 per cent for working-class respondents). The working-class people more often chose 'someone you can always turn to for help' (36 per cent).

We will look first at the number of friends in each class. Willmott found that his middle-class subjects had on average 18.3 friends who had been met socially in the last six months, white-collar 10.4, working-class 8.3. Statistical analysis showed that this could be explained as:

| | |
|---|---|
| basic number of friends | 5.85 |
| further education adds | 6.74 |
| middle-class job adds | 4.59 |
| one car adds | 2.36 |
| second car adds | 2.36 |

However, if frequency of seeing friends was the definition, there were no class differences: all saw an average number of about three friends per week. It follows that working-class people compensated for having a smaller social circle by seeing them more frequently.

Table 4.1 Where friends come from

|  | Middle class | White collar | Working class |
|---|---|---|---|
| Work friends | 4.72 | 3.15 | 2.51 |
| Childhood or school friends | 3.10 | 1.56 | 1.34 |
| Friends met through clubs, churches, leisure, etc. | 2.68 | 0.66 | 1.08 |
| Neighbours who became friends | 1.99 | 1.59 | 1.80 |
| Ex-university or poly | 1.76 | – | – |

Source: Willmott, 1987

Friends have somewhat different origins in each class. Willmott found that, for friends seen in the last six months, origins were as shown in Table 4.1.

Other studies have shown the same pattern – more middle-class friends from work and leisure groups. Often the greatest source of working-class friends has been found to be neighbours and school friends.

How near do they live? Working-class friends live quite a lot nearer – 54 per cent within 10 minutes in this study, while 17 per cent of middle-class friends lived over an hour away. This is by no means an all-or-none difference, more a matter of degree.

Where do they meet? Allan (1979) argued that working-class friends meet at pubs, clubs and similar locations, that they only meet there and do not invite each other home, meet by accident rather than design, and do not have dyadic links with individuals, but rather with the whole group. He later (1989) recognised that this picture applied most to the old, traditional working-class, and not to the newer working-class who have moved out to housing estates. We now know that middle-class people are more likely to find their friends in leisure groups, though they invite them home more, and in this sense get to know them as individuals more than traditional working-class people did. Allan also found that middle-class people deliberately make friends from those they have met in various ways, and then see them in a number of settings including the home and not just in the club. Middle-class homes have more space, are better designed for entertainment and are used to display possessions and for general self-presentation (Allan, 1989).

The traditional working-class pattern was for husbands and wives to have independent social circles. How far is this still the case? Willmott found that 73 per cent of his middle-class couples had 'mainly the same friends', compared with 48 per cent of the working-class sample; only 9 per cent of middle-class couples had 'mainly different friends', compared with 40 per cent of working-class couples. When there were different friends, each spouse usually had friends of the same sex. The middle-class style of life emphasises shared leisure more and middle-class dinner parties are usually based on the entertainment of couples.

How far do people choose friends who are of the same class as themselves? This is important for our understanding of the class system as a whole, how far it consists of segregated layers. In all studies, and in all classes, a preference is found for friends of the same class. Willmott found that overall 61 per cent of friends were from the same broad occupational group. This tendency is strongest at the top and bottom of society compared with the middle. Goldthorpe found that 81 per cent of the friends of class I and II people were also in one of these classes. The extent of this class homogeneity varies between different studies. Laumann (1973) found less in Detroit, while Warner (1953) found a clear differentiation between the classes in Yankee City, a much smaller town. In any case a considerable proportion of friendships are with members of other classes, so the class barriers are far from rigid.

Cross-class friendships arise because other sources of similarity are also important. People choose others who have similar attitudes, are of similar age, family composition or leisure interests. We shall see later that in churches and other leisure groups class differences are to a large extent forgotten.

Friends are a major source of help and social support. Middle-class people receive more help from friends, those in the working class depend more on kin, as some of Willmott's results show (Table 4.2).

Table 4.2 Help by friends and relations

|  |  | Middle class | White collar | Working class |
| --- | --- | --- | --- | --- |
| Advice on a personal matter: | friends | 64 | 67 | 39 |
|  | relatives | 34 | 33 | 58 |
| Source of financial loan: | friends | 26 | 23 | 9 |
|  | relatives | 74 | 73 | 86 |
| Main source of help in child's illness: | friends | 39 | 45 | 19 |
|  | relatives | 56 | 55 | 77 |

Source Willmott, 1987

Friends also provide emotional support, especially to individuals in distress. Veroff found that better-educated people sought friends more often when worried, and that they were less likely to use their family for this purpose when unhappy than less-educated people. Social support from friends has often been found to be beneficial for mental health, regardless of whether stress is present or not, unlike close relationships which become effective in the presence of stress (Cohen and Wills, 1985). However, there is evidence that working-class friends *buffer* stress, i.e. are supportive only when stress is present, as if social support was not a normal feature of working-class friendship (Turner, 1981).

Friends form networks, and these take different forms in each class. Goldthorpe found that in classes VI and VII 'good friends' networks were denser than for other classes – for those naming three good friends, in 39 per cent of cases they all knew one another, compared with 17 per cent for class I. In the Willmott study 25 per cent of working-class friends mostly knew each other, compared with 15 per cent of middle-class friends.

How can we explain these different friendship patterns? Psychological research shows that 'proximity', and resulting frequency of interaction, is one source of interpersonal attraction. 'Proximity' has different meanings for those who have cars and have been accustomed to travelling to see the people they like. A second basis for liking is similarity of attitudes, interests and lifestyles; this seems to be more important for middle-class people, they are more choosey and select their friends from a wider area and from different sources, but especially from work and from leisure groups. A third source of liking is being helped and thus rewarded by the other. In the traditional working class, people were very poor and often needed help; they turned to those living close, in the same street, whom they couldn't avoid knowing. Middle-class folks move about far more in search of education and jobs, do not live so near to their neighbours and have less need for immediate help. Even so, middle-class people make more use of friends for several kinds of help, while working-class people depend more on kin – mainly because they usually have kin who live nearby, since there is so little geographical mobility.

## NEIGHBOURS

With a sample of 132 married couples with children, from two contrasted areas of London, Willmott found that most working-class and white-collar people thought of neighbours as 'the people who live next door' or 'the people who live in the nearest half dozen houses'; middle-class people often meant by neighbours 'people who live in the same street', or further afield. With a national sample MORI similarly found that middle-class people more often regarded neighbours as people who 'live fairly nearby/in the same few streets' (28 per cent v. 17 per cent).

Stacey interviewed fifty people in seven streets in Banbury, over a wide social class range, and found similar differences.

> Broadly speaking, in working class streets near neighbours are the most important source of friendship and of help. . . . In the upper class neighbours are those of the same class who live within a much wider area. . . . Those living nearby of different social class are not included among the 'neighbours'.
>
> (Stacey, 1960, p. 104)

Working-class people have much less choice and accept those living in the nearest houses as neighbours; those of higher social classes do not – they choose their neighbours from a larger area and recognise only those of a similar class.

When we study class differences in relationships with neighbours, we are not comparing the same relationship in each class. The common meaning of neighbour is something like 'people who are known and seen fairly often, mainly because they live fairly near'. The distinction between neighbours and 'friends' now becomes difficult, because in working-class areas they are often the same people. Willmott found that 60 per cent of his sample had a neighbour who had become a friend, and he treated this as a separate category; they were usually not next-door neighbours. There is also some overlap between neighbours and kin, who tend to live quite close in working-class areas, but the two categories are clearly distinct for other people. In all classes, the number of neighbours varies, but the average is about the same – people typically have contact with six or seven neighbours (Willmott, 1987).

Field studies in traditional working-class areas in industrial cities found these neighbourhoods very dense, homogeneous and tightly-knit, and found that there was a great deal of solidarity, gossip, mutual help and reciprocity, especially in times of crisis and especially by young mothers. People would pop in without knocking. Much of this has been lost in moving to the new housing estates. Middle-class neighbourhoods were quite different, no popping in, less help, a greater desire for privacy, more formal relations with neighbours and more awareness of who it was suitable to know (Bulmer, 1986). This picture has been confirmed by social surveys. Table 4.3 shows some of the differences.

It is lower-class people who visit the homes of neighbours, or call round

*Table 4.3* Interaction with neighbours (percentages)

|  | AB | C1 | C2 | DE |
|---|---|---|---|---|
| Visit home of a neighbour daily or more | 6 | 10 | 13 | 16 |
| Call round for a chat, daily or more | 9 | 14 | 21 | 21 |
| Have in for a meal, ever | 43 | 29 | 16 | 13 |
| Have in for a drink, ever | 62 | 53 | 40 | 36 |
| Know neighbours best | 21 | 27 | 33 | 37 |

*Source:* MORI, 1982

|  | I | III–V | VI–VII |
|---|---|---|---|
| Number of neighbours known 'well' or met 'fairly often' | 3.2 | 1.8 | 1.4 |

*Source:* Goldthorpe, 1987

for a chat most often – 21 per cent have a chat daily in DE. But middle-class individuals ask neighbours round for a meal or a drink, though not very often. In DE 87 per cent have never had a neighbour in for a meal. And working-class people more often say that they know their neighbours best, compared with friends and others. On the other hand, in the Goldthorpe study respondents in class I said that they knew more neighbours well, 3.2 v. 1.4 in classes VI and VII. This perhaps represents their choice of 'neighbour' from a wider geographical area, not just the people next door.

People meet other local residents on the doorstep and over the garden fence, but also in the street, and at pubs, churches and other meeting places. There is some evidence that for working-class people these are usually chance encounters, while for middle-class people they are more often arranged (Goldthorpe).

The traditional picture of working-class life was of poor people helping each other out, lending money and sugar, looking after children and so on. Recent studies however do not confirm this picture. Neighbours, in all classes, are mainly sources of minor rather than major help – with shopping and looking after pets or plants, rather than lending money, or looking after those who are ill. In many areas of help there is little class difference, but what differences there are go in the opposite direction.

These two surveys found very similar differences. Whenever there was a class difference in help for neighbours, it was middle-class people who did more. This help was mainly to do with the house – pets, plants, maintenance,

*Table 4.4* Helping neighbours (percentages)

|  | AB | C1 | C2 | DE |
|---|---|---|---|---|
| Looked after pets or plants over the last year or so | 58 | 47 | 46 | 31 |
| Provided help or advice in household maintenance/ repairs | 49 | 44 | 39 | 28 |
| Looked after house key for tradesmen/emergencies | 62 | 55 | 55 | 44 |
| Helped with items of food, when you ran out | 49 | 43 | 42 | 35 |
| Never helped | 9 | 11 | 11 | 22 |

*Source:* MORI, 1982

|  | Middle class | White collar | Working class |
|---|---|---|---|
| Shopping | 10 | 6 | 6 |
| House maintenance | 19 | 17 | 6 |
| Little or no help | 3 | 11 | 12 |

*Source:* Willmott, 1987

etc., which can be seen as more middle-class concerns. But even lending food is more common for middle-class neighbours. And more working-class people provide no help at all for their neighbours.

Nevertheless the effects of neighbours and neighbourhood groups on happiness and mental health are actually greater for those who are lower-class, old or living alone. And they have a greater need for social support – loneliness is more common: 6 per cent of class AB feel lonely once a week or more compared with 22 per cent in C2, DE (MORI).

This is different from earlier accounts of traditional slums in London, New York and elsewhere.

> I suppose people who come from outside think it's an awful place, but us established ones like it. Here you can just open your door and say hello to everybody.
>
> (Young and Willmott, 1957)

Exactly the same was found in a slum in New York: neighbours were very important. People met in local bars and settlement houses, and people felt 'at home' in their own street, where they often sat and talked when the weather was warm. Do such friendly, helpful slums still exist? In the MORI survey several different kinds of housing were distinguished; one was 'very poor quality, older terraced housing', which 8.4 per cent of the sample lived in, so we can see how this group compared in neighbourliness with the groups looked at so far. They had a high score on 'know neighbour best' (34 per cent), a little more than for urban local authority housing (32 per cent), and modern family housing for manual workers (28 per cent). And they were more likely to visit the home of a neighbour daily, 17 per cent, compared with 12 per cent for local authority housing. On the other hand, the level of help was about the same as for the other two working-class groups. There was another group who knew their neighbours even better: people living in rural areas – 43 per cent knew their neighbours best, compared with 37 per cent for the DE group and 21 per cent for AB, but different classes in the country were not separated here.

Most of those traditional terraced slums have now been demolished, and their occupants have moved to modern council estates and some to the suburbs. Sociologists made gloomy predictions about suburbs too – they would develop a tribal-like conformity, with limited social involvements and attachments. In fact American suburbs have more active social life and involvement in the neighbourhood than other parts of American cities, more localised friendships, but less contact with the kin left behind. British suburbs and housing estates are not all so neighbourly. It depends on the availability of community centres and other social facilities.

Another part of the traditional view of traditional working-class life was that people formed close networks with those living close to them. That is, if an individual knows two or three others, they will also know one another.

How far is this borne out by research on social networks? Goldthorpe did find this, for 'spare-time associates'. For men who reported three such associates, in his classes VI and VIII, 77 per cent all knew each other, but in I it was only 35 per cent. Similar differences were found for 'good friends'. The same has been found in American studies. They have also found that for lower-class people dense networks are more supportive, perhaps because they are more controllable and can provide rapid help; middle-class networks are more helpful when they are varied and less dense – and can meet a variety of needs (Fischer, 1977).

## LEISURE GROUPS

There is a large class difference in belonging to leisure groups and voluntary organisations of most kinds. Young and Willmott found that 69 per cent of their professional and managerial class belonged, compared to 36 per cent of their semi- and unskilled groups. Goldthorpe found that his class I men belonged to an average of 3.6 clubs, compared to 1.7, 1.6 and 1.5 for the

Table 4.5 Belonging to clubs (percentages)

|  | AB | C1 | C2 | DE |
|---|---|---|---|---|
| *Know best* | | | | |
| 1. members of sporting club | 15 | 7 | 6 | 4 |
| 2. members of club associated with hobby or interest | 12 | 9 | 7 | 7 |
| 3. members of a voluntary organisation | 4 | 3 | 2 | 3 |
| 4. people you meet at a local pub or club | 11 | 11 | 19 | 21 |
| *Speak to weekly* | | | | |
| 1. members of sporting club | 25 | 19 | 15 | 8 |
| 2. members of club associated with hobby or interest | 30 | 23 | 20 | 15 |
| 3. members of a voluntary organisation | 17 | 12 | 10 | 9 |
| 4. people you meet at a local pub or club | 33 | 35 | 39 | 37 |

Source: MORI, 1982

|  | Prof. & man. | Clerical | Skilled | Semi-skilled and unskilled |
|---|---|---|---|---|
| Active members of at least one club or association | 69 | 51 | 49 | 36 |
| Officers or committee members | 28 | 16 | 13 | 4 |

Source: Young and Willmott, 1973

three lower groupings. Similar differences are found for where the people known best are met and for the people who are spoken to at least weekly (Table 4.5).

However, it makes a difference which kind of club we are talking about. Working-class people know more people and meet them more often at pubs and social clubs, though they belong much less to sports clubs, hobby and interest groups, voluntary organisations, churches and political organisations. American studies have found the same, though the interest of researchers there has been in political groups and groups which are trying to exert influence in some way (Laumann, 1973).

There is an even greater difference in the class of those who become officers or committee members. Most clubs have members from a range of social classes, and it is those from the higher classes who become the leaders and run them.

To what extent do clubs produce a social mix, and succeed in integrating members of different classes? Nearly all clubs draw members from more than one class, but equally nearly all are exclusive in not attracting or encouraging members from other classes. Lloyd Warner (1963), in 'Yankee City', found that the leisure groups there often spanned three or four of his six classes, though some groups were drawn exclusively from one or two adjacent classes, and women favoured these more exclusive groups. Over half of the groups had under twenty members, so that contact would be quite close. Wild (1974) carried out a similar study of 'Bradstow', a small town in New South Wales, which is perhaps more stratified than most Australian cities. He found 108 associations, and the classes found in the main ones, from 'gentry' (mainly big sheep farmers) to 'no-hopers', are shown in Figure 4.1. The only club the latter group were able to join was evidently the Rugby League Club. Again it can be seen that, although the clubs are stratified and keep people out or fail to attract them, they all have members from more than one of the six classes that Wild identified.

But do the members really mix freely and accept one another? Bottomore (1954) studied the 125 leisure groups in a small English town, and found that fewer than half contained members from all of the three main classes distinguished; most drew members from only one of those broad classes. When there was a mixture of classes, Bottomore found that social integration went furthest when there was a definite activity (i.e. not just a 'social' club) and where the meetings were fairly small, informal and frequent. It might be expected that other conditions favouring integration may be wearing a shared costume or uniform (e.g. tennis), cooperation (e.g. music), intimacy (e.g. dancing) or ideological support (e.g. church, left-wing politics).

I have recently surveyed 200 clubs in Oxford. They had a similar degree of social mix to the studies just described. It was also found that 47 per cent of people said their relationships with club members were as close as other

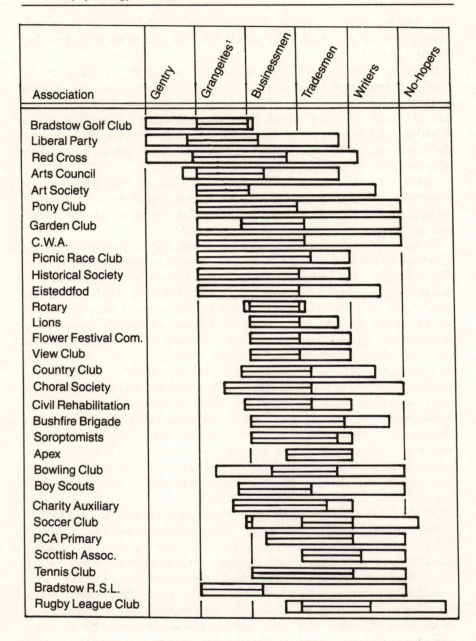

*Figure 4.1* Office holders and members of thirty associations distributed among the status groups. (The open bars indicate membership, the hatched areas indicate that members are also officials.)
*Source:* Wild, 1974
*Note:* 1. Live in a smart suburb called Grange.

friendships, while 13 per cent said they were closer. Some of these club friendships may be with people from other social classes.

Why are middle-class people so much more active in leisure groups of most kinds? Note first that working-class people spend more time in pubs and in 'social clubs' (which are often not very different). Middle-class people go to clubs where there is some physical or mental activity; this may be because they are less tired after work, can afford the expense involved in e.g. golf, are more able to travel to where the club is or have developed the necessary skills or interests during the course of education. They become leaders, sometimes because they are democratically elected because they appear to have useful skills or contacts. Many of these clubs however are quite undemocratic, and do not have real elections; the leaders elect themselves, and it is very interesting that no one seems to object. As long as the club is efficiently run they are happy for others to do the work.

## KINSHIP

In primitive and Third World countries, and in Europe before the Industrial Revolution, kinship was the main source of relationships and help. Families lived in larger units, including at least three generations, as they still do in parts of Italy. The Industrial Revolution is usually credited with the rise of the smaller, nuclear family unit, consisting of the parents and children, and a much smaller number of children at that. Kinship has for a long time been an important source of help and support for working-class people. Agriculture was always uncertain because of the weather, and industry because of trade fluctuations and times of high unemployment. The family provided a major source of financial support for its non-working members (Humphries, 1977). We shall see later how in working-class families in particular, women ganged together in mutual help and protection.

In this section we shall discuss relationships between kin outside the nuclear family – siblings, grown-up children and their parents, and to a lesser extent cousins, aunts, uncles and grandparents.

Frequency of meeting such kin is much greater for working-class people: class I met 1.5 close kin, classes III(m)–VII 3.6, at least once a week (Goldthorpe, 1987). The corresponding numbers of kin who were associates in leisure activities were 1.9 for I, 3.0 for VI and VII. Willmott found the similar average numbers of 2.08 and 3.37, with his broader class groupings. American studies find a further difference: middle-class wives keep up contacts both with their own kin and their husbands', working-class wives only with their own. Working-class wives keep up very close links with their own mothers, daughters and sisters; their husbands don't bother (Adams, 1968).

The greater frequency of contact between working-class kin is linked with greater proximity. Willmott and Young (1960) found that people in

*Table 4.6* Proximity to kin in Woodford and Bethnal Green (percentages)

|  | Woodford | Bethnal Green |
| --- | --- | --- |
| Same dwelling | 10 | 24 |
| Within 5 minutes | 6 | 23 |
| Outside borough | 63 | 43 |

(nearest married child, people below pension age, Willmott and Young, 1960)

middle-class Woodford lived further away from kin than in working-class Bethnal Green (Table 4.6).

We showed earlier how working-class people in London turned to kin for help and advice more than middle-class people did; the latter made more use of friends. The closer links between working-class kin have also been found in American studies. However, a recent British study of 507 women during and after pregnancy in small English towns found that middle-class women had more contact with parents and kin (though not with their sisters) during the period of childbirth (Oakley and Rajan, 1991). The authors suggest that this reflects the decline of traditional working-class communities, where kin lived very close to one another.

In a much-cited American study of fifty-eight working-class families, Komarovsky (1964) found that many working-class women had no friends at all, belonged to no organisations and depended entirely on kin for advice and support. At an earlier period female kin formed a 'female trade union' to give each other mutual support (p. 80). Traditionally working-class kin helped each other a great deal, when someone was ill, with baby-sitting, shopping or lending things.

Inheritance is mainly to kin, so are the most valuable gifts at birthdays and Christmas. Middle-class people do more here, including helping children buy houses, paying for school fees of grandchildren or making loans, though financial help is given by all classes (Firth *et al.*, 1969).

Kin constitute part of the social network, which also includes friends, neighbours and others. For middle-class people kin are kept apart, while for working-class people they are more integrated. Willmott found that 25 per cent of his working-class kin knew 'all or most' of respondents' friends, compared with 12 per cent for white-collar and 15 per cent for middle-class people. In London and in Northern California (Fischer, 1982) middle-class people are found to have social networks that are larger, but less dense and more varied. It is as if working-class people have less choice, and accept many of the kin and neighbours who live nearby as friends and associates, where middle-class people are more selective.

Nuclear families are by some definitions of the same social class. Larger family structures however can vary, as the result of social mobility, up and down. How far does this weaken kinship bonds? Are kinship ties strong enough to withstand class divisions?

It is found that there is less frequent contact with their families by those who have been mobile. The percentages seen in the last week were:

downwardly mobile    41%
upwardly mobile      60%
non-mobile           70%

(Firth *et al.*, 1969)

Goldthorpe found reduced frequency of meeting for upwardly mobile men, compared with the level of kin contact in their class of origin; this was mainly due to increased distance between them, and was most marked for joint leisure. The upwardly mobile had two separate social networks. Willmott and Young (1960) found that there was reduced contact with parents by children who had been socially mobile, but especially for fathers and sons compared with mothers and daughters. Contact between fathers and sons was reduced more when the son was downwardly mobile; perhaps the feeling that a son has failed is more serious than the feeling that the father has been 'outstripped'. Mobile children name their own children less often after family members (Rossi, 1965).

When one sibling is upwardly mobile this has more effect on sibling contact than it has on parent–child relations. In an American study frequency of meeting outside the home fell by 42 per cent. However, the effect is most marked for two brothers, least for two sisters: 59 per cent of the brothers felt less close, in cases of different mobility, compared with 23 per cent of sisters, while 61 per cent of sisters where one had been mobile felt *more* close than earlier (Adams, 1968). We conclude that there are a lot of kinship ties which reach across class divisions between kin, where one has been socially mobile. Although there is some reduction in kinship ties, the majority remain intact and still operate for help, if not for leisure.

The basis of kinship bonds is quite different from friendship. The latter depends on similarity of interests and values, and frequent interaction. Kinship is more due to powerful bonding experiences in the family, social norms about attitudes to kin and perhaps also to the effects of shared genes. Kinship bonds often last forever, in the absence of shared interests or values, and are thus able to survive class differences caused by social mobility, more than friendships can. The greater dependence of working-class people on kin reflects fundamental class differences in style of life, such as the greater proximity and lesser geographical mobility of the working class, together with their greater need for help and the greater need of working-class women for defence against husbands, leading to a high level of contact and help between female kin.

## MARRIAGE

Most people get married in all classes, though more in higher ones, probably because more couples in lower classes live together unwed. In class I 93 per

Table 4.7 Marriage

|  | I | II | IIn | IIIm | IV | V |
|---|---|---|---|---|---|---|
| Percentage women married under age 20 (1971) | 0 | 17 | 19 | 21 | 25 | 23 |
| Median age of bride at marriage (1979) | 26.4 | 24.0 | 21.6 | 21.2 | 20.4 | 22.0 |
| Divorce rate, per 1,000 husbands under 59 (1971) | 7 | 12 | 16 | 14 | 15 | 30 |
| Percentage divorced whose marriages lasted less than 7 years (wife married 20–25) (1970–1) | 10 | 27 | 23 | 36 | 37 | 25 |

Sources: Reid, 1989; Argyle and Henderson, 1985

cent of men are married by the age of 40 v. 74 per cent of class V. On the other hand, more lower-class individuals marry early: 24 per cent of IV and V women, but almost no class I women, marry under 20. The median ages of brides at marriage are shown in Table 4.7.

Working-class young people have intercourse earlier, and many more first births are conceived before marriage (see Table 4.10). In a number of cultures, over a long period, middle-class people have been better informed and more effective in the use of contraception (Blood, 1972). On the other hand, more middle-class couples live together before marriage – though the most recent studies have found little difference. We shall discuss children later. Meanwhile we note that working-class couples have children much sooner after marriage, when the mother is younger, and they go on to have more children, especially in class V (see Table 4.10). Middle-class marriages are less likely to end in divorce (Table 4.7), and last longer.

I thought it worth while to set out these basic statistics, since they give a strong factual basis for the analysis of class differences in marriage. They show that middle-class people marry later, spend over three years together before there are children, have fewer children and are more likely to stay married.

We shall see in Chapter 11 how working-class young people have more pre-marital intercourse. The combination of the boys' lack of restraint and the girls' ignorance of birth control are probably responsible for the high rate of early working-class pregnancies. The marriages that follow are more the result of chance encounters at dance halls and pubs than middle-class marriages made more carefully in colleges, churches and clubs (Slater and Woodside, 1951). But how do the marital relationships compare? The traditional working-class pattern of marriage was that the couple led fairly separate lives, husbands going to the pub in the evening and to football on Saturdays. Wives stayed at home, and were given housekeeping money, but looked after the children and ran the home single-handed. Wives developed a kind of 'female trade union' in defence of themselves and their children, that is they mobilised the support of female kin, mothers, daughters and sisters. Middle-class couples expected to share their leisure and friends, and expected a high level of companionship, mutual help and support.

Research in the USA and Japan has found that better-educated couples talk to each other more, for example they discuss the day's news and what the day's events have been for each. In Komarovsky's sample (1964) some working-class couples said that they would like to talk to each other but did not have anything to say. The better-educated husbands were rated as having greater understanding and empathy with their wives. Other American studies have found more self-disclosure in middle-class couples.

In Britain Young and Willmott found that middle-class couples have more shared friends, though the class difference is not very large. Other research has found that men benefit more from marriage, in terms of better health and mental health. The explanation is probably that wives are better listeners and confidantes than husbands (Vanfossen, 1981). Wives depend more on their female kin for such support. This is especially true of working-class couples, where many husbands do not seem to be very good at it. Much has been said about the increased value placed on intimacy and partnership. However Veroff *et al.* (1981), with a large American sample, found that the better-educated saw marriage more often as consisting of two separate people (Table 4.8).

Middle-class couples share more leisure activities, e.g. belong to the same leisure groups, go to theatres and restaurants together.

We turn to equality of spouses. Traditionally, and in all cultures, husbands have been the dominant partners. In working-class couples this is usually still the case, but in middle-class couples there is more equality, especially when the wife is well-educated, or has a good job, or holds leadership positions in organisations like churches and voluntary groups (Blood, 1972).

There have been widespread social changes during this century. Young and Willmott saw a shift towards the 'symmetrical family', especially in the

*Table 4.8* Marriage and intimacy (percentages)

|  | Grade school | Some high school | High school graduate | Some college | College graduate |
|---|---|---|---|---|---|
| See marriage as two separate people | 11 | 20 | 26 | 36 | 40 |
| Nicest thing about marriage: relationship | 42 | 49 | 56 | 60 | 67 |
| Marital happiness: very happy | 51 | 42 | 51 | 58 | 64 |

*Source:* Veroff *et al.*, 1981

*Table 4.9* How symmetrical are families? (percentages)

| | Prof. and managerial | Clerical | Skilled | Semi-skilled and unskilled |
|---|---|---|---|---|
| Husband helps, other than washing up | 70 | 80 | 73 | 64 |
| Wife's job interferes with home and family | 58 | 30 | 22 | |
| Husband's job does not interfere with home or family | 47 | 60 | 69 | 75 |
| Husband does not work shifts or weekends | 74 | 66 | 51 | 44 |
| Wife present at last meeting with friend | 68 | 60 | 58 | 51 |

*Source:* Young and Willmott, 1973

working class, that is a shift towards greater equality, partnership and cooperation between husbands and wives. To test this thesis they interviewed nearly 2,000 people in London and the South of England to find out.

*Control of money.* Previously working-class husbands kept control of cash, spent quite a lot of it on drink and tobacco and were usually secretive about the family finances. This position has greatly improved, partly because many women earn money themselves, while mothers receive child benefits and other allowances, and more expenditure is for joint entertainment and activities etc., rather than for the husband's tobacco and drink (Young and Willmott, 1973).

*Housework.* For a long time women did all of it. Now some husbands help, a few more in the middle class (Table 4.9). Wives are also helped by better equipment – deep freeze, dishwashers, etc., and more prosperous families have more of it. Oakley (1974) found that working-class wives liked housework more; many middle-class wives disliked it, though they liked looking after the children. The working-class wives identified more with the housewife role, in the 'Who am I?' test, perhaps because it was the most important thing they did. But despite the demands made by educated women for equality of career opportunities, it is lower-class women who work most, presumably because the need for a second income is greater. Middle-class husbands have longer hours of work and travel to work, and find their work more mentally but less physically tiring; however, work interferes less with home life, partly because they do less shift work (Table 4.9).

The 'female trade union' may be less active than it was, but wives still have much more contact with kin than husbands do, and working-class families make most use of kin as a source of help, as opposed to friends (p. 69).

Several typologies of marriages have been put forward. A common division is into (1) traditional marriage, with 'benevolent male dominance coupled with clearly specialised roles', (2) egalitarian marriage, usually with dual careers, alternate or shared jobs, and rejection of the traditional marriage roles, (3) modern marriage, an intermediate position, with less husband dominance and less role specialisation than in traditional marriage (Peplau, 1983). It looks as if more working-class marriages are traditional, more middle-class marriages are modern, while a few are egalitarian. The traditional family has survived longer in working-class culture, and is supported by husbands who are at the receiving end of hierarchical work structures where they have little power and are too tired in the evening to be bothered by housework.

Marriages are happier for middle-class people, see Table 4.8. More educated people admitted to having had marital problems and feeling inadequate as spouses, but seemed to have the skills for handling marital conflicts (Locksley, 1982). Better-educated people have been found to be more open with each other, less controlling and to respect others' feelings more. We have already seen that the divorce rate is much higher in lower classes – 37 per cent in IV and 7 per cent in I (Table 4.7). In the USA less-educated working-class couples are more likely to settle their quarrels by violence and drink than by talking it out and only moderate flare-ups (Komarovsky, 1962).

Why are middle-class marriages on the whole happier and more long-lasting? We have seen that middle-class partners are chosen more carefully and married later. And middle-class couples are under less stress, have more money, larger houses, fewer children, more domestic help and more energy to pursue their leisure interests and social life together.

Spouses are usually similar to one another in social class, whether measured by class of origin, education or occupation. When both have jobs, these are often at the same level, especially for classes I, II and VI, the top and the bottom (Reid, 1989). Differences are created however by the different distributions of men and women between occupational classes – especially the greater number of women in II and III (n), so that husband in I, wife in II, or husband in III (m) and wife in III (n) are quite common combinations.

If the couple are of different classes, by origin, education or job, the main effect is that the marriage is less happy and more likely to end in divorce. An American study found the following percentages of married couples rated as having 'good' adjustment (Roth and Peck, 1951):

| Same social class | Husband higher class | Wife higher class |
|---|---|---|
| 53 | 35 | 28 |

Table 4.10 Birth of children

| | I | II | IIIn | IIIm | IV | V |
|---|---|---|---|---|---|---|
| Percentage first births conceived before marriage (1980) | 9 | | 11 | 20 | 25 | |
| Illegitimate (1983) | 5 | | 6 | 12 | 16 | |
| Median interval in months between marriage and first birth (1985) | 37 | | 33 | 26 | 18 | |
| Percentage mothers under 20 at first birth (1977) | 6 | 10 | 12 | 28 | 31 | 38 |
| Mean family size (1984) | 2.04 | 1.99 | 1.86 | 2.20 | 2.24 | 2.47 |

Source: Reid, 1989

Another study found that 45 per cent of husbands were violent when the wife was better educated, as opposed to 9 per cent when he was better educated or when they were equal (O'Brien, 1971). If the husband is of higher class, his wife may be very attractive or have other desirable qualities, but she may also commit social errors, be an unsatisfactory conversationalist and prove not fully acceptable to his family and friends. It is worse when the wife is of higher social class; she may have to put up with a lower standard of living, suffer a drop in social position and see her children deprived of what she had as a child. She is also discontented if she has been socially mobile through her own career (Argyle and Henderson, 1985).

## PARENTS AND CHILDREN

Working-class couples have many more first births which were conceived before marriage, or born 'illegitimate', the first child is born much sooner after marriage and mothers are younger when the first child is born (Table 4.10).

It follows that many working-class children were not planned, probably not wanted, that the parents are less experienced and that couples have had little time to establish the marital bond before it is disrupted by childbirth. Working-class families are larger than middle-class ones, but not much larger, now that birth control has become widely practised. There are more working-class one-parent families, mostly the mother with one or more children, as the result of the higher divorce rate and higher rates of illegitimacy (Reid, 1989). More middle-class families, mainly childless ones, adopt children and the children are mainly of working-class origin. Most fostered children on the other hand are taken into working-class families.

We turn now to class differences in child-rearing. I shall draw particularly on the studies by John and Elizabeth Newson, of 700 4–year-old children (1968) and of 697 7–year-olds (1976) in Nottingham. A large range of issues were explored, and many difference between classes found.

(1) Love and warmth. Parents of all classes love their children; mothers

play whole-heartedly with them at 4. More middle-class mothers have stories, songs or prayers at bed-time and they express a little more affection at 7.

(2) *Child-centredness*. Middle-class mothers of 4-year-olds were more child-centred, e.g. 'mother is invariably or mostly responsive to the child's demands'. And middle-class mothers of 7-year-olds had much higher scores on ten questions about child-centredness, like being sympathetic to child not wanting to go to school and keeping child's drawings; 60 per cent of class I mothers had high scores v. 16 per cent for class V. More middle-class parents said they often shared an interest with the child at age 7.

(3) *Involvement of father in child care*. Middle-class fathers do quite a lot more for their children. They have longer hours of work and travel to work, but are much less often on shift or weekend work. Oakley (1974) found that 40 per cent of middle-class fathers had 'high' participation in child care, compared with 10 per cent of working-class fathers. The Newsons report that 47 per cent of I and II fathers of 7-year-olds participated a lot in child care, compared to 34 per cent of V, when the children were aged 7, and similar differences at ages 4 and 1.

(4) *Discipline*. In British and American studies, over a number of years, research has found more physical punishment by working-class parents (p. 163). Many American studies have found that middle-class parents instead use reasoning, isolation, appeals to guilt and other methods involving threat of loss of love.

Middle-class mothers are generally stricter – e.g. early bed and better table manners at 4, insisting on obedience at 7, though they are less concerned over rudeness or bad language than working-class mothers. American studies also find that working-class parents place greater emphasis on obedience, and that they give heavier punishment when a child's disobedience has serious consequences. Middle-class parents may decide to punish depending on their interpretation of the child's intentions (Kohn, 1963).

Many class I families, and some in class II, employ nannies, au pairs or other live-in domestic help, especially when the children are young and both husband and wife are working. When the youngest child is 0–4, 30 per cent of class I women are working full-time and 27 per cent part-time, which is usually made possible by domestic help, compared with 1 per cent and 46 per cent for class V. When the youngest child is 10 or over, 61 per cent of class I women are working full-time, compared with 1 per cent for class V (*Social Trends*, 1992). However, there is evidence that nannies, in the recent and remembered past at least, came from a lower social class and used working-class styles of child-rearing, which were strict, prudish and puritanical, concerned with cleanliness, obedience and conformity. Some of their charges became very attached to their nanny rather than their mother, and were very disturbed when she left (at age 5) or they were sent away to school (at 7) (Gathorne-Hardy, 1985).

There are class differences in handling adolescents. American studies have found that working-class parents are more likely to use authoritarian methods, rather than 'democratic', and that authoritarian parenting is not seen as good and reasonable by the children, and leads to them feeling unwanted (Elder, 1962).

(5) *Parental values*. As we show in Chapter 7, middle-class parents are a lot more concerned with educational achievement, spend longer reading to children and stimulating intellectual development. They encourage and reward independent achievement at an early age and set high levels of aspiration (p. 165). Some of the consequences can be seen in the Newsons' data. At age 7, more middle-class children read books a lot at home, wrote at home for their own pleasure, had specific collections and possessed their own toys.

American studies have concluded that the goal of middle-class parents is for their children to internalise the values of achievement, responsibility and respect for others, while working-class parents are more concerned that their children shall be obedient, conforming and respectable (Bronfenbrenner, 1958).

Why are there these differences in child-rearing? It is partly a matter of cultural lag; middle-class parents are the first to read new books and to start the new fashions. They were the first to read Spock, the first to adopt feeding infants on demand and to be permissive about infant sexuality. Working-class fathers may do less for their children because they are physically tired or on shift work. They may pass on the more authoritarian supervision which they experience at work to their children.

## WORK RELATIONSHIPS

These can be very important relationships, and are a common source of friendships. In the MORI survey, 30–35 per cent of people in class A–C said they knew best people from their place of work, but only 18 per cent in DE. Goldthorpe similarly found that his class I males saw 2.4 work colleagues regularly outside work, compared with 1.5–1.7 for classes below this. It should be added that over 50 per cent of people did not see any work-mate outside work regularly. The greater level of contact in the higher classes is despite the greater distance which can be assumed to separate them.

Relationships at the workplace also vary with social status. Veroff, in the USA, found that affiliative satisfaction at work was greater in higher status jobs.

Table 4.11 shows that manual jobs provide less affiliative satisfaction. However, intermediate status jobs like sales and service, which involve a lot of contact with other people, provide even higher levels. There are also gender differences – women at work report high levels of this kind of satisfaction. Friendships are made more easily at work by those who work

Table 4.11 Percentages reporting affiliative satisfaction at work

| | Professional | Managers | Clerical | Sales | Skilled | Operatives | Service | Labourers | Farmers |
|---|---|---|---|---|---|---|---|---|---|
| Men | 27 | 36 | 29 | 40 | 7 | 12 | 48 | 9 | 6 |
| Women | 50 | 54 | 34 | 81 | 9 | 7 | 41 | – | 9 |
| | College graduates | Some college | High school graduates | Some high school | Grade school | | | | |
| Both | 39 | 28 | 31 | 18 | 18 | | | | |

Source: Veroff et al., 1981

in small, segregated work teams, less by those on noisy assembly-lines or working in isolation. Managerial and professional jobs often involve a lot of social life with colleagues and clients, as part of the job (Argyle, 1989).

We go into work more fully in Chapter 5. However, social relationships at work are clearly rather different at each level. Those in more senior jobs report greater affiliation and other kinds of job satisfaction. They find the work 'mentally tiring' – 88 per cent for professional and management, 40 per cent for semi- and unskilled (Young and Willmott, 1973). A lot of the mental strain of higher-level jobs is probably from relations with work-mates. Rosemary Stewart (1967) found that managers spend a great deal of time with other people, 32 per cent of their time with one other person and 34 per cent with two or more.

Relations with superiors are often experienced as stressful, unless they are socially skilled, because of their greater power and capacity to criticise and direct. Relations with subordinates are easier, but relations with equal-status colleagues can be very competitive, as well as requiring cooperation. An obvious explanation of the greater affiliative satisfaction of higher-status individuals is that they have greater power and receive more respect.

There is a positive side to the enjoyment of relations with work-mates, at all levels – informal contacts, especially during work-breaks. Homans proposed a theory about how the two kinds of social activity are related. He argued that people come to work in order to get the work done and to be paid for it; they have to cooperate with other people, discover that they like some of them and start engaging in extra social activity with them. A number of studies of small working groups have found that manual workers often have a lot of fun, with jokes, games, gossip and rituals (Argyle, 1989). When people make friends at work, this is manifested in such informal activities, but also in help and cooperation at work. It probably happens at all levels.

## THE OVERALL PATTERN OF RELATIONSHIPS

The study of social relationships, mainly by social psychologists (e.g. Duck, 1988), makes almost no reference to class differences. Yet, as we have seen, these are quite large, e.g. middle-class people have over twice as many friends and are given more help by them, while working-class people live much closer to their kin, see them more often and are helped more by them. Working-class marriages are less equal and three and a half times as likely to end in divorce. What is meant by a 'neighbour' or 'friend' is somewhat different in each class. And the nature of the relationship can be very different, as in marriage.

Several studies have looked at the total pattern of relationships and social support in different classes. Oakley and Rajan (1991), in their study of 507 pregnant women in small towns in England, found that middle-class women had 12 per cent more contact with their mothers than working-class women, more contact with their fathers, less with their sisters, twice as much contact with close friends, and overall received considerably more help from other people. We shall show later that class differences in mental health in women can partly be accounted for by the lower level of social support for working-class women, especially from spouse or boyfriend (p. 276). We also show that class differences in happiness can partly be explained by the greater amount of middle-class social activity with friends and membership of leisure groups (p. 280). Working-class people may receive more support from kin, but these networks have been found to be 'child-related and practical', compared with their white-collar counterparts (Cochran *et al.*, 1990). Research in other cultures has also found that middle-class people have larger networks and receive more overall social support, but that the balance of different relationships varies.

We have suggested explanations for many of these differences, and these fall into several different types.

*Ecology.* Working-class people live nearer together and are less geographically mobile. Kin in particular live near, and the whole network is denser, especially traditional working-class communities. Middle-class people form relationships over a larger area and exercise more choice.

*Wealth.* Having more money makes it easier to go out to social events, join sports clubs, entertain people at home and travel greater distances. Fischer (1977) found that income was the best predictor of number of friends, with education held constant. People with a background of poverty or economic insecurity are accustomed to keeping a close network of kin, neighbours and friends who can be relied on for help.

*Education.* This passes on new ideas, for example, about how to bring up children and about the role of women in marriage. Women's education is particularly important and leads to increased wealth and influence of women.

*Work experience.* Middle-class people are used to being treated well at work, to being consulted and to democratic decision-making. Working-class people are more likely to be at the lower end of a hierarchy where they have no say at all. These styles are likely to be passed on to the family.

*Personality and social skills.* Middle-class people, partly as a result of their jobs, are more socially skilled, used to dealing with strangers and therefore able to make friends easily. The same may apply to some sociable service occupations, too.

*Class lifestyles.* The lifestyles and values of each class are closely linked to the kinds of relationships formed. Middle-class couples, for example, value joint leisure and shared friendships; working-class couples are concerned with more immediate problems and see relationships primarily as sources of help. Middle-class people value individual achievement and responsibility, working-class people are more collectivist and depend on the group.

*Table 4.12* Homogeneity of different kinds of relationship

|  | Percentage from same class | Correlation between own and other's class |
|---|---|---|
| Kin | 38 | .29 |
| Work-mates | 40 | .51 |
| Friends  : neighbourhood | 39 | .43 |
| : childhood | 40 | .51 |
| : other | 36 | .37 |
| Leisure groups | 54 | .66 |

*Source:* Fischer, 1977

We have seen that individuals tend to have relationships with others of the same class as themselves. This effect varies with different kinds of relationship, and is greatest for work and leisure group associates, least for kin and neighbours, as found by Fischer in Detroit (Table 4.12).

There were similar differences for homogeneity of age. It follows that some relationships, more than others, are able to span class barriers. The most striking cases of this which we have found are certain kin relations, especially between sisters, and mothers and daughters, where class differences resulting from social mobility do not seem to affect the relationship.

Some aspects of class are more permeable to friendship than others. Wright and Cho (1992) found that differences of property were most difficult to cross, followed by differences of expertise and authority – in the USA, Canada and Norway. In Sweden, however, expertise was the greatest barrier and property less important.

## REFERENCES

Adams, B.N. (1968) *Kinship in an Urban Setting*. Chicago: Markham.

Allan, G.A. (1979) *A Sociology of Friendship and Kinship*. London: Allen & Unwin.

Allan, G.A. (1989) *Friendship: Developing a Sociological Perspective*. New York: Harvester Wheatsheaf.

Argyle, M. (1989) *The Social Psychology of Work*. 2nd edition. Harmondsworth: Penguin.

Argyle, M. and Henderson, M. (1985) *The Anatomy of Relationships*. Harmondsworth: Penguin.

Blood, R.O. (1972) *The Family*. London: Collier Macmillan.

Bottomore, P. (1954) Social stratification in voluntary organisations. In D.V. Glass (ed.) *Social Mobility in Britain*. London: Routledge & Kegan Paul.

Bronfenbrenner, U. (1958) Socialization and social class through time and space. In E.E. Maccoby, T.M. Newcomb, and E.L. Hartley (eds) *Readings in Social Psychology*. 3rd edition. New York: Holt.

Bulmer, M. (1986) *Neighbours: The Work of Philip Abrams*. Cambridge: Cambridge University Press.

Cochran, M., Gonnarson, L., Gräbe, S. and Lewis, S. (1990) The social networks of coupled mothers in four cultures. In M. Cochran *et al.* (eds) *Extending Families:*

*The Social Networks of Parents and their Children.* Cambridge: Cambridge University Press.

Cohen, S. and Wills, T.A. (1985) Stress, social support, and the buffering hypothesis. *Psychological Bulletin, 98,* 310–57.

Duck, S. (ed.) (1988) *Handbook of Personal Relationships.* Chichester: Wiley.

Elder, G.H. (1962) Structured variations in the child rearing relationship. *Sociometry, 25,* 241–62.

Firth, R., Hubert, J. and Forge, A. (1969) *Families and their Relatives.* London: Routledge & Kegan Paul.

Fischer, C.S. (1977) *Networks and Places.* New York: Free Press.

Fischer, C.S. (1982) *To Dwell among Friends.* Chicago: University of Chicago Press.

Gathorne-Hardy, J. (1985) *The Rise and Fall of the British Nanny.* London Weidenfeld & Nicolson.

Goldthorpe, J.H. (with the assistance of C. Llewellyn and C. Payne) (1987) *Social Mobility and Class Structure in Modern Britain.* 2nd edition. Oxford: Clarendon Press.

Humphries, J. (1977) Class struggle and the persistence of the working class family. *Cambridge Journal of Economics, 1,* 241–58.

Kohn, M.L. (1963) Social class and parent–child relationships: an interpretation. *American Journal of Sociology, 68,* 471–80.

Komarovsky, M. (1962) *Blue-Collar Marriage.* New Haven: Yale University Press.

Laumann, E.O. (1973) *The Bonds of Pluralism.* New York: Wiley.

Locksley, H. (1982) Social class and marital attitudes and behavior. *Journal of Marriage and the Family, 39,* 479–90.

MORI (1982) *Neighbours and Loneliness.* London: Market Opinion and Research International.

Newson, J. and Newson, E. (1968) *Four-years Old in an Urban Community.* London: Allen & Unwin.

Newson, J. and Newson, E. (1976) *Seven-years Old in an Urban Community.* London: Allen & Unwin.

Oakley, A. (1974) *The Sociology of Housework.* London: Routledge & Kegan Paul.

Oakley, A. and Rajan, L. (1991) Social class and social support: the same or different? *Sociology, 25,* 31–59.

O' Brien, J.E. (1971) Violence in divorce-prone families. *Journal of Marriage and the Family, 33,* 692–8.

Peplau, L.A. (1983) Roles and gender. In H.H. Kelley *et al., Close Relationships.* New York: W.H. Freeman.

Reid, I. (1989) *Social Class Differences in Britain.* 3rd edition. London: Fontana.

Rossi, A.S. (1965) Naming children in middle-class families. *American Sociological Review, 39,* 499–513.

Roth, J. and Peck, R.F. (1951) Social class mobility and factors related to marital adjustment. *American Sociological Review, 16,* 478–87.

Slater, E. and Woodside, M. (1951) *Patterns of Marriage: A Study of Marriage Relationships in the Urban Working Class.* London: Cassell.

Stacey, M. (1960) *Tradition and Change.* Oxford: Oxford University Press.

Stewart, R. (1967) *Managers and their Jobs.* London: Macmillan.

Turner, R.J. (1981) Social support as a contingency in psychological well-being. *Journal of Health and Social Behavior, 22,* 357–67.

Vanfossen, B.E. (1981) Sex differences in the mental health effects of spouse support and equity. *Journal of Health and Social Behavior, 22,* 130–43.

Veroff, J., Douvan, E. and Kulka, R.A. (1981) *The Inner American.* New York: Basic Books.

Warner, W.L. (1963) *Yankee City.* New Haven: Yale University Press.

Wild, R.A. (1974) *Bradstow: A Study of Status, Class and Power in a Small Australian Town*. Sydney: Angus & Robertson.

Willmott, P. (1987) *Friendship Networks and Social Support*. London: Policy Studies Institute.

Willmott, P. and Young, M. (1960) *Family and Class in a London Suburb*. London: Routledge & Kegan Paul.

Wright, E.O. and Cho, D. (1992) The relative permeability of class boundaries to cross-class friendships: a comparative study of the United States, Canada, Sweden, and Norway. *American Sociological Review*, 57, 85–102.

Young, M. and Willmott, P. (1957) *Family and Kinship in East London*. Revised edition. Harmondsworth: Penguin.

Young, M. and Willmott, P. (1973) *The Symmetrical Family*. London: Routledge & Kegan Paul.

# Chapter 5

# Work, leisure and lifestyle

## WORK

Members of different classes do different kinds of work – this is how class is usually defined. As we have seen, there are a number of different schemes for classifying occupations. The Registrar General's is widely used:

1 Professional (e.g. employers and managers of large establishments).
2 Intermediate (e.g. school teachers, nurses, employers and managers of small establishments).
3 (N) Skilled non-manual (e.g. clerical, sales, cashiers).
4 (M) Skilled manual (e.g. miners, police, cooks, supervisors, car workers).
5 Semi-skilled (e.g. agricultural, postmen, barmen).
6 Unskilled (e.g. labourers, office cleaners, dustmen).

The jobs higher up this scale differ from those lower down in a number of ways.

### Working conditions

These are very different at different levels: some are shown in Table 5.1. This adds up to a most undesirable situation for many manual jobs – standing or walking around, in poor conditions, in the open, etc. Refuse collectors, miners, steel workers, oil-rig workers, especially the divers, have work which is also dirty and dangerous, in some cases bad for health. At the top end of the scale things are far better. Managers and professional people have nice warm offices, to themselves if they are above a certain level of seniority. However, these jobs can be very demanding and stressful as well – for politicians, surgeons, TV producers and barristers, for example.

The more senior an individual is at work the more he or she is free to do it their own way, when they want, and the greater freedom they have to choose what they do (Cyert and MacCrimmon, 1968). We show later that this is an important source of job satisfaction. And the more senior a person is, the less they are under the direction of others.

*Table 5.1* Working conditions for British men (1979) (percentages)

| | Levels of skill | | | | | | | |
|---|---|---|---|---|---|---|---|---|
| | 1 | 2 | 3 | 4 | 5 | 6 | 7 | 8 |
| All working time spent standing or walking about | 2 | 16 | 27 | 28 | 32 | 69 | 79 | 89 |
| Working conditions poor or very poor | 2 | 12 | 6 | 10 | 11 | 29 | 27 | 40 |
| At work before 8 a.m. or at night | 15 | 19 | 15 | 20 | 19 | 46 | 50 | 55 |
| Work mainly outdoors | 6 | 8 | 16 | 12 | 20 | 37 | 30 | 63 |
| Subject to one week's notice | 5 | 2 | 12 | 23 | 33 | 52 | 56 | 77 |

*Source:* Reid, 1989

One of the greatest differences in the conditions of work is how much people are paid for it. As we showed earlier, those at the top are commonly paid about three to four times what those at the bottom are paid. Those at the very top, managing directors, are paid far more than this.

As Table 5.1 shows, as many as 77 per cent of those in the least skilled jobs can be sacked at a week's notice. So apparently can a few at the top end of the scale, but they would receive a generous handshake. The unemployed are drawn mainly, though not entirely, from the least skilled (p. 101). Unemployment is a familiar part of working-class experience.

Another important class difference in the nature of work is that those in class I and II jobs are more senior in organisations, that is have a lot of freedom and autonomy as to how they do their work. If they are professional people, like doctors or lawyers, they do not have many subordinates, but they enjoy a lot of influence and responsibility because of their expertise. By contrast, semi- and unskilled workers are under the direction of supervisors, who may or may not be skilled leaders, and who may be authoritarian and unrewarding. Less skilled workers have very little say in how the work is done.

This is one of the causes of class differences in job satisfaction. We shall see in Chapter 7 that position in working hierarchies has a profound effect on personality. Those at higher levels develop a high degree of self-direction, or internal control, and pass it on to their children by their style of child-rearing, copied from the style of supervision experienced at work (p. 167).

There are considerable differences between managers or administrators of different ranks. Spaeth (1989) carried out a 'snowball' network survey, in which a sample of the population of Chicago were interviewed, and named their immediate supervisor, who did the same, thus generating six levels of authority. Class, as measured by the US Census, did not increase beyond level 2, but number of subordinates did (up to 34,000) and monetary control did (up to $670,000). Earnings increased up to an average of $200,000 at the top level, but were not predictable from social class; they could be predicted however from number of subordinates and amount of monetary control.

## The effects of technology

The effects of work, and of work hierarchies, on the experience of work depend on the technology. It can make things much better or much worse for those actually doing the work, and it can give them less power or more power. A key idea here is that the class structure is rooted in the social organisation of work, including the division of labour, and the way that one group of people has authority over another. Goldthorpe and Lockwood (1963) argued that class divisions are greater in mass production industry, like assembly lines and textile factories, where there are remote and impersonal relations between workers and management, and more use of machine-pacing and wage-incentives. Woodward (1965) in England and Blauner (1960) in the USA found that relations were much better under other kinds of technology. In craft-work, printing (at that time) and small-batch production, employees worked in small groups, with little supervision, and working groups were small, though a lot of work was carried out independently. In continuous process technology, as in oil refineries, chemical works and power stations, there was a return to smaller working groups, less close supervision and better relations in the hierarchy.

Since the time of those studies, there have been extensive changes in work technology, notably the introduction of automation and computers. This has had a number of effects on the experience of work. (1) It can lead to loss of jobs; indeed, the long-term outlook is for many fewer industrial workers in the future. It is not only manual workers who have lost their jobs for this reason; banking, insurance and middle management have also shed jobs. (2) It can lead to more skilled and interesting work, for secretaries who use more complex equipment and for shop-floor workers who programme computer-controlled machine tools. It can also lead to 'deskilling' by creating a lot of low-level jobs, entering data into computers or just watching dials for example. (3) It can lead to more power and autonomy for workers, if they control and programme the machines, or less if someone else does; it can also result in closer surveillance by supervisors. Which of these things will happen depends on decisions about how systems are designed. (4) Automation can result in the loss of small working groups and the isolation of workers at isolated work stations. The availability of information technology can lead to more home working, which has many advantages but also results in isolation and less power, and loss of job satisfaction by missing out on the jokes, games and gossip at work.

## Job satisfaction

It is not surprising that job satisfaction is higher for those in the better jobs. Percentages of those who, when asked if they would choose the same work again, say they would are given in Table 5.2.

*Table 5.2* Percentage who would choose the same work again

| | |
|---|---|
| Mathematicians | 91 |
| Lawyers | 83 |
| Journalists | 82 |
| Skilled printers | 52 |
| Skilled car workers | 41 |
| Skilled steel workers | 41 |
| Textile workers | 31 |
| Unskilled car workers | 21 |
| Unskilled steel workers | 16 |

*Source:* Blauner, 1960

Putting the question in this way produces larger occupational differences than other job satisfaction measures. If workers are asked 'Taking into consideration all things about your job, how satisfied or dissatisfied are you with it?', the percentages saying 'very satisfied' in an American national sample were as shown in Table 5.3.

Both sets of findings show that job satisfaction is much less lower down the job hierarchy. Other studies have shown that job satisfaction is low when there is little autonomy, the work is monotonous, with a small repeated cycle, and machine-paced, and there have been moves to improve this kind of work by various kinds of job enlargement and enrichment, such as increasing the number of tasks done and including repairs and inspection (Argyle, 1989). Clerical workers come lower than expected – this is a kind of work which has low satisfaction probably because of the low autonomy.

Job satisfaction has several components; one of the most important is 'intrinsic' job satisfaction, that is enjoying the work itself. It is high when the work is interesting and challenging, uses skills and is believed to be worthwhile. Although managers and professional people may enjoy such interesting and challenging jobs, this is less true for manual workers, many of whom work just for the pay. Csikszentmihalyi (1975) studied several groups of people who were very involved in their work, such as surgeons, and others who had serious leisure activities, such as rock climbers. The basis of such absorption is not known, but one process is probably the undertaking of tasks which provide challenges that are commensurate with the skills possessed. Perhaps the reason that mathematicians, scientists and others have such a high level of job satisfaction is because they have a high degree both of absorption and use of their skills.

Affiliative satisfaction, with social contacts at work, is another source of job satisfaction. It is greater for women than men, and is high for those in small work teams. It is high for workers in sales and service occupations – jobs that are mainly with people, as an American national survey shows (Table 5.3). Satisfaction with achievement and recognition is also greater at higher levels of skill, as the same study showed. On the whole this is higher

Table 5.3 Occupational differences in job satisfaction (USA, 1976) (males/females)

| | Professional | Managers | Clerical | Sales | Skilled | Operators | Service | Laborers | Farmers |
|---|---|---|---|---|---|---|---|---|---|
| **Overall job satisfaction:** | | | | | | | | | |
| Very satisfied | 33/43 | 37/20 | 24/29 | 28/27 | 26/27 | 18/19 | 22/29 | 19/- | 32/9 |
| **Source of satisfaction:** | | | | | | | | | |
| Affiliative | 27/50 | 36/54 | 29/34 | 40/81 | 7/9 | 12/7 | 48/41 | 9/- | 6/9 |
| Economic | 3/3 | 12/7 | 10/13 | 16/12 | 18/46 | 22/23 | 9/10 | 31/- | 13/46 |
| Achievement | 52/38 | 38/30 | 26/22 | 23/12 | 33/27 | 10/16 | 11/16 | 12/- | 23/0 |

Source: Veroff et al., 1981

for men. The percentage who were satisfied mainly by the pay is greatest lower down the scale; this brings us to class differences in the motivation to work.

## Class differences in the motivation to work

Goldthorpe and colleagues (1968) surveyed 250 male industrial workers at three factories in Luton, making cars, ball bearings and chemicals. They found that these workers had a strongly instrumental attitude towards their work: it was a means to an end – making money. They were not interested in friendship at work and had little hope of promotion; they were interested mostly in earning for the home. These workers were seen as typical of an emerging 'new working class'. The main criticism that has been made of this study is about its representativeness. The men studied were all married, between 21 and 46, and most had children. They had recently moved to Luton from other parts of the country, many from areas of high unemployment. It has been argued that they were at a point in the life cycle when they needed money most, as well as having had experience of poverty.

However, later studies have found that an instrumental attitude to work is common among manual workers, especially young men with families (Blackburn and Mann, 1979). A recent survey found that 34 per cent of those in employment saw their present job as nothing more than a means of earning a living – but the other 66 per cent thought it was more than that, valuing especially sociability with colleagues and the use of skills. The instrumental attitude was more widespread for those in lower-status, less-skilled jobs (Table 5.4).

In other words, many manual workers have an instrumental attitude to work because they can't find a more interesting job or lack the skills to do one. In this study people were asked to nominate three activities which they enjoyed when they were not at work; 73 per cent thought that work was at least as important as these other activities, or more so – and there was no variation with class.

*Table 5.4* Instrumental orientation to work (percentages)

|  |  | 1 | 2 | 3N | 3M | 4 | 5 | 6 |
|---|---|---|---|---|---|---|---|---|
| Just a means of earning a living | M | 9 | 15 | 30 | 50 | 57 | 50 | – |
|  | F | 10 | 13 | 29 | 39 | 39 | 61 | – |

Those who gave an instrumental response were asked the reason; the replies are given below.

|  | 1 | 2 | 3N | 3M | 4 | 5 | 6 |
|---|---|---|---|---|---|---|---|
| No interesting jobs locally | 25 | 22 | 18 | 32 | 38 | 46 | 50 |
| Respondent lacks skills for interesting work | 0 | 22 | 28 | 35 | 40 | 31 | 0 |

*Source:* Marshall *et al.*, 1988

If 66 per cent of workers, and more than this at higher levels, work for more than economic reasons, what are these? It may be that middle-class people have a stronger Protestant Work Ethic, that is an internalised motivation to work for its own sake. It may be that middle-class people have a stronger achievement motivation, the motivation to attain standards of excellence and accomplish things. We shall see later that there is evidence for such class differences (p. 164). Another explanation is that most middle-class people think in terms of 'careers', which are of great importance to them, define their life's work and give them their identity. Professionals and managers have careers, manual workers on the whole have jobs. There are class differences here: middle-class adolescents think in terms of careers, working-class adolescents are more likely to think of jobs – perhaps offering good pay and job satisfaction, but not promotion. Middle-class youth have higher job aspirations – derived from the norms of school and home (p. 189), and say that these jobs seem 'more interesting'. Working-class youth recognise that the jobs to which they aspire are less well paid than middle-class jobs, but they overestimate the pay of skilled manual workers (Dickinson and Emler, 1992). Careers can be thought of more generally as a sequence of jobs, or as 'stages or steps in a progression toward culturally defined higher rewards' (Schein, 1978). They can be seen as upward mobility through a number of ranks, as in the army. However, during the course of a lifetime there are extensive historical changes which affect the rise and fall of organisations and types of work. Furthermore, to some extent the individual contributes to the changes in the organisations in which he or she works – both are developing together.

As they get older some people become more committed to their work, which becomes more central to their personality, while others become less committed, and spend more time with family and on leisure interests. In mid-career, around the age of 40, managers have been found to be preoccupied with promotion prospects (Sofer, 1970), or to be in a period of crisis, in which they have to come to terms with their limited prospects (Argyle, 1989).

Middle-class people at work are trying to achieve something, and are very concerned with their promotion prospects. For most manual workers the chances of promotion are small. Goldthorpe et al. (1968) found that none of their affluent manual workers thought that their chance of promotion was 'very good', but 13 per cent of the white-collar workers thought so.

Senior members of working organisations become highly committed to their organisation, and the pursuit of success for them. Those in the lowest ranks couldn't care less what happens to the organisation, as long as they are all right – they are often alienated from it, not committed to it. Commitment is greatest for those who have taken part in decisions, have been a long time with the organisation, probably those who have been most rewarded by it. Japanese workers are highly committed to their firms; this may be because they have been guaranteed a job for life or because they have been well looked after by the firm.

## Conflict between ranks at work

There is often conflict between employers or managers and lower ranks of employees, represented by trade unions. This is the main domain of class conflict in society and the main basis of class conflict in general. This conflict is most visible in the form of strikes; there are also go-slows, working to rule and overtime bans, while absenteeism, lateness and labour turnover can be seen as further manifestations of conflict. Over a recent two-year period about one-third of British firms had a strike, and 46 per cent had strikes or other industrial action (Hartley, 1984).

There are common interests between the two 'sides', since all want their firm or organisation to stay in business and hence want it to compete successfully with other firms. On the other hand, there is also a conflict of interests – it is the employees who are laid off when business is slack. And, as we have just seen, the conditions of work are less favourable in a number of ways for the lower ranks, in addition to the considerable pay differentials.

The system of trade union representation and bargaining itself perpetuates the idea that there are 'two sides' in industry, despite the fact that managers are usually salaried employees themselves and the fact that a large proportion of employees occupy intermediate positions.

The amount of conflict, for example the number of strikes, varies a lot between different places of work. When is it greatest? Strikes are mainly about pay, though low pay does not predict them well; strikes occur when pay is felt to be low in comparison with that of some other comparable group of workers. Comparisons are rarely made with the pay of managers.

There is a lot of conflict over lay-offs, workers losing their jobs, and concern with safety and other aspects of working conditions. Trade union leaders are often militant and can initiate strikes or stoppages, but they are unlikely to be successful unless there are widespread grievances. Managers can be more or less skilled in communicating, informing, consulting and persuading and meeting the needs of employees. A strike may fail to develop if minor stoppages are handled tactfully and if managers avoid breaking agreements and other sources of friction. Conflict can be contained by effective channels of consultation and negotiation, and by various forms of industrial democracy (Argyle, 1989).

## Unemployment

Work may be bad (for some), but unemployment is much worse. And it is mainly (though not entirely) a working-class phenomenon. Table 5.5 shows the percentage who were seeking work in Britain in 1981.

*Table 5.5* Percentages seeking work (Great Britain, 1981)

|         | 1 | 2 | 3n | 3m | 4 | 5 |
|---------|---|---|----|----|----|----|
| Males   | 2 | 3 | 5  | 9  | 11 | 21 |
| Females | 3 | 2 | 4  | 5  | 6  | 3  |

The lower rates for women may be because many women do not regard themselves as seeking work if there is little chance of getting it (Reid, 1989). Unskilled males were ten times as likely to be out of work as middle-class males. Many other studies have obtained similar results. Unemployment is much higher for people without qualifications, and lowest for those with degrees or similar credentials. Members of all ethnic minority groups have higher rates of unemployment, two to three times the average for whites.

Unemployment is in some ways worse for middle-class people, especially middle-aged men, because they are more committed to work (Warr, 1987). We have seen that working-class people are lower in such commitment and motivation. Spanish workers are apparently not upset at all by it, probably because the Protestant Work Ethic is very low in Spain. On the other hand, middle-class people are probably able to use their time better, and find other things to do, because of their greater education and development of leisure interests.

## LEISURE ACTIVITIES

Manual workers spend longer hours at work, and are more physically tired when they get home, than non-manual workers. According to some theories, working-class people should seek compensation in leisure for boring or frustrating work. Do they enjoy their leisure more? And if, as we shall shortly see is the case, different classes pursue different leisure activities, why do they? To start with we would expect lower-class people to engage in kinds of leisure which are cheap, and not physically demanding. Is this what happens?

*TV watching* is cheap, and makes minimal demands for physical exertion. Class differences are in the direction expected, and are quite large:

|                  | AB   | C1   | C2   | DE   |        |
|------------------|------|------|------|------|--------|
| *Hours TV per day* | 2.82 | 3.57 | 3.91 | 4.87 | (1988) |

In the case of many leisure activities we can assume that frequency reflects enjoyment. In the case of TV it may be because people have nothing better to do. Heavy TV watchers are less happy than those who watch less (Argyle and Lu, 1992).

People watch TV partly to relax; 60 per cent said it was for 'entertainment or relaxation' (Comstock *et al.*, 1978), while 27 per cent said 'because there's nothing else to do at the time'. Class differences for 1988 were found for watching all four channels, but particularly for ITV – classes D and E watch two-and-a-half times as much as classes A and B (Reid, 1989). In the USA educated people often think that watching TV is a waste of time, and wish that they were doing something else while they are watching it (Kubey and Csikszentmihalyi, 1990).

Audience research in Britain finds that classes D and E spend more time watching soap opera and comedy, while classes A and B prefer the news and other information and general interest programmes. The greatest difference is in the popularity of soap operas: 24 per cent of working-class and 15 per cent of middle-class people are regular watchers (Wober, 1992). Our own research shows that heavy soap opera watching makes people happy. The probable reason is that people become involved with the characters and their lives, and feel that they almost belong to the group, thus gaining secondhand friendship and social support (Argyle, 1992).

American studies have found class differences in the programmes watched. Lower-class and black people like aggressive and action/adventure programmes more than sit coms and family series. However, teenagers from lower-class and black families do like programmes about families, partly to make up for their own lack of families, partly to learn how to cope with common social situations (Comstock *et al.*, 1978).

Press (1991) carried out depth interviews with small samples of American working-class and middle-class women. The working-class women thought that the representation of working-class life in sit coms and soap operas was unrealistic, but accepted portrayals of middle- and upper-class families like *Dallas*, and enjoyed these as a form of escapism. They did not like comedies set in working-class families, since these often showed disruption of the domestic order. Middle-class women on the other hand did not mind the lack of realism and enjoyed comedies such as *I Love Lucy*, since they showed liberated and rebellious women.

*Radio* is another cheap and undemanding activity. However, the findings are quite different from those for TV – people listen to the radio most in AB and DE rather than C, though the differences are very small. But there are very large class differences in the programmes which are switched on. Radio 1 is listened to more by classes D and E and Radio 3 and 4 much more by classes A and B; the latter listen six times as long to both these channels. This reflects the different contents and appeal of the different channels: Radio 4 is serious talks and news, Radio 3 is serious music, while Radio 1 is light entertainment and pop music. Radio 2 appeals to all classes equally.

*Reading.* National daily newspapers are read by 74 per cent of class A, and by slightly fewer of B–D, but only by 52 per cent of E. Sunday papers are

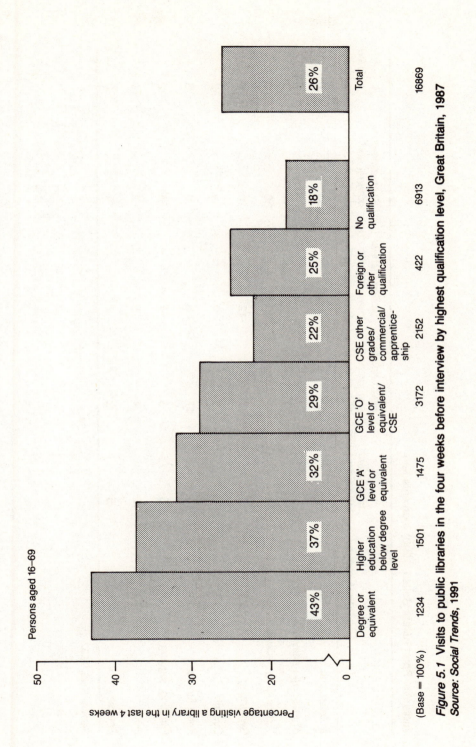

Persons aged 16–69

Percentage visiting a library in the last 4 weeks

| | Degree or equivalent | Higher education below degree level | GCE 'A' level or equivalent | GCE 'O' level or equivalent/ CSE | CSE other grades/ commercial/ apprentice-ship | Foreign or other qualification | No qualification | Total |
|---|---|---|---|---|---|---|---|---|
| | 43% | 37% | 32% | 29% | 22% | 25% | 18% | 26% |
| (Base = 100%) | 1234 | 1501 | 1475 | 3172 | 2152 | 422 | 6913 | 16869 |

*Figure 5.1* **Visits to public libraries in the four weeks before interview by highest qualification level, Great Britain, 1987**
*Source: Social Trends,* 1991

Table 5.6 Sport (Great Britain, 1990) (percentages)

| | Professional | Employers and managers | Intermediate and junior non-manual | Skilled manual, own-account, non-professional | Semi-skilled manual and personal service | Unskilled manual |
|---|---|---|---|---|---|---|
| At least one activity | 79 | 71 | 67 | 66 | 55 | 46 |
| At least one activity excluding walking | 65 | 53 | 49 | 49 | 38 | 28 |
| Swimming | 24 | 17 | 17 | 12 | 10 | 6 |
| Cycling | 13 | 8 | 9 | 9 | 9 | 8 |
| Keep fit/yoga | 11 | 10 | 17 | 6 | 9 | 6 |
| Running, jogging | 11 | 6 | 5 | 4 | 3 | 2 |
| Golf | 13 | 10 | 4 | 5 | 2 | 1 |
| Squash | 9 | 5 | 2 | 2 | 1 | 0 |

Source: GHS, 1992

read a little more. The serious 'good' papers are read only by classes A and B, and *The Times* and *Telegraph* mainly by A. The *Daily Mirror*, the *Sun* and the *News of the World* are increasingly popular lower down the social scale, especially in class D; 37 per cent read the *Sun*, 40 per cent the *News of the World*. Magazines all have their social niche: *True Romances* for example is read by 22 per cent of C1 women, *Practical Motorist* by 22 per cent of C1 men. There are class differences in interest in the news. Middle-class people are more interested in what the government is doing and in political parties (Reid, 1989). The serious papers, like Radio 4, have much more serious discussion of the news, compared with material about scandals, pop stars, crime, etc., in the popular papers.

Middle-class people buy more books, of all kinds. In A and B 40 per cent buy non-fiction hardbacks (E 13 per cent), 52 per cent of A and B buy fiction paperbacks (E 20 per cent). The majority of C–E buy no books at all.

Middle-class people also borrow more books from public libraries (see Figure 5.1).

The percentage of people reporting regular reading fell from 67 per cent and 63 per cent for the top two classes to 33 per cent for skilled and 28 per cent for unskilled men (Young and Willmott, 1973).

*Sport and exercise.* If manual workers are physically more tired after work, we would expect them to engage in less sport. On the other hand, if leisure is a compensation for work (as Marx and others believed), they might be expected to engage in violent sport to release their frustrations at work.

The total amount of sport and exercise is greater for the middle classes, as is their participation in most kinds of sports. Table 5.6 shows the percentages who reported each activity during the four weeks before the interview.

Some of these differences need no explanation – some sports are rather expensive, like golf. Others are simply part of middle-class culture and social life like squash. But there are still large class differences where there is little or no cost, and little dependence on social arrangements, like running, swimming and cycling.

However, there are other sports which show no class differences, or a reversal of the order above.

|  | AB % | DE % |
|---|---|---|
| Dancing | 12.5 | 16 |
| Darts (males) | 11 | 18 |
| Fishing (males) | 5 | 8 |

*Source:* Reid, 1989

The favoured lower-class sporting activities are less violent than most of the middle-class ones. If there is any compensation for work stress, it is for middle-class work.

However, there are some spectator activities which might fit this theory better.

|  | AB % | DE % |
| --- | --- | --- |
| Football pools | 19.5 | 30 |
| Betting (horses) | 5 | 12 |
| Bingo | 1 | 11 |

As we report elsewhere (p. 253), football hooligans are almost entirely male, young and working class, some of them unemployed.

*Social activities*. As we saw in Chapter 4, middle-class people belong to more clubs (3.6 for class I, 1.6 for the other four classes), more of the people whom they know best are from clubs, as are more of the people whom they speak to weekly or more often (p. 74).

In addition, the clubs are different in character: middle-class clubs are for hobby or interest activities, sport, religion, politics or voluntary work, while working-class clubs are more often social clubs where the main activities are talking and drinking. This kind of club is important in traditional occupational communities, where a close-knit social life is centred on clubs, churches and football teams (Abercrombie and Warde, 1988).

Two characteristic forms of working-class leisure are going to pubs and bingo. Public houses spread rapidly in Britain during the nineteenth century, and catered mainly to the new urban, industrialised proletariat. Pubs were, and to a large extent still are, havens of masculine working-class culture, reflecting masculine values of toughness and sensuality, and freedom from the constraints of factory life. Often there was entertainment and games, together with the possibility of sexual adventures, sometimes a setting for the criminal subculture. Pubs were said to have created a 'beer sodden working class', but they also created 'fuddled joy' (Smith, 1983).

Most women feel that they can't go to pubs or clubs alone; many working-class women have found a club for women in the local bingo hall; it is the only place they can go for female sociability, companionship and social support. It is not the winning and losing that counts – the amounts are small and the winnings are often shared, sustaining the network further. Bingo provides a routine where they feel safe, and which is less demanding than more cultural pursuits (Dixey, 1987).

Middle-class people are more active in every kind of club or leisure group which pursues a particular interest. *Voluntary work* is done by 13 per cent of class I, 4 per cent of class VI; indeed, working-class individuals are more often the recipients of it. Many leisure groups also donate money to charities. The kinds of voluntary work which are done vary with class in an interesting way. Professional people do more committee work (52 per cent in the last year v. 22 per cent of unskilled), more advice-giving (16 per cent v. 5 per cent) and more talks, teaching and coaching (Matheson, 1987). This is a good example of the 'spillover' theory of leisure – that people do the same things, use the same skills, as at work. *Amateur music and drama* is done by 6 per cent of class I, 1 per cent of class VI, evening classes by 3 per cent of class I and 1 per cent of class VI. There are similar differences for *church attendance* though not for private religious observance (see p. 255).

Working-class people belong more to *licensed clubs*, but they go to pubs less than the middle class.

| | AB % | C1 % | C2 % | D % | E % |
|---|---|---|---|---|---|
| Belong to licensed clubs | 32 | 36 | 43 | 45 | 29 |
| Go to pub, 2–3 times a week | 14 | 16 | 18 | 16 | 10 |

The government Social Survey defines 'heavy drinkers' as those who consume fifty-one or more half-pint or equivalent units per week. 'Fairly high' drinking is defined as twenty-two to thirty-five units a week. If class is measured by occupation, professionals drink 10.2 units per week, managers 15.0, and semi-skilled manual workers 16.3 (*Social Trends*, 1993). But if class is measured by income, the higher the income the more drinking. In Britain in 1990 35 per cent of men with family incomes over £500 per week were 'fairly high' drinkers, compared with 19 per cent where the family income was under £100 per week (*GHS*, 1992). In the *Health and Lifestyle* survey (see p. 262), it was found that health was poor for the richest group because of their heavy drinking. There are also more lower-class abstainers and 'occasional' drinkers (defined as having one or more drinks between once a year and twice in six months).

The main difference in what is drunk is that the middle classes drink more wine and the working classes draught beer.

*Home-based leisure.* A number of sociologists have argued that working-class life in Britain has become 'privatised', that is leisure is increasingly spent in the home and with the family. This was first noticed by Goldthorpe *et al.* (1968): 62 per cent of the recent leisure activities of these affluent workers and their wives had been in the home. It might be expected that working-class people would spend more leisure at home, because it is not only inexpensive, but may be profitable (e.g. gardening). On the other hand middle-class homes have more gardens and other space and there is more money to pay for expensive hobbies.

We will take the money-saving ones first. Middle-class people do more gardening and DIY, but less dressmaking, needlework or knitting:

|                   | 1 & 2 % | 5 & 6 % |
|-------------------|---------|---------|
| Gardening         | 59.5    | 38.5    |
| DIY               | 59      | 25.5    |
| Dressmaking, etc. | 12.5    | 29      |

Hobbies, and arts and crafts, are mainly class 1 leisure activities:

| 1    | 2–4  | 5 & 6 |
|------|------|-------|
| 21%  | 8%   | 4%    |

Young and Willmott (1973) found that largest class differences were for playing an instrument, collecting stamps or other objects, keeping dogs. Clerical workers had the highest rates of playing cards or chess. There were few class differences for model building, handicrafts or technical hobbies.

We saw earlier that working-class people watch a lot more TV at home, though middle-class individuals read more and listen to radio programmes that require attention.

Entertaining friends or relations is another important home-based activity, and this is something which husbands and wives do together, in all classes. When working-class men go to the pub they usually go alone, as do their wives to bingo (Hill, 1976).

*Holidays and outings.* Middle-class people have a lot more holidays, often two or three per year, while 60 per cent of classes D and E had none at all in 1989 (Figure 5.2). And middle-class holidays are more often abroad.

Middle-class people take a lot of trips into the countryside, for a drive or picnic (Figure 5.3). Middle-class people also make more outings to stately homes, beauty spots, etc. (Table 5.7). This can partly be explained by the greater availability of cars for middle-class families, but perhaps even more because such 'cultural' visits are more part of middle-class culture. In the top two classes 95 per cent of families have one or more cars, compared with 43 per cent for unskilled families. A and B drive 180 miles per week or more (22 per cent), compared with 4 per cent for E (Reid, 1989).

*The unemployed* are mainly, but not entirely, working-class, and are of special interest here. How do they spend their 'leisure'? Like the retired, they appear to have a great deal of it, except that it doesn't seem like leisure

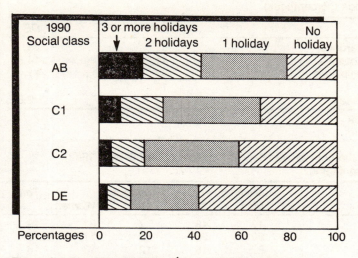

*Figure 5.2* Number of holidays[1] per year by social class
*Source: Social Trends*, 1992
*Note:* 1. Holidays of four nights or more taken by adult residents of Great Britain in Great Britain and abroad.

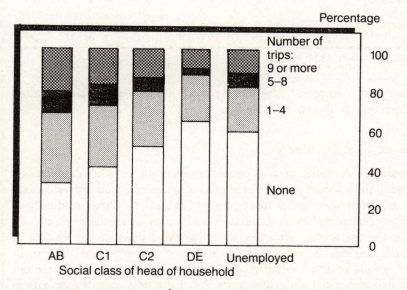

*Figure 5.3* Recreational trips[1] to the countryside by social class of head of household, 1986
*Source:* National Countryside Recreation Survey, Countryside Commission
*Note:* 1. The average number of trips made by respondents during a four-week period.

*Table 5.7* Outings (percentages)

|  | AB | DE |
|---|---|---|
| Beauty spots, gardens | 51 | 23 |
| Stately homes, castles | 41 | 14.5 |
| Art galleries, exhibitions | 41 | 11 |
| Zoos | 16 | 13 |
| Archaeological sites | 15 | 2.5 |

*Source:* Reid, 1989

*Table 5.8* How the unemployed spend their time (Great Britain, 1982)
(percentages)

|  | Morning Men | Women | Afternoon Men | Women | Total |
|---|---|---|---|---|---|
| Housework | 19 | 49 | 7 | 21 | 19 |
| Shopping | 20 | 26 | 9 | 17 | 16 |
| Job hunting | 22 | 16 | 12 | 13 | 16 |
| Visiting friends or relatives | 6 | 10 | 12 | 17 | 10 |
| Gardening | 14 | 2 | 13 | 3 | 11 |
| TV | 4 | 2 | 14 | 12 | 8.5 |
| Reading | 9 | 5 | 8 | 10 | 8 |
| Decorating | 7 | 3 | 7 | 2 | 5.5 |
| Walking | 5 | 3 | 8 | 2 | 5.5 |
| Nothing/sitting around | 3 | 3 | 9 | 6 | 5.5 |
| Staying in bed | 8 | 8 | 1 | 0 | 4.5 |
| Visiting town | 5 | 7 | 3 | 4 | 4.5 |
| Playing sport | 4 | 1 | 4 | 0 | 3 |
| Drinking | 2 | 1 | 3 | 1 | 2 |

*Source: Social Trends,* 1984

to them. How a sample of 1,043 unemployed British people said that they spent their time is shown in Table 5.8.

## Theories of class and leisure

*Compensation.* Do working-class people compensate for other deprivations by enjoying their leisure more? On average the less educated individuals do not, as an American national survey found (Table 5.9). Other studies have found the same, fairly small, differences with other measures of class.

Which are the leisure activities which working-class people engage in more, and can they be interpreted in terms of compensation? The main ones are watching TV, football pools, betting and bingo; there are more visits to licensed social clubs and more darts; the only sporting activity is dancing. TV may operate in this way, to relax, presumably from the strains of work, though it may be just a means of filling time. Gambling is more interesting, it is perhaps an optimistic dream of a solution to life's problems.

*Table 5.9* Leisure satisfaction (USA, 1976) (percentages)

|  | Grade school | Some high school | High school graduate | Some college | College graduate |
|---|---|---|---|---|---|
| Challenging use of leisure | 58 | 62 | 75 | 76 | 76 |
| Value satisfaction through leisure | 47 | 50 | 53 | 61 | 62 |

*Source:* Veroff *et al.*, 1981

*Spillover from work.* Parker also suggested that leisure can be an extension or 'spillover' from work. Young and Willmott (1973) found evidence for this process in 39 per cent of their professional and managerial respondents, either through using similar technical skills (e.g. a brewer making wine at home), a similar interest, mixing business with social life, or using administrative experience (e.g. in running a club). Some of this activity may be preparation for work, or increasing work skills, for example middle-class attendance at evening classes, keeping fit and devotion to reading and serious TV programmes. We saw earlier that much middle-class voluntary work is an example of this process. The most common kind of working-class spillover was of technical skills. However, for the majority of people, in all classes, leisure seems to be independent of work (Argyle and Lu, 1992).

*The origins of serious leisure.* Middle-class people have work which gives great satisfaction from the use of skills, cooperation to attain goals and the pursuit of excellence. They naturally assume that any worthwhile leisure will have similar characteristics.

There is a long-term trend towards shorter hours of work, and fewer years at work, so that leisure is likely to become more important. Many have discussed whether leisure can ever become as satisfying as work often is; the answer appears to be that it can, but only when it has some of the characteristics of work. Some leisure is like this, especially serious leisure done in groups, including voluntary work, fairly serious amateur sport, music, dance and hobbies – the very things that middle-class people do in their leisure (Argyle, 1989).

People acquire many of their leisure interests during childhood and at school or college. Almost any activity can become intrinsically rewarding and hence an enjoyable leisure pursuit, including digging, driving and other activities which are paid work for others. Middle-class people are more likely to have such interests aroused during the course of education; universities and polytechnics provide an amazing range of leisure activities. In later life former students will want to continue these.

Most people have needs and interests which cannot all be satisfied at work. Often young people have difficulty in deciding between two or more careers; they have to choose one, but the others may become leisure interests. They may realise that they can earn their living from banking but not from music, archaeology or tennis, so the last three become hobbies.

*The effects of wealth.* Middle-class people can afford to spend more on leisure. Families earning over £300 per week in 1989 spent £55.46 (18.3 per cent of income) on leisure; those earning under £100 spent £8.18 per week (11.3 per cent). The largest items for the high spenders were holidays, alcohol and meals out.

Young and Willmott (1973) disentangled the effects of wealth and other variables on leisure activities. Using multiple regression they found that married employed men engaged in more leisure activities (1) if they had a car, (2) if they were in professional or managerial jobs, (3) if they had a large income and (4) if they were educated to age 17 or more.

*Conspicuous consumption.* Veblen (1899) in his famous *Theory of the Leisure Class* argued that rich people engaged in conspicuous consumption, and wore clothes quite unsuitable for work, to show that they had no need to work, and had plenty of money and time to burn. It is true that some forms of leisure are exclusive simply because they are very expensive – polo, hunting, grouse-shooting and sailing, as well as golf and skiing, are examples. This has the advantage for those involved that they will meet only the right people in the course of their leisure. In addition most forms of leisure have a well-known social class niche, so that engaging in the activity, even wearing the clothes, could be regarded as a form of self-presentation, as Veblen saw it. An alternative interpretation is that it is not self-presentation at all, but simply conformity to the norms of a social group. A working-class individual who went or tried to go grouse-shooting would be disapproved of by his working-class friends, as would an upper-class person who betted on the dogs, or went to Blackpool, by *his* friends.

*Cultural differences.* There are a number of class-linked leisure pursuits which cannot be explained in terms of the theories discussed so far. Some of the forms of sport favoured by upper income groups are very cheap – jogging and hiking, for example. Some of those favoured by lower income groups are quite expensive – fishing, keeping pigeons and watching football (supporting away matches abroad for example). The explanation must be that there are simply cultural differences, and that particular forms of leisure have become accepted in different strata. If you do the right thing, you meet people like yourself. Taking part in leisure is to identify yourself as a member of a class. We saw earlier how upper-class Americans spent their money quite differently from middle-class ones with similar incomes. The upper-class people spent it on high culture items and events, the middle-class people on swimming pools, boats and big cars (p. 12).

## THE HOME

*Location.* Most people in modern countries live in cities, and these have grown rapidly during this century. To avoid isolation and anonymity people like to live near other people who are similar to themselves, and they form homogeneous neighbourhoods, with their own subcultures. Tryon (1955) studied the 243 census areas of the San Francisco Bay Area; thirty-three demographic measures were available for each, e.g. home ownership, occupation, education. Cluster analysis generated eight types of area, with very similar social class characteristics within each. These areas also had distinctive political, racial and other attitudes – they were occupied by social groups with different cultures. At a later date, the same areas were much the same as before – though different people were now living there. Patterns of housing develop to match or create these subcultures, especially privately owned versus council-rented houses, and houses of different size and cost. The residents find people like themselves and appropriate facilities, such as schools, shops and other institutions, in the location.

Neighbourhoods are usually separated by main roads, railways ('the other side of the tracks') or occasionally walls, as in the notorious 'Cutteslowe wall' in Oxford, built to separate local authority from private housing. Cities often consist of concentric rings, with the decayed inner city and slums in the middle, as in Liverpool, and progressively more prosperous families in the outer suburbs. Some of the inner-city areas are having a second lease of life, through 'gentrification' or rebuilding in London and elsewhere. The Docklands development is a striking example.

Working-class residences are closer together, as in traditional terraced housing, modern apartment blocks or small houses on estates. The richer people are, the larger their houses, the further apart and the higher the walls between them. Working-class people have less choice of neighbours; friends and kin also live nearer.

*Space and crowding.* Middle-class houses have more and larger rooms. Overcrowding has been defined as not having enough bedrooms, i.e. one for a married couple, and other individuals of 21 or more, no more than two children to a room and sexes separated after the age of 10 (Gray and Russell, 1962). In class I 83 per cent of homes are above this standard, in class VI 66 per cent are. Only 6 per cent of white families are below it, but 25 per cent of Asians and 14 per cent of West Indian families are. Only 1 per cent of white families have more than one person per room, but 9 per cent of ethnic families and 32 per cent of Pakistani/Bangladeshi families are like this (*Social Trends*, 1991). Houses which are seriously overcrowded, or which are damp, or lack basic amenities, are found only among the poorest families (Blaxter, 1990). There is central heating in 94 per cent of class I homes, 64 per cent of class VI. Most families have sole use of bath and WC. Most have access to a garden.

Middle-class families are much more likely to occupy a detached house (52 per cent of those earning over £400 per week, 8 per cent for those under £50). Working-class people are more likely to live in a terraced house (30 per cent v. 16 per cent), or a flat (37 per cent v. 7 per cent), but equally likely to be semi-detached.

*Members of the household*. The composition of the household is different, on average, in different classes. As we showed in Chapter 4, working-class couples have more children, and are more likely to split up, so that there are more single-parent families. There are also more kin living in the house – 24 per cent compared with 10 per cent of middle-class families, typically a widowed parent. Working-class wives more often have jobs, and the husbands have longer hours and are more often on night work, so that for several reasons the parents are absent more; they also pursue their leisure activities separately. However, kin are more likely to live within 5 minutes' travel, for 23 per cent v. 6 per cent for middle-class households, in addition to those in the house (Young and Willmott, 1973). Working-class people live so close to their neighbours that they are almost part of the family – 21 per cent have neighbours who call round for a chat every day, and they are a major source of help.

In earlier times, and in other countries today, middle-class people employed servants some of whom lived in, and became part of the family, though sometimes 'below stairs'. In 1895, there were about 2 million domestic servants in Britain, a tenth of these nannies. Middle-class families commonly had three or more such servants living in. By 1939 there were still about 140,000 nannies; there are fewer today, though au pair girls have partly taken their place (see Gathorne-Hardy, 1985, and p. 85).

*The meaning of home* is similar in all classes. The most common meaning is 'centre of family life' (I 52 per cent, VII 48 per cent). However, more of class I see the home as 'a retreat' (55 per cent v. 37 per cent for VI and VII) or as 'a financial asset' (19 per cent v. 11 per cent) or 'self-expression' (16 per cent v. 12 per cent); lower-class people see the home more often as 'simply a roof' (19 per cent in VI, 7 per cent in I) or as 'freedom, independence' (27 per cent of VII, 16 per cent of I), while class IV see the home as the 'centre of my life' more than other classes (13 per cent v. 6 per cent for I, 8 per cent for VII) (Marshall *et al.*, 1988).

Working-class people pursue their social life in the home more than higher classes, especially the women. However, it is kin rather than friends whom working-class people entertain there. Middle-class homes are designed more for entertainment, and for self-expression. Some middle-class homes are minor museums, art galleries or libraries. Two contrasting types have been observed in Boar's Hill, a wealthy suburb of Oxford. In houses belonging to younger, prosperous business people, everything is new and

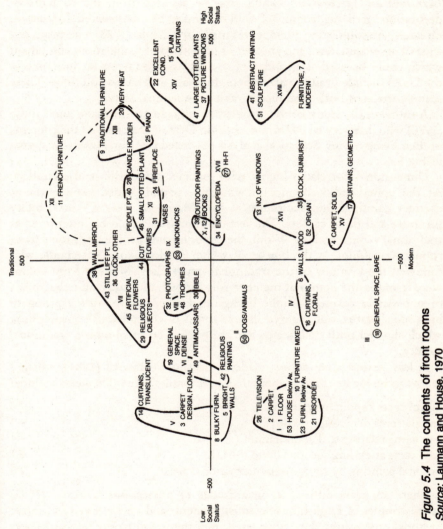

*Figure 5.4* The contents of front rooms
*Source*: Laumann and House, 1970

expensive, 'as if some high pressure jet of money had turned its nozzle on everything in sight'. In the houses of older, academic families there are 'some decent paintings, velvet curtains and Persian rugs' and 'on the shelves you glimpse a lifetime of memorabilia' (Snow, 1991).

*Furniture and decoration.* Could class be assessed from the contents or decoration of living rooms? Could an index be constructed for use in research? An interesting attempt was made by Chapin (1928) who produced a list of seventeen items and another of fifty items of living-room equipment which could be used as an index of social class. The items (at that time in the USA) included radio, newspapers, fireplace and hardwood floor. These scales correlated both with income and occupational status.

A more recent study of this problem was made by Laumann and House (1970) who interviewed 897 white adults in Detroit and checked the contents of their living rooms. Statistical analysis produced two dimensions, as shown in Fig 5.4.

Dimension I correlated highly with income, occupation and education. At the upper end were picture windows, potted plants, plain curtains, abstract paintings and sculpture; at the lower end were TV sets, bulky furniture and floral carpets. The second dimension could be interpreted as traditional versus modern. Within the upper income group, traditional front rooms were found in the houses of white, Anglo-Saxon Protestants, who followed the fashions of the traditional upper class. Modern front rooms were found in the homes of the upwardly mobile, the 'nouveau riche', often of non-Anglo-Saxon, Catholic background. This group were aspiring to high social status, but engaged in new forms of conspicuous consumption, which showed both their status and their rejection of snobbish, traditional society.

A less serious attempt was made to do this by Fussell (1984), which I report more for its entertainment than its scientific value. The items include:

| | |
|---|---:|
| motorcycle kept in living room | −10 |
| any pictures depicting cowboys | −3 |
| any items relating to Tutankhamun | −4 |
| any items attending specifically to the UK | +1 |
| original painting by recognised international artist | +6 |

There are class differences in attitudes to possessions. Dittmar (1992) asked samples of English businessmen, students and unemployed to list five personal possessions they considered important, and to say why each was important to them. The businessmen more often chose photos and other mementoes of sentimental interest, linked to their personal history and relationships with others, or which had intrinsic value, e.g. antiques and works of art. The unemployed more often chose things of basic utility, such as clothes or furniture, because of their financial value, their immediate utility or emotional use, such as for escapist leisure. The students chose more diaries, musical instruments, records and tapes. Where the businessmen emphasised the symbolic value of material possessions, the unemployed focused on their utilitarian properties.

*Meals.* In higher social classes the meals are more formal and elaborate. They take place in a separate dining room, with a large table, not in the kitchen or living room. There may be ceremonies, like saying grace, or moving to other rooms for part of the meal, as in Oxford colleges. Middle- and upper-class meals are more complex, especially when there are guests. There are more elaborate rules, about where people should sit, who is served first, how the drink is passed, even who should be talked to. There are more courses, made of more expensive ingredients and cooked in more elaborate ways. Drinks too are more refined and expensive. Peasant food has always been simple and nourishing, by contrast. 'The rich live to eat, the poor eat to live' (Goody, 1982). We saw earlier that middle-class individuals drink a lot of red wine, while working-class people consume a lot of brown sauce (p. 13).

## CLOTHES

Clothes are one of the most obvious signs of social class, one of the main ways (together with accent) in which class is recognised. The whole system would not work unless people could tell easily where others belong.

Perhaps it was for this reason that for long periods of history in England and elsewhere there were 'sumptuary laws' which prevented the lower orders from wearing extravagant clothes, made of silk or fine linen, or decorated with gold or silver ornaments. There are no such laws today, but there are very strong informal pressures to much the same effect.

Class differences in expenditure on clothing are not very great; class I households spent £21.92 a week on clothes and shoes in 1986, compared with £15.50 in class III and £13.35 in class V (Table 1.7). The difference is not so much in the cost, but in the style. What exactly are the class differences in clothes? At one time it was easy: the upper classes wore top hats, the workers wore cloth caps and clogs; now the differences are more subtle. There are a number of components: middle-class clothes are (1) more fashionable, usually newer, (2) of better material and workmanship, (3) clean and well cared-for, as opposed to dirty and untidy, (4) women add jewellery and other decorations. It is partly that middle-class clothes come from more expensive shops, which are part of the fashion chain, and sustain a class clothes hierarchy. While people are at work there are easily decodable differences, between those who wear 'working clothes' and work with their hands and those who work in offices; there are more subtle differences between the different ranks of white-collar workers.

Experiments in which subjects are asked to judge the class of target individuals find that clothes and accent are the strongest cues. Sissons (1971) carried out an experiment at Paddington station in which an actor dressed up as an obvious member of class I or class V, and was readily recognised as such. However, finer class divisions are less easy to recognise.

Clothes affect the behaviour of others. Many studies have been carried out in which an experimental confederate, dressed to look tidy or untidy, respectable or disreputable, stopped people in the street to request an interview or other help. Other experiments have shown that people wearing suits and white collars are judged to be more competent and intelligent (Kaiser, 1990). Nearly all of these studies found that a conventionally or tidily dressed person elicited more help or cooperation. There is an exception to this principle: if the respondent is himself untidily dressed, he is more responsive to an untidily dressed person – someone who belongs to his own group (Suedfeld et al., 1971). We could say that one of the main things clothes do is to signal group membership, and social class is one of the groups.

Wearing respectable, middle-class-type clothes is also effective in some work situations. Harp et al. (1985) found that newscasters were thought more credible and the news was remembered better when they wore conservative rather than trendy or casual clothes, especially for viewers who wore conservative clothes themselves. Forsythe et al. (1985) showed video-tapes of a woman 'job applicant' for a middle management position wearing four different outfits which varied in masculinity. Personnel administrators gave much higher ratings on forceful, self-reliant, dynamic, aggressive and decisive to the second most masculine outfit. Uniforms may have a special power: someone wearing a vague uniform produced more compliance to requests to pick up a bag, put a coin in a meter or stand on the other side of a bus stop than someone dressed as a milkman or a civilian (Bickman, 1974).

Clothes undergo continuous changes of fashion, and this plays an important role in their connection with class. Skirts get longer and shorter, on a 100-year cycle, with shorter cycles of 20–1 years. There are many other changes, as the history of fashion shows. It was widely believed that fashions 'trickled down' from above, that the upper classes started them, others imitated them to gain social status and the elite then moved to a new fashion in order to distance themselves from their imitators (Simmel, 1904). This was probably a correct description at earlier times. Hurlock (1929) in a survey in the USA in 1928 surveyed 1,500 people and found, among other things, that 25 per cent said that they changed their style of clothes because of fear of disapproval, 100 per cent of men would wait for a new style to be accepted while 19 per cent of women would adopt it at once, 40 per cent of women and 20 per cent of men said they would follow a fashion in order to appear equal to those of higher social status and about half said they changed their styles when their social inferiors adopted it. Veblen's conspicuous consumption theory (1899) applies to clothes. He said that the 'leisure class' wore clothes which were very expensive, frivolously fashionable and hence wasteful, and obviously unsuitable for any manual work, such as patent leather shoes, top hats and high heels.

However, the whole fashion scene has changed in a number of ways. The clothing industry now produces more styles at all price levels simultaneously, so that there is much less fashion lag. The trickle is horizontal, rather than imitating another group. If there are leaders of fashion they are more likely to be pop singers, TV personalities and others in the public eye, rather than a higher class. Some upper-class people don't bother about fashion, wear ancient but expensive clothes and indicate their social status by their charitable activities and country pursuits. Some fashions have even trickled upwards, when the styles of rebellious youth have been imitated.

Nevertheless there is still some fashion lag and some who adopt new fashions earlier rather than later. Fashion innovators, it is found, tend to be well-educated and of high social status, as well as being young, and non-conforming in other ways. However, the groups which they influence most are mainly of their own social class. Being out of fashion is to invite scorn and rejection – and to be perceived as of lower status (Kaiser, 1990).

Clothes indicate quite fine distinctions of rank within various hierarchies. In the armed forces, police, etc., there are badges of rank; those involved may be able to distinguish between several grades of sergeants for example. Inside hospitals the different grades of doctors, and ranks of nurses, are clearly visible to those who work there. And wearing the uniform makes it much more likely that orders will be carried out. In other places of work there may be no such badges of rank, but there are still differences of clothes, which makes status easily recognisable.

People wear different clothes for different situations – for work, social occasions, sport, etc. Each imposes a certain uniformity, though there are status divisions within each – some people are more expensively or fashionably dressed for each situation. In addition, the situations for which an individual dresses carry class meaning themselves, e.g. smart dinners or dances, or for the football ground.

Individuals choose their clothes carefully, once when they buy them and again when they put them on. They choose them because 'they feel right'; we can interpret this as choosing them because they present the right self-image, including the right class image. Sometimes the symbolism is as Veblen (1899) said – rich people wear clothes which are unsuitable for work; or, as Goffman (1956) described it, they wear gold or other ornaments which are obviously expensive. The opposite symbolism is wearing clothes which are clearly designed for manual work. Various deviant youth groups have used this symbolism to project their special self-image:

The Teddy Boy subculture can be 'read' as the theft of an upper-class style to celebrate heavy working-class masculinity . . . skin-head rolled up jeans, cropped-hair, industrial boots . . . can be understood as an attempt to recover and assert the virtues of the traditional working-class community.

(Roberts, 1983, p. 121)

Other fashions derive their meaning from sport – e.g. tweed jackets and cavalry-twill trousers from horse-riding, which has a clear class association. Ties may represent schools, colleges, regiments and other respectable organisations.

## REFERENCES

Abercrombie, N. and Warde, A. (1988) *Contemporary British Society*. Oxford: Polity Press.

Argyle, M. (1988) *Bodily Communication*. 2nd edition. London: Methuen.

Argyle, M. (1989) *The Social Psychology of Work*. 2nd edition. Harmondsworth: Penguin.

Argyle, M. (1992) *The Social Psychology of Everyday Life*. London: Routledge.

Argyle, M. and Lu, L. (1992) New directions in the psychology of leisure. *New Psychologist*, 3–11.

Bickman, L. (1974) Social rules and uniform: clothes make the person. *Psychology Today*, April, 49–51.

Blackburn, R. and Mann, M. (1979) *The Working Class in the Labour Market*. London: Macmillan.

Blauner, R. (1960) Work satisfaction and industrial trends in modern society. In W. Galenson and S.M. Lipset (eds) *Labor and Trade Unions*. New York: Wiley.

Blaxter, M. (1990) *Health and Lifestyles*. London: Tavistock/Routledge.

Chapin, F.S. (1928) A quantitative scale for rating the home and social environment of middle class families in an urban community. *Journal of Educational Psychology*, *19*, 99–111.

Comstock, G., Chaffee, S., Katzman, N., McCombs, M. and Roberts, D. (1978) *Television and Human Behavior*. New York: Columbia University Press.

Csikszentmihalyi, M. (1975) *Beyond Boredom and Anxiety*. San Francisco: Jossey-Bass.

Cyert, R. and MacCrimmon, K.R. (1968) Organizations. In G. Lindzey and E. Aronson (eds) *Handbook of Social Psychology*. Vol. 1. 2nd edition. Reading, Mass.: Addison-Wesley.

Dickinson, J. and Emler, N. (1992) Developing conceptions of work. In J.F. Hartley and G.M. Stephenson (eds) *The Psychology of Influence and Control at Work*. Oxford: Blackwell.

Dittmar, H. (1992) *The Social Psychology of Material Possessions*. London: Harvester Wheatsheaf.

Dixey, R. (1987) It's a great feeling when you win: women and bingo. *Leisure Studies*, 6, 199–214.

Forsythe, G.A., Drake, M.F. and Hogan, J.H. (1985) Influence of clothing attribution on the perception of personal characteristics. In M.R. Solomon (ed.) *The Psychology of Fashion*. Lexington, Miss.: Heath.

Fussell, P. (1984) *Caste Masks: Style and Status in the USA*. London: Heinemann.

Gathorne-Hardy, J. (1985) *The Rise and Fall of the British Nanny*. London: Weidenfeld & Nicolson.

*General Household Survey* (1992) London: HMSO.

Goffman, E. (1956) *The Presentation of Self in Everyday Life*. Edinburgh: Edinburgh University Press.

Goldthorpe, J.H. and Lockwood, D. (1963) Affluence and the British class structure. *Sociological Review*, 2, 133–63.

Goldthorpe, J.H., Lockwood, D., Bechofer, F. and Platt, J. (1968) *The Affluent Worker: Industrial Attitudes and Behaviour*. Cambridge: Cambridge University Press.

Goody, J. (1982) *Cooking, Cuisine and Class*. Cambridge: Cambridge University Press.

Gray, P.G. and Russell, R. (1962) *The Housing Situation in 1960*. London: HMSO.

Harp, S.S., Stretch, S.M. and Harp, D.A. (1985) The influence of apparel on responses to television news anchorwomen. In M.R. Solomon (ed.) *The Psychology of Fashion*. Lexington, Mass.: Heath.

Hartley, J. (1984) Industrial relations psychology. In M. Gruneberg and T. Wall (eds) *Social Psychology and Organizational Behavior*. Chichester: Wiley.

Hill, S. (1976) *The Dockers: Class and Tradition in London*. London: Heinemann.

Hurlock, E.B. (1929) Motivation in fashion. *Archives of Psychology*, III.

Kaiser, S.B. (1990) *The Social Psychology of Clothing and Personal Adornment*. 2nd edition. New York: Macmillan.

Kubey, R. and Csikzentmihalyi, M. (1990) *Television and the Quality of Life*. Hillsdale, NJ: Erlbaum.

Laumann, E.C. and House, J.S. (1970) Living room styles and social attributes: the patterning of material artifacts in a modern urban community. *Sociology and Social Research*, 54, 321–42.

Marshall, G. *et al.* (1988) *Social Class in Modern Britain*. London: Unwin Hyman.

Matheson, J. (1987) *Voluntary Work*. London: General Household Survey. HMSO.

Parker, S. (1983) *Leisure and Work*. London: Allen & Unwin.

Press, A. (1991) *Women Watching Television*. Philadelphia: University of Pennsylvania Press.

Reid, I. (1989) *Social Class Differences in Britain*. London: Fontana.

Roberts, K. (1983) *Leisure*. 2nd edition. London: Longman.

Schein, E.A. (1978) *Career Dynamics: Matching Individual and Organizational Needs*. Reading, Mass.: Addison-Wesley.

Simmel, G. (1904) Fashion. *International Quarterly*, 1, 130–55.

Sissons, M. (1971) The psychology of social class. In *Money, Wealth and Class*. Milton Keynes: Open University Press.

Smith, M.A. (1983) Social usages of the public drinking house: changing aspects of class and leisure. *British Journal of Sociology*, 34, 36–85.

Snow, P. (1991) *Oxford Observed*. London: Murray.

*Social Trends* (1988–93). London: HMSO.

Sofer, C. (1970) *Men in Mid-Career*. Cambridge: Cambridge University Press.

Spaeth, J.L. (1989) Occupational status, resource control, and earnings. *Research in Social Stratification and Mobility*, 8, 203–19.

Suedfeld, P., Bochner, S. and Matas, C. (1971) Petitioner's attire and petition signing by peace demonstrators: a field experiment on reference group similarity. *Journal of Applied Social Psychology*, 1, 278–83.

Tharin, L. (1981) Dress codes, observed attire, and behavior in a recreational setting. Unpublished MS, University of California, Davis. Cited by Kaiser (1990).

Tryon, R.C. (1955) Identification of social areas by cluster analysis: a general method with an application to the San Francisco Bay Area. *University of California Publications in Psychology*, 8, 1.

Veblen, T. (1899) *The Theory of the Leisure Class*. New York: Viking.

Veroff, J., Douvan, E. and Kulka, R.A. (1981) *The Inner American*. New York: Basic Books.

Warr, P.B. (1987) *Work, Unemployment and Mental Health*. Oxford: Clarendon Press.

Wober, M. (1992) *The Use and Abuse of Television*. Hove and London: Erlbaum.

Woodward, J. (1965) *Industrial Organization: Theory and Practice*. Oxford: Oxford University Press.

Young, M. and Willmott, P. (1973) *The Symmetrical Family*. London: Routledge & Kegan Paul.

# Chapter 6

# Speech within and between classes

There are large differences between classes, not only in accent, but also in other aspects of speech style. Speech is one of the main cues to social class, especially in Britain, and is linked to class stereotypes. When people from different classes meet they may accommodate to each other's style, negotiate a certain social distance by means of speech and sometimes have serious communication difficulties.

## ACCENT

It is well-known that there are class differences in accent in Britain and some other countries. We shall see that 'received pronunciation' (RP), i.e. educated Southern English, is generally regarded as the most correct, and various regional accents less so and less prestigious (p. 134). RP is accepted throughout the English-speaking world as the oral component of standard English. There is a Parisian style with similar status in France.

Research by phoneticians has tried to analyse exactly what the class differences in pronunciation are. Trudgill (1974) interviewed people in four areas in Norwich, judged to be of different classes, and recorded sixteen phonetic variables. Large differences were found, for example many more working-class people did not sound the final 'g' in 'running, jumping', etc.

|  | Lower working class % | Middle middle class % |
|---|---|---|
| Sound 'ing' as in 'workin' | 100 | 31 |
| Glottal sounding, e.g. of 'b'utter' | 94 | 41 |
| Dropping 'h' as in 'ammer' | 61 | 6 |

There were many other, though less extreme, class variations in vowel sounds. Middle-class speakers pronounced path to rhyme with 'staff', working-class speakers to rhyme with 'maths'. For several of these variables there was a large gap between manual and non-manual groups.

Women spoke in a more educated way than men. Trudgill suggests that this is because men are rated socially by what they can do, women by how they appear. And, as we shall see later, working-class speech is associated with greater masculinity. The fact that many women are in skilled non-manual jobs may be important – they have more contact with middle-class speakers.

There are also regional variations in accent. However, in Britain there is very little regional variation in pronunciation in higher classes, much more in lower ones, indeed degree of local accent is itself an indicator of class. This is not the case in the USA or Germany, where educated people also have local accents, though probably weaker ones than less-educated individuals.

Accent varies with class in the USA, indeed the study of this topic was started by Labov with his surveys of New York (1966, 1972) and elsewhere. He developed methods of eliciting speech of different degrees of formality, such as asking 264 shop assistants a question to which he knew the answer would be 'fourth floor', in order to sample their pronunciation of two kinds of 'r'. He studied particular sounds, and found large class differences; higher-class people sounded the 'r' in words like 'floor', 'farm' or 'fair' (i.e. at the ends of words and before consonants); there was a smaller effect for the 'r' in fourth. Large class differences were found for other sounds, such as 'th', as in 'thing', which was more often pronounced 't' by working-class people.

What are the origins of these class variations in accent? Accents spread out from certain centres of influence, some of which are prestigious. Oxford and Cambridge have produced 'educated' speech since the sixteenth century, the public schools have given their pupils 'public school accents' since about 1870, the BBC has created and popularised a slightly different version of educated Southern English and the Church of England has given elocution in another. There is a difference between ordinary RP and 'posh', 'affected' or 'marked' RP, which pronounces

man as men,
off as orff
power as pah
hunting as huntin'
stones as staines
India as Indiah etc.                                                    (Honey, 1989)

It is not known where posh accents came from. They could be a hyper-correct version of RP (see p. 125).

Linguistic changes often begin with shifts of population, though the effects may not be straightforward. Labov (1972) carried out an interesting

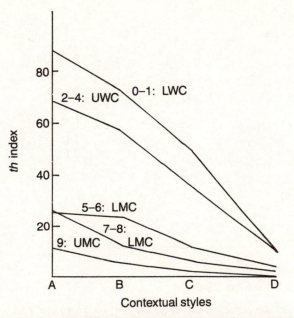

*Figure 6.1* Stratification of the variable *th* for adult speakers born in New York. A, casual speech; B, careful speech; C, reading style; D, word lists
*Source:* Labov, 1966

study of changes in vowel sounds in Martha's Vineyard, a holiday resort popular with New Yorkers. The residents shifted *away* from New York speech in order to differentiate themselves from the visitors. Studies of such language changes have found that they are rarely initiated by high-status groups, but more often by upper-working-class individuals, especially by adolescents, and the changes spread through social networks. If really lower-class groups start a language change, this is stigmatised and avoided by others (Fasold, 1990).

One of Labov's innovations was to obtain speech samples of different degrees of formality – casual speech, careful speech, reading and word lists; one of his main findings was that all classes shift towards a higher-status accent with more formal talk, as is shown for sounding 't' as 'th' (Figure 6.1).

The shift is particularly marked for lower-middle-class speakers, and Labov found 'hyper-correction' for lower-middle-class people in New York, i.e. they went beyond the upper middle class in sounding 'r's' as consonants at ends of words like 'car' and 'beer', or pre-consonantal endings as in 'beard', especially in careful speech like reading lists of words. Hyper-correction was particularly common in those who had already been socially mobile. In general the socially mobile spoke like the next group on the way up; when there is hyper-correction they go beyond it (Figure 6.2).

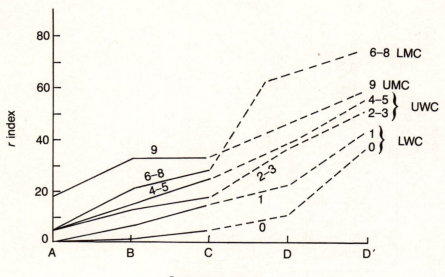

*Figure 6.2* Class distribution of the variable *r* (as in guard, car, etc.) for New York adults
*Source:* Labov, 1966
*Note:* D and D′ are both word-lists.

Trudgill used similar methods in Norwich. He too found that some elements varied both with class and formality of situation, as in the case of sounding the final 'g' in 'hunting' (Figure 6.3). A similar pattern was found for glottal 't' and some vowel sounds, while for some vowels there was a class difference but little variation between situations.

In the case of vowels there is a continuous change with gradual shifts between classes. For a number of consonants there was a large gap between the upper and the lower working class. When there was an effect of situation, for middle-class speakers this was greatest between casual and formal speech, but for working-class speakers the gap was greatest between conversation and reading, as shown for ng in Figure 6.3. Perhaps middle-class people are more aware of the difference between the two kinds of conversation, because they have to shift codes more.

Trudgill suggests that these accent shifts can help us to decide how many social classes there are, and whether there are any sharp discontinuities between them. Although some of his phonetic variables suggest a two-class structure, with the break between manual and non-manual, others suggest that there are three classes, with distinctive accents of their own.

'Code-switching' is where people change accents (or other aspects of speech) according to the person they are talking to or other aspects

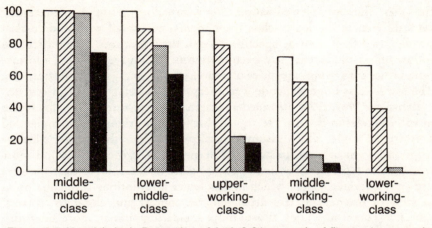

*Figure 6.3* Norwich (ng). Proportion of (ng): [ŋ] in speech of five socioeconomic classes in four styles; word-list (white), reading passage (hatched), formal (dotted), casual (solid)
*Source:* based on Trudgill, 1974

of the situation. Formality, just discussed, is a special case. Another is 'accommodation', where two people move towards one another in speech style. This phenomenon has been studied in connection with different languages. For example Asian immigrants in Britain may speak English in the post office, Punjabi in the home, Arabic in the mosque; at work or shopping they may use English or Punjabi (Bell, 1976). There is code-switching of accents too. School children often use one accent at school, e.g. a public school version of RP, and a different, sometimes more regional accent in the home. They are effectively 'bilingual' for accent.

The research on careful speech shows that most people know the 'correct' way to speak, and are perfectly capable of doing it if they choose. Why don't they do it all the time, since they know that the educated middle-class accent is more prestigious? The answer is that if a lower-class person did this, he would be rejected by his own group. Speech style conveys status, but it also shows group membership. Furthermore, middle-class accents may indicate higher status, but speakers are also judged to be colder, and less tough or masculine (p. 136). People do not usually make conscious choices in these matters but adolescents and members of minority groups have been found to adopt deliberately non-standard accents, apparently to emphasise their distinctive group identity and their distance from middle-class values (Ryan, 1979).

## LINGUISTIC CODES

There are class differences in other aspects of speech – grammar, complexity and other features discriminating 'high' and 'low' versions of language. One of the earliest studies was carried out by Schatzman and Strauss (1955) in the USA. They interviewed people after a tornado, and found an interesting class difference: the lower-class respondents, compared with middle-class people, used their own perspective, so that their accounts were difficult to follow unless the listener had been there too. They gave concrete information, rather than using categories of people or acts, and gave no illustrations. The lower-class linguistic code was interpreted as being more ego-centric.

Bernstein (1961, 1971) presented a comprehensive picture of class differences in speech codes in Britain. He argued that lower-working-class people used a 'restricted' code, which assumes that listeners share the speaker's knowledge and point of view (this can be interpreted as 'ego-centricity'), is more ritualistic and 'predictable', and in a sense more fluent. Middle-class speakers use an 'elaborated' code, which makes fewer assumptions about the point of view of listeners, is less dependent on context and closer to 'correct' speech as taught in school. It uses more standard grammar, more subordinate clauses and a larger vocabulary. Bernstein did not say that working-class people had a language deficit, though he thought that working-class children were at a disadvantage in school, being accustomed to a different style. The two codes developed for different purposes, the restricted code for face-to-face relationships, the elaborated code for accurate transmission of information, for example in professional and managerial settings. Not only is the restricted code better for the former task, it is also used by middle-class people for this purpose. Working-class people meet fewer strangers so don't need the elaborated code. However, this thumb-nail sketch of the sociology of two social classes is a very simplified caricature, and the actual communication needs of each class are much more varied than this.

It is difficult to translate the rather abstract ideas of Bernstein's theory into measurable aspects of speech, though many have attempted to do so. The usual method of research has been to obtain samples of speech or writing from 12–17-year-olds. Bernstein himself (1962) tape-recorded discussions of capital punishment in groups of 16-year-old boys, matched for IQ. He found a number of differences: the lower-working-class boys used fewer subordinate clauses, shorter words and sentences, and paused more. Lawton (1968) used controlled interviews, and found a lot of differences for 15-year-old boys, but not much for 12-year-olds. He used two verbal tasks and also a written one. Robinson and Rackstraw (1972) asked 5–7-year-olds questions and found that the middle-class children took more account of the point of view of the listener, and that their speech was more precise and complex.

To summarise these and other studies, carried out in Britain, the USA, France and Australia, most, though not all, have obtained the results predicted by Bernstein, with almost no reversals, though the differences were often quite small. The most frequently obtained class differences are that working-class speech:

1. has less complex sentences, e.g. fewer subordinate clauses, or complex verb systems
2. has shorter sentences
3. has a smaller vocabulary, less varied adjectives
4. has more personal pronouns and adverbs
5. is less abstract, more concrete
6. takes less account of the different perspective of listeners
7. includes more tags, such as 'didn't I?', and 'you know'.

(Robinson, 1978; Dittmar, 1976)

It is possible that some of these 'class differences' were caused, or partly caused, by working-class children being less familiar with the testing situation, or because they interpreted the demands of the situation differently, or were simply hostile to the testers, as they can be with teachers. One of the most striking differences is that they produced much shorter answers. The apparent differences may be generated by adults, at school and at home. Tizard and colleagues (1983) found that teachers addressed less complex utterances to working-class children, who were quite capable of complex speech and used more of it at home; they changed more between home and school than middle-class children did and appeared to be inhibited from complex utterances at school. Working-class mothers also used less complex and more implicit constructions than middle-class ones.

Bernstein suggested that the informal use of language is different from the formal use, in much the same way that the restricted and elaborated codes differ. It is found in several cultures that individuals of all social classes switch codes to some extent towards a more elaborated code for more formal situations. For example, people speak in a higher code in many work situations, teaching and other places where clear and precise information needs to be given to others who may not be familiar with the matters in hand. Lawton (1968) found that some code-switching was greater for middle-class children, and Collett *et al.* (1981) found working-class children did not shift much to use of the elaborated code in a task where the speaker and listener could not see one another. On the other hand, in everyday life working-class children probably have to shift *more* between school and home (Hudson, 1980). We shall see later that working-class people do shift more for accent.

## SOCIALISATION ORIGINS OF CLASS DIFFERENCES IN SPEECH

A number of studies have investigated possible sources of these class differences in the speech of parents. Robinson and Rackstraw (1972) carried out a major study with 160 children of the ways mothers answer questions from 5-year-olds. Middle-class mothers were more likely to answer questions, gave more information, it was more accurate, and they were more concerned about the truth of the answer. Lower-class mothers in reply to 'why' questions often said 'because they do' or 'because they always have done' but did not give causes or consequences. Two years later, fifty-five girls (now 7) were asked thirty questions; their answers differed as expected between classes and were correlated in quantity and quality with those of their mothers two years earlier. Within the lower-class group there was a weak but positive relationship for general style, complex use of language and for some more specific linguistic features. These links were weaker within the middle-class sample.

Another aspect of maternal behaviour is the way they control children's behaviour. Cook Gumperz (1973) found that working-class mothers more often used threats without explanation; while middle-class mothers referred to the consequences – 'I will have to clear up the mess', 'you will have to clear up the mess', 'you'll cry and Daddy will get angry'. Robinson (1978) concludes that working-class mothers use a restricted code by giving commands without reasons, while middle-class mothers use an elaborated code in giving reasons so that the child can work out for itself what it should do.

Other studies have looked into how mothers instruct and direct children. Hess and Shipman (1965) asked the mothers of 4-year-olds to teach their children how to sort blocks and to etch patterns. Middle-class mothers gave more detailed instructions, and also showed their children how to do it; they appealed less to authority ('because I say so'), and more to reason, and gave more reinforcement; these techniques correlated with successful performance by the children. Mothers were also asked how they would deal with misbehaviour at school; again middle-class mothers said they would not use imperative demands, but rather appeals to reason, and reference to the effect of behaviour on others. These are more than differences in linguistic codes; they show different attitudes to task performance and misbehaviour.

*Grammatical differences.* In all cultures studied so far, members of higher social classes are more likely to use the formal or 'high' version of the language, which in Britain is the elaborated code. These high forms include more 'correct' grammar. On the other hand, the language which is commonly used in lower versions can be described in grammatical terms and may be regarded as an 'alternative' syntax rather than an incorrect one.

The first study of such alternative grammars was by Labov *et al.* (1968) and others into Black English Vernacular (BEV), i.e. Black English. Some of the different 'rules' were:

1 Use of 'be' as in 'the answers always be wrong'.
2 Omission of the copula 'to be' after pronouns, 'She nice'.
3 Omission of -t and -d endings, especially if the next word starts with a consonant, as in 'he kick ball'.
4 Use of multiple negatives, as in 'I don't bother nobody'.

The features of working-class grammar are fairly familiar. Trudgill found that 70 per cent of his lower-working-class subjects in Detroit used double negatives (e.g. 'I can't eat nothing'), compared with 2 per cent of the upper-middle-class speakers. In Norwich 97 per cent of lower-working-class people left off the final 's' from verbs (e.g. 'she like him very much'), compared with 2 per cent of middle-middle-class ones. The difference in Detroit was similar though not so great, 71 per cent v. 1 per cent. Other examples noted by Trudgill of lower-class English grammar are:

'I done it yesterday'
'He ain't got it'
'It was her what said it.'

## LINGUISTIC COMPETENCE

Are there class differences in linguistic competence? To begin with, what is it? I suggest that it should refer to effectiveness in conveying information or in any other purpose for which language is used. Bernstein and others have taken care to avoid suggesting that the class differences in speech which they described constitute differences in competency or that there is a working-class 'deficit'. Nevertheless the differences in code which have been postulated and confirmed look very much like such differences in competence – for one of the main uses of speech, i.e. to convey information.

Heider (1971) found that 10-year-old middle-class children were a little better both as senders and receivers of information to indicate one out of nine abstract shapes, or faces, and that this ability correlated with Bernstein-type variables like use of subordinate clauses and use of many adjectives. A number of later studies with a similar design found similar class differences, with children of different ages. Class differences in communication competence are reduced if IQ is held constant but some studies still found such class differences. Johnstone and Singleton (1977) replicated the Heider study with British 5-year-olds, but with IQ held constant, and found similar class differences in encoding style. Quay *et al.* (1977) found small differences both for encoding and decoding, with 8–9-year-olds, the middle-middle combination doing best. Pozner and Saltz (1974), with American 10-year-olds, used a game in which pairs of children had to describe the positions of pieces on a board invisible to the other. There were no class differences in decoding accuracy, but the working-class children made nearly five times as many errors when sending. These errors could be interpreted as 'egocentric' – sending incomplete information, moving one piece while talking, and giving information e.g. about spatial position in room (e.g. 'near the blackboard') which was correct for the sender but not for the receiver. Heider had observed that the working-class messages were similar to messages intended for oneself or for a friend; perhaps these senders assumed that most people with whom they will have to deal are friends or neighbours.

As Robinson (1978) reminds us, language has a number of other functions in addition to conveying information about the physical world. Are there class differences in competence in these other spheres too?

*Answering questions.* Robinson and Rackstraw (1972) carried out a study of fifty-six 7-year-old girls, and thirty-three boys, who were asked thirty questions, divided into physical and moral. Many class differences were found and, after the effects of IQ and mothers' use of verbal explanations had been partialled out, a number of differences remained. Middle-class children gave more causal answers to physical questions, fewer in terms of regularity, fewer irrelevant answers and their answers were more complete. For the moral questions middle-class children referred more to the effects of behaviour on other people, less to possible punishments or rewards, and appealed to authority less often.

*Dealing with people.* There are several other functions of speech, but there is a whole sphere for which the restricted code may be superior – dealing with others, 'making friends and influencing people'. In Chapter 7 we discuss class differences in social skills, and conclude that those with jobs that involve constantly dealing with people have superior skills. On the whole, middle-class jobs demand more social skill, but so do a lot of class III (n) jobs, while some class I jobs don't need very much.

Labov (1968) argued that the speech of lower-class blacks in New York is, if anything, more complex, and certainly more effective, compared with white speech. He was able to obtain samples of speech by highly informal meetings with subjects and groups of subjects. He reports that BEV, as used by these black youths, is complex, skilled and effective in terms of interpersonal goals. He thought that the most complex speech forms are ritual insults, often consisting of outrageous remarks about another person's mother, but complex, imaginative and sometimes in rhyme.

Some have objected that, on the contrary, ritual insults are clear cases of the restricted code, since they consist of repetition of routine rude remarks, with a stereotyped structure, e.g.:

'Your mother has . . .' (followed by a variety of unlikely and obscene properties)

(Atkinson, 1985)

Lower-class blacks are also said to be good at 'rapping':

a distinctively fluent and lively way of talking, one that is always highly personal in style. It can be a way of creating a favourable impression when first meeting a person, though it can also become rather competitive and lead to a lively repartee.

(Burling, 1970)

Other studies have found that working-class children are good at telling bed-time stories, and other stories, in a way which heightens the tension by insertion of subordinate clauses, and shocks listeners by means of complex and dramatic narratives.

However, this does not really answer the question of whether lower-class people, using the restricted code, are as good or better than middle-class people at dealing with everyday interpersonal situations. It seems very likely that the restricted code is good for dealing with such situations, within a familiar group, just as the elaborated code is better for conveying exact information, especially to strangers. Middle-class people use the elaborated code more often, and are better at this second task. It is possible that working-class individuals are better at the first.

## PERCEPTION OF SPEECH

### Perception of class

Most people speak in the accent and code of their local community, the people with whom they live and work. We have just seen that there are great variations of accent between classes, and also variations in grammar and other aspects of linguistic code. We shall see later that there are status variations within the workplace, for example between nurses of different rank, suggesting that accent can be a quite reliable indicator of social status. How accurately can people judge social class from speech? Putnam and O'Hern (1955) presented 1-minute samples of speech from twelve black Americans from different classes and regions; ranking of social status by judges agreed with objective measures at .80. Ellis (1967) found that this correlation was nearly as high (.65) when the speakers tried to disguise their voices as upper class.

Lambert *et al.* (1960) devised the 'matched guise technique', in which subjects are asked to listen to what they think are different speakers, delivering the same passage, and rate them on a number of dimensions. Actually all recordings are by a single, versatile speaker. This holds everything constant except accent or language. In the original experiments in Montreal messages were given in Canadian-English or French. One of the findings was that both English- and French-Canadian judges rated the English speaker more favourably on a number of traits.

Giles used the matched-guised technique to study this issue in England: the same speaker produced thirteen samples of speech in different accents, which were rated on a number of scales, including the status or prestige of the speaker. The results for 177 12–17-year-old South Welsh and Somerset school children are shown in Table 6.1. The Welsh accent was rated only by Somerset children and vice versa.

The correlation between accent and perceived status was .88, whether presented as a speech sample or simply named as in Table 6.1. This study

Table 6.1 The generalised accent prestige continuum: mean ratings of 13 accents

| | |
|---|---|
| 1. RP (2.1)* | 8. Italian (4.7) |
| 2. Affected RP (2.9)* | 9. Northern English (4.8) |
| 3. N. American and French (3.6)* | 10. Somerset (5.1) |
| 5. German (4.2)* | 11. Cockney and Indian (5.2) |
| 6. South Welsh (4.3) | 13. Birmingham (5.3) |
| 7. Irish (4.6) | |

Note: * Mean for 17-year-olds.

was repeated with 21-year-old students; accent and perceived status now correlated .94 (Giles and Powesland, 1975).

From these and other studies it looks as if British accents fall into several main status groups – received pronunciation, some acceptable local variants like Yorkshire and Scottish, and the stronger accents of industrial towns, including Cockney, together with strong rural accents.

It would be interesting to know how accurately people in Britain can distinguish between the voices of, for example, class II and III (n) voices, especially when there have been different degrees of social mobility. Perhaps listeners can judge both present class and social origins to some extent. Some early acquired accents can be very pervasive, and traces of public school, Scottish, Irish, Yorkshire or American accents for example can persist indefinitely.

Some individuals are better at decoding class from accent than others. Giles found that accuracy increased with age, from 12 to 21. Shuy *et al.* (1969) used half-minute samples of speech and found that middle-class judges were most accurate, and the lower the class of speakers the more accurately they were judged, it was suggested because of various stigmatised speech elements. Giles found that ethnocentric individuals rated regional, i.e. lower-status, accents less favourably and RP accents more favourably.

It would be interesting to know which aspects of speech carry this information. Accent seems the most likely one, as we have seen how greatly it varies with social class. Giles found that 'broader', i.e. stronger, regional accents, Irish, Birmingham and South Welsh, were given lower status than milder versions. There have been one or two attempts to separate the possible speech cues. Ellis (1967) found judgement accuracy of .65 when speakers counted from 1 to 20, thus eliminating everything but accent. Callery (1974) eliminated accent, by transmitting the speech samples used by Putnam and O'Hern, correcting the grammar and spelling; judges could still judge class with an accuracy of .70. This suggests that linguistic code, in the Bernstein sense (apart from grammar), or some other cue such as choice of vocabulary, are also important cues. Normally there is a combination of accent, grammar, other aspects of linguistic code and vocabulary. In addition, a lot of non-verbal evidence is also available, especially clothes, other aspects of appearance and perhaps facial expression.

## Speech stereotypes

In the matched-guise method, judges are asked to rate the social status or features of the speaker; they do not realise that what is being studied is reaction to the accent. Higher-status accents are accorded higher social status, as we have seen; speakers of these accents are also believed to possess a number of other favourable attributes, in other words stereotypes are associated with the accents.

Cheyne (1970) found that English voices were rated, by both English and Scottish listeners, as higher than Scottish voices in:

self-confidence
intelligence
ambition
leadership
prestige and wealth
good looks, height
occupational status
cleanliness.

This kind of result has been widely replicated – speakers of higher-status accents are judged higher on dimensions of competence, such as ability and success, and this stereotype is shared by people who themselves speak in a lower-status style. Similar results have been obtained for English- and French-Canadian speakers in Quebec, in the USA and Australia.

Information about class can be given directly, simply by telling people the target person's occupation. This affects judgements of competence, etc., in just the same way as varying accents (Van Oudenhoven and Withag, 1983). However, when such information is given, accent still influences judgements of status-related traits. In a number of such experiments accent holds its own, indeed is usually the strongest source of positive evaluations, in the presence of information about class, photographs and vocabulary (Giles and Coupland, 1991).

Members of both high- and low-status groups rate users of superior accents as higher in competence, expertise and so on. Lower-status groups may rate users of superior accents as higher in competence, but they rate speakers of their own accent as superior on traits such as:

honesty
friendliness
sense of humour
generosity
likeability
trustworthiness.

This has been replicated in a number of settings, e.g. Ireland and Canada. There seem to be two factors here. (1) People rate those who speak with similar accents to themselves more highly on these 'solidarity' traits. (2) Members of lower-status accents are rated by everyone as higher on these traits (Giles and Coupland, 1977; Ryan and Giles, 1982). A possible explanation of the second point may be that regionally accented speakers are seen as unconcerned with social mobility and economic position, and therefore more community-oriented and socially attractive. Users of high-status accents, like RP, on the other hand may be seen as concealing their true personality, and therefore as insincere fakes, lacking in integrity (Giles and Powesland, 1975).

A further, very interesting, component of accent stereotypes is that lower-class speech is seen as more masculine. We saw earlier that women use a more educated accent, either because of the influence of their white-collar jobs or through greater social insecurity. The result may be that lower-class speech becomes an indicator of masculinity. Trudgill (1974) suggested that middle-class men use working-class speech styles, or 'under-correct', in order to stress their masculinity, the opposite of what women do.

### Reactions to accent

Accents also affect behaviour. Giles and Powesland (1975) carried out experiments in which the same persuasive argument was delivered in different accents, in person or tape, to different audiences. The RP versions were rated as more competent and intelligent, but the greatest attitude change occurred for speakers whose accent matched that of the audience. In other experiments, students and members of the public were asked to help with a psychological experiment. Subjects were more helpful, i.e. they wrote a lot more, when a RP voice was used, typically about 40 per cent more. Do accents affect selection for jobs? Experiments with smart and disreputable clothes have a similar effect (p. 118). Hopper and Williams (1973) found that black–white accents in the USA affected judgements of intelligent-competent, and these affected simulated job selections but only for foremen and managers, not for manual jobs. In later studies candidates with ethnic accents were thought *more* suitable for manual jobs. From my experience of job selection interviews in Britain, I believe that accent, via the associated stereotypes, is often important, since selectors want to choose people like themselves, who will fit in. On the other hand, for technical and scientific jobs, especially for 'back room boys', e.g. in computing, it does not seem to matter.

Does accent damage a child's educational prospects? Bernstein believed that it did, because lower-class children use a different linguistic code from teachers and therefore have communication difficulties. Robinson thought that there is no evidence for this, but points out that working-class children are:

less adept at meeting demands made upon their language skills . . . especially when the tasks required precise and discriminating messages, conceptually difficult abstract speech, and explanations stretching the limits of children's understanding.

(Robinson, 1978, p. 168)

This could be described as weakness in using the elaborated code, or in the representational function of language. A further problem is that, if a teacher forms a poor impression of a child's abilities, this prophecy is likely to be fulfilled, via differential expectations and treatment by the teacher, as shown in the *Pygmalion in the Classroom* experiment by Rosenthal and Jacobson (1968). A number of classroom studies, in Australia and in the USA, have found that teachers do infer differences of ability in children on the basis of differences of accent (Robinson, 1978).

## CONVERSATION BETWEEN PEOPLE FROM DIFFERENT SOCIAL CLASSES

### Accommodation

Two speakers often 'converge' or 'accommodate' to each other, that is they change their speech styles to be more similar – in accent, language chosen, loudness, speech rate, etc. This happens when their speech is different because they belong to different classes. Giles initiated research on this topic, and thought at first that people accommodated when they wanted to be accepted by the other and knew that people prefer those who are similar to themselves. Later he added the motivation of wanting to be understood by the listener and therefore taking account of their point of view (Giles and Coupland, 1991). We might add that individuals may imitate each other and that the demands of synchrony will produce similar speed, loudness and other aspects of speech.

Several studies have shown accommodation of accent between speakers of different social status. In a simple but elegant study Coupland (1984) studied the number of h's sounded by a girl working in a travel agency as she spoke to different clients. The percentage varied from 3.7 per cent to 29.3 per cent, and correlated highly with the percentage of h's sounded by the client.

Thakerar *et al.* (1982) found that senior nurses spoke considerably faster and with a more educated accent than more junior, less well-qualified nurses. When engaged in a cooperative task, where their status differences were relevant, nurses of different status shifted in both speed and accent to what they thought was the style of the other, though actually going too far, which was interpreted as 'subjective convergence'. This is probably unusual, since people often converge only part of the way; there is an optimal degree of it. We shall see shortly that too much convergence may be disliked.

We have seen that accommodation takes place in respect of speech rate and accent. It can also affect the language spoken; this is relevant to social class if there are status differences between those speaking different languages. This has been found in Quebec, in conversations between English- and French-speaking Canadians, and between English and Spanish speakers in the USA (Thakerar *et al.*, 1982). There is probably accommodation in other aspects of speech, and it is likely that it takes place on several levels simultaneously.

It has been found that accommodation is successful in producing favourable attitudes on the part of others. Giles and Smith (1979) prepared eight tapes of a Canadian addressing an English audience, with combinations of accommodation or lack of it on three dimensions – pronunciation, speech rate and message content. English judges thought the speaker most attractive when he converged on speech rate and contents; speech rate was the most effective, but adding accent convergence had a negative effect, perhaps being seen as a caricature. This establishes an important point, that there is an optimal degree of convergence.

It also makes a difference how the listener attributes a speaker's convergence. This is received favourably if it is seen as needing effort, as voluntary and as an attempt to break through cultural barriers, rather than due to situational pressures. Failure to accommodate is reacted to negatively unless it is attributed to lack of ability (Simard *et al.*, 1976).

Lower-status people converge more, for example salespeople more than customers, and foremen converge more towards managers than to workers. This is partly because of the economic consequences, perhaps also through a desire for acceptance by high-status others.

This was found for 6-year-old Chicano (i.e. Spanish speaking) and Anglo-American children: 71 per cent of the Chicanos shifted to English, 17 per cent of the Anglo children to Spanish, though all were bilingual (Aboud, 1976). It depends of course on whether an individual is able to use the other language, dialect, etc. We have seen that many children can speak in more than one class-related accent, and that most people can use a more educated accent if asked to read lists of words. A range of accents is heard daily on radio and TV, and most people can imitate different class-related voices, though this is a caricature of the real thing. It also depends on the strength of desire to be accepted or approved of. It has been found that individuals with a strong social desirability score, indicating general need for approval, converge more. There is also more convergence on the part of extraverts, high self-monitors and cognitively complex individuals (Giles and Coupland, 1991).

However, there are limits to how far a person will accommodate. Giles and Powesland give the example of:

a tough, masculine, rugby-football playing young man seeking the favour of an exceptionally feminine and coy young lady. One might suppose that he would not advance his courtship by modelling his manner on hers but would be wiser to maintain or even exaggerate his own virile and masterful style of speech and behaviour.

(Giles and Powesland, 1975, p. 167)

This is an instance of two people in a cooperative situation, maintaining distinctive roles and, therefore, not converging.

## Identity and self-presentation

We have seen that people often converge, both up and down, in accent and speech style; both want to be understood and both want to be liked and accepted by the other. However, lower-status people converge more, probably due to 'self-presentation', i.e. sending signals to create a favourable impression on the other. This can bring material benefits, like getting a job, or it can add to self-esteem, if it leads to acceptance as a member of a superior group. This may be particularly true of accents, since accent is one of the clearest indicators of group membership (Welsh, American, etc.) and of social class. Accent is more than an indicator of class, it is part of the meaning and definition of class for most people, it is a kind of badge of rank.

However, we saw earlier that convergence is only partial, speakers do not go all the way. One reason for this is that it is not acceptable to the other party, since self-presentation of any kind is not just a matter of individuals sending social signals to each other. Self-images presented have to be *negotiated*, that is they depend on what others will believe and accept, there have to be agreed self-definitions for interaction to proceed.

Another factor which restrains convergence is the danger of rejection by one's own group, a loss of acceptance and hence of identity. Although regional or lower-class accents carry a low-status stereotype, they are also seen as friendly, generous and trustworthy. This may help to explain why lower-status accents survive. It is familiar that efforts are made to keep Welsh, Irish, Gaelic, etc., alive, despite the resultant communication difficulties. The same principle probably explains the persistence of Cockney and other low-status accents – they signal membership of a valued group, which has at least some positive stereotypes associated with it.

Giles and Coupland (1991) argue that accent and language are the main ways of indicating and maintaining group identity, that speech style is a valued symbol of group pride. They link it to social identity theory, which proposed that self-image and self-esteem are partly dependent on belonging to groups, and that people keep up their self-esteem by holding favourable beliefs about group members. It is argued that identity is sometimes best served by divergence, rather than convergence: this is when preserving identity is more important that acceptance. Bourhis and Giles (1977) claim to have demonstrated divergence in an experiment in which the ethnic identity of Welsh subjects was threatened by rude remarks about the Welsh language, with the result that they strengthened their Welsh accents. In a similar study Bourhis *et al.* (1979) found divergence by Flemish speakers speaking to French-speaking Belgians in English, but shifting to their own language when the other demeaned the Flemish people. These experiments did find divergence, but only when the speakers' ethnic group had been criticised. And it is clear that experimentally manipulated divergence is perceived negatively, e.g. as insulting, rude or hostile (Simard *et al.*, 1976).

## Dominance, deference and social distance

When two people interact they establish a relationship along two main dimensions – dominance and social distance. Dominance and deference are greatly affected by the social classes of those involved, and by their ages, positions in hierarchies or other sources of power or status. Often individuals of different classes meet where their different power inside an organisation is relevant – it creates a status difference and it creates a social barrier between them. If they meet on equal terms outside the organisation there may still be generalisation and similar styles of relationship adopted. The precise relationship has to be negotiated, but the signals which are used to do this are mainly non-verbal.

Accent and language are among these cues, but other cues for dominance and deference are probably more important. The dominant speech style is loud, 'confident', expressive (i.e. large pitch range), of lower pitch, with more talk and more interruptions. The contents are relevant too: dominant people give orders and they state their views. The deferential, or submissive, style is the opposite – less loud, nervous and high pitched, less expressive, less talk, no interruptions. Questions are asked and tentative suggestions made. The negotiation consists for example of deciding how much each will speak and how loudly (as well as in which accent).

An example is conversation between doctor and patient. It is found that the doctor does most of the talking, initiates 99 per cent of exchanges, while patients ask only 9 per cent of the questions, and the doctor interrupts more (Wiemann and Giles, 1988).

There are other non-verbal cues for dominance and deference, apart from speech, which were discussed earlier – postures, gestures, etc. (pp. 54–5). For example, it is found that the foremen of juries 'elect themselves', mainly by adopting a dominant style. They are usually middle-class males. Dominance is often generated by the situation – when one person is a judge, or barrister, rather than a defendant or witness, where one is a doctor, nurse or patient, and so on.

The second dimension of relationships is the 'social distance' between two people. This term was coined to describe how far Americans would allow members of other national and ethnic groups to associate with them to different degrees, up to marriage. We have seen that there is a certain distance between classes in this sense – individuals from different classes are less likely to become friends or to marry one another (see Chapter 4). More than this there is evidence of a certain amount of hostility between classes (p. 145).

How great is the 'distance' between members of different classes when they meet, in terms of physical distance, or other indicators of psychological separation? We have seen that there can be convergence of accent and other aspects of speech style, in sales situations – where there is an incentive to be accepted by the other, and between nurses – who have a strong feeling of group membership. How far there is convergence or divergence in other natural situations is not known. Distance and closeness are also communicated by other aspects of speech, especially the use of a friendly tone of voice: this consists of a pure and not discordant tone, higher pitch and upward pitch contour. Again there are a number of other non-vocal signals, especially physical distance, smiling, gaze, touch and lively gestures such as head-nods.

Again there is negotiation of the social distance between two people. For example, a high level of gaze may be reciprocated at first, but if it becomes uncomfortably high it is reduced again. The level and frequency of smiling can be used to keep the relationship at the precise level desired. An example of the effect of status differences on distance is the often-observed tendency of people to back away from important people in public places or at receptions. However, there is little precise research information on the effects of class differences on social distance. An important factor is where the interaction takes place. Different social classes, like different racial groups, can get on very well at work, but are less likely to choose each other's company for leisure. This may be because work is in some sense more scripted, a matter of playing roles. Or it may be that spouses and families are not at work, and so have little contact with the other social class and ethnic groups there.

## Terms of address

In all cultures there are different ways of addressing people to indicate relative status, such as pronouns (e.g. *tu* and *vous*), and first names (FN) and title and last name (TLN), which may be equivalent, in other aspects of speech. Deference is indicated by calling the other 'Sir', using TLN, or occupational title and last name (e.g. Dr X). Superior status is communicated by use of FN, as to children, or to subordinates who do not reciprocate. A senior person has to indicate if and when such reciprocation will be acceptable. In English we have only one second-person pronoun, now that thee and thou have gone, except among some Quakers. In French, German and Italian there are two, and in some languages as many as twenty ways of addressing others.

Within colleges, schools, hospitals and other institutions, use is made of job titles, e.g. 'Bursar', 'President'. The degree of formality depends on the formality of the occasion: the same person may be addressed by job title or FN depending on the situation. Staples and Robinson (1974), in a study of a Southampton shop, found that formality of address varied with the situation. When speaking to one another in front of customers, employees used TLN or Sir; address was less formal in the staff canteen and least formal in the street, in a pub or at a staff dance.

The negotiation of relationships by means of terms of address is illustrated by the following awful story: a white policeman stops a black man in the street.

'What's your name, boy?' the policeman asked.
'Dr Poussaint, I'm a physician . . .'
'What's your first name, boy?'
'Alvin.'

(Ervin-Tripp, 1969)

However, terms of address usually communicate solidarity or closeness as well as power or dominance. The signals for greater power usually indicate closeness as well, e.g. use of FN in English or *tu* in French. Use of FN is therefore ambiguous: it signals closeness only if it is reciprocated (Brown and Gilman, 1960). It is up to the senior person to indicate when this is acceptable. In Hungarian and some Asian languages there are two equivalents of *tu*, for close and less close relationships.

There is little evidence for class differences in how people address each other in Britain. There is an old-fashioned public school and Oxford male style of address by last name only, but this is falling into disuse. Various high-status institutions have special terms of address, such as the House of Commons and Law Courts.

## Politeness

Politeness is not just about how to behave nicely at tea parties; it is an important social skill. Everyone agrees that it is desirable, but what exactly does it consist of? The dictionary is not much help – 'having good manners, being refined, cultivated, courteous' and so on, which does not tell us what to do. How about 'forms of speech which are as far as possible agreeable and rewarding to others'? I say 'as far as possible' because being polite need not require constant flattery and agreement.

Brown and Levinson (1987) proposed that the central purpose of politeness is avoiding 'face threat' to others, and all writers on this subject agree that avoiding loss of self-esteem to others is important. However, they distinguished 'positive politeness' (expression of solidarity, indication that one likes the other and wants the same things) from 'negative politeness' (apologise, defer, avoid coercion, save other's face). From anthropological studies they conclude that members of middle and upper classes use more negative politeness, while members of lower classes use most positive. They think this is due to greater social distance between people at higher levels compared with the denser social networks lower down – especially for women who use most positive politeness.

An important way of avoiding threat to face and avoiding coercion is indirectness of requests, often called 'mitigation'. It is found that these indirect forms are made when social distance is greater, and when addressing a person of higher status, e.g. 'Would you mind passing the salt', rather than 'Pass the salt' or 'Pass the bloody salt' (the 'aggravated' version).

There is evidence that politeness is effective. Linde (1988) found that in air crews with good safety records there was a high level of mitigation, i.e. indirectness, in communication with the captain – this avoided challenging his authority. But in accidents and emergencies, real and simulated, there was less mitigation, and it could lead to disaster, because such messages were much less likely to be acted on. 'Aggravation', e.g. 'watch out for that f . . . . . plane', was more effective.

A number of other aspects of politeness have been proposed, including avoiding rule-breaking by interrupting, breaking into queues or telling unsuitable jokes. Leech (1983) proposed that a speaker should draw attention to the merits of the other rather than himself. We found that it was widely believed that people should be friendly on all occasions, and should try to make encounters pleasant occasions, another possible general principle of politeness (Figure 6.4).

Politeness requires social skill, for example delivering utterances which influence without constraining or offending. At a tutorial, instead of 'Please write notes about what I say', a tutor could say 'Here is some paper in case you need to make notes'.

Rules of politeness vary between situations. In a study which pre-dates the publication of most of these rules we asked subjects to rate the importance of twenty rules for each of eight situations. The results are shown in Figure 6.4.

The rules in the top cluster were thought to apply to all the situations mentioned, and can be regarded as rules of general politeness. The last cluster consists of additional rules for parties, where evidently a further degree of politeness is needed; the party rules did not apply to the other clusters of situations, which were work or informal social situations.

Knowing the politeness rules of different situations is a further aspect of politeness skills. High status organisations often have complex politeness rules of their own – royal courts, the House of Commons, Law Courts, the high tables of Oxford colleges. In university seminars, in Britain at least, it is quite normal for people to disagree sharply, and this is perfectly acceptable if done in a friendly way, but without any 'wrapping up'.

In Japan and other Asian cultures, politeness is very important and the

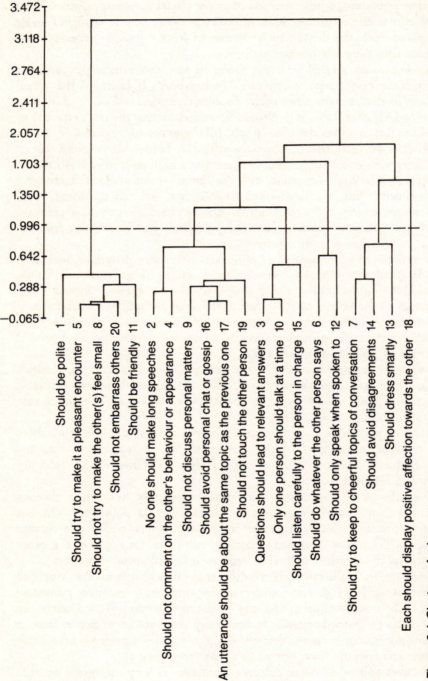

**Figure 6.4 Clusters of rules**
*Source: Argyle et al., 1979*

rules complex. This is probably because of the concern with face, so that rules developed to reduce the risk of loss of face. In Japan it is wrong to ask questions to which the answer might be 'no', since this would lead to loss of face for the initiator of this exchange. Joking and teasing are disapproved of. Disagreement is expressed by changing the subject (Argyle, 1987).

## BREAKDOWNS OF COMMUNICATION BETWEEN CLASSES

People from different social classes often have difficulty talking to and understanding each other. This is an important source of division in society, and we shall explore the main causes of it.

*Language difficulties.*   Pendleton and Bochner (1980) studied interaction between doctors and patients. The doctors reported communication problems in 21 per cent of consultations, and this was much higher for working-class patients. For those patients, consultations were shorter – 5.2 minutes v. over 7 minutes for patients in the highest of three class groupings; there were fewer health-related statements per consultation (patient's plus doctor's), 3.5 per consultation v. 8.25 for the highest class grouping. In the field of mental health these communication difficulties lead to working-class patients being classified as psychotic more often – because psychiatrists find them difficult to understand or empathise with (Wilkinson, 1975). Similarly there can be difficulties talking to industrial workers with broad regional accents, or criminals, who use a lot of criminal slang or 'argot'.

*Different codes.*   We have seen the problems created by lower-class reluctance or inability to use an elaborated code. The restricted code also can be misunderstood: when I was on a jury the following exchange took place:

Barrister:   'And where were you, Mrs X, at 7 o'clock on Friday the 13th?'
Witness:   'I was in the boozer, wasn't I?'
Barrister:   'I don't know, you see I'm trying to find out.'

*Sheer hostility.*   Often there is a lot of convergence, as we have seen, and communication proceeds fairly smoothly. Sometimes however there is so much sheer hostility and distrust that the communication becomes very difficult.

*Non-verbal communication.*   The use of different styles of non-verbal communication is a major problem in intercultural communication. Since ethnic minority groups tend to be lower class, non-verbal communication is therefore relevant to inter-class communications. For example, West Indians take up more space, move about more, smile less and use sudden increases of pitch or volume to add emphasis. Less is known about class differences in non-verbal communication, but these may well be important sources of misunderstanding.

## REFERENCES

Aboud, F.E. (1976) Social developmental aspects of language. *Papers in Linguistics*, 9, 15–37.

Argyle, M. (1987) Rules for relationships in four cultures. *Australian Journal of Psychology*, 38, 309–18.

Argyle, M. (1988) *Bodily Communication*. 2nd edition. London: Methuen.

Argyle, M. (1989) *The Social Psychology of Work*. 2nd edition. Harmondsworth: Penguin.

Argyle, M., Graham, J.A., Campbell, A. and White, P. (1979) The rules of different situations. *New Zealand Psychologist*, 8, 13–22.

Atkinson, P. (1985) *Language, Structure and Reproduction*. London: Methuen.

Bell, R. (1976) *Sociolinguistics: Goals, Approaches and Problems*. London: Batsford.

Bernstein, B. (1962) Social class, linguistic codes and grammatical elements. *Language and Speech*, 5, 221–80.

Bernstein, B. (1971) *Class, Codes and Control*. Vol.1. London: Routledge & Kegan Paul.

Bourhis, R.Y. and Giles, H. (1977) The language of intergroup distinctiveness. In H. Giles (ed.) *Language, Ethnicity and Intergroup Relations*. London: Academic Press, pp. 119–35.

Bourhis, R.Y., Giles, H., Leyens, J.P. and Tajfel, H. (1979) Psycholinguistic distinctiveness: language divergence in Belgium. In H. Giles and R. St. Clair (eds) *Language and Social Psychology*. Oxford: Blackwell, pp. 158–85.

Brown, P. and Levinson, S. (1987) *Politeness: Some Universals in Language Usage*. Cambridge: Cambridge University Press.

Brown, R. and Gilman, A. (1960) The pronouns of power and solidarity. In T.A. Sebeok (ed.) *Style in Language*. Cambridge, Mass.: MIT Press, pp. 253–76.

Burling, R. (1970) *Man's Many Voices: Language in its Cultural Context*. New York: Holt, Rinehart & Winston.

Callery, P.E. (1974) Status perception through syntax. *Language and Speech*, 17, 187–92.

Cheyne, W. (1970) Stereotyped reactions to speakers with Scottish and English regional accents. *British Journal of Social and Clinical Psychology*, 9, 77–9.

Collett, P., Lamb, R., Fenlaugh, K. and McPhail, P. (1981) Social class and linguistic variation. In M. Argyle, A. Furnham and J.A. Graham *Social Situations*. Cambridge: Cambridge University Press.

Cook-Gumperz, J. (1973) *Social Control and Socialization*. London: Routledge.

Coupland, N. (1984) Accommodation at work: some phonological data and their implications. *International Journal of the Sociology of Language*, 46, 49–70.

Dittmar, N. (1976) *Sociolinguistics: A Critical Survey and Theory and Application*. London: Arnold.

Edwards, J.R. (1985) *Language, Society and Identity*. Oxford: Blackwell.

Ellis, D.S. (1967) Speech and social status in America. *Social Forces*, 45, 431–7.

Ervin-Tripp, S.M. (1969) Sociolinguistics. *Advances in Experimental Social Psychology*, 4, 91–165.

Fasold, R. (1990) *The Sociolinguistics of Language*. Oxford: Blackwell.

Giles, H. and Coupland, N. (1991) *Language Contexts and Consequences*. Milton Keynes: Open University Press.

Giles, H. and Powesland, P.F. (1975) *Speech Style and Social Evaluation*. London: Academic Press.

Giles, H. and Smith, P.M. (1979) Accommodation theory: optimal levels of convergence. In H. Giles and R. St. Clair (eds) *Language and Social Psychology*. Oxford: Blackwell, pp. 45–65.

Heider, E.R. (1971) Style and accuracy of verbal communications within and between social classes. *Journal of Personality and Social Psychology*, *18*, 33–47.

Hess, R.D. and Shipman, V. (1965) Early experience and the socialization of cognitive modes in children. *Child Development*, *36*, 869–86.

Honey, J. (1989) *Does Accent Matter?* London: Faber.

Hopper, R. and Williams, F. (1973) Speech characteristics and employability. *Speech Monographs*, *46*, 296–302.

Hudson, R.A. (1980) *Sociolinguistics*. Cambridge: Cambridge University Press.

Johnstone, R.P. and Singleton, C.H. (1977) The ability of middle and working class five-year-olds to encode and decode abstract stimuli. *British Journal of Psychology*, *68*, 237–44.

Labov, W. (1966) *The Social Stratification of English in New York City*. Washington, DC: Center for Applied Linguistics.

Labov, W. (1972) *Language in the Inner City*. Philadelphia: University of Pennsylvania; Oxford: Blackwell.

Labov, W., Cohen, P., Robins, C. and Lewis, J. (1968) *A Study of the Non-Standard English of Negro and Puerto Rican Speakers in New York City*. Vols. 1 and 2. Final Report, Cooperative Research Project 3288. Washington, DC: Office of Health, Education and Welfare.

Lambert, W.E. (1967) A social psychology of bilingualism. *Journal of Social Issues*, *23*, 91–109.

Lambert, W.E., Hodgson, R., Gardner, R.C. and Fillenbaum, S. (1960) Evaluation reactions to spoken languages. *Journal of Abnormal and Social Psychology*, *60*, 44–51.

Lawton, D. (1968) *Social Class, Language and Education*. London: Routledge & Kegan Paul.

Leech, G.N. (1983) *Semantics*. Harmondsworth: Penguin.

Linde, C. (1988) The quantitative study of communication success: politeness and accidents in aviation discourse. *Language in Society*, *17*, 375–99.

Luhman, R. (1990) Appalachian English stereotypes: language attitudes in Kentucky. *Language in Society*, *19*, 331–48.

Pendleton, D. (1983) Doctor–patient communication: a review. In D. Pendleton and D. Hasler (eds) *Doctor–Patient Communication*. London: Academic Press, pp. 5–53.

Pendleton, D. and Bochner, S. (1980) The communication of medical information in general practice consultations as a function of patients' social class. *Social Science and Medicine*, *14A*, 669–73.

Pozner, J. and Saltz, E. (1974) Social class, conditional communication, and egocentric speech. *Developmental Psychology*, *10*, 764–71.

Putnam, G.N. and O'Hern, E. (1955) The status significance of an isolated urban dialect. *Language*, *31*, 1–32.

Quay, L.C., Mathews, M. and Schwarzmueller, B. (1977) Communication encoding and decoding in children from different socioeconomic and racial groups. *Developmental Psychology*, *13*, 415–16.

Robinson, W.P. (1978) *Language Management in Education*. Sydney: Allen Unwin.

Robinson, W.P. and Rackstraw, S.J. (1972) *A Question of Answers*. London: Routledge & Kegan Paul.

Rosenthal, R. and Jacobson, L. (1968) *Pygmalion in the Classroom*. New York: Holt, Rinehart & Winston.

Ryan, E.B. (1979) Why do low-prestige language varieties persist? In H. Giles and R. St Clair (eds) *Language and Social Psychology*. Oxford: Blackwell.

Ryan, E.B. and Giles, H. (eds) (1982) *Attitudes towards Language Variation*. London: Arnold.

Schatzman, L. and Strauss, A. (1955) Class and modes of communication. *American Journal of Sociology*, *60*, 329–38.

Shuy, R., Baratz, J. and Wolfram, W. (1969) *Sociolinguistic Factors in Speech Identification*. National Institute of Mental Health Research Project No. MH-15048–01. Washington, DC: Center for Applied Linguistics.

Simard, L., Taylor, D.M. and Giles, H. (1976) Attribution processes and interpersonal accommodation in a bilingual setting. *Language and Speech*, *19*, 374–87.

Staples, L.M. and Robinson, W.P. (1974) Address forms used by members of a departmental store. *British Journal of Social and Clinical Psychology*, *13*, 131–42.

Thakerar, J.N., Giles, H. and Cheshire, J. (1982) Psychological and linguistic parameters of speech accommodation theory. In C. Fraser and K.R. Scherer (eds) *Advances in the Social Psychology of Language*. Cambridge: Cambridge University Press, pp. 205–55.

Tizard, B., Hughes, M., Carmichael, H. and Pinkerton, G. (1983) Language and social class: is verbal deprivation a myth? *Journal of Child Psychology and Psychiatry*, *24*, 533–42.

Trudgill, P. (1974) *Sociolinguistics: An Introduction*. Harmondsworth: Penguin.

Van Oudenhoven, J-P. and Withag, J. (1983) Influence of social-class information and spelling mistakes on judgment of essays. *Psychological Reports*, *52*, 155–8.

Wiemann, J.M. and Giles, H. (1988) Interpersonal communication. In M. Hewstone, W. Stroebe, J.P. London and G.M. Stephenson (eds) *Introducing Social Psychology*. Oxford: Blackwell, pp. 199–221.

Wilkinson, G. (1975) Patient-audience social status and the social construction of psychiatric disorders: toward a differential frame of reference hypotheses. *Journal of Health and Social Behavior*, *16*, 28–35.

# Chapter 7

# Intelligence and personality

Do members of different classes differ in personality? In other chapters we show that classes differ a lot in attitudes and values, and in speech style. What about more fundamental features of persons like intelligence, extraversion and aggressiveness? We would not expect very large differences here, and we would also expect a large overlap. We shall see an example of such overlap for intelligence in Figure 7.1. If any such class differences are found, the question then arises of the explanation. Are they genetic, are they caused by different kinds of socialisation, are they reactions to different life experiences in each class or perhaps just errors of measurement? We will look at the main dimensions of personality for which there may be class differences.

## INTELLIGENCE

Intelligence has proved difficult to define; sometimes psychologists have given up and said that it is what is measured by intelligence tests. What they have in mind however is a group of abilities to solve problems of different kinds, learn quickly and make rapid perceptual decisions ('inspection time').

Other components are distinguished. Jensen for example separated level I, short-term memory, measured by memory for series of numbers, and level II, conceptual ability, involving verbal knowledge and skills. The Wechsler scales for adults (WAIS) and children (WISC) distinguish verbal and performance measures. Cattell distinguished between 'fluid' intelligence, for solving new problems, which he believed was biologically determined, and 'crystallised', based on culturally acquired skills and ideas.

The intelligence of adults, as measured by such tests, varies with social class, as measured by occupation. Harrell and Harrell (1945) reported the average IQs of 18,782 white males who were called up for the American army. These varied from 128.1 for accountants, 127.6 for lawyers and 126.6 for engineers, to 87.7 for teamsters, 90.6 for miners and 91.4 for farmhands. There are very similar British and French findings, though with smaller numbers of subjects. Accountants, lawyers and engineers were over two

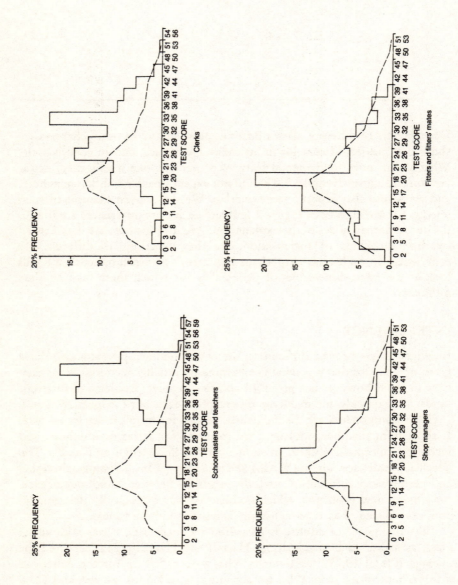

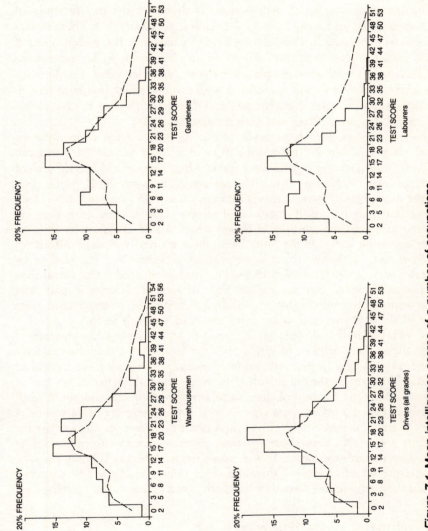

*Figure 7.1* Mean intelligence scores of a number of occupations
*Source*: Himmelweit and Whitfield, 1944

standard deviations above the mean of 100. There is no information about doctors, university teachers or scientists, perhaps because not enough of them were called up. The other occupations come in an approximate skill hierarchy, with least-skilled at the bottom. Nevertheless, there is a wide range of scores within every group. A number of other larger-scale American studies have analysed IQ by the social class of occupation, as shown in Table 7.1.

The extent of overlap of distributions is shown in the British study of 5,000 men called up for the army in World War II (Figure 7.1). These results can also be expressed as a correlation between class and IQ, which is found to be rather higher than the .30–.35 found for children, because social mobility moves intelligent people up the scale, and vice versa. For Jensen's two levels there is a strong correlation with level II, much less with level I. For different sub-scales the strongest correlations with class are for verbal and spatial measures (Scarr and Carter-Salzman, 1982).

Similar analyses have been made of the IQs of children from different social classes. Table 7.1 shows the IQs of a large sample of American children, at different ages, who were tested when Terman and Merrill revised the Binet tests (McNemar, 1942). The correlation between the IQ of children and the social class of their parents is between .30 and .35 (Vernon, 1979). Intelligence tests may be biased in favour of middle-class children, since they are exposed to a larger vocabulary at home, which would explain why they do better on verbal tests. On the other hand, there are nearly as large differences on other tests, including those using abstract problems and intended to be culture free. Stott (1978) studied 15,496 British children aged 7, and found class differences in verbal communication. For the class V children in particular more words were unintelligible, the children were difficult to understand, were more likely to stutter and made more errors in a speech test.

As with the adults, there is a wide range of ability among the children of every social class. Studies of gifted children have found that the majority came from business or professional families and a minority from clerical or manual. However, in the old British 11+, which selected the top 20 per cent in terms of ability, 61 per cent of them came from working-class homes, though the *proportion* of working-class children was lower (there are more working-class children) (Vernon, 1979). It is found that the differences due to class for children are smaller than those for their parents – commonly described as 'regression towards the mean'. This is mainly because parents' IQ only partially predicts the IQ of children – there are other influences. In addition there is mobility after childhood towards jobs which match an individual's intelligence.

## The explanation of class differences in IQ

### Genetics

It is now agreed by all that intelligence is partly inherited. Every aspect of personality requires the contributions both of hereditary properties and of

*Table 7.1* Estimated average IQs for different occupational levels

| Study class | Children | | | | Adults | |
| | Terman-Merrill | Duff and Thompson | Army Alpha | | Cattell | AGCT |
|---|---|---|---|---|---|---|
| I Professional | 116 | 115 | 123 | | 132 | 120 |
| II Semi-professional managerial | 112 | 113 | 119 | | 117 | 113 |
| III Clerical, skilled trades, retail | 107 | 106 | 108 | | 109 | 108 |
| IV Rural owners, farmers | 95 | 97 | 97 | | – | 94 |
| V Semi-skilled, minor clerical | 105 | 102 | 101 | | 105 | 104 |
| VI Slightly skilled | 98 | 97 | 98 | | – | 96 |
| VII Day labourers | 96 | 95 | 96 | | – | 95 |

*Source:* Johnson, 1948

the environment. The point at issue has been which of these is the more important, under the conditions of life which we have, and hence whether intelligence could be raised more effectively by eugenics or by education. There has been much disagreement between those who believe that either genetics or environment is the more important – though the relevant research makes the answer clear enough. Some have cheated, especially Sir Cyril Burt, who seems to have invented both data and research assistants to bolster his hereditarian views. He didn't cheat very much however, and his twin studies show much the same as those of others (Rowe and Plomin, 1978).

From these and other studies it is concluded that the genetic origins of IQ have more weight than environmental ones, and that heredity accounts for up to 70 per cent of the variance (Scarr and Carter-Salzman, 1982; Vernon, 1979).

The genetic explanation of class differences has two further components. It is assumed that there is social mobility of intelligent individuals upwards and less intelligent ones downwards. As we show in Chapter 8, there is clear evidence that this takes place. It is also supposed that there is 'assortative mating', i.e. people marry spouses of similar IQ, which has the effect of increasing class differences between children of different classes. In fact husband–wife IQs correlate at about .40.

However, it does not follow that the difference between classes are due to inheritance – they could be due to systematic environmental differences between classes.

### The effect of environment

*The home.* A number of studies have analysed the effects on the IQs of adopted children of different features of the home environment. Variables such as education of parents, mother's teaching skills, hours spent with child, father reading to child and availability of books have all been found to predict child IQ. Burks (1928), in an early and historic study, found a multiple correlation between such variables and adopted child IQ of .42, i.e. 18 per cent of the variance, which would explain the gain found of 5 points, since the IQ level of the adopting homes was a half to one standard deviation above average. Later studies obtained similar results. Other studies, involving thousands of children, have obtained very similar results (Iverson and Walberg, 1982).

Scarr and Carter-Salzman (1982) showed how mother's IQ is a partial predictor of her teaching skills, but that both affect child IQ (Figure 7.2).

It is variables like these which vary with social class and which can explain the environmental part of class differences in IQ.

*Family size*, i.e. number of siblings, is another family predictor of low IQ. As we saw in Chapter 4, lower-class families tend to have more children.

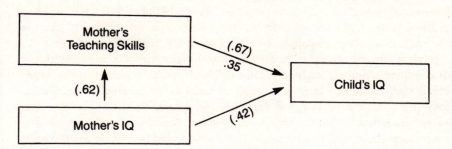

*Figure 7.2* Correlations among child's IQ, mother's teaching skills and mother's IQ (in parentheses); the partial regression coefficient of child IQ on mother's teaching skills with mother's IQ is partialled out
*Source:* Bond and Joffe, 1982
*Note:* ( ) = zero order correlation coefficients.

And family size, with social class held constant, predicts low IQ, with correlations of about −.2 to −.3. Vernon (1951) found that families of one or two had average IQs of 106, and that this declined to 87 for families of thirteen. Douglas *et al.* (1968) followed up all the 3,418 children born in Britain in the first week of March 1946. At the ages of 8 and 11, in families with six or more children, these had substantially lower intelligence than for those in families with one or two children. This was particularly true of verbal measures of intelligence; there was less difference when parents were very interested in their children's progress or when they went to good schools, and there was little difference for the children of unskilled labourers. In a later study of the same group Douglas and colleagues (1968) found that family size continued to affect educational success at age 15; the children from larger families scored lower in attainment tests, were more likely to leave school early (and not just for financial reasons), obtained worse O level grades, and had lower aspirations. In American studies Zajonc (1976) had found a systematic relationship between size of family and low IQ, which he explained in terms of the average intelligence level in the family environment being lower when there are more children.

*Education.* Going to school enhances the IQ of children. It has been calculated that each year of additional schooling adds 2½ points of IQ. In Britain, when the brighter children went to grammar schools, the initial difference of 7 points of IQ compared with secondary modern pupils increased to 12 points after three years (Vernon, 1979). Raz and Bryant (1990) carried out a study of eighty 4–6-year-old children from two social classes. The middle-class children read better and understood spoken speech better; the superior reading was not due to IQ, and appeared only after the children went to school. It was found that reading ability depended on ability to understand spoken prose, and it appeared that school experiences were more important than home experiences here – the middle-class children profited more from school than working-class children, probably because they went to better schools or because they were more attentive.

Such findings have led to large-scale social experiments to raise the ability of deprived children, such as Head Start and similar schemes in the USA. Head Start was a very large-scale multi-million dollar scheme for compensatory pre-school education for deprived and ethnic children. The contents varied according to local needs, and included health care and provision of play materials, as well as education. It was concluded from follow-up studies that Head Start had been a failure. This was partly because, although Head Start children had slightly higher IQs at 4, these gains faded by age 8; it is not clear why. Increases in IQ were retained when there was continued educational support, as given to middle-class children. There were greater gains in Cattell's crystallised intelligence (based on acquired skills) than on fluid intelligence. However, Head Start was not a single scheme but included a wide variety, some of them very minimal and unlikely to have much effect. And other gains from Head Start have been discovered – improved health and better performance in school (Zigler and Seitz, 1982).

Head Start was followed by similar but more intensive schemes, some of them starting earlier at $2\frac{1}{2}$; several of these resulted in gains of IQ of 10–12 points by age 8. In one of them, education was combined with nutritional supplements and health care from 43 months to 87 months. McKay *et al.* (1978) found that four treatment periods led to an average IQ of 92.4, one treatment period to 82.0, a difference of over 10 points by age 8. However, untreated middle-class children still averaged more, 109.2. Middle-class children normally attend both nursery schools and good schools after that, and this is part of the explanation for the class differences in IQ.

## SOCIAL COMPETENCE

Do classes differ in social competence or do they have different kinds of skills? The most careful studies have been carried out with children. Gottman and co-workers (1975) gave 198 8–9-year-old children several measures of social competence. The higher-class children did better on all measures – decoding facial expressions for emotion, seeing another's point. of view and role-playing making friends and giving help. These children also gave more positive reinforcement in class, which was more verbal than non-verbal, gave and received less negative reinforcement, and interacted more with teachers. Pellegrini (1985) gave 100 9–11-year-olds some different tests. The higher-social-class children did better on a measure of interpersonal understanding of filmstrips, were rated by peers as more positive and less isolated and by teachers as less disruptive. They were also more intelligent, but this could not explain the differences in competence, since it had quite a low correlation with them. Gollin (1958) held IQ constant in a study of over 600 10–17-year-olds. At 13½ and 16½, the middle-class children did better on inferences from films, e.g. ascribing motives, and much better on accounting for the behaviour of different children (one good, one bad) in the films. From these three studies there is clear evidence that middle-class children between 8 and 16 have superior social skills, both when measured experimentally and when rated by peers and teachers. The skills include taking the role of the other, rewardingness and social understanding.

At an earlier age, 4.1, it has been found that middle-class children had greater knowledge of rules and conventions (r = .29), and of the rationale for them (r = .33). This was due to interaction with parents, mainly to experience of negative non-verbal reactions to rule-breaking (Johnson and McGillicuddy-Delisi, 1983).

Middle-class adults have the reputation of being more socially competent. We described reactions to accents earlier, and reported that people with middle-class or educated accents are perceived by students as having higher social status, and as more intelligent, ambitious and persuasive.

Do middle-class adults really have better social skills, and if so in which areas of skill? As we showed in Chapter 6, middle-class adults, as well as children, speak with a different linguistic code – with longer sentences, more subordinate clauses and more correct grammar. It has also been found that working-class people take less account of the possibly different point of view of listeners while they are speaking. Schatzman and Strauss (1953) analysed the speech of lower-class speakers describing a tornado. It was found that they failed to take account of the lack of knowledge of the listener. Experiments have shown that middle-class children are more effective in conveying information in a laboratory task (e.g. Heider, 1971).

It is possible that working-class people possess *different* social skills. Bernstein suggested that the 'restricted code' is good for immediate face-to-face communication between people who know each other well (p. 128). Speakers of regional accents may be seen as less intelligent and ambitious, but they are also seen as having a better sense of humour, and as more likeable (p. 135).

We can take a little further the question of the social skills of adults by examining the skills requirements of different jobs.

*Class I.* Some class I jobs demand a high level of social skills, including some difficult ones like public performance (politicians, lecturers), negotiations in conflict situations (lawyers, some managers), complex intimate skills (psychiatry, clergy). Other class I jobs require many fewer social skills – scientists, engineers, computing and accountants.

*Class II.* Nearly all these jobs involve working with people – teachers, social workers, managers, nurses, and generally a high level of social skill is needed and developed.

*Class III (non-manual).* These jobs, too, often require a lot of social contact. Sales is a difficult skill: any job which requires dealing with the public means coping with a wide variety of people, e.g. in post offices, local government, and many secretaries.

*Class III (manual).* Some of these jobs also involve dealing with people. Supervision of working groups is a difficult skill. Hairdressers and bus drivers need much simpler social skills; other skilled manual workers need very little.

*Classes IV and V.* Much less social skill is needed for most of these jobs.

Some confirmation for this model is provided by occupational differences in extraversion, which are shown on p. 159. Extraversion has some correlation with general social competence. What we have suggested here are more specific occupational differences in social skills. Further confirmation is provided by class differences in affiliative motivation (p. 164), if we assume that the motivation to affiliate leads to more practice and hence more skill at doing it.

We can try to explain why middle-class people are more socially skilled. The main explanation for adults is that most middle-class jobs require social skills. For those who are promoted because of their technical skill, e.g. doctors and industrial engineers, special training courses are often provided. For most, success at the job is dependent on skilled social performance, so that there is a major incentive to becoming skilled. Failure at social performance is likely to result in downward mobility. This does not explain however why middle-class children should also be more socially skilled. Part of the reason may be that, because of the occupational demands just described, middle-class culture establishes and passes on such skills to the next generation. Social competence is correlated with intelligence, especially social understanding, so that class differences in IQ may be partly responsible. The greater speech skills of middle-class children may be caused by the greater amount of verbal interaction with parents (p. 84).

## EXTRAVERSION

Extraversion is one of the main general dimensions of personality, and corresponds to sociability and a preference for action rather than thinking. It has been the object of extensive research in Britain as a result of the ideas and measures due to Eysenck. In the earlier questionnaire measures (the Maudsley Personality Inventory and Eysenck Personality Inventory) the extraversion (E) scale included a number of items about impulsiveness, which were transferred to the psychoticism (P) scale in the Eysenck Personality Questionnaire (EPQ). The revised E scale is primarily a measure of sociability, largely purified of impulsiveness items, similar to American measures of extraversion.

Several large-scale studies report data on the E scores of different classes, and most of them find no class differences (Francis and Pearson, 1989). One early study using the EPI found that males in classes IV and V had lower scores (Eysenck and Eysenck, 1975), but this has not been replicated in later studies. There are certainly no differences for children from different classes (Francis and Pearson, 1989).

However, there is evidence that impulsiveness, previously regarded as part of extraversion, but now known to be more closely linked to psychoticism, is higher for working-class people. Sybil Eysenck and Allsopp (1986) compared 282 male students with 264 craftsmen: the craftsmen scored 14.50, the students 12.12 on impulsiveness, and there was a similar difference on psychoticism. Working-class children are found to be more impulsive in problem-solving tasks, where middle-class children are more likely to stop and think before answering, and consequently make fewer mistakes. However, this 'may represent merely the low-SES child's reluctance to sit quietly, listen and to think about school tasks' (Vernon, 1979, p. 126).

Although there is no consistent evidence for class differences in extraversion, there are certainly occupational differences. *The Manual of the EPQ* (Eysenck and Eysenck, 1975) gives norms for a number of different occupations, as shown in Table 7.2.

*Table 7.2* Extraversion and occupation

|  | Males | Females |
| --- | --- | --- |
| Service workers | 16.04 | 15.09 |
| Sales | 15.46 | 13.86 |
| Medical students | 14.04 | 13.33 |
| Student teachers | 13.66 | 13.21 |
| Insurance | 13.62 | |
| Managers | 13.39 | |
| Actors | 12.21 | |
| Telephonists | | 13.03 |
| Receptionists | | 13.02 |
| Secretaries | | 12.55 |
| Population means | 13.19 | 12.60 |

These are all jobs which involve constantly dealing with people and they mostly have well above-average E scores. They belong to a wide range of classes: medical students will soon be in I, student teachers in II, secretaries and sales staff are mostly in IIIn and telephonists in IV, for example. The majority however are probably in II and IIIn. At the introvert end of the scale are scientists, engineers and architects (mostly I), but also machinists and domestic workers (III and IV).

Do extraverts choose sociable occupations, or does the job make them more extraverted? Studies of the job preferences of students find that introverts are much more likely to prefer technical, task-oriented professions – science, engineering and skilled manual work. Extraverts prefer people-oriented jobs like sales, personnel work and teaching, but they also go for traditional high-status professions (Morris, 1979). It is not known whether being a teacher or secretary makes people more extraverted; they would certainly learn some social skills. Headey and Wearing (1991) found that extraversion led to positive experience at work and with friends, and this in turn led to increased extraversion.

Need for affiliation is similar to extraversion. In an American national survey of 1,371 adults, Veroff *et al.* (1960) found that people in higher-status occupations had higher scores, while those working on farms had the lowest, followed by unskilled and semi-skilled workers. There were similar effects of education, especially for women.

## NEUROTICISM, NEGATIVE EMOTIONALITY

This is another classic, well-established dimension of personality. At one extreme it identifies individuals who are suffering from mental disorder, or who could benefit from treatment, about 15 per cent of the population. At the other end of the dimension are those who are exceptionally stable, and able to stand up to stress. The dimension can be measured by the neuroticism scale of the Eysenck Personality Questionnaire (EPQ), by the General Health Questionnaire (GHQ) or by single items.

As we shall show later in more detail, although the EPQ does not show any class differences, other measures do, e.g. the GHQ, measures of depression, a variety of single items, and statistics of diagnosed mental patients. The differences between classes are not great: Veroff *et al.* (1981) in the USA found that, of the poorest group sampled, 25.5 per cent had felt that they were going to have a nervous breakdown, compared with 16.5 per cent for the richest group. Warr and Payne (1982) in Britain found that 7 per cent of classes I–IIIn reported unpleasant emotional strain yesterday, compared with 14 per cent for classes IV and V. The differences in true mental disorder are much greater than this and will be discussed in Chapter 11.

There is of course a lot of variation in neuroticism within each class, but there is evidently a clear, though modest, difference between classes. The causes of this class difference will be discussed later, and we will conclude that it is partly due to the greater stressfulness of working-class life, the lack of resources, social and financial, and to certain personality differences, e.g. in locus of control and coping style. These in turn can be explained through class differences in child-rearing, and are discussed later.

## AGGRESSIVENESS

Aggression is not a broad dimension of personality; it is a particular, and very important, sphere of behaviour. It can be assessed by rating the behaviour, for example, of children at play, by self-report inventories, measures of aggressiveness in the laboratory or records of arrest for violent offenders.

There are some quite substantial class differences here, however aggressiveness is measured.

1 Working-class children are rated as more aggressive in play situations.
2 Football hooligans are almost entirely from the lowest classes (see p. 253).
3 Working-class crime rates are much higher than middle-class ones especially for violent offences, including assault, murder and, in the USA, lynchings (cf. p. 249).
4 Working-class parents use more physical punishment on their children (p. 163).

Some of these forms of aggression are quite rare, such as violent offences. Others are very common: for example 40 per cent of class V parents in Britain make frequent use of physical punishment for 7-year-old children, compared with 21 per cent of class I and II parents (see p. 163).

What are the causes of aggression, and why are they class-linked?

*Inheritance.* Twin studies show that aggressiveness is about 50 per cent inherited (Rushton *et al.*, 1986). In addition a few males have an extra Y chromosome (XYYs) which makes them very aggressive: 1 in 550 in the normal population, but up to 1 in 35 in prisons (Geen, 1990). The higher proportion of violent offenders in lower classes may be partly genetic.

Causal modelling of the generation of aggressiveness (Figure 7.3) shows that early temperamental aggressiveness by boys causes both rejection and permissiveness for aggression by mothers (Olweus *et al.*, 1980).

There are a number of features of children which contribute to rejection or violence on the part of parents – being physically unattractive, overactive, defiant or physically aggressive (Parke and Slaby, 1983). Aggressive boys are found to have high levels of testosterone, but low levels of adrenaline (Olweus *et al.*, 1986).

*Socialization.* There is extensive evidence from several countries showing that aggressiveness is caused by certain kinds of child-rearing:

1 rejection, coldness, hostility v. affection;
2 permissiveness, lax supervision;
3 high levels of physical punishment, threats, outbursts of anger and other power-assertive methods;
4 inconsistent discipline, disagreement between parents over child-rearing.

Unaggressive children have parents who are warm, monitor and discipline aggression, and who reward pro-social and unaggressive solutions to problems.

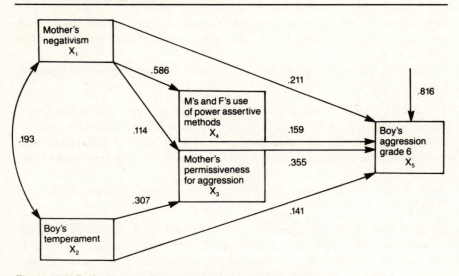

*Figure 7.3* Path diagram for causal model of aggression
*Source:* Olweus *et al.*, 1980

Families contribute to the aggressiveness of children when aggressive patterns of interaction develop in the family, with parents or with peers. Parents become increasingly punitive if a child reacts to discipline by defiance or further aggression. Children can learn aggressiveness by frequent fights with siblings, if parents fail to restrain these (Patterson, 1986). Some children are unresponsive to parental supervision – those who seek immediate rewards, who are not responsive to social stimuli but only to physical ones, or who are lacking in social skills, so that aggression is the only form of influence they know (Parke and Slaby, 1983).

There is a very clear class difference in some of these child-rearing variables – especially in the use of physical punishment. Newson and Newson (1968, 1976) studied families in Nottingham, when the children were 4 and 7, and found differences at both ages (Table 7.3).

Erlanger (1974) re-analysed a number of large-scale American studies of this topic. Middle-class families reported less use of physical punishment, but the differences were small and decreasing with time. The correlation between class and frequency of physical punishment was between .10 and .15. The most educated were least likely to spank, especially those with post-graduate qualifications. Working-class parents however probably punish more severely, for example more used a strap.

Miller and Swanson (1960) studied samples of middle- and working-class American adults and found that the working-class subjects expressed aggression more directly in a projection test, and that this was correlated with experience of physical punishment. Middle-class people expressed aggression indirectly, and this was correlated with experience of psychological,

*Table 7.3* Physical punishment and other forms of discipline (percentages)

|  | I & II | IIIn | IIIm | IV | V |
|---|---|---|---|---|---|
| **Age 4** | | | | | |
| Smacks once a week to once a day | 61 | 68 | 70 | 66 | 79 |
| Uses less than once a week | 33 | 23 | 20 | 24 | 11 |
| Threat of authority figure | 10 | 23 | 29 | 29 | 46 |
| Threat to send away or leave | 10 | 34 | 29 | 27 | 30 |
| **Age 7** | | | | | |
| Frequent use of corporal punishment | 21 | 27 | 34 | 31 | 40 |

*Source:* Newson and Newson, 1968, 1976

i.e. withdrawal of love, discipline. On warmth and rejection, working-class fathers are home less, spend less time with the children and punish them more; middle-class fathers establish a warmer relationship and are more likely to share an interest with them.

We have just seen that parental control of aggression is important. There is restraint of aggression in all classes; it is governed by informal rules, about when, where and how to hit, and with what. However, the restraints on lower-working-class aggression, towards children as towards spouses and others, appear to be less. Indeed aggression is not only normal, but it can be positively valued; being 'macho' is a source of esteem (p. 253).

There are other features of many working-class families which are relevant here. As we showed earlier (p. 84), they are larger, mothers are younger, more often unmarried and more likely to be working. All this makes adequate supervision more difficult. In addition, the pressures on many working-class mothers are likely to make them less patient, and more likely to respond aggressively to their children.

*Situational arousal of aggression.* Aggression is aroused by attacks, insults (attacks on self-esteem), arbitrary frustration, pain, heat and alcohol. Frustration and attacks on self-esteem are more common for low-status people, for example at work, or from being rejected for work, through inadequate housing, transport difficulties, etc. (p. 275). The resulting aggression is likely to be displaced onto targets other than the original source, e.g. white lower-class Americans in the deep South lynching blacks during periods of economic depression. Frustrated or angry people may turn to drink; 64 per cent of violent crimes are committed under its influence. Frustration can be high for children in bad homes – poverty, overcrowding, not enough food, not enough room to play, bad-tempered and drunken parents; this would be expected to result in greater aggressiveness at an early age.

## ACHIEVEMENT MOTIVATION (n.Ach)

This is generally understood as the motivation to succeed, to seek excellence, to work hard to attain goals. This may be at school or college work, at sport, careers and promotion, by making money or in other ways. It is not agreed whether the motive is mainly to seek approval of others or to attain internally defined goals (Zigler and Child, 1969).

McClelland (1987) started the tradition of research into n.Ach, and measured it by a projection test, derived from the Thematic Apperception Test, in which subjects write stories or answer questions about the characters in vaguely drawn pictures, which are then scored for achievement-related themes. Subjects are given high scores if they imagine the characters striving for success, being successful, overcoming obstacles, etc. Projection tests have a bad reputation with most psychologists nowadays, because of the difficulty of scoring, and because subjects can get different scores with different testers, or on different occasions. And there are other, easier measures, such as direct self-report questionnaires. Nevertheless, McClelland presents evidence that the projective measure is a better predictor of achievement behaviour than such other methods.

*Class differences.* A number of American studies have found clear class differences in n.Ach. Veroff and co-workers (1960) carried out an American nation-wide sample survey and found clear though modest differences for different occupational groups as well as for income and education. The occupational differences were larger for affiliative motivation. This could be due, in part, to upward mobility of those high in n.Ach (see p. 187). However, other studies show that class differences are already present in children and students.

Larger class differences were found by Rosen (1956) with a sample of 120 male schoolboys, aged 14–16 (Table 7.4). In a later study Rosen (1959) found that at the highest levels of prosperity n.Ach levels fall again, probably because no further challenges remained. While similar class differences in n.Ach are found for black Americans, their scores do not fall off at the highest levels of prosperity – for them there is still further to climb. However, low-social-class blacks have a very low score (McClelland, 1987).

Douvan (1956) and others have found that offering a ten-dollar reward

*Table 7.4* Achievement motivation and social class of schoolboys

|        | % high n.Ach |
|--------|--------------|
| I, II  | 83           |
| III    | 43           |
| IV     | 30           |
| V      | 23           |

*Source:* Rosen, 1956

had much less effect on the task performance of middle-class compared with working-class children after they had been caused to 'fail'. The conclusion drawn was that the middle-class children were motivated by internalised achievement motivation, not by external incentives, though $10 would mean more to poorer children anyway.

*Explanations of class differences in n.Ach.* The most important known source of n.Ach is socialisation and some of the relevant dimensions of socialisation are also known to vary with social class.

The main socialisation origins so far discovered are:

a. early demands and rewards for independent accomplishment, well before age 8 (Winterbottom, 1958);
b. setting high levels of aspiration, more positive affect and directions and encouragement while performing achievement tasks (Rosen and D'Andrade, 1959);
c. children also need to experience success rather than failure, as well as receiving parental approval;
d. n.Ach will be higher if achievement values permeate the whole home atmosphere and that of the surrounding subculture (Zigler and Child, 1969).

Turner (1970) studied 639 13–14-year-old children, from three different communities. He found a class difference in achievement motivation, but an even greater effect of coming from entrepreneurial (i.e. business) families. N.Ach scores were higher for owners and managers of businesses, but also for blue-collar entrepreneurs like plumbers and small builders who owned their own businesses. The class difference usually found could be due to the greater number of middle-class people in this kind of job.

A number of sociological studies in the USA and Britain have found that middle-class families are more likely to use the pattern of child-rearing described above. They do so because they believe that they should prepare their children for a social setting in which individual competition and achievement is needed for success, and where individuals are personally responsible for success and failure. Manual workers experience a world where external factors, like lay-offs, are important, where individuals contribute to a group product, and there is little individual success or failure (Douvan, 1956; Klein, 1965).

Achievement motivation may also have a biological basis. Boys with higher scores tend to be more mesomorphic, i.e. muscular, which is linked with a higher energy level, but is not known to be connected with social class (Cortes and Gatti, 1966). N.Ach is greater for first-born and only children, and this *is* more common for middle-class children, because of the smaller families. Finally achievement motivation is correlated with early 'ego development', or impulse control, which is also stronger for middle-class children, and is the subject of a later section.

## LOCUS OF CONTROL

Some people believe that they can control what is going to happen, in their own lives, and also that they have some power to influence wider events; these are 'internal controllers'. Others believe that other people, outside events, fate or chance are more important. The internal–external control variable can be measured by a simple questionnaire (Rotter, 1966), and has been found to be a predictor of a wide range of behaviours, and outcomes. The sort of item is:

'Whether I make a success of my life is entirely up to me.'

*or*

'Success is a matter of being lucky enough to be in the right place at the right time.'

(Hampson, 1988)

Many studies have found that middle-class people are more internal and working-class individuals more external.

Some of these studies used the Rotter test (Phares, 1976). Some used a single item: Veroff *et al.* (1981) found that 89 per cent of college-educated people had high internal scores, compared to 66 per cent of those whose education ended at grade school.

Kohn and Schooler (1983), with a sample of over 4,000 US males, used a number of questions in a 2½-hour interview, and then found scores on a factor of self-directedness, which is much the same as internal control and measures 'the belief that one has the personal capacity to take responsibility for one's actions and that society is so constituted as to make self-direction possible' (p. 146). In cross-sectional analyses self-directedness had a high correlation with social class: .68 in 1964, .70 in 1974. Social class was measured by a combination of education, income and occupational status, the latter divided into five levels.

Evans (1988) developed a new measure of perceived powerlessness and found class differences for the three components as shown in Table 7.5.

It can be seen that the greatest class differences are for work-related powerlessness and smaller differences for socio-political and personal powerlessness.

*Table 7.5* Means of dimensions of powerlessness by social class of respondent

| Dimensions of powerlessness | Middle | Means Intermediate | Working |
|---|---|---|---|
| Socio-political | −.52 | .06 | .31 |
| Personal | −.24 | .09 | .09 |
| Work-related | −.43 | .01 | .50 |

*Source:* Evans, 1989

## Explanation of class differences

Kohn and Schooler (1983) showed that self-directedness is a function of work experience. They found class differences in self-directedness and in parental valuation of self-direction. This could be explained by differences in work experience of self-direction: internal self-direction was greatest in men whose work (a) did not involve close supervision, and was (b) complex, and (c) not routine or repetitive. Self-direction was greatest for managers, followed by employers, non-manual and manual workers. Longitudinal analysis over an interval of ten years showed that occupational experience caused self-direction, though there was also a smaller tendency for those high in self-direction to find self-directing jobs. The main findings of this study have been replicated several times, not only in the USA but also in Japan, Poland and elsewhere (Kohn *et al.*, 1990).

The second main cause of internal control so far located is amount of education. We saw above that college-educated individuals tend to be more internal. Kohn and Schooler found that education was a predictor both of self-directedness and of having a self-directed job. Wright and Wright (1976) found that education was a more important source of self-directedness than occupation.

Socialisation is another source of locus of control, which was originally conceptualised as a learned set of generalised expectancies about the causes of rewards. First-born and only children are a little more internal (Falbo, 1981) – and a little more common in the middle class. And socialisation studies have found evidence that internals are more often from homes where mothers were warm and nurturant, externals from homes where children were punished a lot (Phares, 1976).

Internal and external control may be passed on from parents to children. Kohn and Schooler (1973) found that working-class men 'as soon as they have taken off their working clothes . . . they treat wives and children as they are treated by their bosses, demand subjection, service, authority'.

## INTERNALISED GOALS AND RESTRAINTS

### Parental restraints

It has been widely assumed that middle-class children internalise parental values, including parental restraints, more than working-class children. This is supported by the weaker restraints on aggression in working-class boys described earlier and the far higher rate of delinquency, reported in Chapter 10 (p. 249). A number of early American studies found that middle-class children more often accepted their parents' authority and respected their parents, while lower-class children were frequently hostile, dependent and obeyed parental rules rigidly through fear of punishment (Mussen and Conger, 1956).

Perhaps the strongest evidence on this topic comes from studies of class differences in socialisation, since these have known consequences for internalisation. A once widely accepted view of American life was that 'the working class is typically characterised as impulsive and uninhibited, the middle class are more rational, controlled, and guided by a broader perspective in time' (Bronfenbrenner, 1958). And

> The lower class pattern of life ... puts a high premium on physical gratification, on free expression of aggression, on spending and sharing. Cleanliness, respect for property, sexual control, educational achievement – all are highly valued by middle class Americans – are of less importance to the lower class family or are phrased differently.
>
> (Clausen, 1957)

Bronfenbrenner (1958) reviewed a number of studies carried out in the USA between 1932 and 1957, and found that there were considerable changes during this period, as parents became more permissive and working-class parents moved towards middle-class styles. However, throughout the period, working-class parents made more use of physical punishment, while middle-class parents used reasoning, isolation, appeals to guilt and other methods involving threat of loss of love. Many studies have shown that this middle-class style is more likely to produce internalised values and controls (Zigler and Child, 1969). In addition, Bronfenbrenner's review found that middle-class parents were more accepting and egalitarian, working-class ones concerned more with obedience and keeping order. This was confirmed in the large and more recent study by Kohn and Schooler (1983). No class differences have been found in warmth of relationships with mothers, but middle-class children see more of their fathers, and play with them more (p. 85), and middle-class mothers spend about twice as much time 'talking' to their babies during the first year of life (Kagan and Tulkie, 1971).

## Long-term plans and delayed reward

There is some evidence that middle-class children and adults seek longer-term goals, and can wait for larger rewards later. A clear demonstration of this was the study by Schmidt et al. (1978) of 125 German employees, male and female, between 35 and 45. They were asked to describe their hopes and fears, for themselves and more broadly, and the dates when relevant events might take place. The average numbers of years ahead for the most distant events are shown in Table 7.6.

It has often been believed that middle-class young people put up with more deferred gratification, for income and consumption, possibly marriage, because of their long period of education and training. Straus (1962) found that there was deferred gratification for economic independence, but not for sex or consumption. On the other side it can be pointed out that

*Table 7.6* Time span for most distant hopes and fears (years)

|  |  | Middle class | Working class |
|---|---|---|---|
| Personal | male | 15.0 | 7.2 |
|  | female | 13.7 | 13.0 |
| Public | male | 29.8 | 12.7 |
|  | female | 19.9 | 15.5 |

*Source:* Schmidt *et al.*, 1978

middle-class youth, with their years in college, are obtaining more gratification in the spheres of leisure and friendship than many working-class youth, who are already at work.

Some experiments have found that middle-class children will defer gratification now for a larger reward later, but a careful study by Levy (1976) failed to obtain this result, in fact finding a trend in the opposite direction. The widely held theory that middle-class young are more ambitious (Hyman, 1953) may not be entirely correct. It is true that they have a greater desire to go to college, but this is more normal and accessible for them. They hope for good jobs for the same reason. Working-class youth in the USA may gain less from education, and may prefer the immediate and long-term economic advantages of a skilled job (Keller and Zavalloni, 1974).

Among adults, working-class individuals have much higher scores on measures of 'anomie', that is believing that there is little prospect of achieving life goals and hence avoidance of thinking about the future. Anomie is greater among social groups with poor chances in life, including those who are socially isolated, members of minority religions or divorced, but social class is the strongest predictor (Koenig *et al.*, 1981).

## Internalised motivation for work

People in middle-class jobs have a stronger motivation for work, which is not based on the hope of material rewards. For example, in Britain 87 per cent of class I and II feel that work is more than just earning a living (54 per cent of IV and V) (Mann, 1986). In the top three classes 49 per cent think that doing a socially useful job is important (25 per cent in bottom two). On the other hand, only 14 per cent of the top three classes would find extra work for extra pay (21 per cent in lowest two) (Abrams, 1985). Evidently the Protestant Work Ethic is stronger for middle-class workers; we show later than it is also a source of upward social mobility (p. 189).

Research on the motivation to work finds that some individuals are motivated and satisfied by complex and demanding jobs, where they can accomplish something, learn new skills and develop themselves. There is some disagreement about the percentage of workers for whom this is important, but it probably includes most managers and technical staff. There are other workers, paid less and doing more boring work, for whom it is not important and who work mostly for the pay (Goldthorpe *et al.*, 1968), though perhaps too for the social life (Argyle, 1989). While doctors, lawyers and other highly paid professionals no doubt enjoy their work and think it worthwhile, they also charge high fees by the hour, so seem to be enjoying the financial rewards as well. Studies of managers have found that those at higher levels say they are motivated and satisfied most by 'self-realisation', rather than by security, social needs, esteem or autonomy (Porter, 1964). In a survey of 574 households, Agnew (1983) confirmed that working-class individuals were more concerned than middle-class ones with income and job security, and middle-class people with doing 'important work'. However, both were equally concerned with the hope for job advancement.

There is some evidence that these class differences appear earlier in life. Several experiments have found that introducing a monetary incentive makes working-class children try harder at laboratory tasks and tests, but has no effect on middle-class children (p. 165).

### Ego-strength

This Freudian-sounding concept has re-appeared in the work of Block (1971) and others, to mean control of impulsiveness. It has been measured by various questionnaires. There is a little evidence that it is class-related, for example an early British study by Oppenheim (1955) in a survey of 312 13-year-olds. The middle-class children, when choosing a friend, preferred someone who was serious rather than happy-go-lucky, was more emotionally controlled, saved money and was keen on school work.

The topic is being introduced here more as a hypothesis, that there is a substantial class difference, with known roots in socialisation, which can help to account for some of the other differences described in this chapter.

Block (1971) found that ego-control was produced by mothers who were loving, patient, encouraged discussion of feelings and problems, and where the parents were concerned with moral, philosophical or other intellectual interests. An earlier, Russian, tradition of psychological research due to Vygotsky and Luria in this area emphasised the importance of inner speech, directing one's own behaviour by words. The later, American, version has been research on how children learn to use plans and instruct themselves to resist temptations. Training in the use of inner speech has proved to be an effective method of self-control in therapy (Harter, 1983). It seems very likely that there are class differences, partly due to differences in verbal intelligence, but also because middle-class parents talk to their children a lot more (Klein, 1965).

## CONCLUSIONS

We have seen that middle-class children have on average a higher IQ; this is due to a combination of genetics, home environment, and education. Class differences for adults are greater, as the result of social mobility. There are similar differences in social competence, found at age 5. Middle-class people are a little more extraverted, have stronger affiliative motivation, are somewhat less impulsive and on average lower in neuroticism.

Aggressiveness in several spheres is greater for working-class people. This can partly be accounted for by the greater use of physical punishment by parents, but more by the weaker induction of restraints and the frustrations of working-class life.

Middle-class children acquire stronger achievement motivation, especially in business families, as a result of early parental demands for independence and other aspects of child-rearing. Internal locus of control is stronger for middle-class people and has been traced to parental style, in turn caused by experience of autonomy and self-direction at work. Middle-class children internalise parental values and restraints more, and learn to seek long-term rewards.

The explanation of these class differences may be partly genetic, as in the case of intelligence, and physique, which will be discussed in the next chapter. More important however are the effects of class-related styles of parental socialisation. These traditions are partly the result of different cultural values and education, partly due to the different demands and experience of middle-class and working-class jobs. Class differences in personality and ability are partly caused by social mobility, e.g. intelligent people tend to move upwards, as we shall describe in the next chapter.

## REFERENCES

Abrams, M. (1985) Demographic correlates of values. In M. Abrams, D. Gerard and N. Timms (eds) *Values and Social Change in Britain*. Basingstoke: Macmillan.

Agnew, R.S. (1983) Social class and success goals: an examination of relative and absolute aspirations. *Sociological Quarterly*, 24, 435–52.

Argyle, M. (1989) *The Social Psychology of Work*. 2nd edition. Harmondsworth: Penguin.

Bell, W. (1957) Anomie, social isolation and the class structure. *Sociometry*, 20, 105–16.

Block, J. (1971) *Lives through Time*. Berkeley, Calif.: Bancroft Books.

Bond, L.A. and Joffe, J.M. (eds) (1982) *Facilitating Infant and Early Childhood Development*. Hanover NH: University Press of New England.

Bronfenbrenner, U. (1958) Socialization and social class through time and space. In E. Maccoby, T. Newcomb and E. Hartley (eds) *Readings in Social Psychology*. 3rd edition. New York: Holt.

Burks, B.S. (1928) The relative influence of nature and nurture upon mental development: a comparative study of foster parent–foster child resemblance and true parent–true child resemblance. *27th Yearbook of the National Society for the Study of Education*, 27, 219–316.

Chebat, J-C. (1986) Social responsibility, locus of control, and social class. *Journal of Social Psychology*, *126*, 559–64.

Clausen, J.A. (1957) Social and psychological factors in narcotics addiction. *Law and Contemporary Problems*, *22*, 34–51. Cited by Bronfenbrenner, 1958.

Cohen, J. (1985) Protestant ethic and status-attainment. *Sociological Analysis*, *46*, 49–58.

Cortes, J.B. and Gatti, E.M. (1966) Physique and motivation. *Journal of Consulting Psychology*, *30*, 408–13.

Douglas, J.W.B., Ross, J.M. and Simpson, H.R. (1968) *All Our Future*. London: Peter Davies.

Douvan, E. (1956) Social status and success strivings. *Journal of Abnormal and Social Psychology*, *52*, 219–23.

Duckitt, J. (1983) Culture, class, personality, and authoritarianism among white South Africans. *Journal of Social Psychology*, *121*, 191–9.

Erlanger, H.S. (1974) Social class and corporal punishment in childrearing: a reassessment. *American Sociological Review*, *39*, 68–85.

Evans, G.A. (1988) Causal explanation, social class and perceived efficacy. Oxford D. Phil. thesis.

Eysenck, S.B.G. and Allsopp, J.F. (1986) Personality differences between students and craftsmen. *Personality and Individual Differences*, *7*, 439–41.

Eysenck, H.J. and Eysenck, S.B.G. (1975) *Manual of the Eysenck Personality Questionnaire*. London: Hodder & Stoughton.

Falbo, T. (1981) Relationships between birth category, achievement and interpersonal orientation. *Journal of Personality and Social Psychology*, *41*, 121–31.

Francis, L.J. and Pearson, R.R. (1989) The relationship between social class and neuroticism and extraversion among English 16-year-olds. *Journal of Social Psychology*, *129*, 695–7.

Geen, R.G. (1990) *Human Aggression*. Milton Keynes: Open University Press.

Giles, H. and Powesland, P.F. (1975) *Speech Style and Social Evaluation*. London: Academic Press.

Goldthorpe, J.H., Lockwood, D., Bechofer, E. and Platt, J. (1968) *The Affluent Worker: Industrial Attitudes and Behaviour*. Cambridge: Cambridge University Press.

Gollin, E.S. (1958) Organizational characteristics of social judgement: a developmental investigation. *Journal of Personality*, *26*, 139–54.

Gottman, J., Gonso, J. and Rasmussen, B. (1975) Social interaction, social competence, and friendship in children. *Child Development*, *46*, 709–18.

Hampson, S.E. (1988) *The Construction of Personality*. 2nd edition. London: Routledge.

Harrell, T.W. and Harrell, M.S. (1945) Army classification test scores for civilian occupations. *Educational and Psychological Measurement*, *5*, 229–39.

Harter, S. (1983) Developmental perspectives on the self-system. In P.H. Mussen (ed.) *Handbook of Child Psychology*. Vol. 4. *Socialization, Personality and Social Development*. New York: Wiley.

Headey, B. and Wearing, A. (1991) Subjective well-being: a stocks and flows framework. In F. Strack, M. Argyle and N. Schwartz (eds) *Subjective Well-Being*. Oxford: Pergamon.

Heider, E.R. (1971) Style and accuracy of verbal communications within and between social classes. *Journal of Personality and Social Psychology*, *18*, 33–47.

Himmelweit, H.T. and Whitfield, J. (1944) Mean intelligence scores of a random sample of occupations. *British Journal of Industrial Medicine*, *1*, 224–6.

Hoffman, M.L. and Mitsos, S.B. (1958) Achievement striving, social class, and text anxiety. *Journal of Abnormal and Social Psychology*, *56*, 401–3.

Hyman, H.H. (1953) The valvo system of different classes: a social psychological contribution to the analysis of stratification. In R. Bendix and S.M. Lipset (eds) *Class, Status and Power*. Glencoe, Ill.: Free Press.

Iverson, B.K. and Walberg, H.J. (1982) Home environment and school learning: a quantitative synthesis. *Journal of Experimental Education*, 50, 144–51.

Johnson, D.M. (1948) Applications of the standard-score IQ to social statistics. *Journal of Social Psychology*, 27, 217–27.

Johnson, J.E. and McGillicuddy-Delisi, A. (1983) Family environment factors and children's knowledge of rules and conventions. *Child Development*, 54, 218–26.

Kagan, J. and Tulkin, S.R. (1971) Social class differences in child rearing during the first year. In H.R. Schaffer (ed.) *The Origins of Human Social Relations*. London: Academic Press.

Keller, S. and Zavalloni, M. (1974) Ambition and social class: a respecification. *Social Forces*, 43, 58–70.

Klein, J. (1965) *Samples from English Cultures*. London: Routledge & Kegan Paul.

Koenig, F., Swanson, W. and Harter, C. (1981) Future time orientation, social class and anomia. *Social Behavior and Personality*, 9, 123–7.

Kohn, M.L. and Schooler, C. (1973) Occupational experience and psychological functioning: an assessment of reciprocal effects. *American Sociological Review*, 38, 97–118.

Kohn, M.L. and Schooler, C. (1983) *Work and Personality*. Norwood, NJ: Ablex.

Kohn, M.L., Naoi, A., Schoenbach, C. and Schooler, C. (1990) Position in the class structure and psychological functioning in the United States, Japan and Poland. *American Journal of Sociology*, 95, 964–1008.

Levy, M.F. (1976) Deferred gratification and social class. *Journal of Social Psychology*, 100, 123–35.

Lipset, S.M. and Bendix, R. (1959) *Social Mobility in Industrial Society*. Berkeley: University of California Press.

McClelland, D.C. (1987) *Human Motivation*. Cambridge: Cambridge University Press.

McKay, H., Sinisterra, L., McKay, A., Gomez, H. and Lloreda, P. (1978) Improving cognitive ability in chronically deprived children. *Science*, 200, 270–8.

McNemar, Q. (1942) *The Revision of the Stanford-Binet Scale*. New York: Houghton.

Mann, M. (1986) Work and the work ethic. In R. Jowell, S. Witherspoon and L. Brook (eds) *British Social Attitudes: The 1986 Report*. Aldershot: Gower.

Miller, D.R. and Swanson, G.E. (1960) *Inner Conflict and Defense*. New York: Holt.

Morris, L.W. (1979) *Extraversion and Introversion*. New York: Wiley.

Mussen, P.H. and Conger, J.J. (1956) *Child Development and Personality*. New York: Harper & Bros.

Newson, J. and Newson, E. (1968) *Four Years Old in an Urban Community*. London: Allen & Unwin.

Newson, J. and Newson, E. (1976) *Seven Years Old in an Urban Community*. London: Allen & Unwin.

Olweus, D., Mattsson, A., Schalling, D. and Low, H. (1980) Testosterone, aggression, physical and personality dimensions in normal adolescent males. *Psychosomatic Medicine*, 42, 253–69.

Olweus, D., Block, J. and Radke-Yarrow, M. (eds) (1986) *Development of Antisocial and Prosocial Behavior*. Orlando: Academic Press.

Oppenheim, A.N. (1955) Social status and clique formation among grammar-school boys. *British Journal of Sociology*, 6, 503–4.

Parke, R.D. and Slaby, R.G. (1983) The development of aggression. In P.H. Mussen (ed.) *Handbook of Child Psychology*. Vol. 4. New York: Wiley, pp. 547–641.

Patterson, G.R. (1986) The contribution of siblings to training for fighting: a microsocial analysis. In D. Olweus, J. Block and M. Radke-Yarrow (eds) *Developmental of Antisocial and Prosocial Behavior*. Orlando: Academic Press.

Pellegrini, D.S. (1985) Social cognition and competence in middle childhood. *Child Development*, 56, 253–64.

Phares, E.J. (1976) *Locus of Control in Personality*. Morristown, NJ: General Learning Press.

Porter, L.W. (1964) *Organizational Patterns of Managerial Job Attitudes*. New York: American Foundation for Management Research.

Raz, I.S. and Bryant, P.E. (1990) Social background, phonological awareness and children's reading. *British Journal of Educational Psychology*, 8, 209–25.

Rosen, B.C. (1956) The achievement syndrome: a psychocultural dimension of social stratification. *American Sociological Review*, 21, 203–11.

Rosen, B.C. and D'Andrade, R.G. (1959) The psychological origins of achievement motivation. *Sociometry*, 22, 185–218.

Rotter, J.B. (1966) Generalised expectancies for internal versus external control of reinforcement. *Psychological Monographs*, 80, 609.

Rowe, D.C. and Plomin, R. (1978) The Burt controversy: a comparison of Burt's data on IQ with data from other studies. *Behavior Genetics*, 8, 81–4.

Rushton, J-P. *et al.* (1986) Altruism and aggression: the heritability of individual differences. *Journal of Personality and Social Psychology*, 50, 1192–8.

Scarr, S. (1981) *Race, Social Class, and Individual Differences in IQ*. Hillsdale, NJ: Erlbaum.

Scarr, S. and Carter-Salzman, L. (1982) Genetics and intelligence. In R.J. Sternberg (ed.) *Handbook of Human Intelligence*. Cambridge: Cambridge University Press.

Schatzman, R. and Strauss, A. (1955) Social class and modes of communication. *American Journal of Sociology*, 60, 329–38.

Schmidt, R.W., Lamon, H. and Trommsdorff, G. (1978) Social class and sex as determinants of future orientation (time perspective) in adults. *European Journal of Social Psychology*, 8, 71–90.

Stott, D.H. (1978) Epidemiological indicators of the origins of behavior disturbance as measured by the Bristol Social Adjustment Guides. *Genetic Psychology Monographs*, 97, 127–59.

Straus, M.A. (1962) Deferred gratification, social class, and the achievement syndrome. *American Sociological Review*, 27, 326–35.

Turner, J.H. (1970) Entrepreneurial environment and the emergence of achievement motivation in adolescent males. *Sociometry*, 33, 147–65.

Vernon, P.E. (1951) Recent investigations of intelligence and its measurement. *Eugenics Review*, 43, 125–37.

Vernon, P.E. (1979) *Intelligence: Heredity and Environment*. San Francisco: W.H. Freeman.

Veroff, J., Atkinson, J.W., Feld, S.C. and Gurin, G. (1960) The use of thematic apperception to assess motivation in a nationwide interview study. *Psychological Monographs*. 74, 12.

Veroff, J., Douvan, E. and Kulka, R.A. (1981) *The Inner American*. New York: Basic Books.

Warr, P. and Payne, R. (1982) Experiences of strain and pleasure among British adults. *Social Science and Medicine*, 16, 1691–7.

Winterbottom, M.R. (1958) The relation of need for achievement to learning experiences in independence and mastery. In J.W. Atkinson (ed.) *Motives in Fantasy, Action and Society*. Princeton, NJ: Van Nostrand.

Wright, J.D and Wright, S.R. (1976) Social class and parental values for children: a partial replication and extension of the Kohn thesis. *American Sociological Review*, *41*, 527–37.

Zajonc, R.B. (1976) Family configuration and intelligence. *Science, 192*, 227–36.

Zigler, E. and Child, I.L. (1969) Socialization. In G. Lindzey and E. Aronson (eds) *The Handbook of Social Psychology*. 2nd edition. Vol. 3. Reading, Mass.: Addison-Wesley.

Zigler, E. and Seitz, V. (1982) Social policy and intelligence. In R.J. Sternberg (ed.) *Handbook of Human Intelligence*. Cambridge: Cambridge University Press.

# Chapter 8

# Social mobility

Social mobility is the movement of people in adult life to a class which is above or below that of their parents and original family. We shall ask how much mobility there is in Britain, and which individuals are most likely to move. Sociologists have done a great deal of excellent research on social mobility (Ganzeboom *et al.*, 1991), but they have neglected some of the key psychological variables which predict who will rise and who will fall.

Most of the research on social mobility has been about mobility between occupational classes. So education, for example, will be considered as a *cause* of mobility, whereas it could be seen as an example of mobility. Those members of an occupational class who are more educated regard themselves as belonging to a higher class than the less-educated members. In addition, people within a given occupational bracket who adopt a 'superior' lifestyle (in terms of cars, houses, holidays, leisure activities) will have an elevated perception of their social status, partly because they will have friends of a higher class. This could be described as an alternative kind of mobility, 'lifestyle mobility'. However, less is known about this than about occupational mobility, to which we now turn.

How much mobility is there? The Oxford Mobility Study interviewed 10,309 male adults in 1972, and obtained information about their families (Goldthorpe *et al.*, 1987). Overall only 28 per cent of sons were in the same occupational class as their fathers, and 72 per cent had changed class, most by only one class. The percentage change is greater the more classes used; in this study there were seven classes. If just two had been used, manual and non-manual, mobility across this border would be 34 per cent (Heath, 1981). Overall there is more upward than downward mobility because of changes in society during one generation. Another way of putting it is that the correlation between occupational status of fathers and sons is about .40, as a number of different studies in Britain and the USA have found (Kerchoff, 1974).

Let us look at people whose families were in class I and class VII; they ended up as follows:

| Initial class | | | | Final class | | | |
|---|---|---|---|---|---|---|---|
| | I | II | III | IV | V | VI | VII |
| I | 45.7 | 19.1 | 11.6 | 6.8 | 4.9 | 5.4 | 6.5 |
| VII | 7.1 | 8.5 | 8.8 | 5.7 | 12.9 | 24.8 | 32.2 |

This shows that 45.7 per cent of children born into class I ended up in class I compared with 7.1 per cent of those from class VII. Another way of looking at it is to see where adult members of each class came from.

| Final class | | | | Class of origin | | | |
|---|---|---|---|---|---|---|---|
| | I | II | III | IV | V | VI | VII |
| I | 25.3 | 13.1 | 10.4 | 10.1 | 12.5 | 16.4 | 6.5 |
| VII | 2.4 | 2.5 | 6.0 | 7.7 | 9.6 | 35.2 | 36.6 |

This shows, for example, that 25.3 per cent of individuals who ended up in class I came from this class, compared with 2.4 per cent who came from class VII (Goldthorpe *et al.*, 1987). There is more upward mobility because there has been an expansion of jobs at the top, in class I, and white-collar service jobs (II and III), and a decline in manual jobs (Payne, 1992).

Class I looks quite open, since about three-quarters of its members were born in a lower class, including 12 per cent in VII; 45.7 per cent of sons stay in this class, compared with 7.1 per cent from VII. Class I has much more mixed origins than classes VI and VII. However, class I here refers to quite a large group including 10–15 per cent of employed males. If a really upper-class group is examined – people in *Who's Who* or company chairmen, for example – a much more closed circle appears. The chance of getting your name in *Who's Who* is seventy-five times greater if your father did, and your chance of being the director of a bank is 200 times more if father was one (Heath, 1981). We discussed this closed, upper-class group earlier (p. 15).

Many people occupy other classes *between* the one they began with and the class they ended in. Figure 8.1 shows the findings of the Oxford Mobility study. This shows, for example, that, of men initially in classes I or II in 1928–47, 38 per cent stayed in this class throughout. Another 32 per cent fell into classes III–IV for their first job, but 16 per cent later returned to I or II.

It has been suggested that the line between manual and non-manual is some kind of 'barrier' to mobility. However, we have seen that 34 per cent pass through it, more going up than down. On the other hand, some of those opting for white-collar jobs are paid less than some skilled manual

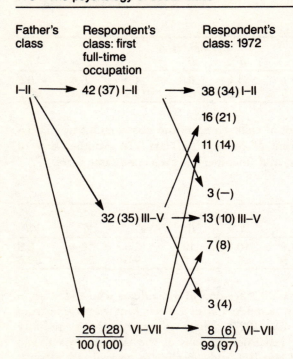

Figure 8.1 Initial, intermediate and final social class of males born into classes I and II
Source: Goldthorpe et al., 1987
Note: Respondents born 1928–47 (N = 588) (results for respondents born 1928–37 (N = 234) in brackets)

jobs, so it is questionable how much 'upward mobility' there has really been.

In Chapter 2 we looked at mobility rates in different countries. Britain is in the middle of the range, about the same as the USA, with more mobility than Poland, Ireland or Italy, but less than Australia or most Communist countries (p. 36).

## EDUCATION

Education is one of the main routes to upward mobility. Those with better education are likely to end up in better jobs, as Table 8.1 shows.

This shows that 63 per cent of class I men (and 80 per cent of women) have a degree or equivalent, while 82 per cent of class VI men have no credentials. Part of the explanation is obvious; many class I jobs actually require a degree or equivalent – doctors, lawyers, university teachers, for example. Other jobs require lower educational qualifications.

In Britain and most other countries there are said to be equal opportunities, so that all children can be educated, if they are bright enough to benefit

*Table 8.1* Education and later social class (Great Britain 1989 and 1990 combined) (percentages)

| | Professional | Employers and managers | Intermediate non-manual | Junior non-manual | Skilled manual and own-account non-professional | Semi-skilled manual and personal service | Unskilled manual |
|---|---|---|---|---|---|---|---|
| *Males* | | | | | | | |
| Degree or equivalent | 59 | 17 | 31 | 5 | 1 | 0 | 1 |
| No qualification (inc. no CSE, or 'O' level) | 2 | 19 | 11 | 26 | 42 | 58 | 77 |
| *Females* | | | | | | | |
| Degree or equivalent | 72 | 15 | 17 | 2 | 2 | 0 | 0 |
| No qualification (inc. no CSE, or 'O' level) | 2 | 21 | 13 | 32 | 49 | 62 | 80 |

*Source: General Household Survey, 1992*

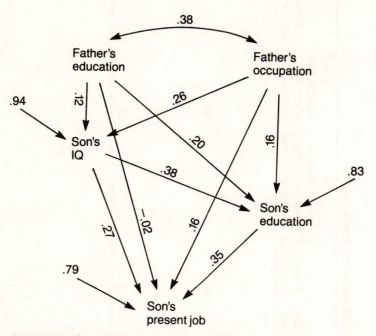

*Figure 8.2* IQ and the attainment process
*Source:* Heath, 1981

from it. And in most countries the more intelligent children are more likely to get to university or other places of training for good jobs. However, another determinant of education is the family's social class, quite independently of the intelligence of children.

Figure 8.2 shows the strengths of various paths to occupational success in Britain, from different sources compiled by Heath (1981). It can be seen that education (type of school) is predicted by IQ (r = .38), but also by fathers' education (.20) and occupation (.16). Children of similar ability do better in examinations if they come from middle-class homes. Douglas (1964) compared the success at 'O' level of children of similar ability but different class. Among the most intelligent group 77 per cent of upper-middle-class and 37 per cent of lower-working-class children obtained good 'O' levels. This is partly because middle-class children receive more encouragement at home, partly because they go to better schools.

The effect of class on education begins before school age, by middle-class parents reading more to their children and the greater availability of books and educational toys (p. 154). Middle-class children receive better education at every stage, and receive more education. Many more class I and II parents send their children to private primary schools, which have smaller classes and usually better facilities. The same parents are also much more likely to

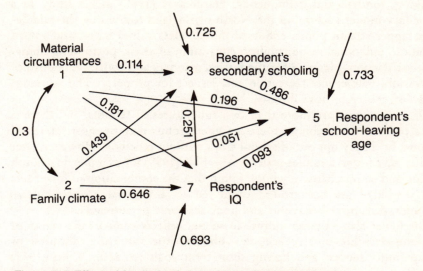

*Figure 8.3* Effect of family background on school leaving age
*Source:* Halsey *et al.*, 1980

send their children to fee-paying secondary schools, either public schools, fee-paying day schools or, in some areas and at certain periods, to selective direct grant or grammar schools, rather than to comprehensive or other kinds of state school. Parents very often send their children to the same kinds of school they went to themselves. Halsey and colleagues (1980) analysed the causal paths leading to choice of fee-paying secondary school: this depended partly on parental values and wealth (Figure 8.3).

In Britain there is an important 'branching point' at age 16, when compulsory education ceases. So 70 per cent of class I and II children stay on at school after 16 v. 17 per cent for VI–VII; 29 per cent of I and II were still there at 18, compared with 3 per cent of the others. Many more middle-class children stay on at school, and this can be predicted from attending a private school, parental wealth and IQ. Examination success at secondary school can also be predicted from the same variables (Halsey *et al.*, 1980). For a working-class child to stay on at school when most of his or her friends have started work and are earning money incurs obvious costs. To opt for further education puts people into a different social circle and a different lifestyle from friends and family, which is a major disincentive (Boudon, 1974).

While at school, middle-class children are likely to pay more attention, work harder and do what they are told. A proportion of working-class children do not, and join a 'counter-culture' of children who reject school and relieve their boredom by insubordination, disruption and generally 'having a laff'. They are more interested in life outside school – smoking, drinking, football and delinquency. Hargreaves (1967) in his study of a secondary modern school in the North of England found that the middle-class, upper-stream pupils endorsed middle-class values more, and valued ambition, individual responsibility, cultivation of skills, postponing imme-diate satisfaction, planning for the future, manners and courtesy, control of aggression, wholesome recreation and respect for property. The working-class, lower-stream boys did not.

Of course there are more than two subcultures in schools, and there is not a perfect correlation with class. Other groups may be most interested in sport or simply opt out of school work without rebellion. However, later studies have found a similar pattern. Abraham (1989) for example, in a South of England comprehensive school, found that the combination of lower sets and working-class background often led to anti-social counter-culture attitudes, disruptive behaviour and poor academic performance.

The lower-class counter-culture in school reflects some of the values of working-class life outside school – placing little value on education or occupational success and having short-term goals (p. 230). Willis (1977) described a group of rebellious working-class school children and observed similarities with shop-floor culture – e.g. avoiding work, lack of respect for authority (and they saw school as an unintended preparation for work in this way) – though others have objected that adult manual workers often take pride in their work and enjoy recognition from management for doing it well.

Part of the reason for the emergence of class-linked school subcultures is that teachers categorise and label children. In a study of an American primary school it was found that the teachers had done this by the eighth day, and placed children at different tables, supposedly by ability, but actually more by appearance and knowledge of the families children came from (Rist, 1970). Being labelled affects the self-image and subsequent performance at school. Rosenthal and Jacobson (1968) carried out an experiment in which teachers were told that one in five of their children were very bright, though these were actually chosen at random. The nominated children not only did well but actually gained in IQ. However, children may try to fight against the label, as Fuller (1984) found with a group of black girls in a London school.

Middle-class children are much more likely to go to university, as Table 8.2 shows. Those who do not go to university in Britain have a choice between Youth Training Schemes (YTS), employment and various vocational courses. It has been found that 50 per cent of professional-class children took an academic route, few did a YTS course, while 43 per cent of children from unskilled families did YTS followed by unemployment, and another 15 per cent YTS followed by a job. Intermediate-class children often (26 per cent) did vocational training, e.g. for secretarial or for hotel and catering work, which require deference, impression management and acceptance of

Table 8.2 Class of origin and education (Great Britain 1989 and 1990 combined) (percentages)

| | Professional | Employers and managers | Intermediate non-manual | Junior non-manual | Skilled manual and own-account non-professional | Semi-skilled manual and personal service | Unskilled manual |
|---|---|---|---|---|---|---|---|
| **Males** | | | | | | | |
| Degree or equivalent | 45 | 21 | 27 | 19 | 7 | 6 | 4 |
| No qualification (inc. no CSE, or 'O' level) | 6 | 18 | 11 | 17 | 36 | 47 | 55 |
| **Females** | | | | | | | |
| Degree or equivalent | 26 | 12 | 16 | 9 | 3 | 2 | 1 |
| No qualification (inc. no CSE, or 'O' level) | 8 | 21 | 16 | 26 | 46 | 55 | 67 |

Source: General Household Survey, 1992

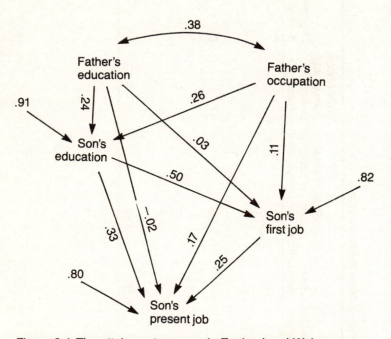

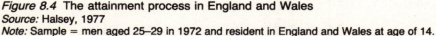

*Figure 8.4* The attainment process in England and Wales
*Source:* Halsey, 1977
*Note:* Sample = men aged 25–29 in 1972 and resident in England and Wales at age of 14.

authority. Working-class youngsters from a subculture which values tough-ness, racism, sexism and rejection of authority do not seek such jobs nor would they be acceptable (Banks *et al.*, 1992).

Educational aspirations, high or low, are influenced not only by parents and their education and jobs, but also by the peer group and their parents, who are likely to have jobs in the same status bracket (Kerbo, 1983).

Education has powerful effects on social mobility, and the causal process has been analysed, by Halsey (1977), and is shown in Figure 8.4. This shows that son's education has a strong effect on first job (.50) and also a direct effect on promotion to present job (.33). Father's education affects son's job only via son's education; father's occupation influences son's education, but it also has some effect on his present job.

American studies of mobility have separated the different components of class – income, occupation and education. Coleman *et al.* (1979) found that the main impact of family background and advantages was on education (as in Britain) which in turn influences occupation and then income. Family had less direct effect on job or income, or education on income.

These are interesting and quite strong effects. Evidently education is one of the main ways in which parents' class influences the class of their children.

However, there is still a lot of unexplained variability, and Jencks (1972) puts this down to a large measure of luck, for example bumping into an old friend who gives you a good job, and to on-the-job competence of a kind which turns out to be very useful.

Education predicts success partly because it selects the brightest and most hard-working children, awards them good exam results at each stage, and employers then choose them for good jobs. As we have seen, however, there is not in fact equality of opportunity: intelligence predicts success, but then so does family social class. Employers like people with good A levels and good degrees, but they also like people who have been to the 'right' schools and colleges.

In Britain public schools seem to confer some advantage – going by the high proportions of bishops, judges, conservative MPs and company directors who went to them (Reid, 1989). Oxford and Cambridge have a similar effect - but at least it takes a high level of secondary school success to get in. Going to these schools and colleges no doubt provides good education, but in addition they produce a certain set of values, a social style and accent, and a set of social contacts. They also produce a certain self-image and self-confidence. All these things help social mobility. The effect on income is less striking, since there are a lot of well-paid skilled manual jobs, as well as well-paid jobs in business or finance which need little education, and there are less well-paid professional jobs which need a lot.

## INTELLIGENCE

As we showed in Chapter 7 there are substantial differences between the average intelligence of people in different occupational classes or with different incomes. There is a correlation between class and IQ of about .30 to .40. The different members of a family have similar IQs, as a result of shared genes and background, but there are also differences of IQ within families, and there are wide variations within each social class. Do the more intelligent individuals become upwardly mobile?

A number of studies have been carried out in which the difference between the IQs of sons and fathers has been taken as the predictor variable. When sons have a higher IQ than their father, they are likely to be upwardly mobile; if they have a lower IQ they will be downwardly mobile (Table 8.3). (No-one has studied mothers or daughters yet, but they are probably very similar.) Mascie-Taylor and Gibson (1978) measured IQs of fathers and sons and found a linear relationship – the more IQ difference the more mobility, and that the effect was greater for differences of verbal IQ than of visuo-spatial ability on the Wechsler.

Gibson (1970) found that Cambridge science faculty (class I) had mostly been upwardly mobile, were more intelligent than their fathers and often the fathers had also been upwardly mobile.

*Table 8.3* Social mobility and IQ scores

| No. of steps | n | VIQ | | PIQ | | TIQ | |
|---|---|---|---|---|---|---|---|
| | | $\bar{x}$ | sd | $\bar{x}$ | sd | $\bar{x}$ | sd |
| **Upwardly mobile** | | | | | | | |
| +1 | 15 | +4.27 | 6.78 | +4.47 | 14.49 | +3.87 | 7.82 |
| +2 | 14 | +7.14 | 7.27 | +10.00 | 14.33 | +8.71 | 7.02 |
| +3 | 6 | +11.67 | 10.42 | +14.17 | 13.66 | +13.67 | 12.11 |
| Total | 35 | | | | | | |
| **Downwardly mobile** | | | | | | | |
| −1 | 10 | +.40 | 6.67 | −9.80 | 13.47 | −4.80 | 7.57 |
| −2 | 6 | −8.67 | 7.17 | −15.83 | 10.83 | −13.33 | 5.75 |
| −3 | 1 | −10.00 | − | −22.00 | − | −15.00 | − |
| Total | 17 | | | | | | |

*Source:* Mascie-Taylor and Gibson, 1978

Intelligence affects social class partly by its effect on educational success, measured by level attained or years of education completed. Models of the causal pathway have been constructed in the USA and Britain, with very similar results. Typical weights for two of the paths were shown in Figure 8.2. This shows that IQ operates partly via education, but also has a direct effect on occupational status. The stronger effect is on education, which in turn has a strong effect on job, as we saw earlier.

Some sociologists think that class differences in intelligence are found because class influences intelligence, for instance a longer period of education may enhance IQ. However, the analysis above shows that son's present job is predicted directly by his earlier IQ, and that this is a more important factor than the class of his family, as measured by his father's education or occupation.

What are the predictors of intelligence? It is correlated with that of parents, typically at about .60, but this leaves a lot of room for differences between parent and child, and between siblings. How far is intelligence providing new information, which can make better predictions of social mobility possible, and how far is it redundant, since it correlates with other variables? Heath (1981) showed that for the lower end of the social class scale, it is the same people who lack intelligence, have uneducated parents, parents in lower-class jobs and other disadvantages; they are disadvantaged in a number of inter-connected ways. However, at the upper end of the scale the predictor variables are more independent of one another: *some* class I fathers are highly educated, *some* of their sons have high intelligence, *some* have a good education. The more of these attributes a son has, the more probable he will end up in class I.

## MOTIVATION AND AMBITION

Achievement motivation (n.Ach) is the motive to seek excellence, to do well, for its own sake. This may be in exams, at work, by making money or in other spheres. It has usually been measured by a projection test in which subjects imagine what will happen to people in vaguely drawn pictures. There are clear class differences, the higher up the social scale, the higher the n.Ach. American Blacks in the lowest class have the lowest score (McClelland, 1987) (see this book p. 164).

Upwardly mobile people have higher scores too. Crockett (1962) found that this was true of men of class III and IV origins who had been mobile, even with education held constant. For class I and II men affiliative motivation was higher and education was essential, but n.Ach had no effect. It is possible that holding a better job increases achievement motivation. However, the studies to be described shortly were longitudinal ones, so that this objection does not apply to them. No consistent effect on academic performance has been found, using the McClelland projective measure of n.Ach. However, Cassidy and Lynn (1991) in Britain did find such a relationship. They used a questionnaire measure of achievement motivation in a study of 451 young people who were tested at ages 16 and 23. Achievement motivation predicted social class, mainly via academic performance, especially the sub-scales for competitiveness and status aspiration. This is shown in Figure 8.5.

In another longitudinal study, this time using the projective method, McClelland and Boyatzis (1982) found that managers who had high n.Ach

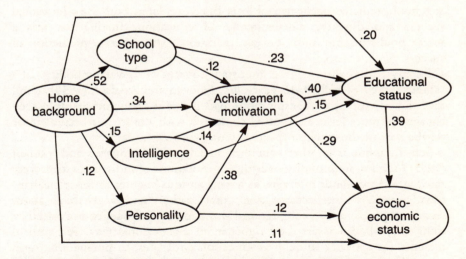

*Figure 8.5* Path analysis of the effects of achievement motivation and other variables on social mobility
*Source:* Cassidy and Lynn, 1991

when they entered a large company later received more promotion for up to sixteen years, to level 3 management, but not to higher grades. It was suggested that power motivation becomes more important at this level (McClelland and Boyatzis, 1982). Other occupational studies have found that n.Ach is higher for entrepreneurs, sales managers and managers of investments, more than for other managers. This can be accounted for by the theoretical link between n.Ach and individual effort, especially where moderate risks are involved.

Another McClelland-inspired motive is the need for power, i.e. the need to influence other people, to be assertive and to acquire social prestige. A projection test measure devised by Winter (1973) has been widely used. He found that male students with high scores aspired to socially influential and prestigeful occupations such as teaching, the church and journalism. McClelland and Boyatzis (1982) in their study of the careers of managers over a period of sixteen years found that the men promoted to the highest levels had a particular pattern of motivation – high power combined with low affiliation. This was more predictive of promotion to higher levels than achievement motivation. These are men who want to influence people and are less concerned about whether they are liked, which may be what is most effective in higher management. On the other hand, the same motive pattern was associated with being an unsatisfactory husband, and having an impaired immune system, and hence worse health.

Ambition is the desire, hope, intention or expectation of doing well, in education, occupation, finances or in other ways. Porter (1976) followed up nearly 15,000 American high school children, and found that ambition while at school predicted occupational level five years later, both via educational success and directly, independently of education. Intelligence was a better predictor, but ambition gave additional and separate prediction of success.

Energy and vitality may be important sources of upward mobility. In a sample survey of 518 14–16-year-olds, Douvan and Adelson (1958) found that those with upward aspirations had more energy, for example they engaged in more leisure activities, compared with a more apathetic attitude on the part of those who expected to move downwards.

Self-discipline is another source of social mobility. Snarey and Vaillant (1985) found more mobility over three generations of individuals who were rated after a two-hour interview as having various 'mature' defence mechanisms, especially 'intellectualisation', that is the capacity to think about emotional problems in a cool, rational way and not to get angry at work; they think they should assert their rights in an unemotional way. Self-control includes the capacity to defer gratification until later, to pursue long-term goals. This is a familiar part of middle-class culture, with its long period of education and long, slow career ladder later (p. 188). There is more sexual restraint among middle-class young people. The socially mobile also show this pattern of restraint, as Elder found (1969), though Kinsey interpreted it as anticipating the mores of the class being joined (pp. 243–4).

The Protestant Work Ethic (PWE) was identified by Max Weber (1904) as a combination of beliefs, values and motivation – with the goal of wealth and material gain, for its own sake, by means of hard work, self-discipline and an ascetic way of life. The Protestant reformers taught that people would be judged on the basis of their life's work, of which their 'calling' was the most important part. Hard work and success were signs of belonging to the elect, and some believed that God caused the elect to prosper (Furnham, 1990). The PWE is still alive today, and Protestants score higher than Catholics (Jews even higher), and middle classes more than working classes.

Does the PWE produce social mobility? There is some evidence for this from Lenski's survey (1961) of 656 people in Detroit, and a thesis by Weller on 1,100 adults in towns in northern US states. In both studies Protestants were more upwardly mobile than Catholics, or likely to stay in a higher class, while Catholics were more likely to be downwardly mobile. Among the Protestants, regular church attenders were more upwardly mobile than others. Cohen (1985) carried out a longitudinal study and found that PWE predicted mobility though the effect was not strong, and it was via its effect on education.

## INFLUENCE OF THE HOME

### Parental encouragement

There is no question that children do better – in school and jobs – if they are encouraged by their parents. However, we need to know whether this is still true when variables like intelligence and social class of parents are held constant. Porter's study of 15,000 American high school children found that influence of parents and friends still predicted educational success and ambition, both of which predicted occupational success. Crockett (1962) reviewed a number of other American studies and suggested that parents select the children who seem likely to be successful (from their personalities and abilities) and then encourage these children.

Cohen (1987) carried out a massive follow-up study over fifteen years of 5,500 American school children, to compare the effects of parental encouragement and modelling (i.e. copying of parental education). He found that both kinds of influence affected educational aspiration and educational success, but that encouragement had the greater effect. Working-class parents had almost no modelling effect, and middle-class children modelled themselves more on their mothers' education than on their fathers'.

British research has been mainly on the effects of parental encouragement on education. Halsey et al. (1980) report part of the Oxford mobility study, of 8,529 males. They found that parental values had a major influence on choice of secondary school, but a much weaker effect on length of education or educational success. However, type of secondary school was an important determinant of both of these, so that parental values operated mainly through choice of secondary school. Jackson and Marsden (1963) had found with a small sample that mother's education had more effect than father's on reported educational encouragement. However, the Oxford study found that either parent having been to a good school affected choice of child's school to the same extent (Halsey *et al.*, 1980).

Douvan and Adelson (1958), in their study of 518 young people, found that those with upward aspirations were on good terms with their parents, had internalised their standards, but had become independent of them; they had rarely been given physical punishment, though some had received psychological. Those with downward expectations were hostile and dependent, and had more often been given harsh and inconsistent discipline. However, studies of entrepreneurs have also found that they are more likely to come from homes where the parents rejected them or preferred their siblings (Kets de Vries, 1977).

## Parental wealth

This is itself part of social class, but it also varies within occupationally defined classes, so can be used as an additional predictor of the mobility of children. In the Oxford Mobility Study wealth of parents was a predictor of choice of primary school, and even more of (usually fee-paying) secondary school. The children of richer parents stayed on at school longer and were more successful in examinations; however, examination success was more due to type of school, with little direct influence of parental wealth (Halsey *et al.*, 1980). From the same source of data, for men from class VII, those from homes with no domestic amenities (telephone, refrigerator, inside lavatory, fixed bath or shower) and rented accommodation were more likely themselves to end in class VII (46.6 per cent v. 41.8 per cent).

Mobility research in a number of countries has found that one of the greatest sources of general *lack* of mobility is the extent of inheritance, of wealth, property and family businesses (Ganzeboom *et al.*, 1991). There is a high degree of 'occupational inheritance' – by a variety of social processes children often go into the same or similar occupations as their parents. At the top of the social scale, people are unlikely to get into the élite groups within class I if their father was not rich, famous or powerful, as we saw earlier.

## Parental education

This varies between classes as we have seen, but it also varies *within* classes, so can be seen as a possible source of social mobility. Heath (1981) used the

Oxford Mobility Study data to show that, with father's occupation and IQ held constant, father's education still predicted son's education and also, via education, his present job (Figure 8.2). At the upper end of the scale 26.7 per cent of sons of class I men are in class I; 39.3 per cent were in class I if one of their parents had a degree or equivalent. At the other end of the scale 17.2 per cent of the sons of class VII males were also in this class; however lack of education made no difference since there is a large overlap between being unskilled and being uneducated.

## Number of siblings

Lower-class families have more children (p. 84); children in larger families have lower IQs, and leave school earlier (pp. 154–5). The Oxford Mobility Group data showed that, among people from lower class families, having more than four siblings is a (small) disadvantage: 41.8 per cent were in class VII compared to 34.8 per cent for those from smaller families. For those from class I families, those with one sibling or none were themselves more likely to be in that class – 47.1 per cent v. 39.5 per cent for those from larger families.

## PHYSICAL FEATURES

### Height

Those in higher classes are on average taller; there is a linear relationship; the average height in class I is two inches greater than in class V. This was found in a study of 33,000 people in Britain (Boldsen and Mascie-Taylor, 1985) (Figure 8.6). There is of course a great deal of variation within classes.

Is this due, or partly due, to upward mobility by tall people or downward mobility by short ones? There is evidence from the USA and from European countries that tall males have an advantage when competing for jobs. In one American study it was found that students over 6'2" were given starting salaries 12.4 per cent higher than those under 6' (Deck, 1968). In a survey of 800 men and women in jobs, the taller men had better jobs and salaries, but it made no difference for women (Quinn cited by Hatfield and Sprecher, 1986). In a study of 416 West Point students, height made little difference to rank twenty years later; however generals tended to be taller, while very short people did less well (Mazur et al., 1984). Perhaps height is most important at the top – American Presidents are usually taller than the rival candidates, and bishops in the Church of England taller than other clergy.

Tall women have been found to do better at work, and make socially mobile marriages (Tanner, 1989). On the other hand, men like women to be shorter than themselves. Women like men to be 5–6" taller than

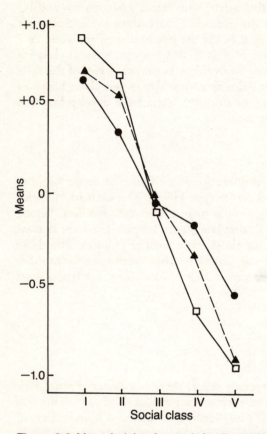

*Figure 8.6* Mean heights for each family position by social class as deviations (inches) from the grand mean (□ = fathers, ● = mothers and ▲ = children)
*Source:* Boldsen and Mascie-Taylor, 1985

themselves, but not too tall, and on the whole they prefer medium-sized men (5′9″ – 5′11″) (Graziano *et al.*, 1978).

Why do tall people have an advantage at work? There seems to be a stereotype that tall people are also leaders, perhaps derived from the advantage that large boys or animals have when battling for dominance. In groups of children height is a predictor of informal leadership. It may derive from the correlation between height and intelligence found in children (about .30: Tanner, 1989), which is partly due to age or maturational differences affecting both. The stereotyped beliefs about tall people are illustrated by Wilson's experiment (1968) in which he briefly introduced a 'Mr. England, a student from Cambridge' or some other rank. When he was said to be 'Dr England, a senior lecturer from Cambridge', his height was guessed to be 5″ more than when he was a mere student.

What makes people tall or short? It is mainly due to inheritance, but is also affected by diet. Children tend to be shorter if their parents are poor, unemployed or uneducated, if there are many other children in the family or if the home is overcrowded (Tanner, 1989). Class differences in height are established by age 7, and social factors have little effect after this age (Mascie-Taylor, 1991).

## Obesity

In Britain and the USA, many studies have found that women who are obese or overweight are more likely to belong to lower classes (Sobal and Stunkard, 1989). In one Swedish study there were eight times as many obese women in the lower of the four classes distinguished than in the highest; obesity was very rare in the top class. The effect for men is much weaker, and in some studies has not been found at all. The effect is less marked for children too, since obesity usually develops after adolescence. In Third World countries the effect is actually reversed, because the richer people can afford to eat more.

This class difference in the modern world is partly generated by the upward mobility of slim females and the downward mobility of fat ones. In a big British study, 3,322 6-year-olds were interviewed and measured by a nurse. For the women, 20.6 per cent of those in class V were obese, compared with 3.4 per cent in class II. The upwardly mobile women were less likely to be obese (4.7 per cent) than the downwardly mobile ones (11.2 per cent). The effects for men were similar but smaller (Braddon *et al.*, 1986). In the Mid-town Manhattan Study, of 1,660 New Yorkers, 12 per cent of the upwardly mobile were obese, compared with 22 per cent of the downwardly mobile (Goldblatt *et al.*, 1965). Note that in both studies *some* fat women were upwardly mobile, perhaps because they had higher intelligence or other assets.

Could it be the other way round? Is it possible that those who are, for example, upwardly mobile adopt the ways and eventually the shape of their new class? This is perfectly possible, and a predictive study is needed to prove that shape leads to mobility rather than vice versa. It does seem very likely however that thin people are likely to move upwards and fat people downwards, in light of the studies to be reviewed later showing that there is prejudice against fat people and that thin people are preferred by those who do selection for jobs.

Why are there class differences in obesity? Partly because of different diets: a greater proportion of working-class diet is sugar and carbohydrates. And we have seen that middle-class people take a lot more exercise (p. 104). There are also strong middle-class norms about the importance of being attractive and slim, leading to a different balance of eating and physical activity. People are much more likely to be obese in the USA if they are immigrants, especially from Italy. It takes more than one generation for middle-class habits of diet and exercise to be acquired.

Why are fat people downwardly mobile? In the USA obesity is a stigma, and fat people are rejected. If adolescent girls are asked to form impressions of women shown in photographs, fat women are liked less and thought to be lazy, greedy, self-indulgent and lacking in self-discipline. The effect is reduced if the judges are told that a fat person has a thyroid problem or has recently managed to lose some weight (De Jong, 1980). Fat people are rejected as friends, and they are rejected for marriage – they are more likely to be single. It is widely reported by obese women that men reject them. They are also rejected for jobs: we have seen that physically unattractive people are less likely to be offered jobs and have lower salaries; obesity is one of the main components of unattractiveness. In a study of 1,000 American firms it was found that 9 per cent of the higher-paid managers were overweight, compared with 40 per cent of lower-paid managers (cited by Hatfield and Sprecher, 1986).

How do people become obese? There is probably an inherited tendency, together with the effects of the home environment on diet, exercise and concern or lack of concern with a slim appearance. As we shall see, this varies with class and culture. Lower-class individuals are likely to have had less education, and lack of medical education is probably important.

## Physical attractiveness

The sociologist Sorokin (1964) thought that there is 'permanent recruiting of beautiful women into the higher social strata . . . a variety of Darwin's sexual selection . . . [so that] higher social layers come to be more handsome than the lower ones'. Is physical attractiveness (p.a.) a basis for social mobility?

The sphere in which p.a. probably counts most is of course love and marriage, and it can certainly result in upward mobility as Sorokin described. It is hardly necessary to document this point by citing research findings. A 'computer dance' was arranged by Walster et al. (1966) who invited 752 students to a freshers' dance and randomly assigned each to a partner; attractiveness was assessed on a seven-point scale by a group of young experimenters. It was found that physical attractiveness was the most important predictor of how much each person was liked by their partner, and how much they wanted to date them again – for males as well as females – with correlations of about .40. Attractive girls have more dates (.61 correlation between p.a. and number of dates); so do attractive young men (.25) (Berscheid et al., 1971). Attractive people are found to be sexually warmer, have more premarital intercourse and are sexually active at an earlier age (Udry and Eckland, cited by Hatfield and Sprecher, 1986). A number of studies have found that attractive girls marry higher-status men and that this correlation is higher for girls who were originally working-class.

Elder (1969) followed up eighty-three American girls, half working-class, half middle-class. The middle-class girls, when at school, were rated by their teachers as more attractive, including ratings for physique, grooming, sex appeal and general appearance. Those who were later socially mobile were initially more attractive, especially in the case of the working-class girls. Physical attractiveness predicted husband's occupational status ($r = .43$), nearly as well as the girls' educational attainments did (.49) and more than did their original social class (.27). This is exactly the process which Sorokin described – attractive girls moving up the social scale through marriage.

Handsome men may also be socially mobile. In a study of 800 employees of American firms, Quinn *et al.* (1968) found that men who were rated as 'strikingly handsome' or 'good-looking' earned on average 18.5 per cent more ($1,809) than those who were 'quite plain' or 'homely'. For women the attractive ones were paid 26.4 per cent more. However, these were not predictive studies, and it is possible that upwardly mobile people pay more attention to their appearance *after* they have arrived, in conformity with the norms of their new class.

A predictive study of mobility was carried out on male West Point cadets. Facial dominance was rated from photographs; this predicted success at the end of the West Point course, but had little effect on final rank twenty years later (Mazur *et al.*, 1984). The evidence of mobility as a result of p.a. comes from younger people, and suggests that p.a. is most important for earlier ages.

There is plenty of evidence that attractive children are preferred by teachers, at school and college, and often given higher marks. Singer (1964) found that attractive female students, especially if they were first-born, were given higher grades in classes in an American college. This was not due to greater intelligence but to using their charms by sitting in the front of classes and speaking to instructors more often. There is evidence that attractive people are preferred for jobs, and not only jobs for which p.a. is relevant (like doing TV commercials).

Experiments on job selection interviews by American companies have found that physical appearance is taken into account, and has a small effect on whether candidates are selected, but especially for jobs with lower professional skills but needing higher social skills like secretaries or receptionists, and not for doctors or financiers (Bull and Rumsey, 1988). However, very attractive women may not be favoured for traditional men's jobs (like car salespersons) (Hatfield and Sprecher, 1986).

Lack of p.a. can lead to downward mobility. We saw earlier that being fat is a stigma which causes a lot of trouble. The same is true of facial blotches, hare lips, bad teeth or other sources of low p.a. Bull (1979) found that people with apparent facial scars were judged to be dishonest and less warm, affectionate, sincere, to have fewer friends and less sense of humour. Rumsey *et al.* (1982) placed a confederate on a busy pavement where people had to wait to cross the road. When she had a strawberry 'birthmark' people stood 100 cm away, with a facial 'bruise' 78 cm and with neither 56 cm. It is most likely that such people are at a disadvantage for love and marriage, and for jobs – though Mr Gorbachev may have popularised strawberry birthmarks.

It is widely believed that criminals have special, unattractive faces (squints, low foreheads, etc.). Furthermore there is evidence that law-breakers really are less attractive than other people. They have scars, tattoo marks and other disfigurements. The explanation may be that such people have suffered from rejection because of their appearance; it is also found that less attractive individuals are more likely to be found guilty by courts or to receive heavier sentences.

Similarly mental patients are less attractive than non-patients. Furthermore it has been found, from rating college photographs, that patients were less attractive than others *before* they became ill, but became even less attractive when they became patients (Napoleon *et al.*, 1980). Criminals and mental patients are further examples of unattractive individuals being downwardly mobile.

Why does being attractive do people so much good? An important part of the explanation is the famous 'p.a. stereotype' – the widely shared belief that attractive males and females are also more sexually responsive, warm, sensitive and nurturant, kind, interesting, strong, poised, modest, sociable, outgoing, have more exciting dates and have a better character than the rest of the population (Dion *et al.*, 1972). Later research has found that very attractive women are thought to have some negative attributes too – vain, snobbish, egotistical, materialistic, more likely to have extramarital affairs and get a divorce (Dermer and Thiel, 1975).

There may be some biological basis for the preference for attractive people, since looking healthy and energetic are constituents of attractiveness. Girls with larger pupils in their eyes are found attractive (Hess, 1965); pupil dilation is a sign of arousal. Perhaps attractive people really do have other desirable qualities. In a study of American students a small tendency was found for attractive women to be happier, higher in self-esteem and less neurotic (Mathes and Kahn, 1975); in another study there was some relationship with assertiveness for men (Reis *et al.*, 1982), but all these effects are rather weak.

More striking is the eliciting of 'attractive' behaviour in a 'self-fulfilling prophecy'. Male students were asked to have a telephone conversation with a female, and were given a supposed photograph of her. When an attractive photograph was given the males behaved differently so that when tapes of the *females* were judged by raters, they were thought to be more gregarious, poised, sociable and self-confident (Snyder *et al.*, 1977).

# THE SOCIAL MOBILITY OF WOMEN

The earlier studies of mobility only dealt with men. It was assumed that the family was the unit of class, that men had the main job and that wives' class depended on their husbands' jobs. All of these assumptions are now partly untrue. More women have jobs than before; husbands are the sole earner in only 19 per cent of families. Husbands' occupational status is helped by wives' education (Kerchoff, 1974); presumably wives are able to help in their spouses' careers in various ways, for example by their social acceptability.

The mobility of women depends partly on marriage. They tend to marry men of similar social class origins, and as many marry 'up' as 'down'. This is slightly greater for women than for men: while 72 per cent of men move into a different class from their fathers, 76 per cent of women end up with a father-in-law of a different class (Goldthorpe *et al.*, 1987). We have just seen that the most attractive working-class girls are likely to marry successful husbands.

If we look at the occupational mobility of women, compared with their fathers, the position is confused by the different job distribution of women. Wives often have jobs of different occupational class, mainly because women have a different pattern of jobs from men – fewer women in I, more in II (teachers, nurses, etc.), many more in III (n) (clerical, shop assistant, hairdressers, waitresses, etc), fewer in III (m) (skilled manual) and fewer in lower manual jobs. Heath (1981) compared the mobility of men in the Goldthorpe study with that of women obtained from the *General Household Survey* (Table 8.4). There was more upward mobility than down for both sexes, but less for women, 27 per cent v. 32 per cent for men, and more women moved down, 26 per cent v. 19 per cent for men. There was upward mobility from manual homes into class III jobs, but these were often not well paid, so that this is more symbolic than real mobility. Women can always avoid moving into class III (m) or below, because there are plenty of white-collar jobs for them.

It is difficult for women to get into class I jobs, partly because of male bias against them. Some jobs like management have been a kind of male preserve where women have had difficulty fitting in. But do women really want to be at the top? Obviously some do, but research on achievement motivation suggests that this drive works differently for women, and that 'success' for them may be defined primarily in terms of social competence and social acceptance. It was believed for a time that women had a 'fear of success', but later research found that this was only fear of losing femininity through success at male jobs (Janman, 1985). However, if this fear is widespread it would reduce the motivation of women to enter many class I jobs. Other studies have found that women are more cooperative but less competitive and less assertive – characteristics often needed to get to the top (Argyle, 1991).

Table 8.4 Single men and women: origins and destinations

|  | Father's class | | Respondent's class | |
|---|---|---|---|---|
|  | Men | Women | Men | Women |
| I } | 17.5 | 23.5 | 10.2 | 13.1 |
| II } |  |  | 12.1 | 24.9 |
| III | 9.8 | 12.2 | 16.5 | 40.3 |
| IV | 6.7 | 4.1 | 1.0 | – |
| V | 4.8 | 5.4 | 4.1 | 1.4 |
| VI | 34.6 | 27.6 | 28.6 | 4.5 |
| VII | 26.7 | 27.1 | 27.6 | 15.8 |
| Total | 100.1 | 99.9 | 100.1 | 100.0 |
| N | 315 | 221 | 315 | 221 |

Source: GHS, 1975
Sample: single men and women aged 25–64 in 1975 who reported income.

How about single women? There is a surplus of single women in II, about twice as many as the proportion of men, and a few more in I. There are 'good' women's jobs in II – teaching, nursing and social work, but it may mean sacrificing marriage and family to stay in them. Perhaps the women concerned have decided to stay single rather than marry 'down'. In any case they are probably very committed to their work.

We have seen that there are many cross-class marriages. Husband in I and wife in II or III (n) is quite common, so is husband in III (m) and wife in III (n) (Heath, 1981). However, men in class III jobs are paid about twice as much as women, and men in III (n) are much more likely to be in a career or promotion pattern than women (60 per cent v. 35 per cent) (Marshall et al., 1988). This is an interesting and possibly important source of integration of different classes.

# REFERENCES

Abraham, J. (1989) Testing Hargreaves' and Lacey's differentiation-polarisation theory in a setted comprehensive. British Journal of Sociology, 40, 46–87.

Argyle, M. (1991) Cooperation. London: Routledge.

Banks, M. et al. (1992) Careers and Identities. Milton Keynes: Open University Press.

Berscheid, E., Dion, K., Walster (Hatfield), E. and Walster, G.W. (1971) Physical attractiveness and dating choice: a test of the matching hypothesis. Journal of Experimental Social Psychology, 7, 173–89.

Boldsen, J.L. and Mascie-Taylor, C.G.N. (1985) Analysis of height variation in a contemporary British sample. Human Biology, 57, 473–80.

Boudon, R. (1974) Education, Opportunity and Social Inequality. New York: Wiley.

Braddon, F.E.M. et al. (1986) Onset of obesity in a 36 year birth cohort study. British Medical Journal, 293, 299–303.

Bull, R. (1979) The psychological significance of facial deformity. In M. Cook and G. Wilson (eds) Love and Attraction. Oxford: Pergamon.

Bull, R. and Rumsey, N. (1988) The Social Psychology of Facial Appearance. New York: Springer-Verlag.

Cassidy, T. and Lynn, R. (1991) Achievement motivation, educational attainment, cycles of disadvantage and social competence: some longitudinal data. *British Journal of Educational Psychology*, *61*, 1–12.

Cohen, J. (1985) Protestant ethic and status-attainment. *Sociological Analysis*. *46*, 49–58.

Cohen, J. (1987) Parents as educational models and definers. *Journal of Marriage and the Family*, *49*, 339–51.

Coleman, R.P., Rainwater, L. and McClelland, K.A. (1979) *Social Standing in America*. London: Routledge & Kegan Paul.

Crockett, H.J. (1962) The achievement motive and differential mobility in the United States. *American Sociological Review*, *27*, 191–204.

Deck, L. (1968) Reported in *Journal of College and University Personnel Association*, *19*, 33–7.

De Jong, W. (1980) The stigma of obesity: the consequences of naive assumptions concerning the causes of physical deviance. *Journal of Health and Social Behavior*, *21*, 75–87.

Dermer, M. and Thiel, D.L. (1975) When beauty may fail. *Journal of Personality and Social Psychology*, *31*, 1168–76.

Dion, K., Berscheid, E. and Walster, E. (1972) What is beautiful is good. *Journal of Personality and Social Psychology*, *24*, 285–90.

Douglas, J.W.B. (1964) *The Home and School*. London: MacGibbon & Kee.

Douglas, J.W.B., Ross, J.M. and Simpson, H.R. (1968) *All Our Future*. London: Peter Davies.

Douvan, E. and Adelson, J. (1958) The psychodynamics of social mobility in adolescent boys. *Journal of Abnormal and Social Psychology*, *56*, 31–44.

Elder, G.H. (1969) Appearance and education in marriage mobility. *American Sociological Review*, *34*, 519–33.

Fuller, M. (1984) Black girls in a London comprehensive school. In M. Hammersley and P. Woods (eds) *Life in School: The Sociology of Pupil Culture*. Milton Keynes: Open University Press.

Furnham, A. (1990) *The Protestant Work Ethic*. London: Routledge.

Ganzeboom, H.B.G., Treiman, D.J. and Ultee, W.C. (1991) Comparative inter-generational stratification research: three generations and beyond. *Annual Review of Sociology*, *17*, 277–302.

Gibson, J.B. (1970) Biological aspects of a high socio-economic group. *Journal of Biosocial Science*, *2*, 1–16.

Goldblatt, P.B., Moore, M.E. and Stunkard, A.J. (1965) Social factors in obesity. *Journal of the American Medical Association*, *192*, 1039–44.

Goldthorpe, J.H., Llewellyn, C. and Payne, C. (1987) *Social Mobility and Class Structure in Modern Britain*. Oxford: Clarendon Press.

Graziano, W., Brothen, T. and Berscheid, E. (1978) Height and attraction: do men and women see eye-to-eye? *Journal of Personality*, *46*, 128–45.

Hällström, T. and Noppa, H. (1981) Obesity in women in relation to mental illness, social factors and personality traits. *Journal of Psychosomatic Research*, *25*, 75–82.

Halsey, A.H. (1977) Towards meritocracy? The case of Britain. In J. Karabal and A.H. Halsey (eds) *Power and Ideology in Education*. New York: Oxford University Press.

Halsey, A.H., Heath, A.F. and Ridge, J.M. (1980) *Origins and Destinations*. Oxford: Clarendon Press.

Hargreaves, D.H. (1967) *Social Relations in a Secondary School*. London: Routledge & Kegan Paul.

Hatfield, E. and Sprecher, S. (1986) *Mirror, Mirror, On the Wall*. Albany: State University of New York Press.

Heath, A. (1981) *Social Mobility*. London: Fontana.

Hess, E.H. (1968) Attitude and pupil size. *Scientific American, 212* (4), 46–54.

Jackson, B. and Marsden, D. (1963) *Education and the Working Class*. London: Routledge & Kegan Paul.

Janman, K. (1985) Achievement motivation, fear of success, and occupational success. D. Phil. thesis, Oxford University.

Jencks, C. (1972) *Inequality*. Harmondsworth: Penguin.

Kerbo, H.R. (1983) *Social Stratification and Inequality*. New York: McGraw-Hill.

Kerchoff, A.C. (1974) Stratification processes and outcomes in England and the U.S.A. *American Sociological Review, 39,* 789–801.

Kets de Vries, M. (1977) The entrepreneurial personality: a person at the crossroads. *Journal of Management Studies, 14,* 34–57.

Kohn, M.L. and Schooler, C. (1982) Job conditions and personality: a longitudinal assessment of their reciprocal effects. *American Journal of Sociology, 87,* 1257–86.

Lenski, G. (1961) *The Religious Factor*. City Gardens, NY: Doubleday.

McClelland, D.C. (1987) *Human Motivation*. Cambridge: Cambridge University Press.

McClelland, D.C. and Boyatzis, R.E. (1982) The leadership motive pattern and long term success in management. *Journal of Applied Psychology, 67,* 737–43.

Marshall, G., Rose, D., Newby, H. and Vogler, C. (1988) *Social Class and Modern Britain*. London: Unwin Hyman.

Mascie-Taylor, C.G. (1991) *Biosocial Aspects of Social Class*. Oxford: Oxford University Press.

Mascie-Taylor, C.G.N. and Gibson, J.B. (1978) Social mobility and IQ components. *Journal of Biosocial Science, 10,* 263–76.

Mathes, E.W. and Kahn, A. (1975) Physical attractiveness, happiness, neuroticism and self-esteem. *Journal of Personality, 90,* 27–30.

Mazur, A., Mazur, J. and Keating, C. (1984) Military rank attainment of a West Point class: effect of cadets' physical features. *American Journal of Sociology, 90,* 125–52.

Napoleon, T., Chassin, N. and Young, R.D. (1980) A replication and extension of 'physical attractiveness and mental illness'. *Journal of Abnormal Psychology, 86,* 41–6.

Payne, G. (1992) Competing views of contemporary social mobility and social divisions. In R. Burrows and C. Marsh (eds) *Consumption and Class*. London: Macmillan.

Phares, E.J. (1976) *Locus of Control in Personality*. Morristown, NJ: General Learning Press.

Porter, J.N. (1976) Socialization and mobility in educational and early occupational attainment. *Sociology of Education, 49,* 23–33.

Quinn, R., Tabor, J. and Gordon, L. (1968) *The Decision to Discriminate*. Ann Arbor, Mich.: Survey Research Center.

Reid, I. (1989) *Social Class Differences in Britain*. 3rd edition. London: Fontana.

Reis, H.T., Wheeler, L., Spiegel, N., Kernis, M.H., Nezlek, K.J. and Perri, M. (1982) Physical attractiveness in social interaction: II. Why does appearance affect social experience. *Journal of Personality and Social Psychology, 43,* 979–96.

Richardson, C.J. (1977) *Contemporary Social Mobility*. London: Pinter.

Rist, R. (1970) Student social class and teacher expectations: the self-fulfilling prophecy in ghetto education. *Harvard Educational Review, 40.*

Rosenthal, R. and Jacobson, L. (1968) *Pygmalion in the Classroom*. New York: Holt, Rinehart & Winston.

Rumsey, N., Bull, R. and Gahagan, D. (1982) The effect of facial disfigurement on the proxemic behavior of the general public. *Journal of Applied Social Psychology, 12,* 137–50.

Singer, J.E. (1964) The use of manipulation strategies: Machiavellianism and attractiveness. *Sociometry*, *27*, 138–50.

Snarey, J.R. and Vaillant, G.E. (1985) How lower- and working-class youth become middle-class adults: the association between ego defense mechanisms and upward social mobility. *Child Development*, *56*, 899–910.

Sobal, J. and Stunkard, A.J. (1989) Socioeconomic status and obesity: a review of the literature. *Psychological Bulletin*, *105*, 260–75.

Sorokin, P.A. (1964) *Social and Cultural Mobility*. New York: Free Press.

Snyder, M., Tanke, E.D. and Berscheid, E. (1977) Behavioral confirmation in social interaction from social perception to social reality. *Journal of Personality and Social Psychology*, *35*, 656–66.

Tanner, J.M. (1989) *Foetus into Man*. 2nd edition. Ware: Castlemead.

Walster, E., Aronson, V., Abrahams, A. and Rohmann, L. (1966) Importance of physical attractiveness in dating behavior. *Journal of Personality and Social Psychology*, *4*, 508–16.

Weber, M. (1904) *The Protestant Ethic and the Spirit of Capitalism*. New York: Scribner.

Willis, P. (1977) *Learning to Labour*. Farnborough: Saxon House.

Wilson, P.R. (1968) Perceptual distortion of height as a function of ascribed academic status. *Journal of Social Psychology*, *74*, 97–102.

Winter, D.G. (1973) *The Power Motive*. New York: Free Press.

Zajonc, R.B. (1976) Family configuration and intelligence. *Science*, *192*, 227–36.

# Chapter 9

# Inter-class attitudes

In this book we are looking at detailed research on social class, which is available only from Britain, the USA and other industrial societies, and from the recent past. This is the place and time that we are in, so it concerns us most, but it confines us to a limited section of the human story. The results are not necessarily true for other times and places.

## SELF-PERCEIVED CLASS

As we saw in Chapter 1, about 95 per cent of people in Britain are able to place themselves in some social class. They recognise that there is a class system and have some idea of their place in it. On the other hand, as we also saw, self-perceived class has a far from perfect correspondence with class as assessed by social scientists. The main reason for this is that, while social scientists in Britain define class by occupation, those concerned use a number of other criteria as well, like accent, appearance and style of life.

However, not everyone is closely identified with the class they think they belong to. Gurin *et al.* (1980) found that only about 28 per cent of men with middle-class or working-class jobs felt closely identified with those classes. The remainder were equally divided between those who identified with their class, though not strongly, and those who did not identify with it at all. This was an American study, and those who were black identified more strongly with the black group.

Furthermore people may have a very hazy idea of what belonging to a class means. Runciman (1966) found that many of his sample of manual workers could not think of 'any sorts of people doing noticeably better at the moment than you and your family'. In the 'affluent worker' study (Goldthorpe *et al.*, 1968), Luton car workers saw little opposition between themselves and the employers, disapproved of the connection between the unions and the Labour party and enjoyed their work because they were well paid. These individuals too showed little understanding of their membership of the working class.

'Class consciousness' is a complex idea, and has several components. Being able to name the class one belongs to is the first stage, followed by different degrees of identification with it. Other components, for the lower classes especially, are discontent with power, a belief that the situation is illegitimate and being prepared to take collective action (Gurin *et al.*, 1980). Some writers think that holding class-related political attitudes is part of class consciousness; however, the correlation here is far from perfect, as we shall see below.

## Images of classes

Most people recognise that there is a class system of some kind, though they have different views of what it is like. They may recognise different numbers of classes. Only 5 per cent of people think that there is only one class. Many people recognise two classes, 59 per cent in Newby's study of farm workers (1977). When asked to place themselves, 36 per cent say they are middle-class, 46 per cent working-class, which makes up 82 per cent of the population. On the other hand, people are able to place occupations in order of social status, so they evidently do recognise finer divisions.

How are the members of different classes perceived? We saw earlier that the main criteria used in Britain are way of life, family, job, money and education (p. 5). Centers (1949) carried out a survey of 1,100 adult Americans, and asked them the criteria other than occupation for including a person in each class. He found that different criteria were used by members of different classes.

*Table 9.1* Criteria for class membership: what would you say puts a person in each social class? (percentages)

|  | By own class | National |
|---|---|---|
| *Upper class* | | |
| Wealth, income | 34.5 | 66.8 |
| Education | 31.0 | 24.1 |
| Family origins, family position, etc. | 34.5 | 13.9 |
| Attitudes and beliefs | 20.7 | 5.9 |
| *Middle class* | | |
| Money, income, etc. | 39 | 36 |
| Not rich, not poor, live comfortably, all necessities and some luxuries | 20 | 13 |
| Education | 18 | 13 |
| Family | 13 | 9 |
| *Working class* | | |
| 'Working for a living' | 37 | 26 |
| Manual, common, mill or factory work or labour | 20 | 23 |
| Lack of income | 14 | 14 |
| Being an employee or wage earner | 11 | 10 |

*Source:* Centers, 1949

It can be seen that upper-class individuals were generally simply seen as rich, but saw themselves also as people who are educated, from good family and holding certain attitudes and beliefs. Middle-class people (nearly 40 per cent of the sample) saw themselves much as others did. But working-class individuals saw themselves primarily as people who work for their living.

People also have images of the kinds of people in their own and other classes. Dittmar (1992) asked students to rate the personalities of target persons, whose possessions had been described or shown on video and experimentally varied. Rich people were perceived as more forceful and in control of their environment, while poor people were seen as friendly, warm and unselfish, high in individuality and self-expression. We saw earlier (p. 135) that target persons with an educated middle-class accent were perceived as having more intelligence, ambition, self-confidence and leadership; the same speaker, using a regional accent, was seen as more honest, friendly, generous, likeable, trustworthy and having a better sense of humour.

In this chapter we shall consider several other aspects of class awareness, such as the images which people have of different classes, perceived injustice and willingness to engage in collective action on behalf of a class.

Lockwood (1966) interpreted a lot of British sociological research on class to show that there are three kinds of worker, with different images of the class system.

(a) 'Traditional workers', like miners and dockers, lived in close-knit communities, with strong links between workers, were a radical working-class proletariat and saw society as consisting of two classes, 'us and them', divided by differences of power.

(b) 'Deferential workers' were employed in small firms, had direct contact with employers or managers, and often accepted their right to manage. They saw the class system as a hierarchy of status, lifestyle and social acceptance, with three, four or more classes. On the other hand, most of Newby's farm workers held the two-class power model. Agricultural workers are in a special situation: they are basically in a two-class system where the farmers have a lot of power and the workers have very little. And there are few people in between.

(c) 'Privatised workers' were those in mass-production factories, living in new housing estates, who thought of work as a source of instrumental reward and had weak bonds with work-mates or neighbours. Living in the new housing estates with many other 'ordinary people who work for a living', all belonging to the new working class or new middle class, the main differences between them were of money and possessions, and this is how they saw class. In the 'affluent worker' study 54 per cent held this money model of classes rather than the other two (Goldthorpe *et al.*, 1968).

Leahy (1981) surveyed 720 American children aged 6–17. He asked them to describe rich and poor people, and the differences between them. The youngest children mainly used peripheral attributes like possessions, the older ones increasingly referred to central categories like traits and thoughts. Lower-class subjects referred more to the thoughts of the poor, perhaps taking their point of view, while upper-class children used the traits of the poor, perhaps seeing them as 'others'. In a Canadian study Baldus and Tribe (1978) found that 8–12-year-olds thought that poor people were tough, rough, lazy, irresponsible, drank a lot and likely to have unlikeable and unsuccessful children. Rich people were thought to be well-mannered, cheerful, nice, intelligent and happy, though some children thought they were also greedy and bossy.

*Table 9.2* Percentage of people rating explanations for poverty in their country

| United Kingdom (27%) | |
| --- | --- |
| 1. Laziness | 45 |
| 2. Chronic unemployment | 42 |
| 3. Drink | 40 |
| 4. Ill health | 36 |
| 5. Too many children | 31 |
| 6. Old age and loneliness | 30 |
| 7. Lack of education | 29 |
| 8. Lack of foresight | 21 |
| 9. Deprived childhood | 16 |
| France (40%) | |
| 1. Old age and loneliness | 50 |
| 2. Deprived childhood | 44 |
| 3. Ill health | 38 |
| 4. Lack of education | 37 |
| 5. Chronic unemployment | 36 |
| 6. Drink | 31 |
| 7. Too many children | 26 |
| 8. Laziness | 15 |
| 9. Lack of foresight | 15 |
| Germany (39%) | |
| 1. Deprived childhood | 47 |
| 2. Ill health | 42 |
| 3. Lack of education | 41 |
| 4. Chronic unemployment | 38 |
| 5. Old age and loneliness | 32 |
| 6. Drink | 31 |
| 7. Laziness | 30 |
| 8. Lack of foresight | 18 |
| 9. Too many children | 17 |

*Source:* EEC, 1977
*Note:* The % brackets after the country's name refers to the percentage of people in the respective countries who maintain that they have seen people in poverty.

## Lay explanations and attributions

Members of different classes give different explanations for wealth and poverty, unemployment, success and failure. An EEC survey of perceptions of poverty in different European countries found somewhat different views in different places. The results for the UK, France and Germany are given in Table 9.2. These can be seen as the views of the majority about the poor minority, i.e. the lower working class. The differences between countries here may reflect real differences between social conditions or may be due to different stereotypes.

Different explanations for poverty are given by rich and poor. Feagin (1975), in a large American survey, found that middle-class people blamed the poor themselves (lack of thrift, lack of effort, lack of ability, loose morals and drunkenness, sickness and physical handicaps). The poor on the other hand explained poverty in terms of structural features of society (low wages in some industries, failure of society to provide good schools, racial prejudice, failure of private industry to provide jobs, being taken advantage of by rich people). The poor also attached more importance to bad luck. Individualistic explanations, i.e. blaming the poor for their poverty, are also more widespread among older people and those with conservative political views (Furnham, 1988).

These studies show that middle-class people think the poor are poor because they are thriftless, idle, lacking in ability, etc. How do people see the rich? A number of studies in Britain, the USA and Australia have found the most widely held explanations are:

| | |
|---|---|
| 1 *Individualistic:* | hard work |
| | careful money management |
| | very intelligent |
| 2 *Societal*: | high wages in some jobs |
| | family influence |
| 3 *Fatalistic*: | inherited wealth |
| | having a lucky break |
| | born with a good business sense |

(Furnham, 1988)

In these studies, individualistic explanations were rated as more important by richer people and by conservative voters, while the opposite was found for societal explanations; there was less difference for fatalistic ones.

Similar results were obtained in a comparison of British boys at a public (i.e. fee-paying) and a state school. The public school boys attributed failure by one of their own group to lack of effort rather than lack of ability, but the reverse for a state school boy. State school boys attributed failure by one of their own group to bad luck. The public school boys emphasised their intellectual ability and higher academic standards, while the state

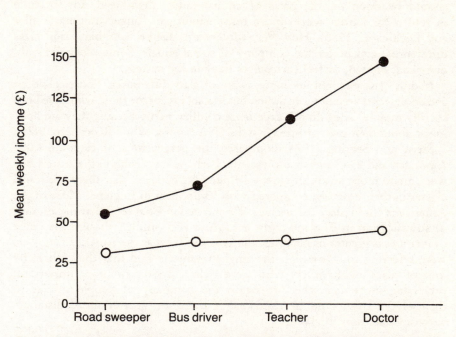

*Figure 9.1* Income estimates for each occupation by middle-class and working-class children; ●—● middle class; ○—○ working class
*Source:* Emler and Dickinson, 1985

school boys pointed to the privilege of a public school education (Hewstone *et al.*, 1982).

## The development of class attitudes and beliefs

A number of studies have shown the development of ideas about class with age. At 5–6 children recognise the difference between rich and poor, from observation of the size of houses, cars and other possessions. By 10 they recognise an intermediate class and a hierarchy of occupations of different pay, calling for different abilities and effort. Emler and Dickinson (1985) found that 7–12-year-olds realised that there were pay differentials between four occupations; however the middle-class children thought (correctly) that these differences were a lot greater than working-class children thought (Figure 9.1).

Adolescents have an increased understanding of class, realise that differences are partly due to ability and effort, as well as to social factors outside the individual. There is greater acceptance of the legitimacy of differences in rewards. The majority of children agree that there should be unequal distribution of income and goods, especially older children. They think this should be done on the basis of equity rather than need, for example in return for harder work, more responsibility or longer training (Emler and Dickinson, 1985). However, adolescents dislike 'snobbery' and class differences, and prefer the company of social equals. Some recognise only one class, or two, or feel themselves outside the system.

Middle-class children are more aware of class differences. Poorer children and adolescents are not more aware, but less so, except for those who have been socially mobile. They do not experience conflict, partly because they are optimistic about their own prospects, in the USA (Simmons and Rosenberg, 1971).

Stern and Searing (1976) compared the perceptions of class of 1,090 American and 834 English adolescents. Perhaps surprisingly, the Americans were much more aware of class – 74 per cent believed that there are social classes in their country, compared with 53 per cent in England. More of the Americans could place themselves. We showed in Chapter 2 that the amount of stratification in England and the USA is very similar, though the range of incomes is greater in America. Perhaps this is what the American subjects were referring to. However, the English subjects said that they felt more 'out of place' with others who were richer, poorer or more important, preferring more than the Americans the company of people similar to themselves. This could be explained if there are greater *social* distances between classes in England.

## SOCIAL DISTANCE AND HOSTILITY BETWEEN CLASSES

Marx thought that lower classes had a relationship of hostility and deference to those above them. In this section we will examine the present degree of hostility between classes. A recent British Social Attitudes Survey (Smith, 1989) found that 52 per cent in Britain perceived that there are strong or very strong conflicts between rich and poor (USA 59 per cent); and 20 per cent perceived such conflict between the working and middle classes (Italy 45 per cent). National Opinion Polls found that a majority thought that there is a class struggle in this country (AB 66 per cent, DE 72 per cent) (Reid, 1989). And this proportion is not falling over time, in fact it has gradually increased since 1964, when it was only 48 per cent (Abercrombie and Ward, 1988).

Zingraff and Schulman (1989) found that, among textile workers in the American South, awareness of class conflict was greatest in workers of low income, or who were black, members of unions and those dissatisfied with their jobs. Marshall and colleagues (1988) asked which issues were thought to cause class conflict. The overwhelming answer was 'money, generally (including envy of a particular lifestyle)' 65 per cent, followed by lack of understanding or communication, ignorance 8.2 per cent, public verses private services (in health, education, etc.) 6.9 per cent, employment versus unemployment 5.6 per cent.

How much hostility is there between members of different social classes? In times of revolution, the heads of the rich may roll and the streets run with blood. During recent strikes in Britain the only actual warfare has been between the strikers and police. The police may be seen as defending the middle class and their property, but most police are themselves working-class, in education and lifestyle if not in pay or social attitudes. There is a lot of working-class crime, but, as we have seen, little of it is directed against members of higher classes. Runciman (1966) found that only 23 per cent of manual workers disapproved of other people being paid more. And many people accept the need for pay differentials and are not opposed to the status quo.

Feather (1989) found indirect evidence of hostility to those who are better off and more successful. He investigated attitudes in Australia to the fall of 'tall poppies', i.e. individuals who had occupied a high position and failed, fallen from the top of the ladder. He found that Australians were more pleased when people fell from the top rather than from the middle of the ladder, e.g. in a stock market crash, or when a politician was caught out in a misdemeanour, especially when that person was felt not to have earned his position in the first place. There was greatest satisfaction on the part of individuals who were themselves low in self-esteem and held left-wing attitudes.

How great is the 'social distance' between members of different classes? Vignettes describing people of different classes, races, etc., can be presented, and subjects asked to indicate how close a relationship they would accept with each individual. Triandis and Triandis (1960) used a scale with items

From: 1. I would marry this person
To: 2. I would be willing to participate in the lynching of this person.

They found that race created more social distance than class, and that the people who expressed the greatest distance from other classes were those who were prejudiced against out-groups in general. We studied cross-class relationships in Chapter 4, and found that most friends, neighbours, etc., come from the same or adjacent classes, especially for those in the highest and lowest classes. However, many friends do not come from the same class, 39 per cent in one of Willmott's studies in London. There are two major exceptions to this within-class exclusiveness. One is the people known through leisure groups, all of which provide some degree of social mix. Research on race relations has found that racial prejudice can be reduced by sheer contact with members of the other race. However, the contact has to be of the right kind – equal status, cooperative, intimate and with pleasant members of the other group. Leisure groups can provide exactly these conditions; status within the club is equal. There is an additional positive factor – leisure group activities are very enjoyable, so that contact with the other group is strongly reinforced. Research shows that inter-class contact is most successful in leisure groups when they are engaged in a definite activity, and when the club is fairly small and informal (Bottomore, 1954). The wearing of costume, e.g. for sport or dancing, may help to conceal class differences.

The second exception is relations between kin who have ended up in different classes as the result of social mobility. The result is typically to weaken the relationship, and reduce frequency of meeting, though not very much. And in the case of sisters, and mothers and daughters, there is very little change in the relationship.

## DEFERENCE AND RESPECT

Traditional working-class people, sociologists believe, 'knew their place', behaved in a way that was cooperative and deferential towards their superiors. How far do working-class people hold deferential attitudes today? We have just seen that working-class people perceive middle- and upper-class people as richer, better educated and doing professional and managerial jobs. We saw earlier that they rate speakers with RP accents higher in education, leadership, ambition, etc. (p. 135). Some working-class individuals explain the wealth of the rich as being due to hard work, intelligence and careful money management (though others put it down to inheritance or luck). We saw similarly that the upper and middle classes see members of the working class as poor, uneducated, doing manual jobs, and explained poverty as being due to lack of ability, effort, etc.

It is likely that such attitudes vary between different sections of the working class. Newby (1977) studied a very traditional section, agricultural workers in East Anglia. He found that most of them had an image of a two-class society, the farmers and the farm-workers, and thought that mobility was impossible. They had some very conservative attitudes, e.g. 47 per cent thought 'the best leaders of the country come from an upper-class background'. They recognised their powerlessness, and 50 per cent saw relations with employers as basically conflicting. They interacted with their employers in a deferential way – because of the latter's power to hire, fire and reward. However, Newby concluded that only 15 per cent had a genuinely deferential and subordinate attitude to their employers. Comparisons with industrial workers showed that the latter are much less deferential in their attitudes. In their study of 'Yankee City', Warner and Lunt (1947) found that those who lived there had no difficulty in assigning higher or lower status to various groups of people. Some were regarded as 'superior', others as 'inferior', some were given a 'high' position, others 'low'. It was believed that those from the lower groups had an inferior lifestyle with low sexual morals and behaviour that was regarded as ludicrous and uncouth. The 'classes' were looked up to, the 'masses' were despised (p. 5).

It does not tell us whether the 'deference' described affects behaviour.

Warner and colleagues reported that people knew their place when thinking of joining a club or association – they knew where they would be acceptable, and many didn't even know of the existence of some of the highest-status clubs. We describe elsewhere how the leadership of clubs of all kinds tends to be drawn from the higher class members (p. 75), suggesting a kind of deference, perhaps based on the belief that they have more knowledge or skill, or would do it better.

A similar kind of deference is found in the election of the foremen of juries. Middle-class people usually become foremen, and they are usually male and middle-aged as well. A number of laboratory experiments have been carried out to find the cues which result in someone becoming an informal leader. Three alternatives have been investigated: (1) knowledge of occupational status, (2) dominant non-verbal style and (3) concern with task issues. Each of these variables has been shown to be important in different studies. But social class is likely to be manifest by both status and demeanour, under normal conditions: both have the power of creating deference (see p. 53).

Deference is common between the ranks of social organisations – privates salute officers, nurses do what doctors tell them. In any social organisation those in the higher ranks have more power, more status and usually more pay than those lower down. Subordinates have to do what they are told, and usually behave in a respectful and deferential manner. Often they actually do respect their seniors, since the latter have been promoted because of their competence. If the boss simply inherited his position, he is still the source of employment.

Deference is a feature of most sales situations, where 'the customer is always right', and deference is likely to lead to more sales. It is also true of other personal service occupations, like hairdressers, waiters and others. Often these sales and personal service workers are themselves prosperous and middle class, but put on a deferential act for work. But it is this deferential relationship which may have created the traditional social inferiority of 'trade'.

## PERCEIVED JUSTICE OF THE INCOME DIFFERENCE

We have seen that there are large class differences in income and wealth. How far is this accepted as just, and how far is it seen as unfair? Recent large-scale surveys in Britain have found that most people think that things are not fair. A British Social Attitudes Survey found that 75 per cent of people in Britain agreed that income differences were too large (this compares with 56 per cent in the USA, 86 per cent in Italy) (Smith, 1989).

Gallie (1983) found that 60 per cent of a sample of 196 English oil refinery employees, and rather more French, believed that there is 'a great difference in living standards', and 74 per cent that there is a 'great' or 'quite a lot' of

*Table 9.3* Class differences in perception of fairness (Great Britain, 1984)
(percentages)

| | I | II | III | IV | V | VI | VII | All |
|---|---|---|---|---|---|---|---|---|
| *Distribution of wealth and income is not perceived as fair* | 69 | 66 | 72 | 56 | 76 | 75 | 78 | 71 |
| *Why not?* | | | | | | | | |
| Gap between haves and have nots is too wide | 57 | 59 | 63 | 64 | 55 | 63 | 63 | |
| Pay differentials are too wide | 21 | 19 | 19 | 19 | 26 | 21 | 19 | |
| Some people acquire wealth too easily (unearned income etc.) | 13 | 16 | 13 | 13 | 20 | 10 | 9 | |

*Source:* Marshall *et al.*, 1988

difference in respect, between classes (Gallie, 1983). In this study 48 per cent of the English employees thought that the richest had not deserved it. This was mostly because of inheritance, though some thought it was due to exploitation or fraud. On the other hand 49 per cent thought that the rich have deserved it. Marshall and colleagues (1988) found that 70 per cent of British adults thought that the distribution of income and wealth was unfair; 27 per cent thought it *was* fair.

How far does concern with unfair income differences vary with social class? Not as much as we might expect. Little variation with class was found in the large, representative British survey by Marshall *et al.*, using the seven Goldthorpe classes. Class IV (self-employed) thought the distribution was fairer than other groups did; class V (lower grade technicians) thought pay differences were too great (Table 9.3).

Marshall and colleagues carried out a further analysis of this problem. They made up an index of six questions about topics related to income re-distribution, e.g. support for incomes policy to favour the low paid. This new index was found to be clearly related to social class, both current class and class of origin.

Perception of unfairness of income distribution is clearly related to support for political parties. In a British sample survey, respondents were asked how they felt about the gap between the lowest paid and the highest paid in the workplace. Again it was found that only about 30–40 per cent thought that the gap was too great, but the percentage with this point of view was higher for Labour supporters (47.5 per cent) than for Alliance or Conservative (both 31.5 per cent).

| | Conservative (M/F) | Alliance (M/F) | Labour (M/F) |
|---|---|---|---|
| Much too big | 28/35 | 34/29 | 51/44 |
| About right | 63/50 | 54/55 | 35/39 |
| Too small | 4/4 | 9/– | 4/3 |

Evans (1992) re-analysed the data from this survey, and found that social class was indeed correlated with class identity and with attitudes clearly related to class interests, such as taxes on company profits, but not to other egalitarian attitudes like helping the low paid and unemployed at cost to self. He concludes that such working-class attitudes reflect instrumental self-interest, not egalitarianism, or any affective class loyalty. It is interesting that a lot of the population think that things are fair.

Runciman (1966) found that many manual workers were quite contented with their salaries. Asked 'Do you think there are any sorts of people doing noticeably better at the moment than you and your family?', about 25 per cent did not. The proportion was highest for the better-paid manual workers (39 per cent). Asked to give a 'proper income' for self or husband, 56 per cent of this group named a figure less than their present salary. Manual workers were more satisfied with their wages than non-manual workers with a similar wage, since they compared themselves with other manual workers, most of whom were paid less, while the non-manual workers compared themselves with better paid non-manual workers. Asked what consumer goods they would like, the non-manual workers had higher aspirations than the manual workers. We do not know that choice of reference group caused satisfaction with pay – it could be the other way round, for example discontented workers might seek better-paid groups to support their sense of grievance.

We should note that many of Runciman's manual workers were well aware of the benefits of middle-class life. About one third would like a son to be a teacher, or have some other non-manual job, rather than have a better-paid job as a foreman, and would like a son to go to a fee-paying school. Emler and Dickinson (1985) found that poorer children thought salary differences were less legitimate. School provides an introduction to the occupational and class hierarchy, as it channels pupils towards different careers and social futures related to their ability and efforts. Most people when they have left school accept the existence of and need for a class hierarchy, except for the drop-outs who join the counter-culture (Furnham and Stacey, 1991).

Although a majority think that things are unfair, some are egalitarians. Indeed, 26 per cent think that 'large differences in prosperity are necessary for material prosperity' (Smith, 1989). About half of the subjects in the Marshall survey thought that the income gap in the workplace was about right. How do people think that incomes should be distributed? One theory is that incomes should be distributed in proportion to merit, to what individuals contribute to society. Another theory is that income should be related to need. Alves and Rossi (1978) conducted a very interesting study with an American sample of 522 using fifty vignettes, describing individuals of different sex, marital status, number of children, education, occupation and annual earnings; subjects were asked to judge how far those individuals were overpaid or underpaid, to find out what people thought was the fair salary.

The average salary thought to be fair for individuals was $19,000 p.a. Was merit or need considered more important?

*Merit*

*Occupation* made a difference of $5,600 for men, $4,700 for women, comparing the top and bottom of the occupational scale.
*Education* added $195 for each year of education, college added $779, the whole range was $1,370. This means that the best jobs combined with the best education were thought to be worth $22,485 and the worst $15,515, a ratio of nearly 1.5:1, i.e. the best-paid would get about 50 per cent more.

*Need*

*Children*. Each child added $325, six children added $1,950.
*Marriage*. In a similar study Jasso and Rossi (1977) found that fair rates for married men in the middle of the range were $1,700 more than those for single men.

It seems that both merit and need were taken into account, but merit counted more than need. Richer people in particular thought that merit counted more, poor people that need did. Gender and ethnicity were not counted at all. In this and other studies there is a consensus that there should be both lower and upper limits on incomes, in this case of $13,187 and $34,593 respectively for couples where at least one is working (Jasso and Rossi, 1977), which is to some extent brought about by taxation and welfare.

Studies of children also show that older children increasingly accept the legitimacy of different pay for different occupations (Hook and Cook, 1979).

Emler and Dickson (1985) asked British children how much they thought various occupations should be paid. Middle-class children of 11 thought that doctors should be paid 2.64 times as much as road sweepers, while working-class children of the same age thought they should be paid 1.61 times as much. The authors conclude that these class differences reflected the social representations and prejudices of their cultural milieux.

In his study of 720 American children, Leahy (1983) found that children increasingly challenged poverty from 6–11, and wealth from 6–14, but that 17-year-olds had greater acceptance of wealth differences. Dickinson (1991) found that half of a group of London students thought that wages should depend on need, while 53 per cent referred to effort, 34 per cent to training and 29 per cent to importance to the community. A third thought that wage differentials should be increased or stay the same.

Another way of tackling the problem is to see how far objective characteristics of people or their jobs are in fact reflected in salaries. Jobs have been analysed in this way to remove sex inequalities. A committee awards points for different aspects of jobs, e.g. the skills required, the effort, responsibility and the job conditions. The total points are found to correlate well with actual salaries. The points for a range of jobs are plotted against salaries to give the best-fitting line and salaries of particular jobs can then be deduced (McCormick and Ilgen, 1985). Another idea didn't work so well. Jaques (1961) proposed that a key feature of jobs is the 'time-span of responsibility', i.e. the period of time which may elapse before a worker's supervisor can know whether he or she is working efficiently (Jaques, 1961). In practice this is the length of the longest job performed. These predictions were tested on 141 managers in an American firm. It was found that the correlations between pay and time-span were positive but were extremely small, in the range of .1 to .2, thus providing very weak support for the theory as stated (Goodman, 1967).

Satisfaction with pay depends very much on how far it is thought to be fair. In a study of employed men in Madison, Wisconsin, Berkowitz et al. (1987) found that perceived inequity was a major predictor (−.49) of satisfaction with pay. Perception of equity depends mainly on comparisons with other people of similar qualifications or in similar jobs. Rupert Brown (1978) found that industrial workers said they would prefer a wages situation where they received £2 per week less, if this would increase their differential over a rival group to £1 per week.

## PERCEIVED LEGITIMACY OF POWER AND OTHER CLASS DIFFERENCES

As well as being paid less, working-class people have less power, or think that they do. It is believed for example that 'the laws favour the rich' by 72 per cent of manual workers and 59 per cent of white-collar workers (Goldthorpe et al., 1968). Similar differences are found for 'big business has too much power', but the opposite for 'trade unions have too much power' (Mann, 1970). In the American study by Gurin et al. (1980) 52 per cent of working men thought that their group had too little influence, compared to 31 per cent of middle-class people. Similar differences are found for the perception that there are equal opportunities or that getting ahead depends on luck and influence rather than hard work (Mann, 1970).

How far are people willing to do something about inequality of incomes? Social identity theory (see p. 223) suggests several alternative kinds of action. Some leave the low-status groups and become socially mobile. Some are prepared to try to bring about radical social change by militant methods. There have of course been such revolutions in many parts of the world; the nearest to such a revolution in Britain may have been the General Strike in 1925. Since then there has been a decline in such militancy, and the main remaining source of militant action is some of the trade unions, and an attempt at a revolution took place in 1984–5 in the miners' strike. The decline in working-class militancy is partly because the gap between rich and poor has become smaller (pp. 9–10), partly because the Labour party has abandoned revolutionary ideas in favour of parliamentary political action, and the unions have pursued specific improvements in working conditions rather than widespread political changes. Meanwhile management has improved things for workers by job enrichment, teamwork and other methods. Furthermore there are fewer manual workers (p. 19), many of them are now black (which arouses other kinds of conflict) and in any case there is conflict between unions, and conflict of interest between those who are union members and those who are not, so that there is little working-class solidarity (Abercrombie and Warde, 1988; Scase, 1992).

A number of studies have found a stronger collectivist orientation, a willingness to take group action, among manual workers. Gurin *et al.* (1980) found that 44 per cent of those who identified with working men had such views, compared with only 14 per cent of middle-class people. Of those who identified with blacks, 61 per cent had such a collectivist attitude.

One reason that the underprivileged usually do nothing about their position is that many of them believe the system is fair, as we have seen. And one reason for this is that there are social forces which are able to 'legitimate' inequality.

## The legitimation of inequality

We have seen that all human societies have class systems, in which some groups of people have higher status and receive greater rewards than others. Why do the lower orders on the whole accept such unfair distributions of rewards? In very primitive societies we saw that greater esteem and rewards were given to those most skilled at hunting and at dealing with supernatural powers, because of the greater contribution they made to the general welfare. In the Roman Empire slaves were kept in their place partly by the force of law, but also by the belief that they were inferior and this was their proper place. In caste systems the lowest caste accepted their lot, and kept their place for fear of losing their jobs in this world or worse to follow in the next life. In feudalism military power and law were supported by widespread acceptance of the right of kings and others to rule. These are all ways in which inequality is 'legitimated', in which those who receive lesser rewards are persuaded that this is just. We have seen that most people nowadays think that there should be differences in income, depending on education, occupation, age and sex. People apparently believe in equity theory, that rewards should be in proportion to 'inputs' in some way, but there may be disagreement on which inputs count. Being male now counts for less than before, for example. Some people think that 'need' is more important than 'merit'; lower-status people emphasise need where higher-status people think that merit should count for more.

Della Fave (1980) used self-esteem as the key to how legitimation works. He argues that self-evaluation is based on how people are treated at work, by the state in giving welfare, etc., and by other people in general, in other words on their social class (we have seen that this is partly true). Higher-status individuals have more subordinates to provide positive feedback, they can manipulate situations so that they can present themselves positively. By the real nature of their work, and by sheer impression management, high-status individuals create the perception, both in their own minds and the minds of others, that they should be evaluated positively, and are therefore worth more and deserve greater rewards, though this is largely a self-fulfilling process (Kerbo, 1983).

Widespread belief that there is equal opportunity for education, or for good jobs, adds to the legitimation process. Those who are doing badly now have only themselves and their lack of ability or effort to blame. Lane (1962) interviewed American working men; they believed that their low status was due to some defect in themselves.

Durkheim (1897) argued that the strains in society have increased now that everyone is seeking the same goals of wealth and success. In feudal and caste systems it was possible for people at all levels to obtain self-respect by pursuit of the socially defined goals for their group. Sociologists from Durkheim onwards have seen the importance of rituals and ceremony, for strengthening social bonds and for strengthening hierarchical social structures, since members play out their proper roles in these ceremonies. Religious beliefs, in the after-life and the virtue of poverty, give further legitimation for inequality (p. 256).

There is a positive side to awareness of differentials – the more prosperous agree to some amount of re-distribution. Marshall *et al.* found that 64 per cent of classes VI and VII were in favour of taxes on company profits to create jobs v. 24 per cent of class I. Over 30 per cent of classes V–VII supported taxes to finance increased welfare benefits v. 24 per cent of class I. But only 23 per cent overall were willing to accept pay restraint to reduce wage differentials. To this can be added the 45 per cent of the salariat who do not vote Conservative (Table 9.4), but instead vote Labour or Liberal/SDP. We shall see that there are people with working-class origins or who work in certain kinds of jobs who, for one reason or another, think it right to vote against their own class interests.

## POLITICAL BEHAVIOUR, POLITICAL ATTITUDES AND CLASS

### Class-linked voting

Individuals of higher social class, and especially those who are better educated, are more likely to vote or take part in other kinds of political activity. In one American election, those with degrees had a rate of voting

38 per cent higher than those with less than five years' education (Kinder and Sears, 1985). In Britain middle-class people are also more willing to attend demonstrations, join boycotts and occupy buildings (Phillips, 1985). Middle-class people are more politically active in more conventional ways too: 40 per cent of AB, compared with 22 per cent of C and 15 per cent of DE, reported that they had engaged in five or more political activities such as helping raise funds, taken an active part in a campaign or contacted a councillor or MP (Reid, 1989). Working-class people have less faith in politics and are more likely to think that parties are all the same (Marshall *et al.*, 1988).

Part of the reason for this working-class lack of participation in politics is that many working-class people do not trust politicians or the political system, do not believe that anything they do can have any effect, as many surveys have shown (Mann, 1970). Why do they hold such views? It may be part of a broader syndrome of beliefs described elsewhere as 'external control', produced by experience of inability to control events at work or elsewhere (p. 166).

The main effect of class on politics however is that working-class people are more likely to vote for left-wing parties, middle-class people for right-wing parties. By 'left-wing' is meant favouring more equal distribution of income and wealth, the nationalisation of industry and state provision of health, education and welfare. The extent of this class linkage is quite strong, as is shown in the results of the 1959 and 1987 elections. However, there is obviously a lot of 'deviant' voting – many working-class people vote Conservative and many middle-class people vote Labour. Alford (1962) suggested an index of class-linked voting: the percentage of the working class voting left minus the percentage of the middle class voting left. The index is 40 per cent for 1959, 24 per cent for 1987, and Alford claims that there has been a steady decline in class-linked voting. It is possible to use this index to compare the effect of class on voting in different countries. The average Alford index since the last war is:

| | |
|---|---|
| UK | 41% |
| Australia | 34% |
| USA | 16% |
| Canada | 8% |

It looks as if British and Australian voting is much more strongly class-linked than that in the USA or Canada.

The Alford index suggests that class-linked voting has declined in Britain during recent years, and some political sociologists agree. There has certainly been a decline in the Labour party, and in the number of working-class people who support it. On the other hand, the working class itself has become rather smaller, and there has been a rise of the Liberal party and its successors. Heath and colleagues (1991) argue that Liberal supporters are of

Table 9.4 Voting and occupational class (percentages)

|  | Conservative | Labour | Liberal and SDP |
|---|---|---|---|
| Salariat | 55 | 13 | 31 |
| Routine non-manual | 53 | 20 | 27 |
| Petit bourgeoisie | 71 | 12 | 17 |
| Foremen and technicians | 44 | 28 | 28 |
| Working class | 30 | 49 | 21 |

Source: Heath et al., 1991

similar social class to Conservative party supporters and should be included in the middle-class vote. The total in-class voting on this basis declined from 70.7 per cent in 1964 to 66.3 per cent in 1987, a very small amount of 'de-alignment'.

These authors also favour a five-class and three-party breakdown (instead of two), but using classes which are theoretically associated with left and right voting. A 1987 British survey found the breakdown given in Table 9.4.

This shows that there is still a strong link between class and voting intentions. In addition, the most conservative group were the 'petit bourgeoisie', i.e. employers and self-employed, which includes a lot of small shop-keepers, owners of small businesses, farmers and self-employed manual workers.

### Deviant working-class voting

As we said, a major factor in the political scene is deviant voting by working-class voters, i.e. in Britain not voting Labour. It is found that self-assigned class predicts voting when objective measures of class are held constant. Some of the working class as defined by social scientists think they are middle class, and as a result do not vote Labour: this is largely the 'new' working class. Several factors have been found to predict non-Labour voting by working-class people (from Robertson, 1984; Heath et al., 1991).

1 House owners v. local authority tenants. Buying a house leads to an 8 per cent fall in Labour voting; other house buyers had shifted already.
2 Not belonging to a trade union makes a difference of at least 10 per cent in Labour party support. Since trade union membership is mostly not voluntary for working-class people, this is mainly a causal effect.
3 Nature of job. We saw that the self-employed vote Conservative. Robertson (1984) compared a number of working-class jobs in detail and found that Conservative voting was associated with all aspects of status – non-manual v. manual and authority v. subordinate.
4 Income makes little difference to voting within the working class. Heath et al. found that it was only at the upper end of the income scale, the top 4 per cent, that income was associated with Conservative voting.

Goldthorpe and colleagues' 'affluent' car workers did not feel at all middle class, and most of them voted Labour (1968). However, Robertson found that certain patterns of *consumption* did correlate with voting – having a telephone, a car, private health insurance and domestic help. Although this was found within all classes, these kinds of expenditure are very typical of a middle-class lifestyle, compared for example with spending the same money on beer or tobacco.

5 Receiving state benefits increases Labour voting; there is 22 per cent more Labour voting for those who receive over 5 per cent of their income from this source, though this correlates with other sources of Labour voting (Marshall *et al.*, 1988).

6 Working in the private sector as opposed to the public, i.e. government and nationalised industry, produces about a 7 per cent fall in Labour voting.

7 Experience of unemployment produces a large increase in expressed support for Labour, but also a large fall in political participation; the unemployed are less likely to vote.

8 Living in the South of England, in recent years, especially as opposed to Scotland and Wales, has a strong link with Conservative voting.

9 Ethnic minority groups vote Labour much more strongly than whites.

(Heath *et al.*, 1991; Marshall *et al.*, 1988)

So manual workers and their families who own their houses, employ other workers or domestic help, have private health insurance, etc., often fail to vote Labour. Perhaps this is because they see themselves as middle-class; working-class people (defined as doing manual jobs) who think they are middle-class are much more likely to vote Conservative (Heath, personal communication; Butler and Stokes, 1974). Perhaps they really *are* middle-class, not only in terms of how they see themselves, but also in their lifestyle and how others see them. Self-perceived class depends a lot on which groups people are accepted by, which in turn depends on money and lifestyle (p. 5).

There is still a core working-class proletariat, who vote solidly Labour – living in council houses, belonging to unions, employed in low-status, manual jobs, in the public sector, receiving state benefits, with experience of unemployment, living in the North or in Wales or belonging to ethnic minority groups.

Another cause of working-class Conservative voting is 'deference'. McKenzie and Silver (1968) found that these voters preferred a hypothetical upper-class to a working-class parliamentary candidate, on the grounds that they liked to be set an example and have someone to look up to. Agricultural workers, and people in personal service, often have similar attitudes, an almost feudal acceptance of the power and status of those whom they serve.

Table 9.5 Occupational divisions within the salariat 1987

|  | Conservative | Alliance | Labour | Other | N |
|---|---|---|---|---|---|
| Public sector | 40 | 32 | 26 | 2 | (212) |
| Private sector | 57 | 29 | 13 | 2 | (281) |
| Specialists | 44 | 31 | 24 | 2 | (266) |
| Technocrats | 56 | 29 | 14 | 2 | (287) |
| Welfare and creative | 32 | 33 | 34 | 1 | (162) |
| Business and administrative | 58 | 28 | 12 | 2 | (391) |
| Economically inactive | 63 | 26 | 9 | 1 | (299) |

Source: Heath et al., 1991

## Deviant middle-class voting

There are also divisions within the middle class. We saw that employers and owners are very Conservative. The 'salariat', or 'service class', of managers, businessmen and higher professionals vote Conservative a little less, Labour and Liberal more than routine white-collar workers, but there are other, and bigger, divisions within the middle class for predicting voting.

1 Jobs. The greatest occupational division within the middle class is that 'welfare and creative' workers are the least Conservative and the most pro Labour and Liberal (Table 9.5).
2 Public sector workers are similar, partly because they include some of the same people – in health, universities, etc.
3 University education produces a considerably lower rate of Conservative support (39 per cent v. 60 per cent in 1987) and more support for the other two parties.
4 Religion. Within the middle class, members of the Church of England vote Conservative most, non-conformists support the Alliance party, Catholics and atheists support Labour.

There have been changes over the last twenty years over the relative importance of those divisions in the middle class, as predictors of voting. Higher education has become a stronger predictor, as have belonging to welfare and creative occupations, and belonging to unions (Heath et al., 1991).

It was believed for a time that 'Yuppies' had a distinctive political outlook. Research on American Yuppies shows that they are liberal on social issues (e.g. marihuana, gun control), but conservative on economic issues (e.g. reduce taxes). However, this constellation of attitudes is typical of people with the Yuppy combination of characteristics – young, urban, and professional (Carpini and Sigelman, 1986).

## Explanations of the effects of class on voting

What is the explanation for the effect of class on voting? There are several possible explanations.

(1) The most obvious is that voters make 'consumer' choices and select the party whose policies best match their political views. This was supported by evidence that from twenty-one political attitude statements voting could be predicted with about 85 per cent accuracy – though much less than this for Liberal voters (Himmelweit *et al.*, 1985). However, later and more rigorous tests of this approach have not confirmed it (e.g. Heath *et al.*, 1991). Marshall *et al.* (1988) asked people why they would vote for the party of their choice. The most common reason was 'Like general policies of party'. Heath *et al.* (1991) found that a number of attitudes predicted Conservative v. Labour voting, and that these attitudes correlated with social class. So, for example, both the Labour party and working-class people favour more income re-distribution and are against trade union reform. Such differences must be part of the explanation of class differences in voting.

However, in addition to a left–right attitude scale, they found a second liberal–authoritarian dimension. It has often been found in research on political attitudes that there are two, independent dimensions and that liberals score on the second and are neutral on the first (Eysenck, 1954). So attitudes and issues are part of the explanation. Moreover, the effect of issues on voting has increased over recent years (Heath *et al.*, 1991).

(2) The other main theory is that people in different classes identify with certain parties, so that working-class people see themselves as Labour party supporters. Butler and Stokes (1974) found that 95 per cent of people identified with a party, most of them strongly, and that those who did so voted accordingly. Labour voters are more likely to give class links with the party as their reason for party choice. However, strength of attachment to all parties has declined over recent years, and there has been some increase in the 'volatility' of voters, i.e. likelihood of changing vote from one election to another (Heath *et al.*, 1991).

(3) An important source of deviance in all classes is social influence from members of other classes. Social mobility is an example. Marshall *et al.* (1988) analysed voting intention by present social class and class of origin (Table 9.6).

It can be seen that class of origin is just as strong a predictor as present

*Table 9.6* Percentage Labour voting intention by present class and class of origin

| | | Class of origin | | |
| | | Service | Intermediate | Working |
|---|---|---|---|---|
| Present class | Service | 13 | 19 | 31 |
| | Intermediate | 21 | 15 | 33 |
| | Working | 27 | 55 | 59 |

class. Middle-class Labour party supporters more often have fathers who voted Labour (60 per cent v. 37 per cent for all salaried workers) or who were working-class (47 per cent v. 33 per cent); they are also more likely to have degrees (48 per cent v. 28 per cent) (Heath and Evans, 1988).

Trade union membership is another example, as is belonging to different kinds of working organisations. Some working-class Conservatives have no contact with the world of industrial trade unions, but work in small firms or organisations, with middle-class people (Parkin, 1971).

## Social identity theory

Festinger (1954) proposed a theory of social comparisons: that there is a drive to evaluate abilities and attitudes by comparison with others who are similar. He proposed that there is also an ego-enhancing drive upwards in the case of abilities, so that comparisons are made with others who are a little better, usually members of their own group. Tajfel (1978) proposed an extension of this theory, that individuals also make comparisons with other groups, and that self-esteem partly depends on the characteristics of groups to which people belong.

Research found that Festinger was right, and that people do make comparisons with those who are similar, or in the case of abilities a little better. However, only a minority of people make comparisons with others who belong to other groups, e.g. some of Runciman's manual workers compared their pay with that of managers. Some black Americans compare themselves with whites (Brown, 1988). Some studies, though not all, found that making biased judgements in favour of an in-group had the effect of raising self-esteem (Oakes and Turner, 1980).

Gaskell and Smith (1986) interviewed 206 young people, and asked which social groups they felt they belonged to. The answers were 'youth', 'black', 'unemployed' and so on. It was found that the higher the social status of the membership group, the more important was this group to its members – confirming the idea that groups are a source of self-esteem. Young blacks saw their own group as of higher status than that of blacks in general.

Runciman (1966) argued that relative deprivation could be 'egoistic' or 'fraternal', i.e. be based on comparisons between self and members of some group or between one's group and other groups. It is found that both kinds of relative deprivation are important, but that fraternal deprivation is a little more strongly associated with the hostile attitudes towards authority, such as the police for blacks in England (Smith and Gaskell, 1990). This is similar to Tajfel's idea that self-esteem depends on perceived group properties, in relation to other groups.

A further part of social identity theory is that in-group bias will lead to collective action if there is also conflict and ideological support. We have just seen that blacks and working men are more willing to engage in some kind of collective action.

Social identity theory has been widely accepted as an explanation of racial prejudice and stereotypes. Can it be used equally successfully for social class?

Social psychologists have been more concerned with relations between racial than class groups, but the race model fits classes quite well. In both cases (1) groups reject other groups and are biased towards the in-group; (2) there are negative stereotypes about the other groups; (3) difficulties are experienced interacting with the other groups, and social relationships are less likely than with the in-group; (4) there are differences of status, and of prospects, between groups. There is some intersection between race and class differences, since ethnicity contributes to social class. However, there are some differences between class and race relations. (1) Social mobility between classes is much easier, and is very common. (2) Classes are arranged in a clear hierarchy.

Social identity theory proposes that an individual's identity and self-esteem depend partly on the properties of groups to which he or she belongs. This explains why people make biased judgements in favour of members of the in-group; they also exaggerate the difference between in-group and out-group members. It is accepted, though not emphasised, that self-esteem also has individual, personal components, based for example on comparisons with other members of the group. A number of studies have looked at in-group bias and favouritism between groups of different power or status. For real groups (as opposed to minimal laboratory ones) there is more bias for members of low-status groups, though high-status groups are more biased for relevant attributes, low-status groups for irrelevant ones (Mullen *et al.*, 1992).

An important part of the theory deals with the reaction of low groups to their inferior position and consequent threats to their self-esteem; several alternatives are proposed (Tajfel, 1978).

1 Individuals may leave the low-status group and join a higher group. Blacks may try to 'pass' as whites, Jews as gentiles. It is probably easier for a person to move to a different class than to a different race, though it requires more than changing accent and clothes to do this, that is to be accepted by the new class. As we have seen, a considerable proportion of individuals born into lower-status groups succeed in moving out of them: 67 per cent of those born into class VII moved up, as did 45 per cent of those born into class VI (p. 177).

2 If it is impossible to move out people may passively accept the status quo, including accepting the low valuation placed on themselves. However, if they feel that the status system is illegitimate, and also unstable, i.e. possibly changeable, they will engage in one or other of several different

strategies. There may be direct social action in the form of violence or political action. In the racial sphere violent action has been common in South Africa, in American cities and elsewhere. Gay people have staged demonstrations. We have just seen that there is a strong tendency for working-class people to vote for left-wing parties, though we have also seen that many of them do not, especially if they own houses, don't belong to unions, etc.

3 Low-status groups can improve their position by persuading people to re-evaluate characteristics of the group which were previously devalued. The 'black is beautiful' movement and attempts to revive the Welsh language are examples. A social class example is the high valuation placed on manual skills by workers, associating them with masculinity, or with productivity, as compared with the effeminate and unproductive paper-pushing of white-collar workers.

4 A more subtle kind of 'social creativity' is the discovery of positive traits which the low-status group possesses. Blacks have shown that they excel at certain kinds of sport and at jazz music. Women show that they are kind and caring. East African Asians believe that, though economically inferior, they are more religious (Mann, 1963). Lower-status nurses think that they are more cheerful. A good social class example is the perception of regional accent speakers, by those of similar class, as friendly, generous and honest. A common theme of these examples is the belief by lower-status groups that they have superior inter-personal qualities. This makes sense since other members of the same class are found to be more friendly and helpful. Recent research has found that out-groups are not always rejected; minority groups and low-status groups often acknowledge the superiority of the out-group. This is recognised as a serious problem for social identity theory. Part of the solution is that out-group favouritism occurs only on dimensions of little importance to the in-group (Mummendey and Simon, 1989).

5 Lower-status groups can compare themselves with others who are in a similar position. It has been found that in the USA blacks who compare themselves with blacks have higher self-esteem than those who compare themselves with whites (Rosenberg and Simmons, 1972). When lower-status groups do compare themselves with higher-status ones, this immediately produces feelings of inequity. We shall see that black children in segregated American schools often have higher self-esteem than whites – there are no whites about to compare themselves with. Runciman (1966) found that many working-class people in Britain did not compare themselves with those who were better off, and were in complete ignorance of the better material prosperity of middle-class people. In trade union disputes over wage differentials, concern is with the relative pay of other workers, not with the managers.

We have seen that working-class people have lower esteem than the middle class, though the effect overall is weak, perhaps as a result of the processes just described, perhaps because of the segregation of social classes, which weakens comparison processes.

However, we are left with some very puzzling findings, and puzzling not only for social identity theory. Subordinate groups are very likely simply to accept their inferior status. Black American children in 1947 chose white rather than black dolls as 'nicer to play with', and 'nice doll', while they thought that black dolls 'looks bad'. But by 1970 black children much preferred black dolls (Hraba and Grant, 1970). We have seen that lower-status groups not only accept their position in the hierarchy, but agree that middle-class people are superior in intelligence, leadership and other desirable qualities. And about a third of lower-class people accept the class system as just and legitimate, have no desire to change it and vote Conservative.

We have seen that most people think it right and proper that some people should be paid more than others. Part of the explanation may be that social comparisons with other groups will only take place if those groups are sufficiently visible. People spend most of their time, at home, in leisure, and frequently at work, with members of the *same* group. Workers are unlikely to compare themselves with managers if they know nothing about their lifestyle. The media, especially TV, are one source, and some popular soap operas give an exaggerated picture of life among the very rich. Perhaps it is for this reason that many groups are not very interested in each other, they do not reject them or compete with them and do not compare themselves with them. It seems that self-esteem is based on group comparisons only in groups which are in competition with each other – sports teams, political groups – and racial groups, but not in juries, therapy groups or families (Hinkle and Brown, 1990). This is a serious problem for social identity theory, and means that it has rather a limited range of applications.

A second line of explanation is in terms of subjective social mobility. It is difficult to change your racial group, but much easier to change your self-perceived social class. We have seen that manual workers who are able to adopt a middle-class lifestyle do not vote Labour, and probably see themselves, and may be perceived by others, as middle-class. This can be added to the social identity theory repertoire of forms of social creativity.

This still leaves the problem of why people accept hierarchies and unequal distribution of rewards. Part of the answer must lie in the legitimation processes described earlier, and part of it in ignorance and lack of interest in social groups who are rarely encountered, except in public and superficial social contacts.

# REFERENCES

Abercrombie, N. and Warde, E. (1988) *Contemporary British Society*. Cambridge: Polity Press.

Alford, R.R. (1962) A suggested index of the association of social class and voting. *Public Opinion Quarterly*, 26, 417–25.

Alves, W.M. and Rossi, P.H. (1978) Who should get what? Fairness judgments of the distribution of earnings. *American Journal of Sociology*, 84, 541–64.

Bachman, J.G. and O'Malley, P.M. (1977) Self-esteem in young men: a longitudinal analysis of the impact of educational and occupational attainment. *Journal of Personality and Social Psychology*, 35, 365–80.

Baldus, B. and Tribe, V. (1978) The development of perceptions and evaluations of social inequality among public school children. *Canadian Review of Sociology and Anthropology*, 15, 50–60.

Berkowitz, L., Fraser, C., Treasure, F.P. and Cochran, S. (1987) Pay equity, job qualifications, and comparisons in pay satisfaction. *Journal of Applied Psychology*, 72, 544–51.

Blauner, R. (1960) Work satisfaction and industrial trends in modern society. In W. Galenson and S.M. Lipset (eds) *Labor and Trade Unions*. New York: Wiley.

Bottomore, P. (1954) Social stratification in voluntary organisations. In D.V. Glass (ed.) *Social Mobility in Britain*. London: Routledge & Kegan Paul.

Brown, Rupert (1978) Divided we fall: an analysis of relations between sections of a factory workforce. In H. Tajfel (ed.) *Differentiation between Social Groups*, London: Academic Press.

Brown, Rupert (1988) *Group Processes*. Oxford: Blackwell.

Butler, D.E. and Stokes, D.E. (1974) *Political Change in Britain*. 2nd edition. London: Macmillan.

Carpini, M.D. and Sigelman, L. (1986) Do yuppies matter? Competing explanations of their political distinctiveness. *Public Opinion Quarterly*, 50, 502–18.

Centers, R. (1949) *The Psychology of Social Classes*. Princeton, NJ: Princeton University Press.

Della Fave, L.R. (1980) The meek shall not inherit the earth: self-evaluation and the legitimacy of stratification. *American Sociological Review*, 45, 955–71.

Dickinson, J. (1991) Values and judgements of wage differentials. *British Journal of Social Psychology*, 30, 267–70.

Dittmar, H. (1992) *The Social Psychology of Material Possessions*. Hemel Hempstead: Harvester Wheatsheaf.

Durkheim, E. (1897) *Suicide: A Study in Sociology*. 1951 edition. Glencoe: Free Press.

EEC (1977) *Perception of Poverty in Europe*. Brussels: Commission of the European Communities.

Emler, N. and Dickinson, J. (1985) Children's representation of economic inequalities: the effects of social class. *British Journal of Developmental Psychology*, 3, 191–8.

Evans, G. (1992) Is Britain a class-divided society? A re-analysis and extension of Marshall *et al.*'s study of class consciousness. *Sociology*, 26, 233–58.

Eysenck, H.J. (1954) *The Psychology of Politics*. London: Routledge & Kegan Paul.

Feagin, J. (1975) *Subordinating the Poor*. Englewood Cliffs, NJ: Prentice-Hall.

Feather, N.T. (1989) Attitudes towards the high achiever: the fall of the tall poppy. *Australian Journal of Psychology*, 41, 239–67.

Festinger, L. (1954) A theory of social comparison processes. *Human Relations*, 7, 117–40.

Furnham, A. (1982) Explanations for unemployment in Britain. *European Journal of Social Psychology*, 12, 335–52.

Furnham, A. (1988) *Lay Theories*. Oxford: Pergamon.

Furnham, A. and Stacey, B. (1991) *Young People's Understanding of Society*. London: Routledge.

Gallie, D. (1983) *Social Inequality and Class Radicalism in France and England*. Cambridge: Cambridge University Press.

Gaskell, G. and Smith, P. (1986) Group membership and social attitudes of youth: an investigation of some implications of social identity theory. *Social Behaviour*, *1*, 67–77.

Gecas, V. and Seff, M.A. (1989) Social class, occupational conditions, and self-esteem. *Sociological Perspectives*, *32*, 353–64.

Goldthorpe, J.H., Lockwood, D., Bechofer, F. and Platt, J. (1968) *The Affluent Worker: Industrial Attitudes and Behaviour*. Cambridge: Cambridge University Press.

Goodman, P.S. (1967) An empirical examination of Elliott Jaques' concept of time-span. *Human Relations*, *20*, 155–70.

Gurin, P., Miller, A.H. and Gurin, G. (1980) Stratum identification and consciousness. *Social Psychology Quarterly*, *43*, 30–47.

Heath, A. and Evans, G. (1988) Working-class conservatives and middle-class socialists. In R. Jowell, S. Witherspoon and L. Brook (eds) *British Social Attitudes: The 5th Report*. Aldershot: Gower.

Heath, A. and Topf, R. (1987) Political culture. In R. Jowell, S. Witherspoon and L. Brook (eds) *British Social Attitudes: The 1987 Report*. London: Gower.

Heath, A. *et al.* (1991) *Understanding Political Change*. Oxford: Pergamon Press.

Hewstone, M., Jaspars, J. and Lalljee, M. (1982) Social representations, social attribution and social identity: the intergroup images of 'public' and 'comprehensive' schoolboys. *European Journal of Social Psychology*, *12*, 241–69.

Himmelweit, H.T., Humphreys, P. and Jaeger, M. (1985) *How Voters Decide*. Revised edition. Milton Keynes: Open University Press.

Hinkle, S. and Brown, R. (1990) Intergroup comparisons and social identity: some links and lacunae. In D. Abrams and M.A. Hogg (eds) *Social Identity Theory: Constructive and Critical Advances*. New York: Harvester Wheatsheaf.

Hook, J.G. and Cook, T.D. (1979) Equity theory and the cognitive ability of children. *Psychological Bulletin*, *86*, 429–45.

Hraba, J. and Grant, G. (1970) Black is beautiful: a reexamination of racial preference and identification. *Journal of Personality and Social Psychology*, *16*, 398–402.

Jaques, E. (1961) *Equitable Payment*. London: Heinemann.

Jasso, G. and Rossi, P.H. (1977) Distributive justice and earned income. *American Sociological Review*, *42*, 639–51.

Kerbo, H.R. (1983) *Social Stratification and Inequality: Class Conflict in the United States*. New York: McGraw-Hill.

Kinder, D.R. and Sears, D.O. (1985) Public opinion and political action. In G. Lindzey and E. Aronson (eds) *Handbook of Social Psychology*. 3rd edition. Hillsdale, NJ: Erlbaum.

Lane, R. (1962) *Political Ideology*. New York: Free Press.

Leahy, R.L. (1981) The development of the conception of economic inequality. I. Descriptions and comparisons of rich and poor people. *Child Development*, *52*, 523–32.

Leahy, R.L. (1983) The development of the concept of inequality. II. Explanations, justifications and concepts of social mobility and change. *Developmental Psychology*, *19*, 111–25.

Lockwood, D. (1966) Sources of variation in working-class images of society. *Sociological Review*, *14*, 249–67.

McCormick, E.J. and Ilgen, D. (1985) *Industrial and Organizational Psychology* (8th edn). London: Allen and Unwin.

McKenzie, R.T. and Silver, A. (1968) The working class Tory in England. In P. Worsley (ed.) *Angels in Marble*. London: Heinemann.

Mann, M. (1963) The social cohesion of liberal democracy. *American Sociological Review*, 35, 423–39.

Marshall, G., Newby., H., Rose, D. and Vogler, C. (1988) *Social Class in Modern Britain*. London: Hutchinson.

Mullen, B., Brown, R. and Smith, C. (1992) In group bias as a function of salience, relevance, and bias: an integration. *European Journal of Social Psychology*, 22, 103–22.

Mummendy, A. and Simon, B. (1989) Better or different? III The impact of importance of comparison dimension and relative in-group size upon intergroup discrimination. *British Journal of Social Psychology*, 28, 1–16.

Newby, H. (1977) *The Deferential Worker*. Harmondsworth: Penguin.

Oakes, P.J. and Turner, J.C. (1980) Social categorisation and intergroup behaviour: does minimal group discrimination make social identity more positive? *European Journal of Social Psychology*, 10, 295–301.

Parkin, F. (1971) *Class Inequality and Political Order*. London: MacGibbon & Kee.

Phillips, D. (1985) Participation and political values. In M. Abrams, D. Gerard and N. Timms (eds) *Values and Social Change in Britain*. Houndsmill, Hants: Macmillan.

Porter, L.W. (1964) *Organizational Patterns of Managerial Job Attitudes*. New York: American Foundation for Attitude Research.

Rawls, J. (1972) *A Theory of Justice*. Cambridge, Mass.: Harvard University Press.

Reid, I. (1989) *Social Class Differences in Britain*. 3rd edition. London: Fontana.

Robertson, D. (1984) *Class and the British Electorate*. Oxford: Blackwell.

Robinson, R.V. (1983) Explaining perceptions of class and racial inequality in England and the United States of America. *British Journal of Sociology*, 34, 344–66.

Rokeach, M. (1968) *Beliefs, Attitudes and Values*. San Francisco: Jossey-Bass.

Rosenberg, M. (1965) *Society and the Adolescent Self-Image*. Princeton, NJ: Princeton University Press.

Rosenberg, M. and Simmons, R.G. (1972) *Black and White Self-Esteem in the Urban School Child*, Washington, DC: American Sociological Association.

Runciman, W.G. (1966) *Relative Deprivation and Social Justice*. London: Routledge & Kegan Paul.

Scase, R. (1992) *Class*. Buckingham: Open University Press.

Simmons, R.G. and Rosenberg, M. (1971) Functions of children's perceptions of the stratification system. *American Sociological Review*, 36, 235–49.

Smith, P. and Gaskell, G. (1990) The social dimension in relative deprivation. In C. Fraser and G. Gaskell (eds) *The Social Psychological Study of Widespread Beliefs*. Oxford: Clarendon Press.

Smith, T.W. (1989) Inequality and welfare. In R. Jowell, S. Witherspoon and L. Brook (eds) *British Social Attitudes: Special International Report*. London: Gower.

Stern, A.J. and Searing, D.D. (1976) The stratification beliefs of English and American adolescents. *British Journal of Political Science*, 6, 177–201.

Tajfel, H. (1978) *Differentiation Between Social Groups*. London: Academic Press.

Triandis, H.C. and Triandis, L.M. (1960) Race, social class, religion and nationality as determinants of social distance. *Journal of Abnormal and Social Psychology*, 61, 110–18.

Warner, W.L. and Lunt, P. (1947) *The Status System of a Modern Community*. New Haven, Conn.: Yale University Press.

Zingraff, R. and Schulman, M.D. (1984) Social bases of class consciousness: a study of southern textile workers with a comparison by race. *Social Forces*, 63, 98–116.

# Chapter 10

# Values, sex, crime and religion

## VALUES

A value can be defined as 'an enduring belief that a specific mode of conduct or end-state of existence is personally or socially preferable to its opposite or converse' (Rokeach, 1973). It is a belief about the goals of life. The most extensive study of values was that by Rokeach. He developed lists of

*Table 10.1* **Class differences in values**

|  | Middle class |
|---|---|
| *Terminal values* | |
| A sense of accomplishment | (8) |
| Wisdom | (7½) |
| Mature love | (5½) |
| *Instrumental values* | |
| Imaginative | (5½, 8 with educational level) |
| Intellectual | (7) |
| Responsible | (6) |
| Logical | (3½) |
|  | **Lower class** |
| *Terminal Values* | |
| A comfortable life | (10½) |
| Salvation | (10) |
| Equality (income level only) | (7) |
| Happiness (income only) | (5) |
| Pleasure (educ. only) | (4) |
| *Instrumental values* | |
| Clean | (14½) |
| Courageous | (9)   (with income only) |
| Cheerful | (7½) |
| Polite | (4) |
| Obedient | (3½) |

*Note:* The numbers in brackets are the differences in rank order, out of 18 from the top to bottom class. They are an average of the different ranks for education and income classes.
*Source:* Rokeach, 1973

eighteen terminal values (or goals) and eighteen instrumental values (or means). Subjects were asked to place the eighteen values in each list in rank order. An American national sample was tested in 1968, with 1,409 subjects. Clear class differences were found (Table 10.1). The greatest difference was for the instrumental value 'clean', which was ranked 14½ places higher by the lowest compared with the highest social class (seven social classes were used).

The interpretation of this finding is unclear. Rokeach suggests that higher-class individuals take cleanliness for granted, while for those living in squalor it is a real problem. Lower-class people also value a comfortable life much more highly, perhaps because they haven't got it, as well as 'salvation' (confirming our discussion of religion later). The poor value being courageous and cheerful, equality and happiness, while the uneducated value pleasure. Those from the upper end of the scale value most a sense of accomplishment, wisdom, and being intellectual, imaginative and responsible (rather than clean, polite or obedient).

These thirty-six values were factor analysed to produce seven factors. The class difference can be described in terms of the factors. People of higher class value delayed gratification, competence and being inner-directed, lower-class people value immediate gratification, religious morality, self-control and being other-directed.

A British study of values was carried out by Abrams *et al.* (1985). A sample of 1,231 adults was interviewed, and a rather different range of values explored: six 'traditional' values, in the spheres of religion, sex, family, patriotism, work and property. Some class differences were found: working-class people held more traditional views about the family, middle-class people about work. In the following section I shall look at the best studies of class differences in the main value areas.

*Work values.* The Rokeach survey found that middle-class Americans valued 'a sense of accomplishment' much more highly, as well as being more 'responsible', 'intellectual' and 'imaginative' than lower-class individuals. Abrams *et al.* (1985) also found that middle-class British people valued a number of work values more (Table 10.2).

*Table 10.2* Class differences in work values (percentages)

|  | A, B, C1 | C2 | D,E |
|---|---|---|---|
| Achievement important | 68 | 60 | 45 |
| Take a pride in work | 84 | 78 | 70 |
| Use of ability important | 56 | 45 | 35 |
| Use of initiative important | 62 | 42 | 38 |
| Chance of promotion important | 40 | 35 | 30 |
| Socially useful job important | 49 | 31 | 25 |
| Find extra work for extra pay | 14 | 24 | 21 |

*Source:* Abrams *et al.*, 1985

Working-class people work primarily to be paid for it; middle-class people value pay too, but they also want to achieve something, use their ability, get promoted and do something socially useful. In Britain 87 per cent of class I and II feel that work is more than just earning a living (54 per cent of IV and V) (Mann, 1986). Evidently the Protestant Work Ethic is stronger for middle-class workers; we showed earlier that it is also a source of upward social mobility (p. 189).

Research on the motivation to work finds that some individuals are motivated and satisfied by complex and demanding jobs, where they can accomplish something, learn new skills and develop themselves. There is some disagreement about the percentage of workers for whom this is important, but it probably includes most managers and technical staff. There are other workers, paid less and doing more boring work, for whom it is not important, and who work mostly for the pay (Goldthorpe *et al.*, 1968), though perhaps too for the social life (Argyle, 1989). Studies of managers have found that those at higher levels say they are motivated and satisfied most by 'self-realisation', rather than by security, social needs, esteem or autonomy (Porter, 1964). In a survey of 574 households, Agnew (1983) confirmed that working-class individuals were more concerned than middle-class ones with income and job security, and middle-class people with doing 'important work'. However, both were equally concerned with the hope for job advancement.

*Education* is valued more by middle-class parents. This is demonstrated by their help and support for their children's education.

|                            | AB  | C1  | C2  | DE  |
|----------------------------|-----|-----|-----|-----|
| Members of PTA             | 47% | 36% | 25% | 15% |
| Does not help with homework| 5%  | 7%  | 13% | 17% |

*Source:* Reid, 1989

Douglas (1964) found that middle-class English parents took a lot more interest in their children's education. They visited the school more often, saw the head, father went as well as mother, and they had greater educational aspirations for their children. In an American study Kinloch (1987) found that middle-class parents wanted an 'idealistic, thought-provoking, and ability-developing' type of education for their children, while working-class parents wanted a vocational, skill-oriented and job-related education for them. American surveys consistently find that middle-class parents place far more value on college education for their children (Hyman, 1953).

We reviewed research in the USA earlier, showing that middle-class parents produced higher achievement motivation in their children by encouraging independent accomplishment and high levels of achievement

(p. 164). This achievement would be mainly in the sphere of school work.

Schools often have a division between those children who accept the goals of school, and get on with the educational process, and those, mostly working-class, who do not. Some of the later form a 'counter-culture' which rejects school values; they break the rules and are highly resistant to being educated (Chapter 8, pp. 181–2).

*The 'culture of poverty'.* Hyman (1953) showed that working-class people not only valued education less, they also valued professional jobs less, and thought that they had less opportunity of promotion. We discussed the theory of the 'underclass' earlier (pp. 18–19). Part of this theory is that there is a culture of poverty, consisting of present rather than future orientation, preferring immediate gratification, and fatalism. One objection to this doctrine is that class differences in these values are not 100 per cent, and many working-class people accept middle-class values. There is also another interpretation of these differences: some sociologists have argued that differences of behaviour in this sphere are not due to internalised cultural values but rather to situational pressures. For example, poor people may have a short time perspective because they cannot expect future benefits like promotion, home ownership or steady employment. Some working-class men would like to be able to provide for their families and be effective fathers; if they are not able to earn enough money to do so they may turn instead to the street corner life of drinking, gambling, aggression and sexual adventure (Liebow, 1967). The objection to *this* interpretation is that the alternative pattern must exist in working-class culture to provide an alternative male role (Haralambos and Holborn, 1990).

What does the social psychological research say? There certainly may be the kind of situational pressures just described, but there is also evidence that working-class people, on average, do have different scores on personality dimensions like achievement motivation, internal control and ego-strength – which give a capacity to control immediate impulses in favour of long-term goals (p. 167). The origins of these personality differences can be found partly in the socialisation methods used by parents, on which there are also class differences, and which are in turn partly derived from experiences at work in different kinds of jobs. Another source of these personality differences is in experience of being able or not being able to control events, and this is very similar to the Liebow doctrine of situational constraints.

*Post-materialism.* It has been argued by Inglehart (1971) and others that in affluent societies many people come to value non-material goals as much or more than material ones. Inglehart's scale used the following non-material values – a friendlier and less impersonal society that honours ideas more than money, protects freedom of speech, and widespread participation in

*Table 10.3* Class differences in preference for post-material goals (percentages)

|  | Britain | Germany | Italy |
|---|---|---|---|
| Lower | 6 | 7 | 10 |
| Middle | 8 | 11 | 14 |
| Upper-middle | 10 | 26 | 32 |
| Upper | 15 | 44 | 27 |

decision making. Respondents are asked to compare these with material values – maintaining order, economic growth and strong defence. Class differences are found in the countries that have been surveyed (Table 10.3).

Younger people endorse post-material values more strongly, but there is a class difference for every age group (Inglehart, 1981). When successive surveys have been carried out a gradual historical trend has been found for increasing support for post-material values.

Wuthnow and Schrum (1983) reports a series of American surveys, showing that professional and technical workers had more post-material values than managers: they valued the quality of life, the limitation of growth, concern for the underdog, scientific expertise and government spending and regulation. This division within the middle class appears also in political attitudes, between managers and employers, on one hand, and educational, scientific and creative workers, on the other (p. 221). Kilwein *et al.* (1974), in a study of 865 American high school seniors, found that the middle-class ones expressed greater willingness to take account of environmental issues – like limiting family size and the use of electrical appliances.

*Concern for others.* All classes do voluntary work, but middle-class people do more. The *General Household Survey* found the following percentages reporting doing some voluntary work during the past four weeks (Gerard, 1985).

| I | II | III | IV | V | VI |
|---|---|---|---|---|---|
| 13% | 13% | 12% | 6% | 5% | 4% |

There is a big break between classes III and IV. The percentages doing *some* voluntary work in the course of a year vary similarly (Figure 10.1).

The kinds of voluntary work done vary. Professional people do more committee work (52 per cent), as do employers (49 per cent), compared with 22 per cent for unskilled manual workers. Middle-class people do a greater variety of voluntary activities, but especially those involving teaching, talks and administration (Matheson, 1987).

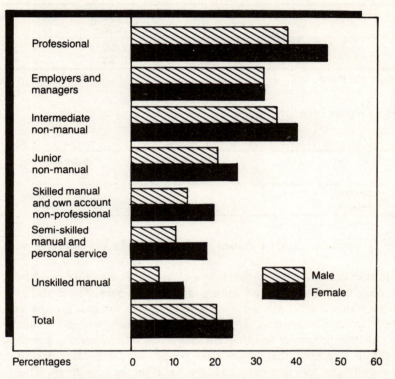

*Figure 10.1* Participation in voluntary work by sex and socioeconomic group, Great Britain, 1987
*Source: Report on Voluntary Work.* Office of Population Censuses and Surveys

There is prejudice and hostility towards ethnic minority groups in all classes, but more for the working class. The percentages who agree that the country should 'stop all future immigration into Britain' were:

| A,B,C1 | C2 | D,E |
|---|---|---|
| 58% | 71% | 75% |

*Source:* Reid, 1989

It is difficult to obtain honest answers to questions in this area. A projective question asked 'Do you believe that there is a lot of prejudice towards ...?'

|         | 1/2 % | 3(n) % | 3(m) % | 4/5 % |
|---------|-------|--------|--------|-------|
| Asians  | 54    | 56     | 59     | 62    |
| Blacks  | 52    | 53     | 53     | 46    |

*Source:* Airey and Brook, 1986

Asked to report their own prejudice the same people admitted:

|        | Non-manual % | Manual % |
|--------|--------------|----------|
| Asians | 13           | 18       |
| Blacks | 8            | 4        |

Evidently prejudice against Asians, rather than blacks, increases with class.

American studies have found that lower-class people are more anti-black, while there is more anti-Semitism among middle-class ones. The most likely explanation is that social groups are liable to be hostile towards groups with which they are in competition. This process is evidently stronger than the opposite one, that proximity and frequent interaction lead to positive attitudes.

It might be expected that lower-class people would be less patriotic, because they might feel that their country has done less for them. This is not what is found, however.

|                                          | A,B,C1 % | C2 % | D,E % |
|------------------------------------------|----------|------|-------|
| Very proud to be British                 | 51       | 55   | 60    |
| Willing to fight for country             | 61       | 66   | 59    |
|                                          |          |      | (Abrams, 1985) |
| Reintroduction of National Service: good idea | 65  | 77   | 81    |
| Task force to Falklands: right           | 74       | 73   | 67    |
|                                          |          |      | (Reid, 1989) |

There is in fact very little class difference in answer to questions tapping patriotism. Lower-class people are more proud to be British, and more in favour of National Service.

*Family values.* The Abrams survey found that working-class people place more value on the family.

|                                          | A,B,C1 % | C2 % | D,E % |
|------------------------------------------|----------|------|-------|
| More emphasis on family life would be good | 82       | 84   | 86    |
| Regardless of faults, respect parents      | 44       | 58   | 68    |
| Parents duty to do their best for their children | 68  | 70   | 76    |
| Divorce unjustified                        | 46       | 52   | 52    |

On the other hand, middle-class people seem to value *marriage* more.

|                                     | AB | C1  | C2  | DE  |
|-------------------------------------|-----|------|------|------|
| Marriage is an out-dated institution | 9% | 11% | 16% | 17% |

*Source:* Brown *et al.*, 1985

On divorce, several British surveys found that middle-class people think divorce is too easy, and they also have a much lower rate of divorce.

There appears to be a double class difference here. Working-class people value family in the sense of parents, children and kinship, while middle-class people value marriage more. This is entirely consistent with the findings on class differences in relationships which we discussed in Chapter 4. Working-class people live nearer to their relatives, and receive more help from them. Middle-class people have happier marriages and get divorced less.

*Liberal moral values.* Phillips and Harding (1985) report the class differences found in the Abrams survey. They found three factors of moral attitudes. Factor I, personal/sexual morality, consisted of attitudes to topics like prostitution, divorce, homosexuality and abortion. There was a strong class linkage – middle-class people held more tolerant views. However, on factor II, self-interest, middle-class people were stricter: it consisted of attitudes to cheating on tax, keeping money you have found, avoiding paying fares, etc. Middle-class people were also stricter on factor III, legal: attitudes to fighting with the police, taking bribes, falsely claiming state benefits.

It is broadly true that the working class is more authoritarian, the middle class more liberal. We shall discuss authoritarianism in the next section. Liberal values include, for example, the acceptance of homosexuality. The British Social Attitudes Survey found that 20 per cent of the salariat but only 7 per cent of foremen and technicians did so. Although such views are associated with political parties there are still large class differences within each political party. Salariat Labour supporters are much more liberal than working-class Labourites. Salariat Labourites are thus more 'liberal', or perhaps more 'radical' on the new agenda. They are also more radical on the traditional agenda, i.e. re-distribution of wealth and the rest (Heath and Evans, 1988).

Himmelstein and McRae (1988), reporting an American survey of 2,876 respondents, found that most aspects of liberalism increased with education, especially attitudes to marihuana, abortion and pornography, but also nuclear power, minorities and the environment. Income had a different effect – it was correlated with conservative political attitudes.

It is interesting that class is especially associated with liberal views about sex. In addition to the items listed by Phillips and Harding above, there was a similar class difference on extramarital affairs, although working-class people have more of them (p. 246) (Abrams, 1985).

The British Social Attitudes Survey studied views about various kinds of dishonesty. These included asking for or offering bribes, fiddling travelling expenses, illegally helping friends and relations. The class differences were all quite small.

Punishment of offenders is approved by all, but especially by working-class people, although they break the law more.

|  | Degree % | Prof. qual. % | A/O levels % | None % |
|---|---|---|---|---|
| Death penalty for: |  |  |  |  |
| terrorists | 51 | 76 | 75 | 82 |
| killing policemen | 49 | 69 | 70 | 77 |
| other murders | 31 | 36 | 63 | 75 |

Source: Airey and Brook, 1986

These results show quite large class differences, e.g. 75 per cent v. 31 per cent for the death penalty for 'other murders'.

## Conclusions and discussion

There are many substantial class differences in values. In the sphere of *work*, working-class people are concerned primarily with pay and job security, though also with taking a pride in their work. Middle-class people are more concerned with achievement and promotion, and find more intrinsic satisfaction with their work. This is probably because middle-class work is more skilled, interesting and responsible, and because there is more chance of promotion. Working-class parents value *education* if it leads to a job; middle-class parents want education to develop abilities, and they give more support and encouragement for their children's education. There is evidence for the existence of a *'culture of poverty'*, consisting of short-term goals, immediate gratification and fatalism, which is at least partly due to class differences in personality, but may also be due to the poor future prospects of poor people. In prosperous industrial countries there has been a growth of 'post-materialism' – concern for various non-material values, like freedom of speech, social cohesion and the environment. This is more common among those from higher classes, especially in the USA and Germany, where such people will have satisfied their material needs.

*Concern for others* is such a non-material value. Middle-class people do much more voluntary work, especially women, perhaps because they do not need to work. There is a little more racial prejudice for the working class, mainly towards Asians in Britain, but no less patriotism. Working-class people value the *family* more; we saw earlier that kin are more important for the working class (p. 77). However, the middle class value *marriage* more; we saw earlier that middle-class marriages are happier and more successful (p. 79).

Middle-class individuals hold more *liberal moral attitudes*, on deviation from traditional sexual rules, drugs, pornography, etc., though they keep these rules themselves more than the working classes. This kind of liberal attitude is most closely linked with education, which perhaps teaches liberality on such non-criminal kinds of deviance. Middle-class people hold *stricter* views on honesty and law-breaking, though again they keep the rules more themselves; the only exception to the class difference in strictness is that lower-class people are much more in favour of capital punishment.

This pattern of class-linked values can be explained (a) by the more immediate material needs of lower-class people, (b) by the effects of education in creating wider concerns and sympathies and (c) the effects of cultural lag, for example in attitudes to capital punishment and the environment.

## Authoritarianism

This dimension of personality was originally developed in connection with the study of racial prejudice, but was found to embrace a wide range of attitudes – hostility to racial minority groups and foreigners, anti-democratic beliefs and lack of sympathy for under-dogs. It was found that the holders of this package of attitudes also had a certain kind of personality – ready acceptance of institutional authority, cognitive rigidity and dogmatism, and a number of psychoanalytically inspired properties, such as 'anti-intraception' (i.e. opposition to the imaginative), destructiveness and cynicism. Authoritarianism was measured by the F-scale, which consisted of items reflecting the proposed features of personality (Adorno *et al.*, 1950).

Authoritarianism, and similar measures of illiberal, prejudicial, anti-democratic attitudes, is stronger for working-class people. In fact, the strongest link is with lack of education. Educational differences for a brief

Table 10.4 Educational differences in authoritarianism

| | College (n = 217) | High school (n = 545) | Grammar school (n = 504) |
|---|---|---|---|
| **Agree that:** | | | |
| The most important thing to teach children is absolute obedience to their parents | 35% | 60% | 80% |
| Any good leader should be strict with people under him in order to gain their respect | 36 | 51 | 66 |
| Prison is too good for sex criminals. They should be publicly whipped or worse | 18 | 31 | 45 |
| There are two kinds of people in the world: the weak and the strong | 30 | 53 | 71 |
| No decent man can respect a woman who has had sex relations before marriage | 14 | 26 | 39 |
| Believe cancer is contagious | 9 | 12 | 27 |
| Know what a nuclear physicist does | 50 | 16 | 5 |
| Think the world is better off as a result of man's ability to exploit atomic energy | 58 | 40 | 25 |
| Believe that most people can be trusted | 77 | 70 | 52 |
| Mention reading as a favourite activity | 62 | 43 | 33 |
| Thinks it's more important for government to guarantee jobs than to assure opportunities | 24 | 39 | 51 |
| Rate interest in work as most important thing in choosing a job | 44 | 34 | 21 |
| Rate financial return as most important thing in choosing a job | 9 | 12 | 21 |

*Source:* Hyman and Sheatsley, 1954

version of the F-scale are shown in Table 10.4. Otherwise expressed, the correlation between the F-scale and education is between −.45 and −.54. The F-scale also correlates strongly and negatively with IQ, though with education removed at about −.20 (Hyman and Sheatsley, 1954).

Kohn and Schooler (1983), in a study to be described later, used an interview measure of 'authoritarian conservatism' − 'at one extreme, rigid conformance to the dictates of authority, and intolerance of nonconformity; at the other extreme open-mindedness'. With a sample of 3,100, the correlation with class was −.65 in 1964, −.64 in 1974.

As originally conceived, authoritarianism was linked with right-wing, fascist political views. It was later suggested that Communism was a kind of 'authoritarianism of the left', so that Communists too would be expected to have a similar personality, despite different political ideas. Eysenck (1954) proposed that there are two dimensions of political attitudes: a Radical–Conservative factor and a Tough–Tender one. He and colleagues found that members of the British fascist party were, as expected, Tough and Conservative. However, members of the Communist party, although Radical, were not very Tough-minded, in fact they endorsed quite a lot of the Tender items, of a humanitarian kind (e.g. did not agree that 'Coloured people are innately inferior to white people'). Rokeach (1960) made a similar proposal, for a dimension of authoritarianism which is politically neutral, which he called Dogmatism. A small sample of British Communists had the highest scores on dogmatism of any political group, although they did not score high on the F-scale (Brown, 1965).

So part of authoritarianism, as it has usually been studied, is a right-wing ideology, even though Rokeach's dogmatism, and perhaps Eysenck's tough-mindedness are politically neutral. Since working-class people are more likely to support *left-wing* parties, there is no correlation between being lower-class and supporting political conservatism, part of authoritarianism. The correlation is with the non-political parts − hostility to minority groups and foreigners, anti-democratic views, approving the death penalty and other illiberal ideas. But are the *personality* components also class-related? We shall see later that authoritarianism is partly genetic in origin, and we have already seen that it is linked with intelligence, so it seems very likely that the whole underlying structure is associated with social class.

To explain the connection between authoritarianism and class we need to examine its causes in general.

*Inheritance.* It has long been known that children resemble their parents in authoritarianism. Scarr (1981) found that the F-scale scores of biological children correlated .44 with parents, while those of adopted children correlated only .06 − and they had been adopted early, on average at 2.6 months. This shows a strong genetic tendency; these figures are similar to those for IQ, and suggest a stronger inheritance than extraversion. Further analysis showed that inheritance was mainly via IQ, which was strongly inherited and strongly linked to (low) authoritarianism. Other inherited aspects of personality, unrelated to IQ, were also involved.

*Socialisation.* This is the weakest part of the original research, since the data were obtained from the memories of subjects; a later study however by Frenkel-Brunswik (1954) with prejudiced and unprejudiced children produced similar results. The parents of authoritarians were found to be strict, rigid and punitive, they used power and coercion, without discussion or explanation. Research on class differences in socialisation has consistently found that working-class parents are more punitive, use less discussion and that discipline is intended to produce obedience and respectable conformity, where middle-class parents try to inculcate concern for others, self-control and curiosity (see p. 167).

*Unsophisticated subcultures.* We showed above that authoritarianism is strongly linked to lack of education. Lipset (1960) suggested that this aspect of lower-class culture is responsible – little reading or education, and little membership of clubs, resulting in little exposure to a variety of ideas and a simplified view of the world. More liberal ideas and wider sympathies require more complex considerations.

Political scientists in America have taken this idea further, and have concluded that 'The clearest evidence about the social origins of illiberal ideas is that they result from socialization in lower-status, less educated, fundamentalist Protestant, Republican, small town or farm circumstances' (Sears, 1969, p. 413). This is in conflict with the ideas we presented earlier about the effects of genetics on personality; it remains to be seen which is more important.

*Job conditions.* As with external locus of control, which will be discussed later, authoritarianism is affected by jobs where there is close supervision, repetition and where obedience to authority is required. This can explain some of the class differences in adults.

## SEXUAL BEHAVIOUR

The main general finding is that working-class people are less restrained in matters of sex and engage in a greater variety of sexual activities before and during marriage. Eysenck (1976) constructed a scale of attitudes towards sexual behaviour – such as approval of wife-swapping and thinking physical sex the most important part of marriage. There was a clear class difference, and he concluded that 'working class people are more earthy, middle class people more moral' in matters of sex, and that working-class people have 'more libido' but do not get more satisfaction from it. In Britain in the nineteenth century there were probably similar class differences; at least the middle classes believed that there were and they were worried about the 'sexual rampancy and immorality' of the lower orders and engaged in efforts to teach them the values of ordered family life (Weeks, 1981).

Rushton and Bogaert (1988) counted up Gebhard and Johnson's revised version of the Kinsey findings, and concluded that for twenty-four out of forty-one comparisons college-educated people were more restrained than the less educated, over a wide range of sexual behaviour. Some of the findings will be given shortly. However, the black/white differences for most kinds of sexual behaviour were greater than the class differences. There were some reversals, for example there is more middle-class masturbation. We will now look in more detail at class differences for different aspects of sex.

*Early sexual behaviour* consists first of masturbation, then kissing, breast stimulation and genital stimulation short of intercourse. I shall cite first the very extensive Kinsey data. This was a massive survey, though the sample was overloaded with students and criminals. It was revised by Gebhard and Johnson (1979) and extended to over 11,000 interviews, with 300 questions, carried out in the USA between 1943–49 (see Table 10.5).

It can be seen that many working-class people had intercourse before the age of 17, while the middle-class ones engaged in more masturbation and heavy petting. One possible explanation is given in the bottom line – the greater moral and religious restraints reported by the men.

These data are now dated. The 'sexual revolution' of the 1960s, consisting mainly of greater premarital sexual activity, meant that the middle-class young to a large extent caught up with the working-class young. However, some class differences still remained. Schofield (1965) reported a study of 1,873 English adolescents in 1962–3, and found that middle-class adolescents did more deep kissing, and that middle-class children who stayed on at school engaged more in sexual activities short of intercourse than the working-class early school leavers – who also had earlier intercourse. Gorer (1971) surveyed 1,831 English people aged 16–45, and found that 15 per cent of DEs had had intercourse before the age of 17, compared with 4 per cent of the ABs; more of the DEs had more than three premarital partners, 11 per cent v. 6 per cent for the ABs. Recent attitude surveys show that only 24 per cent of people now think premarital intercourse is wrong, 50 per cent think it isn't and the rest are not sure (Reid, 1989).

Another intriguing finding from the Kinsey *et al.* study (1948) is that socially mobile males adopt the sexual behaviour of their new class – but do so *before* they have moved into it. This could be because sexual restraint is part of a broader personality trait of inner control, which leads to upward mobility. Another explanation is that upwardly mobile males, at college for example, are likely to meet girls from a higher social class. When

Table 10.5a Early sexual behaviour (percentages)

| | Male | | Female | |
|---|---|---|---|---|
| | College | Non-coll | College | Non-coll |
| Masturbation, frequency per week (age 16–20) | 2.41 | 2.09 | 1.12 | 1.01 |
| Premarital petting to orgasm (16–20) | 41.7 | 34.5 | 22.5 | 22.0 |
| Premarital french kissing (much) | 68.6 | 45.7 | 62.9 | 50.8 |
| First intercourse before 17 | 20.9 | 48.6 | 6.0 | 12.6 |
| Moral or religious restraint on PMI (much) | 53.9 | 40.0 | 79.0 | 79.6 |

Source: Gebhard and Johnson, 1979

Table 10.5b Premarital sexual behaviour at 16–20, by later adult status (percentages)

| | Unskilled | Semi-skilled | Skilled | Lower white-collar | Upper white-collar | Professional |
|---|---|---|---|---|---|---|
| Premarital intercourse | 79 | 77 | 66 | 39 | 39 | 35 |
| Weekly frequency | 0.9 | 1.1 | 0.6 | 0.3 | 0.2 | 0.2 |
| Masturbation (climaxes due to) | 38 | 29 | 44 | 64 | 67 | 70 |

Note: These are the figures for men who were born into and stayed in these classes.
Source: Kinsey et al., 1948

Table 10.6 Class differences in enjoyment of marital sex (percentages)

| | Middle class | | Working class | | | |
| | | | Less segregated | | Segregated | |
| | Husbands | Wives | Husbands | Wives | Husbands | Wives |
|---|---|---|---|---|---|---|
| Great interest and enjoyment | 78 | 50 | 72 | 64 | 55 | 18 |
| Socio-emotional closeness and exchange | 75 | 89 | 52 | 73 | 16 | 32 |
| Psychophysiological pleasure and relief only | 25 | 11 | 48 | 27 | 84 | 68 |
| Negative to sex, or sexual relations | | 14 | | 32 | | 68 |

Source: Rainwater, 1966

they do so they are found to engage in lower levels of sex than when with girls at home from their own class, because the relationship is dominated by the girl (Ehrmann, 1959).

*Marital sex*. Middle-class people do it less often, according to the Kinsey data, 3.05 times per week for males in their early twenties compared with 3.45 for the non-college group (Table 10.6). There was no difference for females, suggesting that the initiative lay with husbands. On the other hand, middle-class couples enjoy their sex life more. An American study by Rainwater (1966) found large differences (Table 10.6).

It can be seen that marital sex was enjoyed much less by working-class people, especially those in 'segregated' marriages, where couples did not do many things together; working-class marriages in the past were often like this, though they are now changing to the middle-class style, with more companionship and joint participation. In Rainwater's segregated working-class couples the wives complained about their husbands' lack of consideration in relation to sex; 38 per cent regarded it simply as a duty. Slater and Woodside (1951) in Britain reported that working-class couples found their sex life monotonous, boring and habitual – 'It's something that's got to be done, and the quicker the better'.

Kinsey found that his college-educated subjects had much longer foreplay, preferred it in the dark and in the nude. On the other hand the non-college group more often practised oral sex.

*Extramarital sex*. In the Kinsey data, many more non-college males had extramarital intercourse (EMI), but there was no difference for the females. Many more expected to have it in the future, had it during the first year of marriage or with prostitutes (Table 10.7). Perhaps this is because their sex life at home is so monotonous.

Recent British surveys have found that about 80 per cent of people think EMI is wrong, and there are no class differences here (Airey, 1984; Airey and Brook, 1986).

*Homosexuality*. In the Kinsey data homosexuality is more common for the non-college male subjects, and the number of orgasms per week is far higher

*Table 10.7* Extramarital intercourse (percentages)

| | Males | | Females | |
|---|---|---|---|---|
| | College | Non-coll | College | Non-coll |
| Had EMI | 29.8 | 47.1 | 28.4 | 24.6 |
| During first year of marriage | 15.2 | 22.8 | 7.8 | 11.6 |
| Expectation of future EMI | 26.7 | 36.0 | 16.0 | 11.9 |
| Prostitute contact more than incidental | 8.4 | 17.4 | 0 | 0 |

*Table 10.8* Homosexuality (percentages)

|  | Males | | Females | |
|  | College | Non-coll | College | Non-coll |
|---|---|---|---|---|
| Expectations of future homosexual contacts | 13.2 | 19.5 | 7.8 | 5.7 |
| Amount of homosexual contact: extensive | 9.9 | 12.7 | 3.7 | 2.4 |
| Orgasms per week, for never-married (21–5) | 1.17 | 2.88 | 1.23 | 1.87 |

(Table 10.8). In Britain it may be more common among middle-class men, especially those from boarding schools. Schofield (1965) found that 28 per cent of his boarding-school boys sample reported taking part in it, compared with 3 per cent at day schools. In Britain there have been prominent homosexual circles in upper-middle-class society, and the members have commonly chosen short-term working-class partners. Autobiographies report a fascination with crossing the class divide in this way, and with jokes like 'buggers can't be choosers' (Weeks, 1981). Attitude surveys consistently show that more working-class people think it is wrong, about 70 per cent, compared with 60 per cent of the middle class (Airey, 1984; Airey and Brook, 1986).

*Prostitution.* In the Kinsey research, 10.9 per cent of college and 19.9 per cent of non-college men had more than incidental contact with prostitutes. And prostitutes themselves are mostly working-class, though there are also some middle-class women who can't get jobs after graduation and end up in massage parlours or as call-girls (Giddens, 1989).

What is the explanation of the variation of sexual behaviour with class?

Weinrich (1977) offered an explanation of this whole pattern of class differences in terms of sociobiology. In the animal kingdom, those species with an uncertain food supply are more promiscuous, and males invest less in a single sexual relationship. This is the best way of making sure that their genes are reproduced. It can be assumed that working-class people are in a somewhat similar situation over the food supply, or material needs in general. This could explain the greater level of pre- and extramarital intercourse, by males, and also the greater investment in marriage in the form of male domestic work.

Sexual motivation is commonly aroused, but it is not allowed to be expressed a lot of the time, because social rules forbid it – in the interests of public order and social stability. However, such rules are ineffective without internal restraints, which are normally acquired in the home. We have seen that there are class differences in child-rearing and consequently in personality. This provides a second line of explanation of working-class sexual permissiveness. Middle-class socialisation methods produce greater internal control, less impulsiveness and deferred gratification. From a purely rational or economic point of view, one can understand why people who do not anticipate very much gratification in the future should not be prepared to delay gratification in order to obtain it. This set of attitudes is stronger in the black population in Britain and the USA, where the amount of sexual permissiveness is very high, and marriage is very short-lived. In the Kinsey data blacks had higher rates of PMI, EMI and a number of other kinds of sex, though not for homosexuality.

Anthropological studies have found that families make greater efforts to control the sex-life of their children in societies in which women can inherit property, especially land, because of the need to control the family's fortunes (Goody, 1976).

During feudal times there were strong social pressures among the propertied classes for young people to marry within their own class and conserve family property. It didn't matter what the peasants did. In the nineteenth century, historians tell us, the middle classes placed much greater value than the working class on family stability, responsibility and domesticity. 'Sexual responsibility expressed the aspirations and lives of the middle class' (Weeks, 1981). This is not the whole story however and some middle-class Victorian diaries describe the use of prostitutes and pornography, and suggest that for some marriage was primarily a contract, love and romance had to be sought elsewhere (Abercrombie and Turner, 1978). For poor people, whose experience of home was of poverty and ill-treatment, it would not be expected that they would value family very highly.

Middle-class families today are less concerned about inheritance of property but are still concerned that their children shall continue in a similar lifestyle, to avoid causing a social breach with them. Similar considerations apply to Jewish families, and to other religious and ethnic groups. The control of the partners of the young is achieved in a number of ways in different cultures – child marriage, segregation, supervision and organisation of social life.

## Conclusions and discussion

The main class difference is that lower-class and less-educated people engage in more premarital intercourse, and do it earlier, more extra-marital intercourse and have more contact with prostitutes but enjoy marital sex less. The black population is even less restrained. There are a number of possible explanations – the biological pressure for gene propagation in an uncertain environment, stronger middle-class restraints and deferred gratification imparted during socialisation, while middle-class parents may do this because of a concern for family stability and continuity, and concern for inheritance of property.

*Table 10.9* Percentage juvenile delinquency rates,[1] by social class and sex

| | Social class (NS) | | | | | | |
| | UM | LM | UW | LW | U/C[2] | All boys | Girls |
|---|---|---|---|---|---|---|---|
| Any offence | 2.7 | 8.3 | 9.7 | 18.7 | 8.6 | 12 | 1.6 |
| Non-indictable/trivial offence only | 1.9 | 4.1 | 3.6 | 4.9 | 1.5 | 4 | 0.6 |
| One or more indictable/serious offence | 0.8 | 4.2 | 6.1 | 13.8 | 7.1 | 8 | 1.0 |
| More than one indictable/serious offence | – | 0.7 | 1.8 | 5.6 | 2.6 | 2.8 | 0.03 |

*Notes:* [1] That is, either cautioned or sentenced for type of offence indicated; [2] Unclassified.
*Source:* Douglas *et al.*, 1966

## CRIME AND DEVIANCE

The percentages of working-class people who are caught and punished for breaking the law are far higher than for the middle classes. For example, the official juvenile delinquency rates in Britain in 1966 were as seen in Table 10.9.

Those in prison are mostly from the lowest social class. And a classic study of delinquent subcultures in Chicago found that the percentages of delinquents rose from 1.8 per cent in the outer suburbs to 11.9 per cent in the inner city (Shaw and McKay, 1942).

West and Farrington (1977) and Farrington (1991) report a longitudinal study of 411 boys from a working-class part of London, from the age of 8. By the age of 32 37 per cent had been convicted of criminal offences and 20–5 per cent were persistent offenders. Although all were from working-class backgrounds, criminality was more common among those from poorer homes and with criminal parents. These boys didn't only break the law, the persistent criminals in particular had an anti-social personality, including heavy drinking, reckless driving, promiscuity, neglect of children, unemployment, violence and debt.

The relation between class and crime has been found in many studies, in many countries. Braithwaite (1979) reviews 300 of them. However, doubts have been raised about these findings. Studies of self-reported crime find far higher rates of law-breaking, but smaller class differences. The offences reported are mostly minor ones like riding a bicycle without a light (c. 80 per cent), trespassing on railway lines or private gardens (65 per cent) or smoking under the age of 15 (c. 40 per cent). There are smaller class differences with self-reported crimes than for official statistics, partly because middle-class people report more of their minor offences and working-class people fewer of them. If only serious offences are considered, the link between class and crime is as strong as before. Elliott and Ageton (1980) developed a measure of self-report for a wide range of crimes, the main class difference was for crimes against persons: working-class youth committed nearly four times as many of these, and the difference was mainly due to the rates of crime of frequent offenders. West and Farrington (1973) used careful interviews, rather than questionnaires, and found that self-reports located many of the same people who had also been caught, and that self-reported crime was more common among boys from poorer homes. They also concluded that law-breaking is more closely related to poverty than to class in the occupational sense. Class differences are found in objective studies, based on direct observation, behaviour in school and laboratory tests of lying, cheating and stealing. American studies have found that working-class people under-report their offences to a greater extent, so it looks as if there really is a class difference in crime (Kleck, 1982).

The correlation with official rates on the other hand may be too high, because of police bias or the way in which the courts work. This has been shown in many American studies. In California 46.5 per cent of young people who are arrested go to juvenile court, but in the Lafayette district only 17 per cent – 'For the same offense, a poor person is more likely to be arrested, and if arrested charged, than a middle- or upper-class person' (Reiman, 1984, p. 82). Poor, black and young defendants are more likely to be found guilty by the courts, partly because they have less competent lawyers, perhaps also because judges or juries are biased against them. Middle-class people are more likely to be cautioned rather than charged, to be got off by good lawyers or to commit 'white-collar crimes', which are very difficult to detect (see pp. 253–4).

The connection between crime and class is different for different kinds of crime. Class differences are greatest for murder, rape and other crimes of violence, while the class difference is lower for crimes of property, in American studies. Class differences are greater for adult crime than for juvenile delinquency. The victims of crimes of violence are predominantly working-class, whereas the victims of crimes of property are those with more property (Thornberry and Farnworth, 1982; Horwitz, 1984).

Is the relation between class and crime due to innate or environmental factors? Van Dusen and colleagues (1983) carried out a massive study of 14,427 adopted children in Denmark, and related their criminal records to the class of their biological and adoptive parents (Table 10.10).

Since the children were adopted shortly after birth, the influence of biological parents must have been entirely or nearly entirely genetic. The findings show that class affects crime about equally via inheritance and environment; for boys the environment had more effect, for girls inheritance had. Only property offences were affected by class in Denmark, crimes of violence were not.

There is strong evidence that crime is partly due to socialisation experiences. Glueck and Glueck (1950) showed that delinquent boys were much more likely to have been rejected by their fathers, to have received harsh and

*Table 10.10* Delinquency rates by class of biological and adoptive parents
(percentages)

|  |  | Biological parents | | Adoptive parents | |
|  |  | Males | Females | Males | Females |
| --- | --- | --- | --- | --- | --- |
|  | *high* | 11.64 | 0.99 | 11.58 | 2.01 |
| Class | *medium* | 14.31 | 2.56 | 15.62 | 2.43 |
|  | *low* | 16.00 | 2.95 | 17.19 | 3.19 |

*Source:* Van Dusen *et al.*, 1983

inconsistent discipline and to have parents who were themselves offenders. Of course some of these differences may be due to reversed causation, i.e. some boys may have been rejected *because* they were delinquent. Farrington (1991) also found that the boys in his London sample were more likely to become offenders if they had received harsh and erratic discipline, and came from large families, or where there was marital disharmony. A re-analysis found a possible effect of labelling, by the conviction of a parent or an early conviction of a child (Hagan and Palloni, 1990).

Class differences in law-breaking can be partly explained by class differences in socialisation. We show elsewhere in this book that working-class parents use more punitive discipline, are more authoritarian, have larger families, that there is less contact with fathers and that there is less use of reasoning or related methods likely to produce internalised controls. This is likely to produce a negative attitude to authority, to the sources of rules. Parents from underprivileged sections of society will themselves have less respect for authorities who treat them badly, for unskilled and authoritarian supervisors at work or for a society which does not give them fair rewards.

Crime and class are related in all of the many countries in which the problem has been studied, but the effect is stronger in some countries than others. Several studies have found that homicide rate correlates with measures of economic inequality, at about $r = .40–.50$. This is still true when attempts are made to hold overall prosperity constant, though there are still a number of other confounding variables. To eliminate these, studies have been made of 100 or more American cities. The findings are clear: the gap between rich and poor correlates with all forms of crime, but the number of poor people does not (Braithwaite, 1979). Harer and Steffensmeier (1992) found that the numbers of arrests for crimes of violence, including murder and rape, correlated strongly with such measures, for different areas of the USA, for whites but much less for blacks. We shall see in the next chapter that overall happiness levels are lower in countries with greater economic inequality (p. 280).

## The sociological explanation of class differences in crime

A number of sociological theories have been put forward to explain the link between class and crime. It is beyond the scope of this book to go into all these theories, and the evidence for and against them. However, the main ideas are as follows:

1 Working-class people are oppressed and frustrated by an unfair economic system, they feel exploited and become disillusioned with the concept of property, hate the rich (Marx, Engels). A recent version of this theory is that social imbalance leads to envy, manifested for example in damaging expensive cars, abusing or attacking expensively dressed people (Schoeck, 1987).

2 Working-class people have the same aspirations for material success as middle-class people, but their aspirations are blocked, so they seek illegitimate means to these goals (Merton).

3 Criminal behaviour is more likely when there are illegitimate opportunity structures, for example a criminal subculture (Cloward and Ohlin).

4 Failure at school leads to a group solution to pursue alternative goals, of toughness, apathy and impulse gratification (Cohen).

5 Law-breaking is an acting out in an exaggerated manner of lower-class values of toughness, masculinity and the need for excitement.

6 Some working-class areas are 'socially disorganised', i.e. have a shifting population, many problem families, overcrowding, poor housing, high unemployment and poor leisure facilities: these become 'delinquency areas' (Shaw and McKay).

7 If a young person is arrested, e.g. for a drugs offence, this 'labels' him as a law-breaker, affects his self-image and puts him outside mainstream society (Becker).

8 Working-class homes have more social pathology in the form of divorce, out of work fathers who have little power in the family, low intelligence and poor child-rearing methods.

The association of class with crime is rather different for different forms of crime. We will look at three very interesting kinds.

*Football hooliganism and vandalism.* Vandalism is the most common offence, and football hooliganism causes a great deal of trouble and needs a lot of policing. It takes the form mainly of the supporters of the two teams threatening and insulting each other inside the ground, sometimes charging and attacking each other in large groups, invading the pitch, attacking members of the other side outside the ground and doing miscellaneous damage. The fans are more or less restrained by large numbers of police.

Marsh *et al.* (1978) offered an interesting interpretation of these phenomena. They said that it is ritual, symbolic aggression, in which no one gets seriously hurt, because there are rules against injuring people. The aim is more to frighten the other side and make them look ridiculous. The fans enjoy the reputation, invented by the media, of being dangerous and violent. Evidence for shared rules against injury was obtained from interviews with hooligans, and supported by the very small number of injuries at the Oxford United ground. However, this view has been disproved by events – a series of disasters, at which English fans have been responsible for a number of deaths, especially at international matches, as at the Huissell stadium in Brussels. And in fact there always was quite a lot of real violence, outside the ground if not inside, especially at more important games than those of Oxford United.

The main activity of these groups is pursuing their rivalries and vendettas with other groups. Status is gained by the team winning or by the humiliation of the other team's supporters. The insults are to the effect that the others are weak, non-masculine, 'wankers' and so on. Elias and Dunning (1986) point out that nearly all football hooligans, especially the ones convicted of violence at matches, are unskilled or unemployed working-class young men. They come from lower-working-class estates where parents do not restrain aggressive behaviour, the children often see violence between adults, and macho behaviour and 'hardness' are valued, one of the main sources of reputation and status among youth who have failed to achieve any success in the educational or occupational spheres.

There have been a number of other social movements among working-class youths in Britain during recent years – teddy boys, skinheads, rockers, punks, etc. All have had flamboyant costumes and been associated with leisure activities, sometimes with styles of music; each has had its own culture and ideology. All have been on the edge of delinquency, e.g. drugs and violence, and expressed defiance of adults and of middle-class society (Abercrombie and Warde, 1988). Their appearance can be seen as symbolic of their self-image (p. 120). These movements can be seen as reactions of working-class youth to their underprivileged place in society in a way which gives them a positive self-image.

Labelling plays a part here. Football hooligans come to see themselves as dangerous, drunken and uncontrollable, hippies as dirty and promiscuous. This process does not explain how a person starts breaking the law, but it provides part of the explanation of why he keeps on doing it.

*White-collar crime.* This is mainly financial, such as embezzlement, insider dealing, bribery, computer crime, transfer of pension funds and other swindles. On a smaller scale it includes tax evasion, and the copying of computer software and videos. There is also corporate crime where the whole organisation breaks the law. The victim may be the public at large, members of a pension fund or a particular firm. This kind of crime is mostly carried out by middle-class people, who have the expertise to do it and whose jobs put them in a position to do it. The *number* of white-collar crimes is far smaller than the number of burglaries for example, but it is estimated that the amount of money lost is forty times as great as that from ordinary crimes against property. In some white-collar crimes many millions of pounds may be embezzled from pensions or other funds. There may be other serious consequences to employees or to the public, from cutting corners on safety regulations or tests for new drugs for example (Giddens, 1989).

A great deal of white-collar crime goes undetected, and those who do it are often either not found out, or not prosecuted, or not given very heavy sentences. Computer frauds for example are often hushed up.

The sentences for white-collar crime are lighter than those for typical working-class crimes. In the USA the average number of months in prison for the crimes of the poor are:

| | |
|---|---|
| robbery | 131.3 |
| burglary | 63.4 |
| larceny/theft | 31.0 |

The sentences for white-collar crime were much shorter:

| | |
|---|---|
| embezzlement | 18.8 |
| fraud | 22.0 |
| tax evasion | 15.5 |

(Reiman, 1984)

*Black crime*. In British prisons about 10 per cent of the inmates are West Indians, who make up only 1 per cent of the population. There is no over-representation of Asians (Reid, 1989). In the USA the black rate of crime is considerably higher than that for whites, and the association with social class is stronger (Thornberry and Farnworth, 1982). Defenders of blacks say that this is partly because of police prejudice, harassment and selective enforcement of the law, though it is accepted that there is *some* black/white differential. There is a particular form of black crime – mugging on the streets. The explanation usually offered for black crime, both in Britain and in the USA, is that they have a very high rate of unemployment, and the jobs they can find tend to be badly paid and dirty jobs – the ones whites don't want to do. Crime is simply an alternative way of earning a living.

An additional factor may be that blacks are less likely to accept the legitimacy and authority of the state and its laws. They feel they are not being given a fair deal and have no say in the way things are done. Crime is a kind of political protest, a way of hitting back at society. And the police are often seen as the enemy. The same theory can be applied to Catholics in Northern Ireland, militant coal mining unions and student protests at various times in the past.

However, a weakness with the political protest theory is that the victims of crimes tend to be blacks or unskilled manual workers themselves; these two groups are more likely to be mugged or murdered than middle-class whites (Lea and Young, 1984).

## RELIGIOUS BELIEFS AND BEHAVIOUR

One of the largest class differences found in the Rokeach survey was in the value attached to 'salvation', which was placed much higher by working-class people. As part of the Abrams survey, Gerard (1985) used the results of a factor analysis to develop a combined index of religious commitment, based on questions about acceptance of traditional Christian beliefs, reported perception of oneself as a religious person, and needing prayer and contemplation, drawing comfort and strength from religion. With this measure lower-class people come out again as much more religious.

| | Under £3,840 % | £3,840– £7,199 % | £7,200 and over (in 1981) % |
|---|---|---|---|
| High score | 26 | 21 | 15 |
| Medium-high score | 25 | 17 | 13 |
| Low scores | 15 | 19 | 28 |

Source: Gerard, 1985

This is consistent with American research showing that working-class people more often hold traditional, fundamental beliefs (Argyle and Beit-Hallahmi, 1975). However, this index includes more than such beliefs, and puts its emphasis on reported commitment and devotional activities.

However, if we turn to religious *behaviour* it is the middle classes who appear to be more active.

Church attendance is more frequent higher up the social scale. This has been a very stable finding in Britain and the USA for a long time. The levels of weekly attendance reported in Britain 1978 were:

| AB | C1 | C2 | DE |
|---|---|---|---|
| 17% | 11% | 8% | 9% |

Source: Reid, 1989

However, church attendance may not be the best measure of religious commitment – it omits private prayer for example.

Different classes to some extent belong to different churches. In Britain the Church of England tends to be middle-class, non-conformists lower-middle-class, Roman Catholics come from all classes and small sects are drawn mostly from the working class and ethnic minority groups. In the USA there is a clear social hierarchy of churches, with the Congregationalists (now United Reformed) at the top, followed by Episcopalians, Presbyterians, Jews, other Protestant churches, Roman Catholics and small fundamentalist sects at the bottom (Argyle and Beit-Hallahmi, 1975).

Marxism says that religion should appeal to the poor and oppressed by offering compensatory rewards in heaven, or after the Second Coming, and making a virtue of poverty. It also says that religion is used as a source of control of the lower orders; slave owners in the American Southern states welcomed the conversion of their slaves, believing it would make them easier to control (Haralambos and Holborn, 1990). As we have seen, in Britain, although the poor and oppressed go to church less, they believe more and have a more intense devotional life.

The Church of England and other middle-class churches are formal and restrained, often interpreted as 'secularised'. Protestant sects are noisy, spontaneous and emotional, and have avoided secularisation by separating themselves from the world. Their beliefs are likely to appeal to the poor, emphasising the virtues of poverty, and they offer acceptance as equals and status within the religious group; they regard themselves as a spiritual élite. A high level of commitment and beliefs is demanded (Argyle and Beit-Hallahmi, 1975). The Catholic church somehow succeeds in appealing to all social classes: it is both formal and ritualistic, and it is colourful and emotional; perhaps it has different appeals to different classes.

## Conclusions and discussion

There is a very interesting contradiction here – lower-class people go to church less, but report a greater interest in 'salvation', more belief in traditional, fundamentalist ideas, more prayer and contemplation. Middle-class religion is more public, working-class religion more private. Church, and especially the Church of England, is like a middle-class club. The number of people who claim to engage in daily prayer in Britain (about 40 per cent) is much higher than the numbers who go to church weekly (now about 9 per cent), and many of these non-church-going prayers are presumably working-class.

If churches are social clubs, then as with other clubs there are different ones for different classes, reflecting the different interests and needs of each. The Protestant sects offer salvation, and a better life to come, while immediate frustrations are met by an intense devotional life. Middle-class churches offer impressive spectacles, good music, interesting sermons, like a club which has concerts, lectures and improving pep talks.

## REFERENCES

Abercrombie, N. and Turner, B.S. (1978) The dominant ideology thesis. *British Journal of Sociology*, 29, 149–70.

Abercrombie, N. and Warde, A. (1988) *Contemporary British Society*. Oxford: Polity Press.

Abrams, M. (1985) Demographic correlates of values. In M. Abrams, D. Gerard and N. Timms (eds) *Values and Social Change in Britain*. Basingstoke: Macmillan.

Abrams, M., Gerard, D. and Timms, N. (eds) (1985) *Values and Social Change in Britain*. Basingstoke: Macmillan.

Adorno, T.W., Frenkel-Brunswick, E., Levinson, D. and Sanford, N. (1950) *The Authoritarian Personality*. New York: Harper.

Agnew, R.S. (1983) Social class and success goals: an examination of relative and absolute aspirations. *Sociological Quarterly, 24,* 435–52.

Airey, C. (1984) Social and moral values. In R. Jewell and C. Airey (eds) *British Social Attitudes: The 1984 Report*. Aldershot: Gower, pp. 121–56.

Airey, C. and Brook, L. (1986) Interim report: social and moral issues. *British Social Attitudes*. Aldershot: Gower, pp. 149–72.

Argyle, M. (1989) *The Social Psychology of Work*. 2nd edition. Harmondsworth: Penguin.

Argyle, M. (1992) *The Social Psychology of Everyday Life*. London: Routledge.

Argyle, M. and Beit-Hallahmi, B. (1975) *The Social Psychology of Religion*. London: Routledge & Kegan Paul.

Axenroth, J.B. (1983) Social class and delinquency in cross-cultural perspectives. *Journal of Research in Crime and Delinquency.* 20, 164–82.

Box, S. (1981) *Deviancy, Reality and Society*. London: Rinton & Winston.

Braithwaite, J. (1979) *Inequality, Crime, and Public Policy*. London: Routledge & Kegan Paul.

Brown, J. *et al.* (1985) Marriage and the family. In M. Abrams, D. Gerard and N. Timms (eds) *Values and Social Change in Britain*. Basingstoke: Macmillan.

Brown, R. (1965) *Social Psychology*. New York: Free Press.

Dittmar, H. (1992) *The Social Psychology of Material Possessions*. Hemel Hempstead: Wheatsheaf.

Douglas, J.W.B. (1964) *The Home and the School*. London: MacGibbon & Kee.

Douglas, J.W.B., Ross, J.M., Hammond, W.A. and Mulligan, D.G. (1966) Delinquency and social class. *British Journal of Criminology*, 6, 294–302.

Ehrmann, W.W. (1959) *Premarital Dating Behavior*. New York: Holt.

Elias, N. and Dunning, E. (1986) *The Quest for Excitement*. Oxford: Blackwell.

Elliott, D.S. and Ageton, S.S. (1980) Reconciling race and class differences in self-reported and official estimates of delinquency. *American Sociological Review*, 45, 95–110.

Eysenck, H.J. (1954) *The Psychology of Politics*. London: Routledge & Kegan Paul.

Eysenck, H.J. (1976) *Sex and Personality*. London: Open Books.

Farrington, D. (1991) Antisocial personality from childhood to adulthood. *The Psychologist*, 4, 389–94.

Frenkel-Brunswick, E. (1954) Further explorations by a contributor to 'The Authoritarian Personality'. In R. Christie and M. Jahoda (eds) *Studies in the Scope and Method of 'The Authoritarian Personality'*. Glencoe, Ill.: The Free Press.

Gebhard, P.H. and Johnson, A.B. (1979) *The Kinsey Data*. Philadelphia: W.B. Saunders.

Gerard, D. (1985) Religious attitudes and values. In M. Abrams, D. Gerard and N. Timms (eds) *Values and Social Change in Britain*. Basingstoke: Macmillan.

Giddens, A. (1989) *Sociology*. Oxford: Polity Press.

Glueck, S. and Glueck, E. (1950) *Unraveling Juvenile Delinquency*. Cambridge, Mass.: Harvard University Press.

Goldthorpe, J.H., Lockwood, D., Bechofer, F. and Platt, D. (1968) *The Affluent Worker: Industrial Attitudes and Behaviour*. Cambridge: Cambridge University Press.

Goode, W.J. (1959) The theoretical importance of love. *American Sociological Review*, 24, 38–47.

Goody, J. (1976) *Production and Reproduction*. Cambridge: Cambridge University Press.

Gorer, G. (1971) *Sex and Marriage in England Today*. London: Nelson.

Hagan, J. and Palloni, A. (1990) The social reproduction of a criminal class in working-class London, circa 1950–1980. *American Journal of Sociology*, 96, 265–99.

Haralambos, M. and Holborn, M. (1990) *Sociology*. 3rd edition. London: Unwin Hyman.

Harer, M.D. and Steffensmeier, D. (1992) The differing effects of economic inequality on black and white rates of violence. *Social Forces*, 70, 1035–54.

Heath, A. and Evans, G. (1988) Working class conservatives and middle class socialists. In R. Jowell, S. Witherspoon and L. Brook (eds) *British Social Attitudes: The 5th Report*. London: Gower and SCPR.

Himmelstein, J.L. and McRae, J.A. (1988) Social issues and socioeconomic status. *Public Opinion Quarterly*, 52, 492–512.

Horwitz, A.V. (1984) The economy and social pathology. *Annual Review of Sociology*, 10, 95–119.

Hyman, H.H. (1953) The value system of different classes: a social psychological contribution to the analysis of stratification. In R. Bendix and S.M. Lipset (eds) *Class, Status and Power*. Glencoe, Ill.: Free Press.

Hyman, H.H. and Sheatsley, P.B. (1954) The 'Authoritarian Personality' – a methodological critique. In R. Christie and M. Jahoda (eds) *Studies in the Scope and Method of 'The Authoritarian Personality'*. Glencoe, Ill.: The Free Press.

Inglehart, R. (1971) The silent revolution in Europe: intergenerational change in post-industrial societies. *American Political Science Review*, 65, 990–1017.

Inglehart, R. (1981) Post materialism in an environment of insecurity. *American Political Science Review*, 75, 881–900.

Kilwein, J.H., St. Denis, G.C. and Hall, W.T. (1974) The social class of young adults and their views on the environment: how much would you sacrifice? *Journal of School Health*, 44, 196–7.

Kinloch, G.C. (1987) Social class and attitudes towards education. *Journal of Social Psychology*, 127, 399–401.

Kinsey, A.C., Pomeroy, W.B. and Martin, C.E. (1948) *Sexual Behavior in the Human Male*. Philadelphia: W.B. Saunders.

Kleck, G. (1982) On the use of self-report data to determine the class distribution of criminal and delinquent behavior. *American Sociological Review*, 47, 427–33.

Kohn, M.L. and Schooler, K.A. (1973) Occupational experience and psychological functioning: an assessment of reciprocal effects. *American Sociological Review*, 38, 97–118.

Kohn, M.L. and Schooler, K.A. (1983) *Work and Personality*. Norwood, NJ: Ablex.

Lea, J. and Young, J. (1984) *What is to be Done about Law and Order?* Harmondsworth: Penguin.

Liebow, E. (1967) *Tally's Corner*. Boston: Little, Brown.

Lipset, S.M. (1960) *Political Man*. Garden City, NY: Doubleday.

Mann, M. (1986) Work and the work ethic. In R. Jowell, S. Witherspoon and L. Brook (eds) *British Social Attitudes: The 1986 Report*. Aldershot: Gower.

Marsh, P., Rosser, E. and Harré, R. (1978) *The Rules of Disorder*. London: Routledge & Kegan Paul.

Matheson, J. (1987) *Voluntary Work*, supplement to *General Household Survey*. London: HMSO.

Merton, R.K. (1968) *Social Theory and Social Structure*. New York: Free Press.

Phillips, D. and Harding, S. (1985) The structure of moral values. In M. Abrams,

D. Gerard and N. Timms (eds) *Values and Social Change in Britain*. Basingstoke: Macmillan.

Porter, L.W. (1964) *Organizational Patterns of Managerial Job Attitudes*. New York: American Foundation for Attitude Research.

Rainwater, L. (1966) Some aspects of lower class sexual behavior. *Journal of Social Issues*, 22, 96–108.

Reid, I. (1989) *Social Class Differences in Britain*. 3rd edition. London: Fontana.

Reiman, J.H. (1984) *The Rich get Richer, and the Poor get Prison*. New York: Wiley.

Rokeach, M. (1960) *The Open and Closed Mind*. New York: Basic Books.

Rokeach, M. (1973) *The Nature of Human Values*. New York: Free Press.

Rushton, J-P. and Bogaert, A.F. (1988) Race versus social class differences in sexual behaviour: a follow-up test. *Journal of Research in Personality*, 22, 259–72.

Scarr, S. (1981) *Race, Social Class, and Individual Differences in IQ*. Hillsdale, NJ: Erlbaum.

Schoeck, H. (1987) *Envy. A Theory of Social Behavior*. New York: Liberty Fund.

Schofield, M. (1965) *The Sexual Behaviour of Young People*. London: Longman.

Sears, D.O. (1969) Political behavior. In G. Lindzey and E. Aronson (eds) *The Handbook of Social Psychology*, Vol. 5. 2nd edition. Reading, Mass.: Addison-Wesley.

Shaw, C.R. and McKay, H.D. (1942) *Juvenile Delinquency and Urban Areas*. Chicago: University of Chicago Press.

Slater, E. and Woodside, M. (1951) *Patterns of Marriage: A Study of Marriage Relationships in the Urban Working Classes*. London: Cassell.

Sugarman, B. (1970) Social class, values and behaviour in schools. In M. Craft (ed.) *Family, Class and Education*. London: Longman.

Thornberry, T.P. and Farnworth, M. (1982) Social correlates of criminal involvement: further evidence on the relationship between social status and criminal behavior. *American Sociological Review*, 47, 505–18.

Tittle, C.R., Villemez, W.J. and Smith, D.A. (1978) The myth of social class and criminality: an empirical assessment of the empirical evidence. *American Sociological Review*, 43, 643–56.

Van Dusen, K.T., Mednick, S.A., Gabrielli, W.E. and Hutings, B. (1983) Social class and crime in an adoption cohort. *Journal of Criminal Law and Criminology*, 74, 249–69.

Weeks, J. (1981) *Sex, Politics and Society*. London: Longman.

Weinrich, J.D. (1977) Human sociobiology: pair-bonding and resource predictability (effects of social class and race). *Behavioral Ecology and Sociobiology*, 2, 91–118.

West, D.J. and Farrington, D.P. (1973) *Who Becomes Delinquent?*. London: Heinemann.

West, D.J. and Farrington, D.P. (1977) *The Delinquent Way of Life*. London: Heinemann.

Wuthnow, R. and Shrum, W. (1983) Knowledge workers as a 'new class': structural and ideological convergence among professional-technical workers and managers. *Work and Occupations*, 10, 471–87.

# Chapter 11

# Health, mental health, happiness and self-esteem

The rich may have more money, members of higher classes may have bigger houses and cars, but do they feel any better for it? Do they have better health, mental health, happiness or self-esteem? To answer this question we will look at four indices of well-being to study the class differences. We shall ask how large they are, how they can be explained and how the lot of the less fortunate groups could be improved. This might require major social or economic changes, but perhaps it could be achieved in other ways.

## SOCIAL CLASS AND HEALTH

### Measurement

We should consider both how well people feel and how well the doctor thinks they are. The best measure of health is probably an interview and physical examination by a doctor, together with medical tests for blood pressure, etc. However, some people never see a doctor, and different doctors may apply different standards. In the *Health and Lifestyle* study 7,414 people were interviewed, and a nurse made a number of physiological measurements (Blaxter, 1990). Several social surveys have been carried out with questions like 'Do you have any limiting long-standing illness?' (17 per cent in 1985) as used by the *General Household Survey*, which interviews 24,000 people. However, it has recently been found that subjective reports of feeling well or ill correlate more with unhappiness and neuroticism than with physiological measurements. Subjective reports of ill-health may be due to negative emotions causing people to attend more to bodily symptoms, and to be more sensitive to them, while important bodily conditions like high blood pressure go unnoticed (Watson and Pennebaker, 1989). The way to avoid these biases is to ask objective questions about days off last year, number of visits to the doctor, medicines taken and restriction of activities caused by illness. A measure which is not affected by subjective bias is whether people live or die, and we will begin with class differences in longevity.

## Life expectancy and longevity

Life expectancy can be calculated from census data. In Britain class I babies in 1978 would have expected on average to live to 72.2, class V babies to 65. This difference of 7.2 years falls to under 4 years by the time they are 15, since a lot of the differential risk lies in early childhood. By 45 the difference in life expectancies between classes I and V is only 2.3 years (Reid, 1989).

Another way of calculating life chances, and the effects of serious illness, is by the standardised mortality ratio (SMR). This is calculated from the number of observed deaths in a group/number of expected deaths × 100, the expected deaths being based on the whole population. The SMRs from all causes, including child deaths, are shown in Table 11.1. It can be seen that the rates for both rise steeply in class V.

*Table 11.1* Standardised mortality ratios

|  | *I* | *II* | *IIIn* | *IIIm* | *V* | *A11* |
|---|---|---|---|---|---|---|
| Child deaths | 81.5 | 81.5 | 94 | 95.5 | 116 | 159 |
| Male adults | 66 | 76 | 94 | 106 | 116 | 165 |
| Female adults | 69 | 78 | 87 | 100 | 110 | 134 |

*Source:* Reid, 1989

Class differences in deaths are greater for certain illnesses. For men some of the major differences are:

|  | SMRs | |
|---|---|---|
|  | *I* | *V* |
| Mental disorders | 35 | 342 |
| Injury and poisoning | 67 | 226 |
| Infectious/parasitic diseases | 65 | 215 |
| Diseases of respiratory system | 36 | 210 |
| Diseases of digestive system (inc. cirrhosis and ulcers) | 67 | 204 |
| Diseases of circulation, including heart | 69 | 151 |
| Cancer | 69 | 154 |

*Source: Occupational Mortality,* 1990

The differences for women are similar, but the class differences are smaller, as Table 11.1 shows.

These figures are available from 1949. Although the health of all classes has improved, the *gap* between them, measured by the SMR ratios, has increased. In 1949–52 the mortality of class IV and V males was 23 per cent greater than for those in I and II; in 1970–2 it was 61 per cent greater. A sudden change occurred in 1951: the health of most groups improved, but for the lowest classes there was little or no change. Pneumonia and TB were replaced by heart attacks and lung cancer as the main causes of death during the working years. Lung cancer is primarily due to smoking, while important factors in heart disease are smoking, diet and (lack of) exercise; in all these areas working-class people have much less healthy styles of behaviour (Goldblatt, 1990). Lower-class people have higher death rates for all kinds of illness except car accidents, skin cancer, polio and brain tumours (Black *et al.*, 1988).

Mortality ratios have been examined for different occupations, and large differences found. The highest rates are for electrical engineers (SMR 317, i.e. death rates 3.17 times average), bricklayers' labourers (273), fishermen (171), armed forces (147) and publicans (155). The lowest include engineering foremen (47), paper products makers (50) and clergymen (76). It is also very interesting that the average mortality of the wives of men in these occupations is very similar, e.g. armed forces (150), clergymen's wives (76) (Fletcher, 1983). Some other occupational groups have low rates – supervisors, professionals and others who work for themselves, including farmers (Goldblatt, 1990).

The mortality rate of the unemployed is considerably elevated – by 36 per cent for men and 21 per cent for women in Britain, with age and class held constant (Moser *et al.*, 1984).

## Illness and health

People may live to a great age, but it is also important to know whether they are in good health while doing so. In the *Health and Lifestyles* study (Blaxter, 1990) several indices of health were developed. For a combined index, health was 'good' or 'excellent' for more class I and II people (37 per cent at age 40–59), than class IV and V (24.5 per cent). The effects of class in this study were due more to income than to other aspects of class. The healthiest people were earning £250 per week (£13,000 p.a.) in 1984–5; those on £50 per week had twice the average rate of disability or disease and 50 per cent more illness, for men; those earning over £300 per week were in worse health, nearer the average. The explanation of the poor health of the most highly paid group is that some of the highly paid men, especially young men, had poor health behaviour, mainly drinking a lot. This was most true of owners of small businesses and managers, not professional or technical people.

The class differences in Britain are quite large. The corresponding differences in Sweden for example are much smaller. The ratio of prevalence of long-standing illness in Britain, class VI to class I, is 2.65, in Sweden 1.52 (*Lancet*, 1 July 1989). Class differences increased with age, but these declined again after 60, and in the 70+ age group were much reduced. Only for mental health did class differences continue to increase with age. Class

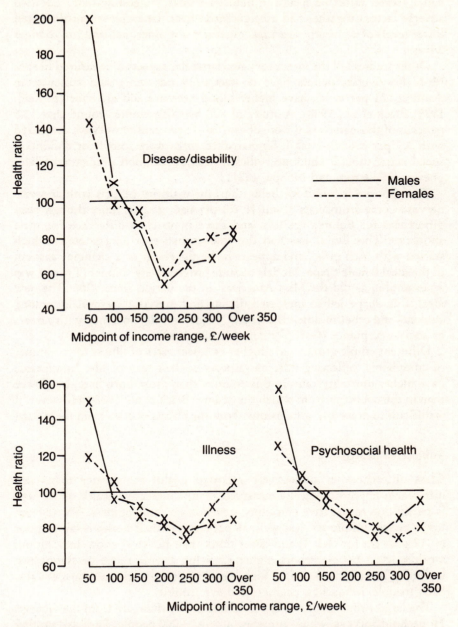

*Figure 11.1* Income and health: age-standardised health ratios, illness and psychosocial health, in relation to weekly income, demonstrating the effect of £50/week increments in household income, males and females age 40–59 (all of a given age and gender = 100)
*Source:* Blaxter, 1990

had a greater effect on health in industrial areas, suggesting that these two adverse factors together had a heightened effect. Unemployment produced lower levels of all health measures, especially for older men and for younger wives.

Other studies tell the same story for particular aspects of measured health. More lower-class people have no teeth (39 per cent), and suffer from deafness (21 per cent), have higher blood pressure and are shorter (Reid, 1989; Black *et al.*, 1988). A study of 800 Swedish women found that 32.5 per cent of those in class V were obese (top 10 per cent of obesity) compared with 3.9 per cent in class I. Similar differences were found for childhood social class, though childhood obesity was not a good predictor of later obesity (Hällstrom and Noppa, 1981).

The opposite is found for being thin: the majority of girls with anorexia nervosa come from class I and II, 70 per cent at one time, though class differences for bulimia are less, and there is no class difference for male anorexics. This illness has had the characteristics of an epidemic, which started with 'rich girls', and appears to be the result of a changing fashion of the ideal female shape. Models became progressively thinner (Twiggy was an example), as did the Miss Americas, in the period since 1960. The new ideal, thin shape led to increased dieting and exercising, especially among students and other middle-class young women much concerned with careers or social acceptance (Garfinkel and Garner, 1982).

Different ethnic groups have higher or lower rates of illness for a number of complaints, reflecting different aspects of their way of life. Immigrants have higher mortality rates in this country than those born here, but lower than in the countries from which they came (Black *et al.*, 1988). However, it is difficult to draw any conclusions about the effects of class from these data.

## Subjective health

Class differences in subjectively reported health are greater than class differences in physiologically measured health. Subjective health, as we saw, is partly due to negative emotions, neuroticism, unhappiness. Those from lower classes simply feel less well: 36 per cent say their health is fair or poor (v. 12 per cent for class I) and fewer think their health is good. In addition, working-class people report higher rates for a wide range of symptoms, including bronchitis, arthritis, high blood pressure, varicose veins, coughs, back trouble, headaches, deafness and eye trouble.

The largest surveys of self-reported health in Britain are from the General Household Surveys, which interview nearly 24,000 people. They ask a rather precise question, about 'limiting long-standing illness', which may reduce the effects of negative emotions. The 1990 results are shown in Figure 11.2. It can be seen that there is little difference for the two younger age groups, but there is a considerable class difference in health for the 45–64 group.

To summarise, there are massive class differences in health, whether this is measured from mortality, physiological measures or self-report. In particular class differences are greater:

1 for men than women
2 for older age groups
3 in industrial areas
4 when class is measured by income
5 for infectious diseases, respiratory and digestive troubles
6 for the lowest social class.

How can this complex pattern of results be explained?

## Explanation

Several different explanations of the link between social class and health have been discussed and investigated. The basic phenomenon is a sociological one, but the explanations lie mainly in psychology, though they draw on knowledge of the conditions of life in different classes.

*Selection and drift.* According to this model unfit people move down the social scale, while fit people move up, or stay up. Unfortunately health has not usually been included in social mobility studies, so that the overall importance of this process is not known. However, parents' age at time of death accounts for only 2.6 per cent of the variance in the longevity of their children, and since alternative explanations have been shown to explain a lot of the class–illness link it must be concluded that selection and drift is a fairly minor part of the story for physical health (Williams, 1990).

*Lifestyle.* There are several aspects of the working-class lifestyle which are known to be linked with poor health. In particular, working-class people:

1 smoke more, as shown in Figure 11.3;
2 take less exercise, e.g. 65 per cent of professional-class people engage in regular exercise, apart from walking, compared to 28 per cent of unskilled (Table 5.6);
3 are more often obese, e.g. 20.6 per cent of British class V women compared to 3.4 per cent of class II (p. 193).

Further details on these topics were given in earlier chapters. Blaxter (1990) found the worst health behaviour for men among manual workers with low incomes; class was more important than income. Women had better health behaviour, but for them income was a more important predictor than occupational class.

Can these differences in lifestyle explain the class differences in health? A study of 17,530 British civil servants found that those in the lowest ranks

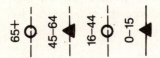

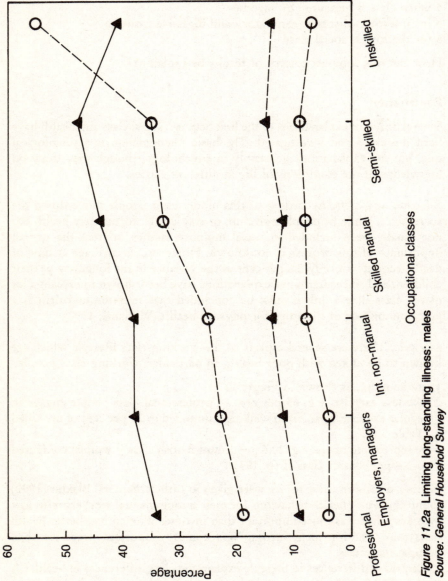

Figure 11.2a  Limiting long-standing illness: males
Source: General Household Survey

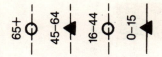

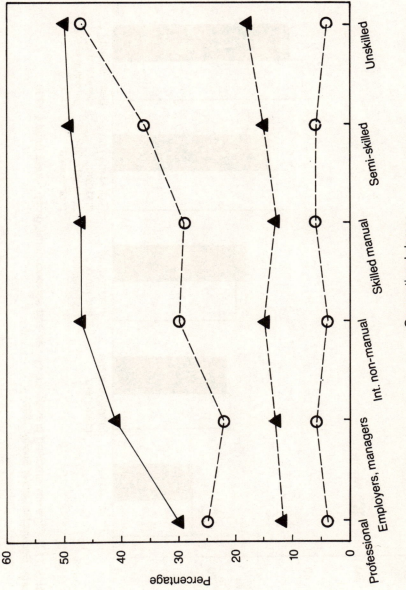

*Figure 11.2b* Limiting long-standing illness: females
*Source: General Household Survey*

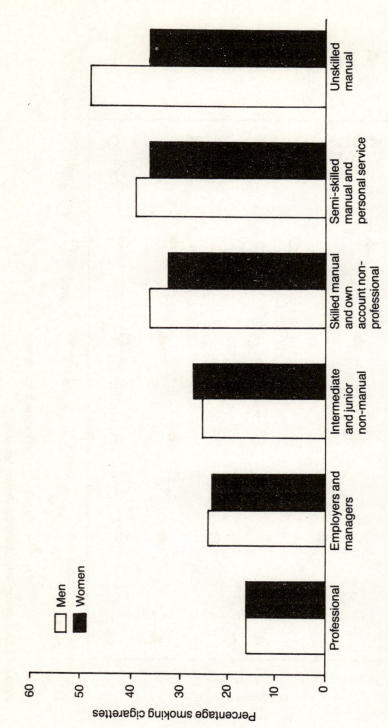

*Figure 11.3* Cigarette-smoking prevalence by sex and socioeconomic group, Great Britain, 1990
*Source: General Household Survey, 1992*

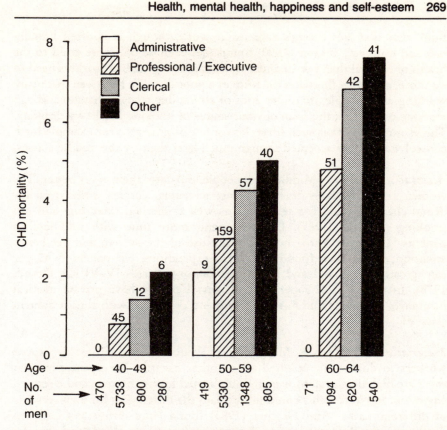

*Figure 11.4* Coronary heart disease mortality (and number of deaths) in seven and a half years by civil service grade and age
*Source:* Marmot *et al.*, 1984

had a 3.6 times greater death rate from heart attacks. The lower ranks consist of people like porters and messengers who would belong to classes IV and V. They also had higher blood pressure, smoked more, had higher blood sugar and cholesterol, were shorter and older. However, these factors could explain only about 40 per cent of the variance in the rate of heart attacks, leaving 60 per cent to be accounted for. The lower ranks also had less active leisure, but this was not quantified nor its effects examined (Marmot *et al.*, 1984).

What is the reason for these class differences in lifestyle? One factor is education, and health education, access to the latest medical news. The serious papers, read by middle-class people, have better coverage of medical matters than the popular papers – more articles, articles which are more informative and based on medical journals and statistics (Kristiansen and Harding, 1988). Smoking, eating fast food, not taking exercise are all part of a working-class cultural style, with many causes. Manual workers may think that they get enough exercise at work, though it is often literally manual; however, Blaxter (1990) found that exercise did more good to the health of manual than non-manual workers. Heavy manual workers need to eat more, and often this takes the form of a poor diet. We have seen that many working-class people are under a lot of stress, due to daily hassles and bad working conditions; this is an obvious source of smoking and heavy drinking. This is not to say that such lifestyles cannot be changed; for example birth control was widely accepted though much later than by the middle classes.

*Access to medical care*. Middle-class people look after themselves better. The women are more likely to have breast screening, cervical smears, go for dental check-ups and use seat belts, as well as dieting, exercising and not smoking (Calman, 1985). Doctors spend more time with middle-class patients. The latter know how to make use of the system and get better attention; it has been found that NHS expenditure per patient is 40 per cent greater for class I and II patients than on classes IV–VI (Le Grand, 1978). In addition, 22.5 per cent of class I people have private medical insurance, ensuring rapid hospital treatment, compared with almost none in class VI.

*Material aspects of work*. Many industrial jobs are dangerous, or expose workers to dust, heat, polluted air or other hazards. We saw earlier that there are high death rates for men in the armed forces, firemen and electrical engineers. However, this could not explain the differences for civil servants of different ranks. And Fletcher (1983) found large differences between death rates for different jobs in the same industry. He also found that the average for wives is very similar to that of husbands. This cannot be explained by material transfer, e.g. of dust particles, since the effect is also true of different jobs in the same industry. He suggests that it could be due to 'psychological transfer' of the risks and stresses associated with jobs, and the resultant similar lifestyles. There are other differences between high- and low-status jobs which could be responsible. In lower-status jobs there is less autonomy, less perceived control over how the work is done. There is often time pressure, e.g. on assembly lines, tedious repetitive work, heavy work, as well as unfavourable work conditions – heat, noise, dust, shiftwork, etc. (Argyle, 1989).

*Home environment*. Young children in poor families have a higher rate of early deaths. This could be due to poor nutrition, lack of heating, damp and unhygienic surroundings and no safe play areas outside the home, making accidents more likely. The health of adults too will be affected by inadequate food, heating, cleanliness and by air pollution, difficulty in getting to the doctor. These conditions could help to explain the very poor health of the lowest classes. Goldblatt (1990) found that, within both manual and non-manual groups, not having a car and not owning a residence were strong predictors of poor health.

Blaxter (1990) found that, in general, exercise, good diet, not smoking or drinking had good effects on health and to some extent could protect against the effects of environment. However, in the case of poor people living in industrial cities, these good health behaviours made little difference: they were more advantageous for those in good environments.

*Social support* is an important factor in health. People in families not only look after each other better, but have a strengthened immune system as a result of the supportive relationship. Working-class people overall have less social support from all sources taken together – more broken marriages, unemployment producing isolation, high job turnover, noisy work inhibiting work relationships, less attendance at church or leisure groups. This is part of the explanation of class differences in health (Williams, 1990).

*The effects of status on health.* We saw that less than half the variance in health could be accounted for by health behaviour (though exercise was omitted). Some more could be explained by environment and by differential access to medical care. However, it is possible that status itself is good for health in a more direct way. This could be by generating feelings of ability to control events, of self-confidence or simply of positive affect. Higher-status people command more respect, both at work and in the community, have more money to do what they like and, as we shall see later in this chapter, are happier and have greater self-esteem.

## Conclusion

The greatest known cause of class differences in health is lifestyle, especially smoking, diet and exercise, accounting for 40 per cent or more of class differences. Also important are the domestic environment, especially heating, hygiene, air pollution and safety. Many manual workers do jobs that are dangerous, stressful or produce industrial diseases. There are class differences in access to medical care and making use of preventive medical services. Middle-class people have more social support, and status probably has a positive effect via self-esteem. Downward drift of the unfit, upward selection of the healthy is a fairly minor factor.

## SOCIAL CLASS AND MENTAL HEALTH

### Introduction

Mental health can be assessed from the number of patients of different kinds known to doctors or psychiatrists as in-patients or out-patients. A difficulty here is that there is probably some bias in diagnosis, linked to social class. Psychiatrists may diagnose more working-class patients as psychiatric cases (Goldberg and Huxley, 1980). It has also been suggested that psychiatrists may diagnose more working-class patients as 'psychotic' and therefore suitable for physical treatment, because of apparent 'communication difficulties', and more middle-class people as 'neurotic' and suitable for psychotherapy. In any case many people who are suffering from mental disturbance are never seen by doctors at all. Another method is sample surveys, asking questions like 'Did you experience unpleasant emotional strain yesterday?' (all of the time . . . not at all), or scales like the twelve items of the shorter version of the General Health Questionnaire. There is no reason to expect any social class bias here, just the usual fear of inaccurate self-reporting.

## Mental hospital patients

A larger percentage of mental hospital patients are in social class V (20.5 per cent of psychotic patients) than the percentage of non-patients who are in this class (9 per cent), giving a patient:non-patient ratio of 2.28:1. Table 11.2 shows how this ratio increases from social class I in Britain (0.78:1), and in the USA from 0.70 to 2.08.

*Table 11.2a* Percentage of non-patients and patients admitted to hospital in Aberdeen, 1963–7, by social class

| Social class | Non-patients | All patients | Psychotic patients | Non-patient: all patients ratio | Non-patient: pyschotics ratio |
|---|---|---|---|---|---|
| I | 5.5 | 5.0 | 4.3 | 0.91 | 0.78 |
| II | 21.0 | 19.7 | 15.4 | 0.94 | 0.73 |
| III | 46.8 | 35.9 | 27.0 | 0.77 | 0.58 |
| IV | 17.8 | 25.4 | 31.9 | 1.43 | 1.79 |
| V | 9.0 | 14.1 | 20.5 | 1.57 | 2.28 |

*Source:* adapted from Birtchnell, 1971

*Table 11.2b* Percentage of patients and non-patients in each social class in New Haven, Connecticut, 1950

| Social class | Non-patients | Patients | Non-patient: patient ratio |
|---|---|---|---|
| I and II (business; professional; managerial) | 11.4 | 8.0 | 0.70 |
| III (white collar) | 20.4 | 13.7 | 0.66 |
| IV (semi-skilled manual) | 49.8 | 40.1 | 0.81 |
| V (unskilled manual) | 18.4 | 38.2 | 2.08 |

*Source:* adapted from Hollingshead and Redlich, 1958

Some mental disorders are more linked to social class than others. Schizophrenia is the most strongly class-linked, working-class people being about five times more likely to be diagnosed schizophrenic. Depression is two to three times more common for working-class women, as found by Brown and Harris (1978) in South London. Several other forms of mental disorder are more common in the working class, especially alcoholism and drug addiction. On the other hand, middle-class people have higher rates of anxiety and psychotic affective disorders (Dohrenwend, 1975).

## Surveys of mental health

Many surveys have found a similar class difference. Some asked simple questions, e.g. Warr and Payne (1982). Others used short scales, assessing degrees of mental disturbance. The *Health and Lifestyle* survey used the General Health Questionnaire; Figure 11.2 shows how poorer people report more ill-health, especially the poorest. And those earning more than £250 per week in 1984–5 (£13,000 p.a.) were in slightly worse mental health than those earning less. In this study class differences were greater for older people, whereas for physical health the difference declined after 60. Cochrane and Stopes-Roe (1980) found that non-manual people reported 3.10 symptoms on average, skilled manual and supervisory 3.74 and semi- and unskilled manual 4.88. Again, it is classes IV and V who show the high rates of disturbance.

American studies have analysed the separate effects of occupational status, education and income: all are related to mental health. Kessler (1982) re-analysed the data from eight national surveys from 1967 to 1976, with 16,000 subjects in all. He found that for men, income, especially earned income,

*Table 11.3* Class differences in strain and worry

| UK | | Class | |
|---|---|---|---|
| | ABC1 | C2 | DE |
| Reported unpleasant emotional strain yesterday: most or all of the time | 7 | 8 | 14 |
| Had experienced strain for more than a month | | 14.5 | 23.5 |
| USA | | Education | |
| | College | High school | Grade school |
| Worry a lot | 30 | 38 | 40 |
| Feelings of impending nervous breakdown | 16 | 19 | 20 |

*Sources:* Bradburn, 1969; Warr and Payne, 1982.

was the strongest predictor, while for women, especially housewives, education was strongest; occupational status was the weakest predictor for both. Unemployment is very bad for mental health. But does unemployment cause poor mental health, or vice versa. Banks and Jackson (1982) carried out an elegant longitudinal study to tackle this question; they followed up several hundred school leavers for one to two years. Those who found jobs showed reduced scores on the GHQ, while those who didn't had considerably increased scores. In addition, however, there was a small tendency for those with initially poorer mental health not to get jobs. Other studies have found that workers and their spouses often become depressed, anxious and irritable within a few months of job loss, with an average of 11 on the Beck Depression Inventory (v. 5.5 for those at work) in one study (Feather, 1982). In addition, the level of alcoholism goes up: 44 per cent are heavy drinkers (seven glasses once a week or more) v. 28 per cent for those with jobs. The rate of attempted suicide went up by a factor of eight in some studies (Argyle, 1989).

Stott (1978) reports a survey of 15,496 British and 2,527 Canadian school children using the Bristol Social Adjustment Guides, a set of scales for teachers to rate behaviour. The British manual groups had twice the rate of disturbance of children from non-manual families, and class V was particularly high. In the Canadian study over- and under-reacting were separated; class affected only over-reacting, though the overall class difference was less than in Britain. Class differences were found for 7-year-olds, and in the Canadian sample were greater at this age than later, leading Stott to favour a genetic explanation.

Do ethnic groups have worse mental health than majority group members similar in occupation or income? If social class is a causal factor in some way this would be expected. Certainly the overall rates of disturbance among ethnic groups are very high, though varying between different groups. In Britain the Irish and West Indians have high rates, mostly due to their rates of alcoholism and schizophrenia (Table 11.4)

*Table 11.4* Mental hospital admission rates of natives and immigrants in Great Britain, 1971

| (a) Crude rates per 100,000 population | |
| --- | --- |
| Natives | 265 |
| Immigrants | 495 |

| (b) Age-sex standardised rates per 100,000 adults | |
| --- | --- |
| Native | 494 |
| Irish | 1110 |
| Indian | 403 |
| Pakistani | 336 |
| West Indian | 539 |

*Source:* adapted from Cochrane and Stopes-Roe, 1981b

However, much of this difference is because more ethnic group members are of lower social class anyway; what happens if they are compared with native whites of the same occupations and income? In American studies Puerto Ricans are found to have worse mental health than whites of similar social class, but blacks have *better* mental health. In Britain Asians have *fewer* symptoms than whites (like the black Americans) (Cochrane, 1983).

## Explanation

An alternative to social class in some way 'causing' mental disorder is the 'downward drift' theory, that people who are mentally disturbed move downwards in society. If people become disturbed early in life their education or career suffers, and they are likely to be downwardly mobile. It is found that the class differences of patients' parents are less class-linked than the patients themselves, sometimes not class-linked at all, supporting this theory. Another version of it is that mental disturbance makes *upward* mobility more difficult; during recent years the working class has been shrinking, and many have moved out of it – but not the mental patients (Harkey *et al.*, 1976). The downward drift theory applies particularly to schizophrenia (Wheaton, 1978), but also applies to some extent to other forms of disorder. Since schizophrenia in particular is partly genetic, the drift could take place over several generations. Ecological studies find that male schizophrenics in particular often leave their families, presumably because of their personality difficulties, and move into run-down central areas of cities (Kohn, 1973). Part of the explanation for working-class schizophrenia is the gradual accumulation of genes in that class. This raises the possibility that there are some genetic differences between classes, not only in height and IQ, but in schizophrenic tendencies and other aspects of mental health.

Mental patients of all kinds report more stressful events than other people (Angemeyer, 1987). Are working-class people exposed to greater stress than those higher up the social scale? McLeod and Kessler (1990) re-analysed five studies, of nearly 7,000 people, and found that lower-class individuals did experience more unfavourable events of a variety of kinds, especially loss of income and ill-health. Other research shows that they are more likely to be out of work, have frustrating jobs or be in trouble with the law. They have more minor but daily 'hassles', like drunken husbands, bad housing, money problems and several young children at home. Brown and Harris (1978) in their famous study in Camberwell found that the higher rate of severe depression in working-class women could partly be accounted for by these environmental stresses.

In addition, working-class people are more vulnerable to stress – they are more distressed by the *same* level of stress (McLeod and Kessler, 1990). This could be because they have fewer resources or because of some personality-based vulnerability. A missing resource which may be important is lack of education – the main predictor for women. Another may be a weaker level of social support. Brown and Harris found that their working-class women were less likely to have a close relationship with husband or boyfriend. Turner and Noh (1983), in a study of 312 women before and after giving birth, found that the relation between class and distress could be explained by the weaker social support and lower degree of internal control of the working-class women.

A number of personality differences are relevant here: working-class people are lower on *internal control* (Lefcourt, 1976). Internal control is the most important component of hardiness, that is the capacity to resist and not be upset by external stresses. *Self-esteem* is another feature of personality that enables people to stand up to stress (Cronkite and Moos, 1984). We shall see later that there are large class differences in self-esteem. There are also class differences in *coping* style: working-class people are more likely to withdraw, become fatalistic or use passive methods like prayer, where middle-class people are more likely to use active methods, e.g., try to solve the problem or seek informal help (Veroff *et al.*, 1981). Working-class people are also more likely to break the law when under stress and to express their distress in bodily psychosomatic forms.

The origin of these different styles of coping can be found in class-related patterns of socialisation. Children from the lowest level, or underclass, experience poverty, rejection, criminality and chaotic families, leading to many personal problems later. Working-class children in general are more likely to experience rigid, punitive styles of discipline (p. 85). Kohn (1976) suggested that an important factor in the development of schizophrenia in working-class people is a rigid form of upbringing, producing conformity to authority, a fatalistic and conservative world view and inability to cope with problems and stress. This could interact with the class-linked genetic and stress factors we have just described. In addition, poor people repeatedly encounter situations where they have no control, so that a culture of powerlessness and external control is passed on (Hess, 1970), which can lead to learned helplessness and depression. In a study of eighteen neighbourhoods in Sydney it was found that the emotional distress of children was greatest in low-income families, in areas of bad housing, with single parents. The four worst areas stood out; they were inner-city areas with no outside play spaces, the children were lonely, disliked each other, felt rejected and fearful (Homel and Burns, 1989). Withdrawal may also be learnt, for example when confronted by authority at work. Middle-class people more often react with anxiety (Langner and Michael, 1963).

A final hypothesis is that mental health is enhanced by happiness, which can prevent the effects of stress. A number of longitudinal studies have shown that happiness is a cause of mental health, and that there are class differences in happiness, as we shall see in the next section.

## Conclusion

There are extensive class differences in mental health, rather greater than those in physical health. These differences are partly due to greater stress in working-class life, e.g. through poverty, which is the strongest class predictor here. Working-class people are also more vulnerable to stress, because of lower levels of internal control, lower self-esteem and less effective styles of coping, in turn due to different socialisation experiences and lower levels of social support. There is some downward drift, especially of schizophrenics, and probably some effects of lower happiness.

## SOCIAL CLASS AND HAPPINESS

Happiness is now thought to consist of three related components – positive affect, (absence of) negative affect, and satisfaction (with life as a whole). There are a number of self-report measures of each, which agree quite well with one another, and the three components correlate at about .50 (Argyle, 1987). Some of the best-known studies of satisfaction reported that it had a very low correlation with income or other measures of social class, about .15, and furthermore that this correlation was smaller in later American studies (Campbell *et al.*, 1976). Later, a meta-analysis of a number of such studies found that a composite measure of social class correlated a little higher than this, on average .20, income .17 and occupational status .11, with measures of subjective well-being (Haring *et al.*, 1984).

The main result is clear: people of higher social class are somewhat

*Table 11.5* Social class and happiness in the USA

|  | Very happy | Positive affect | Negative affect |
|---|---|---|---|
| **Incomes** | | | |
| less than $2,000 | 18 | .32 | .56 |
| $2,000–3,000 | 16 | .40 | .58 |
| $3,000–4,000 | 15 | .39 | .54 |
| $4,000–5,000 | 24 | .38 | .51 |
| $5,000–6,000 | 35 | .46 | .52 |
| $6,000–7,000 | 33 | .45 | .52 |
| $7,000–8,000 | 33 | .46 | .53 |
| $8,000–10,000 | 38 | .50 | .49 |
| $10,000–15,000 | 41 | .52 | .46 |
| $15,000 or more | 38 | .57 | .46 |
| **Education** | | | |
| Eighth grade or less | 26 | .35 | .52 |
| Part high school | 28 | .41 | .51 |
| High school graduate | 37 | .49 | .51 |
| Part college | 31 | .55 | .52 |
| College graduates | 39 | .56 | .47 |

*Source:* Bradburn, 1969

*Table 11.6* Social class and happiness in Great Britain

|  | Very happy | Positive affect | Negative affect |
|---|---|---|---|
| **Income** | | | |
| High | 44 | 3.2 | 1.2 |
| Middle | 42 | 2.7 | 1.1 |
| Low | 30 | 2.3 | 1.5 |
| **Occupation** | | | |
| Professional and management | 43 | 3.3 | 1.1 |
| Non-manual | 34 | 2.8 | 1.0 |
| Skilled manual | 40 | 2.8 | 0.9 |
| Unskilled manual | 42 | 2.7 | 1.3 |
| Unemployed | 27 | 2.1 | 1.6 |
| Retired | 28 | 2.2 | 1.2 |
| **Education ended** | | | |
| Before 15 | 35 | 2.4 | 1.3 |
| 15 | 40 | 2.5 | 1.2 |
| 16 | 40 | 2.7 | 1.3 |
| 17–18 | 40 | 3.0 | 1.2 |
| 19+ | 36 | 3.0 | 1.1 |

*Source:* Harding, 1985

happier, in whatever way happiness or social class are measured. All that has been disputed is how strong this effect is.

Let us start with an early survey of 6,000 people mainly in Detroit and Washington (Bradburn, 1969) (Table 11.5). The measure of happiness used was a single direct question, positive affect was measured by five questions about positive feelings and negative affect by five questions about negative feelings. It can be seen that income had quite a strong effect on positive affect and happiness, but a weaker effect on negative affect. Education had a strong effect on positive affect, less on happiness.

A recent British study of 1,200 adults obtained similar results (Harding, 1985) (Table 11.6). In this study income affected all three measures of happiness, but mainly at the lower end of the scale, between middle and low income. Occupation mainly affected positive affect, though the unemployed were unhappy on all three measures. Education had no effect on reported happiness, but did influence the two affect scales.

We have established that, in both the USA and Britain, all measures of social class have an effect on happiness. Which aspects of happiness are most affected? Positive emotion is influenced more than negative, and more than satisfaction. The only group with clearly elevated negative emotions are the unemployed. This gives a clue to the explanation of the effect of class on happiness: it may be because a middle-class way of life provides more joyful experiences.

Do different dimensions of class affect happiness differently? Occupation has a smaller effect than income or education. On the other hand, occupational status has a strong effect on job satisfaction. As we showed in Chapter 5, the most satisfying jobs are professional ones, followed by management, other white-collar work, skilled manual and unskilled manual work. There are large differences in job satisfaction, depending how it is measured. If asked 'Would you choose the same work again?', 91 per cent of mathematicians and 83 per cent of lawyers would do so, but only 16 per cent of unskilled car workers (Blauner, 1960). However, the effect of jobs on reported overall satisfaction is less than this, though job satisfaction does influence overall satisfaction (and vice versa).

Income has a greater effect than occupation on satisfaction and positive affect. In addition, people are concerned about how their incomes compare with those of others, indeed this is behind a lot of trade union disputes over wages. There is now a lot of evidence that satisfaction depends on the size of the gap between goals (or aspirations) and achievement and that aspirations depend on the incomes and possessions of other people (Michalos, 1986). White-collar workers are less satisfied than manual workers with the same earnings, because the white-collar workers compare themselves (unfavourably) with other (better paid) white-collar workers (Runciman, 1966). Table 11.5 suggests that income has less effect at the upper income levels. However, there are effects of income at the upper end of the scale too: Diener *et al.* (1985) compared sixty-two Americans earning over 10 million dollars a year with a control group from the same areas. The millionaires scored 15.4 on positive affect, the controls 14.0; the millionaires were happy on average 77 per cent of the time, the others 62 per cent.

The unemployed are particularly unhappy, on all measures but especially negative affect. They become bored and apathetic, can't fill their time, sit around doing nothing and walk slowly (*Social Trends*, 1984). In one British study 19 per cent said that they had become miserable or very unhappy since being out of work (*Social Trends*, 1984).

Education is a strong predictor, especially of positive affect: Veroff *et al.* (1981) found that 40.5 per cent of college graduates said that they were very happy, compared with 23.5 per cent of people with only grade school education. It is found that education has a stronger effect for those who are less well off, possibly because education to some extent frees them from purely material needs, and interests them in non-material concerns (Campbell, 1981).

Members of ethnic minority groups tend to be less happy than the rest of society. In the USA fewer blacks say they are very happy than whites; this is particularly true for younger blacks – only 9 per cent of 21–34-year-olds were very happy in 1976, compared with 36 per cent of whites. However, blacks over 55 were slightly happier than whites, probably because they had accommodated to their situation. The difference is partly due to difference of income, but with income held constant blacks still felt less satisfied in all domains of life (Campbell *et al.*, 1976).

Veenhoven (1990) has analysed happiness data from twenty-eight countries. He found that average happiness in 1979 was greater where there was most economic equality (r = .45). Happiness was also greater where there was less governmental coercion. There are problems about comparing happiness scores in different countries, but these are quite strong statistical relationships.

## Explanation

The explanation of class differences in happiness may lie partly in money leading to a better standard of living, especially at the lower end of the scale where it really makes a difference and for ethnic minority groups. On the other hand, this does not explain why relative income is so important.

We suggested earlier that another explanation may be that middle-class people have more enjoyable experiences in some way. Bradburn found that social activity with friends and 'novelty' (i.e. doing new things, going to new places) correlated with positive affect, and with social class, and partly explained the relation between class and happiness. There are several other features of the lifestyle of the higher classes which could contribute further to the explanation. We have seen that middle-class people engage in much more sport and exercise, belong to more leisure groups, go to church more, do more voluntary work and watch less TV. All of these differences are known to be linked with happiness (Harding, 1985; Argyle, 1992), and between them provide a substantial part of the explanation that we are looking for.

Social relationships are another important source of happiness (Argyle, 1987); are there class differences here which could further elucidate the link between class and happiness? We have seen that there are class differences in friendship. Middle-class people form closer friendships; they turn to friends rather than kin when in need, invite them home. Middle-class marriages are on average closer: couples do more things together, have shared friends, confide more in one another and are more happily married. Working-class people on the other hand have closer links with kin and neighbours, but these relationships are much less important for happiness (Argyle and Henderson, 1985).

In the next section we show that class has a strong effect on self-esteem; self-esteem can be seen either as a component of happiness or as correlated with it. Happy people are found to have a more positive view of themselves and a smaller gap between self and ideal self (Argyle, 1987). A slightly different interpretation is that richer, better-educated people and those with better jobs simply receive more attention. Their clothes and cars attract it, subordinates, servants and the staff of shops and restaurants give it. Better-educated people and those with professional expertise are listened to carefully (Derber, 1979).

Another personality variable that correlates with happiness is internal control (Diener, 1984), and internal control is stronger in people from higher classes, probably because this reflects their experience of being able to control events, at work for example (Kohn and Schooler, 1982). Occupational status produces job satisfaction through more interesting, more skilled and more autonomous work, though this affects those at work more than housewives.

## SELF-ESTEEM

There are several reasons for expecting that class will have an effect on self-esteem:

1 Social comparison with 'inferior' groups should raise self-esteem.
2 Deferential and respectful behaviour from such groups should raise esteem via the process of 'reflective appraisal', the 'looking-glass self' theory.
3 Occupational roles which involve direction of others, or use of expertise, should also raise self-esteem.
4 Applying stereotypes to oneself, about people who attended certain schools or colleges, hold various jobs, etc., should also raise esteem.

The first empirical studies of social class and self-esteem were with children and students. Self-esteem is measured by short self-report scales, like that of Rosenberg (1965) in which people are asked how strongly they agree or disagree with items like 'On the whole I am satisfied with myself' and 'I feel I do not have much to be proud of' (Table 11.7). His classic study of self-esteem in 5,000 high school children found that the children from higher social class families had greater esteem, but this effect was stronger for boys than girls. Since then there have been many further studies using children in different countries. Most of these found the expected positive correlation, though not all, and the correlation was usually quite low, about .20 (Wylie, 1979).

The explanation for this relationship, with children, has been found. In the Rosenberg study described above, it was found that the upper-class fathers were more likely to have close relationships with their sons (65 per cent v. 28 per cent for lower class); there was a similar but weaker effect for

*Table 11.7* Social class and self-esteem

| | Social class | | |
|---|---|---|---|
| Self-esteem | Upper | Middle | Lower |
| High | 51% | 46% | 38% |
| Medium | 23 | 25 | 26 |
| Low | 26 | 29 | 35 |
| Total per cent | 100 | 100 | 100 |
| (Number) | (195) | (2,686) | (340) |

*Source:* Rosenberg, 1965

daughters. And close relationships with father correlated with self-esteem, so that class differences in self-esteem can be partly explained by these differences in family relationships. Whitbeck and co-workers (1991) found that self-esteem correlated .42 for boys and .37 for girls with parental support and involvement, which in turn were caused by the family's economic situation. This was the main causal route from class to esteem; the direct causal route apart from this was quite weak (r = .17).

A second explanation of the effects of class or esteem in children is via their academic success. Bachman and O'Malley (1977) followed up 1,600 young people from age 16 for eight years. At 16 their self-esteem was influenced by their educational success, which in turn was due to their family's social class. In most studies the class of family had little or no direct effect on self-esteem (Maruyama *et al.*, 1981), though Wiltfang and Scarbecz (1990) did find such an effect using non-traditional class measures such as unemployment of father and state of neighbourhood.

Research on adults has found that educational level is the strongest social class predictor of self-esteem. In an American national survey, Veroff *et al.* (1981) found a strong effect of education (see Table 11.8). Weidman *et al.* (1972), with 420 American adults, found that self-perceived competence was most strongly correlated with education, rather than income or occupation.

*Table 11.8* Self-esteem and education

| Grade school | Some high school | High school graduates | Some college | College graduates |
|---|---|---|---|---|
| 27% | 38% | 45% | 48% | 60% |

*Source:* Veroff *et al.*, 1981

The effect of occupational status is smaller, more like .10–.15. However, in twin studies it was found that self-esteem correlates more with job complexity ( .37, .23) and job control (.17, .25) (Gecas and Seff, 1989, 1990). This suggests it is not the status of the job, but the level of competence and the amount of autonomy involved which influence self-esteem.

Unemployment has a powerful effect on self-esteem, as with other aspects of happiness. A British study found that only the negative aspects of self-esteem were affected, with items like 'I haven't got much to be proud of', and there were shifts in this as people moved in and out of employment (Warr, 1984).

The positive relationship between social class and self-esteem was expected; what requires explanation however is why the relationship is so small, usually less than 10 per cent of the variance. Gecas and Seff (1990) found part of the answer. Occupation is not of central importance for everyone; home, leisure or religion may be more important. They found that the correlation between occupational status and self-esteem was higher (.33) for men for whom their job was central, than for those for whom it was not (.12). The effect of job complexity on self-esteem varied even more: .37 when job was central, .06 when it was not. If home was central, control at home correlated .32 with self-esteem. This would be more important for many women than the effects of job. Rosenberg and Pearlin (1978), with 2,300 adults in Chicago, found that if income was of central importance to them it correlated .52 with self-esteem; for those who valued occupational status this correlated .25 with self-esteem.

We can find a further reason for the low effect of class on self-esteem by looking at the self-esteem of ethnic minority groups. There have been many studies of self-esteem of black Americans. In several of the studies with children, blacks had on average *higher* self-esteem (Wylie, 1979). For example, Rosenberg and Simmons (1972) studied 1917 8- to 15-year-olds in Baltimore. At different ages, 12–14 per cent per cent more blacks had high self-esteem. Bachman (1970) found that children in integrated schools were .30 of a standard deviation higher than the white children in self-esteem, those in segregated schools .50 of a standard deviation higher. It is usually found that black children have higher self-esteem only in segregated schools (Wylie, 1979; Gray-Little and Appelbaum, 1979). Rosenberg and Simmons found that 43 per cent of black children thought that blacks are considered the best group in America. The most likely interpretation of these findings is that low-status groups can retain high self-esteem if they are segregated from higher-status groups, and do not make comparisons with them. If self-esteem is based on comparisons with and reactions from others in the immediate group, these can well be positive factors in a black segregated school (Gray-Little and Appelbaum, 1979).

There has been less research on the self-esteem of ethnic adults. Yancey *et al.* (1972) found that black adults in Nashville had higher self-esteem than whites, but in Philadelphia lower self-esteem. In a national survey Campbell *et al.* (1976) found that 32 per cent of blacks and 50 per cent of whites had high self-esteem. The high self-esteem of black Americans has attracted a lot of interest. It has been found that a number of other 'stigmatised' groups do not have the lowered self-esteem which might be expected – women(!), delinquents, the mentally and physically handicapped and those with facial stigmas for example. Possible explanations are that members of such groups attribute rejection to prejudice, make comparisons primarily with members of their own group and devalue themselves only on selected characteristics (Crocker and Major, 1991).

We saw earlier that English manual workers often do not compare themselves with middle-class people; 25 per cent were scarcely aware that there were such people (p. 213). This would certainly be expected to weaken any effects of low class on self-esteem.

A further explanation of the weak effect of class on self-esteem is that there are other more important sources of self-esteem, which can be found in any class, and may even be more important in lower classes. These are:

1 Parental warmth, which is on average greater for middle-class children, though working-class children see more of other kin.
2 Positive reactions from others, and here the immediate group is more important than remote ones, like other social classes.
3 Comparisons with others. Working-class children may do badly at school work, but can succeed at sport or in other spheres. In any case they are less interested in success at school. Lower-status groups may discover different criteria of success on which to evaluate themselves (p. 225).
4 Playing high-status roles. Although work roles are very important here, they are not the only roles which can be sources of self-esteem. Leisure groups, trade unions and the home are also important.

## FINAL DISCUSSION

We have seen that there are large class differences in all four areas of well-being that we have examined here. How could the reduced well-being of lower social classes be improved? Does this necessarily involve radical social changes or are there easier methods?

There is no question that the health and mental health of lower-class individuals would be greatly improved by better housing, less stressful or dangerous jobs and higher incomes. However, health could also be improved by better diet, less smoking, more exercise, less heavy drinking, better access to medical care, though Blaxter (1990) reports that lifestyle in the absence of a decent environment is less effective than when combined with a better one.

Mental health could be improved for lower-class people by decreasing their vulnerability to stress, either through improved socialisation methods or through health education, and greater social support in the community.

Happiness could be improved relatively easily by encouraging greater use of leisure facilities and leisure groups, and more exercise. Social relationships could be improved by making social skills training available.

Self-esteem in the lower classes is directly due to low status and education, but could be raised by closer parent–child relationships and by finding sources of esteem in leisure activities.

## REFERENCES

Angemeyer, M.C. (1987) *From Social Class to Social Stress*. Berlin: Springer-Verlag.
Argyle, M. (1987) *The Psychology of Happiness*. London: Methuen.
Argyle, M. (1989) *The Social Psychology of Work*. 2nd edition. Harmondsworth: Penguin.
Argyle, M. and Henderson, M. (1985) *The Anatomy of Relationships*. London: Heinemann; Harmondsworth: Penguin.

Bachman, J.G. (1970) *Youth in Transition:* Vol.2. *The Impact of Family Background and Intelligence on Tenth Grade Boys.* Ann Arbor, Mich.: Survey Research Center, University of Michigan.

Bachman, J.G. and O'Malley, P.M. (1977) Self-esteem in young men: a longitudinal analysis of the impact of educational and occupational attainment. *Journal of Personality and Social Psychology, 35,* 365–80.

Banks, M.H. and Jackson, P.R. (1982) Unemployment and risk of minor psychiatric disorder in young people: cross sectional and longitudinal evidence. *Psychological Medicine, 12,* 789–98.

Birtchnell, J. (1971) Social class, parental social class, and social mobility in psychiatric patients and general population controls. *Pyschological Medicine, 1,* 209–21.

Black, D. *et al.* (1988) *Inequalities in Health.* Harmondsworth: Penguin.

Blane, D. (1985) An assessment of the Black report; explanation of health inequalities. *Sociology of Health and Illness, 7,* 423–48.

Blauner, R. (1960) Work satisfaction and industrial trends in modern society. In W. Galenson and S.M. Lipset (eds) *Labor and Trade Unions.* New York: Wiley.

Blaxter, M. (1990) *Health and Lifestyle.* London: Tavistock/Routledge.

Bradburn, N.M. (1969) *The Structure of Psychological Well-Being.* Chicago: Aldine.

Brown, G.W. and Harris, T. (1978) *Social Origins of Depression.* London: Tavistock.

Calnan, M. (1985) Patterns in preventive behaviour: a study of women in middle-age. *Social Science and Medicine, 20,* 263–8.

Campbell, A. (1981) *The Sense and Well-Being in America.* New York: McGraw-Hill.

Campbell, A., Converse, P.E. and Rodgers, W.L. (1976) *The Quality of American Life.* New York: Sage.

Cochrane, R. (1983) *The Social Creation of Mental Illness.* London: Longman.

Cochrane, R. and Stopes-Roe, M. (1980) Factors affecting the distribution of psychological symptoms in urban areas of England. *Acta Psychiatrica Scandanavica, 61,* 445–60.

Crocker, J. and Major, B. (1991) Social stigma and self-esteem: the self-protective properties of stigma. *Psychological Review, 96,* 608–30.

Cronkite, R.C. and Moos, R.H. (1984) The role of predisposing and moderating factors in the stress–illness relationship. *Journal of Health and Social Behavior, 25,* 372–93.

Derber, C. (1979) *The Pursuit of Attention.* Boston, Mass.: C.K. Hall.

Diener, E. (1984) Subjective well-being. *Psychological Bulletin, 92,* 542–75.

Diener, E., Horowitz, J. and Emmons, R. (1985) Happiness of the very wealthy. *Social Indicators Research, 16,* 263–74.

Dohrenwend, B.P. (1975) Sociocultural and socio-psychological factors in the genesis of mental disorders. *Journal of Health and Social Behavior, 16,* 365–92.

Feather, N.T. (1982) Unemployment and its psychological correlates: a study of depressive symptoms, self-esteem, Protestant Ethic values, attributional style and apathy. *Australian Journal of Psychology, 34,* 309–23.

Filsinger, E.E. and Anderson, C.C. (1982) Social class and self-esteem in late adolescence: dissonant context or self-efficacy? *Developmental Psychology, 18,* 380–4.

Fletcher, B. (1983) Marital relationships as a cause of death: an analysis of occupational morbidity in the community. *British Journal of Psychiatry, 7,* 475–89.

Garfinkel, P.E. and Garner, D.M. (1982) *Anorexia Nervosa.* Montreal: Brunner/Mazel.

Gecas, V. and Seff, M.A. (1989) Social class, occupational conditions, and self-esteem. *Sociological Perspectives, 32,* 353–64.

Gecas, V. and Seff, M.A. (1990) Social class and self-esteem: psychological centrality, compensation, and the relative effects of work and home. *Social Psychology Quarterly*, *53*, 165–73.

*General Household Survey* (1980, 1983) Nos. 11 and 12. London: HMSO.

Goldberg, D. and Huxley, P. (1980) *Mental Illness in the Community*. London: Tavistock.

Goldblatt, P. (1990) Social class mortality differences. In C.G. Mascie-Taylor (ed.) *Biosocial Aspects of Social Class*. Oxford: Oxford University Press.

Gray-Little, B. and Appelbaum, M.I. (1979) Instrumentality effects in the assessment of racial differences in self-esteem. *Journal of Personality and Social Psychology*, *37*, 1221–9.

Hällström, T. and Noppa, H. (1981) Obesity in women in relation to mental illness, social factors and personality traits. *Journal of Psychosomatic Research*, *25*, 75–82.

Harding, S. (1985) Values and the nature of psychological well-being. In M. Abrams, D. Gerard and N. Timms (eds) *Values and Social Change in Britain*. Basingstoke: Macmillan.

Haring, M.J., Stock, W.A. and Okun, M.A. (1984) A research synthesis of gender and social class as correlates of subjective well-being. *Human Relations*, *37*, 645–57.

Harkey, J., Miles, D.L. and Rushing, W.A. (1976) The relation between social class and functional status: a new look at the drift hypothesis. *Journal of Health and Social Behavior*, *17*, 194–204.

Hess, R.D. (1970) The transmission of cognitive strategies in poor families: the socialization of apathy and under-achievement. In V.L. Allen (ed.) *Psychological Factors in Poverty*. Chicago: Markham.

Hollingshead, A. and Redlich, F. (1958) *Social Class and Mental Illness*. New York: Wiley.

Homel, R. and Burns, A. (1989) Environmental quality and the well-being of children. *Social Indicators Research*, *21*, 133–58.

Kessler, R.C. (1982) A disaggregation of the relationship between socioeconomic status and psychological distress. *American Sociological Review*, *47*, 752–64.

Kohn, M.L. (1973) Social class and schizophrenia: a critical review and reformulation. *Schizophrenia Bulletin*, *7*, 60–79.

Kohn, M.L. (1976) The interaction of social class and other factors in the etiology of schizophrenia. *American Journal of Psychiatry*, *133*, 177–80.

Kohn, M.L. and Schooler, C. (1982) Job conditions and personality: a longitudinal assessment of their reciprocal effects. *American Journal of Sociology*, *87*, 1257–86.

Kristiansen, C.M. and Harding, C.M. (1988) A comparison of the coverage of health issues by Britain's quality and popular press. *Social Behaviour*, *3*, 25–32.

Langner, T.S. and Michael, S.T. (1963) *Life Stress and Mental Health*. Glencoe: Free Press.

Lefcourt, H.M. (1976) *Locus of Control: Current Trends in Theory and Research*. Hillsdale, NJ: Erlbaum.

McLeod, J.D. and Kessler, R.C. (1990) Socioeconomic status differences in vulnerability to undesirable life events. *Journal of Health and Social Behavior*, *31*, 162–72.

Marmot, M.G., Shipley, M.J. and Rose, G. (1984) Inequalities in death – specific explanations of a general pattern. *Lancet*, 1, 1003–6.

Maruyama, G., Rubin, R.A. and Kingsbury, G.G. (1981) Self-esteem and educational achievement: independent constructs with a common cause? *Journal of Personality and Social Psychology*, *40*, 962–75.

Michalos, A.C. (1986) Job satisfaction, marital satisfaction, and the quality of life: a review and a preview. In F.M. Andrews (ed.) *Research on the Quality of Life*. Ann Arbor, Mich.: Institute for Social Research.

Moser, K.A., Fox, A.J. and Jones, D.R. (1984) Unemployment and mortality in the OPCS longitudinal study. *Lancet*, 2, 1324–9.

*Occupational Mortality* (1990) *The Registrar General's Decennial Supplement*. London: HMSO.

Reid, I. (1989) *Social Class Differences in Britain*. 3rd edition. London: Fontana.

Rosenberg, M. (1965) *Society and the Adolescent Self-Image*. Princeton, NJ: Princeton University Press.

Rosenberg, M. and Pearlin, L.L. (1978) Social class and self-esteem among children and adults. *American Journal of Sociology*, 84, 53–77.

Rosenberg, M. and Simmons, R.G. (1972) *Black and White Self-Esteem: the Urban School Child*. Washington: American Sociological Association.

Runciman, W.G. (1966) *Relative Deprivation and Social Justice*. London: Routledge & Kegan Paul.

*Social Trends* (1984–91) London: HMSO.

Stott, D.H. (1978) Epidemiological indicators of the origins of behavior disturbance as measured by the Bristol Social Adjustment Guides. *Genetic Psychology Monographs*, 97, 127–59.

Townsend, P. and Davidson, N. (eds) (1988) *Inequalities in Health*. Harmondsworth: Penguin.

Turner, R.J. and Noh, S. (1983) Class and psychological vulnerability among women: the significance of social support and personal control. *Journal of Health and Social Behavior*, 24, 2–15.

Veenhoven, R. (1990) *World Databook of Happiness*. Dordrecht: Reidel.

Veroff, J., Douvan, E. and Kulka, R.A. (1981) *The Inner American*. New York: Basic Books.

Warr, P. (1984) Reported behaviour changes after job loss. *British Journal of Social Psychology*, 23, 271–5.

Warr, P. and Payne, R. (1982) Experience of strain and pleasure among British adults. *Social Science and Medicine*, 16, 1691–7.

Watson, D. and Pennebaker, J.W. (1989) Health complaints, stress, and distress: exploring the role of negative affectivity. *Journal of Personality and Social Psychology*, 96, 234–54.

Weidman, J.C., Phelan, W.T. and Sullivan, M.A. (1972) The influence of educational attainment on self-evaluation of competence. *Sociology of Education*, 45, 303–12.

Wheaton, B. (1978) The sociogenesis of psychological disorder: re-examining the causal issues with longitudinal data. *American Sociological Review*, 43, 383–403.

Whitbeck, L.B. *et al.* (1991) Family economic hardship, parental support, and adolescent self-esteem. *Social Psychology Quarterly*, 54, 353–63.

Williams, D.R. (1990) Socioeconomic differentials in health: a review and redirection. *Social Psychology Quarterly*, 53, 81–99.

Wiltfang, G.L. and Scarbecz, M. (1990) Social class and adolescent self-esteem: another look. *Social Psychology Quarterly*, 53, 174–84.

Wylie, R. (1979) *The Self-Concept*. Vol.2. Lincoln, Nebr.: University of Nebraska Press.

Yancey, W.L., Rigby, L. and McCarthy, J.D. (1972) Social position and self-evaluation: the relative importance of race. *American Journal of Sociology*, 78, 338–59.

# Chapter 12

# Conclusions, implications and reflections

In this chapter I leave the detailed examination of particular aspects of social class and turn to some broader issues. The points made can all be supported by earlier parts of the book, but will not be referred to in detail; the index will find them.

## IMPLICATIONS FOR SOCIAL PSYCHOLOGY

I write as a social psychologist. For a number of years social psychologists have been saying that we should 'make social psychology more social' and stop carrying out artificial 'experiments in a vacuum'. One of the most important variables in the outside world is surely class, yet it has often been notable by its absence from our work. In this section I shall note some of the main areas where it has been found to be important for the study of social behaviour.

*Class is a major source of variation in social behaviour.* We have seen that 'friendship' has a rather different meaning for different classes. For working-class people friends are those you can turn to for help, for the middle classes friends are those whose company is enjoyed. Working-class friendship is based on proximity and helpfulness, middle-class friends on similarity of outlook and interests, and they are often met at leisure groups. On the other hand, kin are the major source of help for the working class, friends for the middle class. Marriage is also very different: middle-class marriages, we have seen, get off to a much better start, are happier and last longer. They are more symmetrical, with more companionship and conversation. Relationships are a good example of class differences in social behaviour – some of the differences are very significant, they can be explained quite easily, and they have been almost totally overlooked by social psychologists.

Differences in speech between classes have been carefully documented by sociolinguists. Accent differences are very familiar. Differences of speech style have also been found: middle-class people use more accurate syntax, more complex utterances and take more account of the point of view of listeners. In this and other ways middle-class people are usually found to have better social skills, partly because of the demands of middle-class jobs.

*Class as group membership*. Classes are more like categories than groups, but they function as social groups since members are attracted to one another because of their similarity of lifestyle, values and the rest, and they are aware of being members of the same group. They can recognise each other from speech and appearance, they conform to shared norms and they like outsiders less. Social identity theory was introduced to explain the rejection of out-groups, with ethnic groups in mind, but can be applied to classes too, and some of its predictions work. For example, members of lower-status groups re-value characteristics of their own group, e.g. doing skilled manual work, and discover new favourable attributes, e.g. sincerity, generosity and sense of humour. We have suggested two modifications to this theory to deal with some of the empirical findings about class. Individuals do not compare themselves with other classes if they rarely meet them. And social mobility of a new kind is common – 'subjective social mobility', by adopting the lifestyle and self-image of another class.

*Self-presentation* theory had social status in mind – 'keeping up appearances' by the display of symbols. However, a lot of what looks like self-presentation, e.g. adopting the clothes or accents of one's class, may be better interpreted as conformity; the communicative aspect is secondary. When there is deliberate adoption of the lifestyle of another, superior group, this may result in social acceptance by members of that group and thus in real social mobility.

*Attitudes and beliefs*. The attitudes which have been examined most closely here are attitudes to other social classes. This turned out to be a most complex set of attitudes, with many components, including social distance, deference, hostility, perceived justice or legitimacy, lay explanations of social differences, willingness to take group action. No one dimension can do justice to this many-layered attitude.

Political attitudes were expected to vary with class, but are found to do so in a most complex way. More working-class people vote for left-wing parties, but nearly half do not, especially those who regard themselves as middle-class or who have a middle-class lifestyle. Many middle-class people on the other hand vote Labour; going to university is one of several factors responsible. Religious beliefs and behaviour vary with class in a paradoxical way: middle-class people go to church much more, but working-class people believe more and engage in more private devotions.

Values also vary considerably with class. Middle-class people value work for its own sake, education, 'post-materialist' goals, and share liberal values concerning personal morality. Working-class people hold certain family values, like respect for parents, but not marriage, more strongly and they favour severity of punishment for offenders. The 'culture of poverty' is partly a matter of short-term goals, but is partly due to lack of opportunity and the experience of inability to control events.

*Personality*. There are very wide variations within each class, but there are also some overall differences. Middle-class people tend to be more inner-directed, and to have stronger achievement motivation, longer-term goals; working-class individuals tend to be more aggressive and authoritarian. The explanation of these differences lies partly in the different experiences of work and partly in different kinds of parental socialisation; the latter are partly produced by the different situations in each class, e.g. opportunities for careers.

## IMPLICATIONS FOR SOCIOLOGY

Most of the research into class has been carried out by sociologists, though there is no clear border between psychology and sociology. Sociologists sometimes include intelligence as a variable, for example, while psychologists sometimes include social class. The main points that I want to make here concern the importance of psychological factors which sociologists have left out, either as causes of phenomena, or as part of their explanation.

*The meaning and measurement of class*. Sociologists usually, and especially in Britain, measure class by occupation, and this is also used for governmental statistics. However, this is not the way the man or woman in the street assesses class: they go by accent, appearance, the friends people have, where they live, education and income as much as by occupation, which came fourth in the list in one study and sixth for female subjects. Nor does occupation predict subjective class very well. It is not surprising that class as measured by occupation is such a weak predictor of voting. It may be suggested that class should be measured in the same way that other people do it, by weighting the different criteria just mentioned. This has been done in some American studies.

*Social mobility*. This has been a particular success story for sociology, with path analyses showing the effect of various predictors, including two important psychological ones, intelligence and parental encouragement. However, there are several other psychological variables which are at least as important as intelligence which have been left out – achievement motivation, self-discipline, height for men, not being fat for women, physical attractiveness for both. And the whole study of social mobility would be transformed if more adequate measures of social class were used. Mobility by moving to a different kind of occupation is only one kind.

Changing lifestyle, education, moving house, even elocution are other ways of being accepted at a higher level of society.

*The explanation of class differences in behaviour.* Sociologists have documented, very successfully, the class differences in many important aspects of behaviour, including health, mental health, crime, sexual behaviour, leisure activities and behaviour at work. However, nothing can be done with this knowledge to improve the human condition unless we also know the explanation. It may lie in sociology, psychology, or elsewhere.

*Genetic.* Parts of the class difference in mental health, intelligence and height are evidently due to genetics, and are produced by the effects of these characteristics on social mobility, up or down.

*Socialisation.* Much of the class differences in personality can be traced to class-linked styles of child-rearing; this can explain differences in internal control and other aspects of inner direction, achievement motivation, aggressiveness, crime and authoritarianism. Unlike genetics, this is a source of behaviour which is capable of modification.

*Work experience.* It has long been known that work can be a cause of stress and illness, as well as of job satisfaction, and that there are class differences in these variables. We now know that experience at work can produce greater or lesser levels of inner-directedness, and of social skills. Those with better jobs, with authority over others, whose expertise is recognised, have high job satisfaction, which is an important component of happiness; they also experience higher self-esteem, which is another.

*Class differences in lifestyle.* The history of many of the differences here can be traced, including accent, clothes and leisure pursuits. There is a major cultural difference in health behaviour – working-class people take much less exercise, have worse diets, are therefore more often obese and are more likely to drink or smoke heavily. The reasons for these differences are not wholly understood; they are probably due in part to an educational lag in learning about good health behaviour, partly the direct result of stress.

*Effects of inequality.* Some class differences are direct results of the experience of inequality. Crime is much higher among poor people; it is also much higher in areas where there is greater economic inequality; this is especially true of offences against the person. We shall see below that health, mental health and happiness are affected by status, probably by the emotional effects of high or low self-esteem. Left-wing political attitudes, including aggressive and revolutionary attitudes, are stronger among those who are or have been unemployed, ethnic minority groups, manual workers and those who belong to trade unions; income has little independent effect.

Some areas of behaviour are affected by two or more of these factors. In some cases we do not yet know which is the more important. Take sexual behaviour: working-class people engage in much more premarital and extramarital sex, but why do they? It could be due to personality differences

– middle-class youth have stronger internal controls and long-term goals. There is a lower commitment to marriage for working-class people, perhaps because their marriages are on average less satisfying. There are cultural differences in that middle-class families are more concerned about inheritance of property and their children marrying into the right class. There may also be a sociobiological factor; animals with an uncertain food supply copulate more widely to ensure propagation of their genes.

## THE PURSUIT OF HUMAN HAPPINESS AND WELL-BEING

Most aspects of human well-being are closely linked to social class in some way. Plans to enhance human happiness and well-being must take this into account.

*Health.* Working-class people have much worse health, partly because of bad working conditions, bad housing and less access to medical care. (There are some reversals – middle-class people have more anorexia, skin cancer, polio, car accidents and brain tumours.) The main explanation of these class differences is in terms of the differences in health behaviour described above. However, they cannot explain all the differences in health and it seems likely that there are also direct effects of low status via the emotional consequences of low self-esteem.

Psychologists have had considerable success in modifying the health behaviour of individuals by clinical methods, for example smoking, drinking and eating. They have also had some success on a larger scale, in reducing smoking or increasing level of exercise for whole firms, with resultant improvements in health and efficiency (Argyle, 1992). Health education programmes have targeted the lifestyles which are responsible for poor health, and which are most common in the working class. Another area of social improvement is in the enhancement of social support via leisure groups. Community social support can be increased by the provision of leisure centres, with facilities for different leisure groups, and by the organisation of self-help groups for those who share similar problems. Educational programmes are used in America to train parents in better child-rearing methods, and this could be an important way of enhancing hardiness.

*Mental health* is much worse for working-class people overall – five times the rate of schizophrenia, two to three times the rate of depression for women. The schizophrenia difference is partly, perhaps largely, due to downward drift. The prevalence of working-class depression is partly due to the greater everyday stresses of working-class life, but also to greater vulnerability. The amount of social support in the community is less, especially from spouses. Working-class people have less effective coping styles and other aspects of personality – 'hardiness' – which enable people to stand up to stress. This in turn is caused by rigid and punitive styles of child-rearing, and repeatedly encountering situations which cannot be controlled. Industrial experiments have shown that it is possible to train people in stress-management techniques, such as looking at and tackling problems in a different way; exercise and relaxation are also beneficial (Argyle, 1992).

*Happiness* is affected by social class, especially at the lower end of the scale; the unemployed are particularly unhappy, the rich a little happier, compared with others. The most likely explanation is that higher-class individuals enjoy their leisure more, belong to more clubs and leisure groups, engage in more sport and have more friends, while working-class people just watch more TV. A second explanation is that middle-class people receive more attention and respect, and this raises their self-esteem, both at work and in public places. Self-esteem is particularly enhanced by education. Happiness could be increased through better provision of leisure centres, which would lead to more enjoyment of leisure groups and also to more social support. Middle-class job satisfaction is greater, and such benefits can be spread by programmes of job enrichment, team-work and the rest (Argyle, 1989). Happiness depends too on personality – extraverts, positive thinkers and others do better – and this could be enhanced by better socialisation.

## ARE CLASSES INEVITABLE?

Can there be a classless society? We have seen that social inequality has a number of serious consequences for those at the lower end of it. In addition to having less money and all it buys, they have worse jobs, lower self-esteem, are less happy and more likely to break the law. They also have worse health and mental health, which can partly be attributed to low status directly, but are more due to subcultural differences in health behaviour and child-rearing.

However, there never has been a classless society, and in the course of human history most societies have been much more stratified than ours is today. Britain is in the middle of the range in the modern world for rate of social mobility, and at the egalitarian end for income distribution, especially after tax and welfare are taken into account. We are also at the egalitarian end for delegation and consultation at work.

There are several countries which have moved further towards classlessness. The USSR and Eastern Europe up to 1991 abolished private property and its inheritance, there was a high rate of social mobility and income differentials were small. On the other hand, party officials had extensive privileges and a superior lifestyle, and there was quite a lot of occupational inheritance. People in Hungary thought that the degree of egalitarianism still fell short of the ideal, and those of higher occupational class thought they had relatively low social status, compared with similar individuals in Australia for example (Evans *et al.*, 1992).

The Israeli kibbutz is more egalitarian, though social divisions have appeared between the administrators, who have privileges as well as status, those with inherited wealth and full members as opposed to employees. But office holders do not form a class or pass their position on to their children.

Australia has sometimes been claimed to be a classless society, though it has a similar income distribution to other countries; it does have a slightly higher rate of social mobility, and Australians feel they have rejected European feudal traditions and are said to value their lack of respect for authority. The gap between ideal and perceived egalitarianism has narrowed during this century, but is about the same as that in Hungary.

Sweden is one of the most egalitarian countries in the modern world, with a high rate of mobility and small range of incomes. Class differences in health are much smaller than in Britain.

A number of sociologists have argued that stratification is inevitable because of the 'functions' it performs for society. Parsons (1953) thought that societies share the same values, and those who perform well in relation to these values will be evaluated more favourably and rewarded more. The need for administrative hierarchies, especially where there is much division of labour, also creates classes. He believed that stratification was necessary because it integrates society; others have argued that it leads more to divisiveness and hostility.

Davis and Moore (1945) argued that all societies have a number of roles to be performed; some are more functionally important than others, and require special abilities and long training, so need to be rewarded more to motivate people to perform them. Tumin (1970) and others have criticised these ideas in various ways: it is hard to decide which jobs are most important, rewards often do not seem to be closely related to importance, e.g. pop stars v. dustmen, they depend on the power of occupational groups to enhance their salaries and restrict access, and classes act as barriers to the free mobility of labour. Lack of equal opportunities prevents the best people moving into socially important jobs, family members can enjoy the rewards without making any contribution; it is questioned whether economic rewards are necessary in addition to those of status? Wesolowski (1962) agreed that hierarchies of authority are needed in society, but thought that differences of prestige or income are not necessary.

Do social psychologists have any contribution to make to this debate? It does appear that all known groups and societies have so far been stratified, including those that were initially planned as egalitarian, like the kibbutz and USSR. The need for administrative hierarchies in large organisations seems to lead inevitably to social stratification and differences of prestige. The existence of the family seems to make inevitable the formation of groups of different status, not all of whom have made much contribution to society. The same applies in groups of monkeys.

Do some jobs need to be paid more? The rewards of status and better work might be enough to motivate people to do professional and managerial work. The jobs that need extra economic incentives might be rather different ones – those that are dangerous, stressful, unpleasant or very demanding. How great should pay differentials be? In Britain, after tax and welfare, the ratio of the average income of the richest and poorest fifths of families is about 4.3:1, but about 70 per cent of the population think this difference is unfair (the rest think that it *is* fair). An American survey thought that those in the best jobs and with most education should be paid about 50 per cent more. This suggests that income differentials might be reduced, though a very low ratio might not be enough to motivate and compensate for long years of training or for difficult and dangerous work. The reduction of differentials would do a lot to reduce differences of lifestyle, in such domains as education and leisure, perhaps to increase the self-esteem and reduce the criminality and rebelliousness of the under-privileged.

However, there are other aspects of class systems which might be modified more easily. In particular the social distance between classes could be changed, so that social contact between members of different classes would be easier. We have seen that one arena where this happens quite a lot is in certain kinds of leisure groups, especially those engaged in some specific activity, like sport, music and dancing. Different classes also meet at work, but may be separated by different dining rooms, uniforms or other symbols. These could go, and styles of supervision which include consultation and care for subordinates be encouraged.

## REFERENCES

Argyle, M. (1989) *The Social Psychology of Work*. 2nd edition. Harmondsworth: Penguin.

Argyle, M. (1992) *The Social Psychology of Everyday Life*. London: Routledge.

Coleman, R.P. and Rainwater, L. (1979) *Social Standing in America*. London: Routledge & Kegan Paul.

Davis, K. and Moore, W.E. (1945) A conceptual analysis of stratification. *American Sociological Review*, 7, 309–21.

Evans, M.R.D., Kelley, J. and Tarki, T.K. (1992) Images of class: public perceptions in Hungary and Australia. *American Sociological Review*, 57, 461–82.

Parsons, T. (1953) A revised analytical approach to the theory of social stratification. In R. Bendix and S.M. Lipset (eds) *Class, Status and Power*. Glencoe, Ill.: Free Press, pp. 92–128.

Tumin, M.M. (1970) *Readings on Social Stratification*. Englewood Cliffs, NJ: Prentice-Hall.

Wesolowski, W. (1962) Some notes on the functional theory of stratification. In R. Bendix and S.M. Lipset (eds) *Class, Status and Power*. Glencoe, Ill.: Free Press, pp. 64–9.

# Name index

# Subject index